بِسْمِ ٱللَّهِ ٱلرَّحْمَٰنِ ٱلرَّحِيمِ

Al-Imām
Muḥammad Ibn ʿIsā al-Tirmidhī

The SUBLIME BEAUTY of the PROPHET ﷺ

being a translation of his
'Al-Shamā'il al-Muḥammadiyyah'

دار السنة

Umm Ma'bad described the Prophet (ﷺ) saying,

"I saw a radiant man with a luminous face and handsome physique"

Ḥākim 3/9-10

The Sublime Beauty of the Prophet ﷺ

الشمائل المحمدية

Imām Muḥammad Ibn 'Isā al-Tirmidhī

With accompanying Biography of the Prophet ﷺ

by Imām al-Nawawī

دار السنة

Dār as-Sunnah Publishers

BIRMINGHAM

First Edition Published in Great Britain, March 2020 CE / Shaban 1441 AH
by Dār as-Sunnah Publishers

DĀR AS-SUNNAH PUBLISHERS
P.O. Box 9818, Birmingham, B11 4WA, United Kingdom

W: www.darassunnah.com
E: info@darassunnah.com
E: daar-us-sunnah@mail.com

British Library Cataloguing in publication Data.
A catalogue record for this book is available from the British Library.

Title: The Sublime Beauty of the Prophet ﷺ
by Imām Muḥammad Ibn ʿIsā al-Tirmidhī
Translated from the original Arabic

ISBN 1-904336-64-7
Paper-back

First Edition, 1441 AH/2020 CE
Typeset by: Dār as-Sunnah Publishers

CONTENTS

FOREWARD

In the name of Allāh, the Most Gracious, the Most Merciful. All praise belongs to Allāh, the Lord of the worlds, who sent His final messenger Muhammad ﷺ with divine guidance. May the peace, blessings and salutations be upon our beloved Prophet ﷺ, the chosen one, and upon his family and companions. May Allāh bless all those who follow the Sunnah of the Messenger of Allāh ﷺ until the Last Day.

It is with great pleasure that I introduce this new translation of Al-Shamā'il al-Muḥammadiyyah, by the famous Imām Tirmidhī. It has been taught and studied all over the world for well over a thousand years and has been accepted by the Ummah as one of the key works in studying the physical characteristics of the Prophet ﷺ.

Allāh, the Most High said, "Say, 'If you love Allāh, then follow me, Allāh will love you and forgive you your sins. And Allāh is Most Forgiving and Merciful.'" Aali Imran 3:31

The Messenger of Allāh ﷺ said, "None of you will truly believe until I am more beloved to him than his family, his wealth and all of mankind." Muslim #67

As a believer, to love the Messenger of Allāh ﷺ more than anything in this world, even more than our own selves, is a condition of faith and a way to guarantee the love of Allāh. Loving the Messenger of Allāh ﷺ means that we must follow in his footsteps and obey him. For obeying the Prophet ﷺ is obeying Allāh, as he was the appointed Messenger from Allāh to all of mankind.

It is human nature that when we love a person, we seek to know all what we can of them. We are eager to speak about them and mention them to others. We try to emulate them in order to establish our identity in association to them, expressing ourselves through the words and actions of theirs which we admire the most. Therefore, as a sign of true love and obedience of the Prophet ﷺ, the first step is to learn about him.

Before you is a spring of knowledge that every Muslim who claims to love the Messenger ﷺ would do well to drink from. You will be able to better appreciate this sublime man, who was a mercy to the worlds, sent to exemplify and perfect the character of the believers. He singlehandedly changed the course of human history forever, establishing the way for the seeker of truth to escape the depths of darkness and oppression, and discover the light, justice and freedom. Due to his unparalleled contribution to human civilisation encompassing every sphere of life, the Messenger of Allāh ﷺ is still as relevant today, as he has remained throughout time. Thus, the only way to address the numerous issues of this turbulent world of ours, is to study his superlative life and resolve our troubles by following his example.

Those who read through these pages should count themselves as the fortunate ones, for they will learn about the beloved friend of Allāh and the leader of all the children of Ādam. This in-depth study of the greatest man to have ever lived will enrich every soul; it will be a guide for all those who are seeking true guidance, and it will transform the lives of those who choose to follow the best man to have ever lived. I believe every Muslim should own a personal copy of this great work, it should be gifted between people and offered on the shelves of every library, in every corner of the world.

It is important to add that this book also contains an abridged biography of the Prophet ﷺ by the famous Imām Nawawī, which is an additional benefit for reader. Both works are quite unique in their own way, whoever reads through this whole volume will get a very comprehensive understanding of the Prophet's ﷺ life, including details of his physical appearance, personal characteristics, and much more, with the permission of Allāh.

Dār as-Sunnah Publishers originally commissioned this work for translation and publication over a decade ago, but due to many obstacles this work has not seen the light of day until now, all praise be to Allāh.

I personally want to take this opportunity to thank the translator, the Dār as-Sunnah team and the many brothers and sisters, who invested many valuable hours into this work, all for the sake of Allāh and their love for the Prophet ﷺ. May Allāh richly bless them all and unite us all together with our beloved Prophet ﷺ and his companions in the hereafter. *Āmīn.*

Abū Muḥammad Tasaddaq
7th Rabi Al-Akhar, 1441 AH
4th December 2019

MUḤAMMAD IBN ʿĪSĀ AL-TIRMIDHĪ

May Allāh have mercy upon him

His Name and Linage

He is al-Imām, al-Ḥāfiẓ, the expert authority: Abū ʿIsā Muḥammad Ibn ʿIsā Ibn Sawrah Ibn Mūsā Ibn al-Dhaḥāk al-Sulamī Adhrīr al-Bughī al-Tirmidhī.

It is also said he was Muḥammad Ibn ʿIsā Ibn Yazīd Ibn Sawrah Ibn Al-Sakan. He is also said to be Muḥammad Ibn ʿIsā Ibn Sawrah Ibn Shadād Ibn ʿIsā.

His lineage: Al-Sulamī referring to the tribe of Sulaym Mūsāghar, from the clan of Gaylan. As for Al-Bogithen it is a connection to Boogh: a village from the villages of Tirmidhī, attributed to him due to the fact that he died there.

Al-Dharīr: There is a disagreement about whether he was born blind or with sight. Al-Dhahabī said: What is most correct is that he became blind in his old age after his travelling and his writing down of knowledge.

Tirmidhī: Is the famous affiliation he has become known by and is a connection to the city of Tirmidhī, the city in which he grew up. It is located on the northern banks of the river Jahūn (Amodariyah) north of Iran.

His Birth: Historians are not clear about the exact year of his birth, placing it in the first decade of the third century. al-Dhahabī said: He was born near the year 210 AH, maybe even the year 209 AH, due to the fact that most believe he died in the year 279 AH and Al-Dhahabi said: He was seventy years old.

His Background in Knowledge and His Journey to Seek Knowledge

Imām Tirmidhī grew up learning from the scholars of his town and the scholars of Khurasān such as Ishāq Ibn Rahāwayh and Muḥammad Ibn 'Amr Al-Ṣawwāq. He travelled to 'Irāq and the Ḥijāz and took from the scholars of those places. He also travelled to many other places in order to seek knowledge.

Imām Tirmidhī never travelled to Egypt or Shām. Rather he narrated from these two places through a medium. It is also widely believed that he never entered Baghdād. If he had entered it he would have taken from the great Imām Aḥmad Ibn Ḥanbal, however it has not been established that he did. What further strengthens this point is that Khaṭīb al-Baghdīdī never mentioned him in his book: *Ṭārīkh al-Baghdād.*

He spent much of his time travelling and taking knowledge from the scholars. He collected and authored [books] and did so well and benefitted [others], may Allāh have mercy upon him.

His Teachers

Imām Tirmidhī travelled to many places and heard from many people. He also shared many teachers with Imām Bukhārī and among them a group who all the Imāms of the famous six books of ḥadīth (*kutub al-sitta*) narrated from and they are:

- Muḥammad Ibn Bashār (Bandār)
- Abū Mūsā Muḥammad Ibn Al-Muthanāh
- Ziyād Ibn Yaḥyā Al-Ḥassānī
- Al-ʿAbbās Ibn ʿAbdu'l-ʿAzīm Al-ʿAnbarī
- Abū Saʿīd al-ʿAshaj ʿAbdullāh Ibn Saʿīd Al-Kandī
- Abū Ḥafs ʿAmr Ibn ʿAlī Al-Aflaṣ
- Yaʿqūb Ibn Ibrāhīm Al-Darūqī
- Muḥammad Ibn Muʿammar Al-Qaysī Al-Bahranī
- Naṣr Ibn ʿAlī Al-Jahdhamī

He also reached many scholars who were before these scholars [mentioned above], among them:

- Qutaybah Ibn Saʿīd Al-Madanī
- Isḥaq Ibn Raḥawayh
- ʿAlī Ibn Ḥajr Al-Marūzī
- Abū Muṣʿab Aḥmad Ibn Abū Bakr Al-Zuhrī Al-Madanī
- Suwayd Ibn Naṣr Ibn Suwayd Al- Marūzī
- ʿAbdullāh Ibn Muʿāwiyah Al-Jahmī
- Muḥammad Ibn ʿAbdu'l-ʿAzīz Abū Ruzmah
- Muḥammad Ibn ʿAbdu'l-Mālik Ibn Abū Shawārib
- Ismāʿīl Ibn Mūsā Al-Farazī Al-Suddī
- Ibrāhīm Ibn ʿAbdullāh Ibn Ḥātim Al-Ḥarāwī
- And many more

Imām Tirmidhī greatly benefited from the major scholars who were the very pinnacle of memorisation and understanding of ḥadith in his time. However his greatest influence and from whom he benefitted the most was al-Imām, al-Ḥāfiẓ Abū ʿAbdullāh Muḥammad Ibn Ismāʿīl Al-Bukhārī. He was the student of Imām Bukhārī and took knowledge of ḥadith and its understanding. He also met Imām Muslim Ibn Ḥajjāj and learnt from him.

He also met the Imām Abū Dāwūd Sulaymān Ibn Al-ʿAshath Al-Sijistanī, and narrated from him in his own collection. He acquired knowledge of defects of ḥadiths and narrators and other aspects of ḥadith from the Imām ʿAbdullāh Ibn ʿAbdu'l-Rahmān Al-Dārimī, Abū Zurʿah al-Rāzī as he has mentioned toward the end of his collection of ḥadīth.

His Students

Imām Tirmidhī became a distinguished scholar who would benefit others through his knowledge and works. The people that narrated from Tirmidhī were many. Some of them are mentioned in *Al-Tahdhīb*; *Tazkirat ul-Ḥuffāẓ*, and *Siyār ʿAlām Al-Nubala* amongst them are:

- Abū al-ʿAbbās Muḥammad Ibn Aḥmad Ibn Maḥbūb Al-Maḥbūbī Al-Marwazī
- Abū Saʿīd Al-Haytham Ibn Kulayb Al-Shashī
- Ḥamad Ibn Shakir Ibn Sawiyaht Nafasī
- Abū Bakr Aḥmad Ibn Ismāʿīl Ibn ʿAmir Al-Samarqandī
- Abū Ḥāmid Aḥmad Ibn ʿAbdullāh Ibn Dāwūd Al-Marwazī Al-Tājir
- Abū Jāʿfar Muḥammad Ibn Sufyān Ibn Al-Naṣr Al-Nafasī, better known as Al-Amīn

His Standing in Knowledge and the Praise of the Scholars for him

The scholars who are respected are all united in their admiration for him and praise for him. They bear witness to his elevated status in knowledge, memorisation and competence.

The Imām and scholar Abū Saʿīd al-Samānī said about him: 'He is one of the Imāms that were followed in the knowledge of ḥadīth. He authored the book *Al-Jāmiʿ*, a book on history, and hidden defects in ḥadith, like an expert scholar (that he was), and he was used as a symbol of memory and precision.'

Ḥāfiẓ al-Mazī said about him: 'One of the well-known Imāms of memorisation, and someone who Allāh benefited the Muslims with.'

Imām al-Dhahabī said about him: 'The renowned memoriser, Abū ʿIsā al-Tirmidhī, writer of the collection (of ḥadīth), his reliability was unanimously acknowledged'

Mubārak Ibn Al-Asīr said: 'One of the renowned scholars and memorisers, he had a noble role in the field of jurisprudence (*fiqh*).'

Ibn Ḥibbān said: 'He was from those that collected, authored, memorised and reviewed.'

Al-Ḥākim said:' I heard Mālik Ibn 'Alā' say: 'After Bukhārī died, no one was left in Khurasān better than Abū ʿIsā in memorisation, piety and ascetics. He wept until he became blind and remained so for the rest of his life.'

Imām Abū ʿIsā al-Tirmidhī said: 'I was once on the road to Makkah and I had written two volumes worth of narrations from a Shaikh that were with me. It so happened that very same Shaikh had passed by us and so I asked the group of people about him. They said 'he is so and so.' So I eagerly went over to him thinking I have the two volumes with me of his narrations. I enquired about those narrations and he agreed to narrate them to me. I took out the two volumes, only to find the pages were empty. The sheikh started to read the narrations from his memory and looked at me and saw the white empty pages and said: 'Are you not ashamed?' I said 'no,' and told him what had transpired. I have memorised all of what you have said, I infomed him. So he said to me 'read.' So I read to him all of what he had read but he did not believe me. He said 'you have memorised all that before I came?' So I said: 'Narrate something else to me.' So he narrated another forty narrations to me from the rare narrations he knew. Then he said to me 'read.' So I read from the start to the finish and never made a mistake in a single letter. So he said: 'I have never seen the likes of you."

Imām Bukhārī said to Tirmidhī: 'You have not benefitted from me more than I have benefitted from you.'

Tirmidhī himself said that he showed his collection of ḥadīth to the scholars of Ḥijāẓ; 'Irāq and Khurasān and they were all pleased with it. Whoever has this book in his house is as if he has the Prophet in his house talking to him.

Abū Ismā'īl Shaikh al-Islām said: 'The ḥadīth collection of Tirmidhī is more beneficial than Bukhārī and Muslim, because the benefits of those books are only fully appreciated by those well-grounded in knowledge. As for Tirmidhī then everyone is able to benefit from it.'

His Works

Imām Tirmidhī became famous for his works which reflect his great and extensive knowledge and benefit. Among them are:

- *Al-Jāmi'*, better known as *al-Sunan al-Tirmidhī*
- *Al-Shamā'il al-Muḥammadiyyah*
- *Al-'Ilal al-Ṣagīr*—It is an appendix at the end of *Jāmi'* (collection of ḥadīths) and it is the book that follows it. It is a very beneficial book in which it embodies principals in the science of ḥadith and other issues which can be referred to by the one reading his book *Al-Jāmi'* as well as other general principals in the science of ḥadith. This book has been printed along with an explanation by Ḥāfiẓ Ibn Rajab Al-Hanbali.
- *Al-'Ilal al-Kabīr*—This is different from the previous book. He mentions narrations with the chain and then speaks about their hidden defects and this is the book referred by the majority of scholars.
- *Asmā' al-Ṣaḥābah*—The Names of the Companions of the Messenger of Allāh (ﷺ). It begins with the names of the ten companions promised paradise, then it lists all the other companions in alphabetical order by mentioning their names and then their titles.
- *Al-Tārīkh* (The History)—This book has not yet seen the light of day. It has been mentioned as part of his works.
- *Rubā'iyyāt al-Ḥadīth*—This book has been mentioned by the author of the book: *Hadiyat al-'Ārifīn* as part of the worksof Tirmidhī.
- *Al-Zuhd*—Ḥāfiẓ Ibn Ḥajr mentioned it in *al-Tahdhīb* and said: It has not yet been found.
- *Al-Asmā' wa'l-Kunā* (Names and Titles)—Ḥāfiẓ Ibn Ḥajr also mentioned it in *al-Tahdhīb*

- *Kitāb Fī Athār Al-Muwqūfah*—Tirmidhī mentioned it himself at the end of his ḥadith collection (*Jāmi'*) at the very start of the appendix.

His Death

He was an example of piety and devotion, to the point he lost his sight at the end of his life and remained blind for many years. Many have mentioned that he died on Monday the 13th of Rajab 279 AH. He died in the village of Boogh, while others say he died in Tirmidh. There is no contradiction in this as Boogh is in Tirmidh. So whoever said Boogh is being more precise and whoever said Tirmidh is simply being general intending the same place, and this is something known and used a lot.

May Allāh have mercy upon Imām Tirmidhī for indeed he has left behind many beneficial works. May Allāh reward him greatly along with the Imāms of the Muslims who preserved the knowledge and sciences of the religion and conveyed it as they heard it for those that would come after them.

CHAPTER ONE

بَابُ مَا جَاءَ فِي خَلْقِ رَسُولِ اللهِ ﷺ

What has been narrated concerning the Description of the Physical Appearance (*khalq*) of the Messenger of Allah (ﷺ)

١ـ أَخْبَرَنَا أَبُو رَجَاءٍ قُتَيْبَةُ بْنُ سَعِيدٍ، عَنْ مَالِكِ بْنِ أَنَسٍ، عَنْ رَبِيعَةَ بْنِ أَبِي عَبْدِ الرَّحْمٰنِ، عَنْ أَنَسِ بْنِ مَالِكٍ رضي الله عنه، أَنَّهُ سَمِعَهُ يَقُولُ: «كَانَ رَسُولُ اللهِ ﷺ لَيْسَ بِالطَّوِيلِ الْبَائِنِ، وَلَا بِالْقَصِيرِ، وَلَا بِالأَبْيَضِ الأَمْهَقِ، وَلَا بِالآدَمِ، وَلَا بِالْجَعْدِ الْقَطَطِ، وَلَا بِالسَّبْطِ، بَعَثَهُ اللهُ تَعَالَى عَلَى رَأْسِ أَرْبَعِينَ سَنَةً، فَأَقَامَ بِمَكَّةَ عَشْرَ سِنِينَ، وَبِالْمَدِينَةِ عَشْرَ سِنِينَ، وَتَوَفَّاهُ اللهُ تَعَالَى عَلَى رَأْسِ سِتِّينَ سَنَةً، وَلَيْسَ فِي رَأْسِهِ وَلِحْيَتِهِ عِشْرُونَ شَعْرَةً بَيْضَاءَ».

1. Abū Rajā' Qutaybah Ibn Sa'īd informed us; from Mālik Ibn Anas; from Rabī'ah Ibn Abū 'Abdu'l-Raḥmān that he heard Anas Ibn Mālik (*raḍiyAllāhu 'anhu*) saying:

> "The Messenger of Allāh (ﷺ) was neither [excessively] tall, nor short. In complexion, he was neither pale white, nor very dark; neither was his hair tightly curled nor completely

> straight [but slightly wavy]. When he reached the age of forty, Allāh the Exalted granted him Prophethood. He stayed for ten years in Makkah and in Madīnah for ten years. Allāh took his soul upon the completion of sixty years, at that time there were no more than twenty white hairs on his head and beard."[1]

٢ـ حَدَّثَنَا حُمَيْدُ بْنُ مَسْعَدَةَ البَصْرِيُّ، قَالَ: حَدَّثَنَا عَبْدُ الوَهَّابِ الثَّقَفِيُّ، عَنْ حُمَيْدٍ، عَنْ أَنَسِ بْنِ مَالِكٍ ﷺ قَالَ: «كَانَ رَسُولُ اللهِ ﷺ رَبْعَةً: لَيْسَ بِالطَّوِيلِ وَلاَ بِالقَصِيرِ، حَسَنَ الجِسْمِ، وَكَانَ شَعْرُهُ لَيْسَ بِجَعْدٍ وَلَا سَبْطٍ، أَسْمَرَ اللَّوْنِ، إِذَا مَشَى يَتَكَفَّأُ» .

2. Ḥumayd Ibn Mas'adah al-Baṣrī narrated to us; 'Abdu'l-Wahhāb al-Thaqafī narrated to us; from Ḥumayd that Anas Ibn Mālik (*raḍiyAllāhu 'anhu*) said:

> "The Messenger of Allāh (ﷺ) was of a medium stature, he was neither [excessively] tall nor short, with handsome physique (*ḥasan al-jism*). His hair was neither tightly curled nor completely straight [but slightly wavy]. He had a red-coloured complexion (*asmar al-lawn*). When he walked, he would incline forward."[2]

٣ـ حَدَّثَنَا مُحَمَّدُ بْنُ بَشَّارٍ ـ يَعْنِي العَبْدِيَّ ـ قَالَ: حَدَّثَنَا مُحَمَّدُ بْنُ جَعْفَرٍ، قَالَ: حَدَّثَنَا شُعْبَةُ، عَنْ أَبِي إِسْحَاقَ قَالَ: سَمِعْتُ البَرَاءَ بْنَ عَازِبٍ رضي الله عنهما يَقُولُ: «كَانَ رَسُولُ اللهِ ﷺ رَجُلًا مَرْبُوعًا، بَعِيدَ مَا بَيْنَ المَنْكِبَيْنِ، عَظِيمَ الجُمَّةِ إِلَى شَحْمَةِ أُذُنَيْهِ، عَلَيْهِ حُلَّةٌ حَمْرَاءُ، مَا رَأَيْتُ شَيْئًا قَطُّ أَحْسَنَ مِنْهُ» .

---

[1] Bukhārī, #5899, Muslim, #2347 and Tirmidhī, #362.

[2] Bukhārī, #3547, Muslim, #2330, Nasā'ī in *al-Kubrā*, #9311 and Tirmidhī, #1754 and he said: It is ḥasan saḥīḥ gharīb.

3. Muḥammad Ibn Bashshār—al-ʿAbdī—narrated to us; Muḥammad Ibn Jāʿfar narrated to us; Shuʿbah narrated to us; from Abū Isḥāq that he heard Barā'a Ibn ʿĀzib (*raḍiyAllāhu ʿanhu*) saying:

> "The Messenger of Allāh (ﷺ) was a man of medium stature, broad shouldered, with luxuriant hair (*jummah*) reaching the lobes of his ears, wearing a red garment (*ḥullah*). Never have I seen anything more beautiful (*aḥsan*) than him."[3]

٤ـ حَدَّثَنَا مَحْمُودُ بْنُ غَيْلاَنَ، قَالَ: حَدَّثَنَا وَكِيعٌ، قَالَ: حَدَّثَنَا سُفْيَانُ، عَنْ أَبِي إِسْحَاقَ، عَنِ البَرَاءِ بْنِ عَازِبٍ رضي الله عنهما قَالَ: «مَا رَأَيْتُ مِنْ ذِي لِـمَّةٍ فِي حُلَّةٍ حَمْرَاءَ أَحْسَنَ مِنْ رَسُولِ اللهِ، لَهُ شَعْرٌ يَضْرِبُ مَنْكِبَيْهِ، بَعِيـدُ مَا بَيْنَ الْمَنْكِبَيْنِ، لَمْ يَكُنْ بِالقَصِيرِ وَلَا بِالطَّوِيلِ» .

4. Maḥmūd Ibn Ghaylān narrated to us; Wakīʿ narrated to us; Sufyān al-Thawrī narrated to us; from Abū Isḥāq; on the authority of Barā'a Ibn ʿĀzib (*raḍiyAllāhu ʿanhu*) that he said:

> "Never have I seen anyone with a lock of hair flowing below the ears (*limmah*) and wearing red garments (*ḥullah ḥamrā'*) more handsome (*aḥsan*) than the Messenger of Allāh (ﷺ). He had hair touching his shoulders and he was broad-shouldered. He was neither [excessively] short nor tall."[4]

---

[3] Bukhārī, #3551, Muslim, #2337, Abū Dāwūd, #4072, Tirmidhī, #2811 and Nasā'ī, #5232.
[4] Bukhārī, #3549, Muslim, #2337 and Tirmidhī, #1724.

٥ـ حَدَّثَنَا مُحَمَّدُ بْنُ إِسْمَاعِيلَ، قَالَ: حَدَّثَنَا أَبُو نُعَيْمٍ، قَالَ: حَدَّثَنَا الْمَسْعُودِيُّ، عَنْ عُثْمَانَ بْنِ مُسْلِمِ بْنِ هُرْمُزَ، عَنْ نَافِعِ بْنِ جُبَيْرِ بْنِ مُطْعِمٍ، عَنْ عَلِيِّ بْنِ أَبِي طَالِبٍ ﵁ قَالَ: «لَمْ يَكُنِ النَّبِيُّ ﷺ بِالطَّوِيلِ وَلَا بِالْقَصِيرِ، شَثْنُ الْكَفَّيْنِ وَالْقَدَمَيْنِ، ضَخْمُ الرَّأْسِ، ضَخْمُ الْكَرَادِيسِ، طَوِيلُ الْمَسْرُبَةِ، إِذَا مَشَى تَكَفَّأَ تَكَفُّؤًا كَأَنَّمَا يَنْحَطُّ مِنْ صَبَبٍ، لَمْ أَرَ قَبْلَهُ وَلَا بَعْدَهُ مِثْلَهُ ﷺ».

5. Muḥammad Ibn Ismā'īl narrated to us; Abū Nu'aym narrated to us; Mas'ūdī narrated to us; from 'Uthmān Ibn Muslim Ibn Hurmuz; from Nāfi' Ibn Jubayr Ibn Muṭ'im; on the authority of 'Alī Ibn Abū Ṭālib (*raḍiyAllāhu 'anhu*) that he said:

> "The Prophet (ﷺ) was neither [excessively] tall nor short. [He had] sturdy hands and feet.[5] He had [proportionally] large head and limbs, and a long thin line of hair stretching from his chest to his navel. When he walked, he leant forward as if descending a slope. I have not seen anyone, before him nor after him, one who was comparable (*mithl*) to him."[6]

٦ـ حَدَّثَنَا سُفْيَانُ بْنُ وَكِيعٍ قَالَ: حَدَّثَنَا أَبِي، عَنِ الْمَسْعُودِيِّ، بِهَذَا الإِسْنَادِ نَحْوَهُ بِمَعْنَاهُ.

6. Sufyān Ibn Wakī' narrated to us; my father narrated to us; from Mas'ūdī the likes of this with this isnād.

---

[5] This quality is praiseworthy in a man as it denotes strength and courage but is not praiseworthy for a woman.

[6] Tirmidhī, #3637, Ibn Ḥibbān, #6311, Ḥākim, 2/605-606 and Tirmdhī said this ḥadīth is ḥasan ṣaḥīḥ.

٧ـ حَدَّثَنَا أَحْمَدُ بْنُ عَبْدَةَ الضَّبِّيُّ البَصْرِيُّ، وَعَلِيُّ بْنُ حُجْرٍ، وَأَبُو جَعْفَرٍ مُحَمَّدُ ابْنُ الْحُسَيْنِ ـ وَهُوَ ابْنُ أَبِي حَلِيمَةَ ـ، وَالمعْنَى وَاحِدٌ، قَالُوا: حَدَّثَنَا عِيسَى ابْنُ يُونُسَ، عَنْ عُمَرَ بْنِ عَبْدِ الله مَوْلَى غُفْرَةَ، قَالَ: حَدَّثَنِي إِبْرَاهِيمُ بْنُ مُحَمَّدٍ مِنْ وَلَدِ عَلِيِّ بْنِ أَبِي طَالِبٍ رضي الله عنه قَالَ: كَانَ عَلِيٌّ رضي الله عنه إِذَا وَصَفَ رَسُولَ الله ﷺ قَالَ: «لَمْ يَكُنْ رَسُولُ الله بِالطَّوِيلِ الـمُمَغَّطِ، وَلَا بِالقَصِيرِ الْمُتَرَدِّدِ، كَانَ رَبْعَةً مِنَ القَوْمِ، لَمْ يَكُنْ بِالجَعْدِ القَطَطِ، وَلَا بِالسَّبْطِ، كَانَ جَعْدًا رَجِلًا، وَلَمْ يَكُنْ بِالـمُطَهَّمِ، وَلَا بِالـمُكَلْثَمِ، وَكَانَ فِي وَجْهِهِ تَدْوِيرٌ، أَبْيَضُ مُشْرَبٌ، أَدْعَجُ العَيْنَيْنِ، أَهْدَبُ الأَشْفَارِ، جَلِيلُ الـمُشَاشِ وَالكَتَدِ، أَجْرَدُ ذُو مَسْرُبَةٍ، شَثْنُ الكَفَّيْنِ وَالقَدَمَيْنِ، إِذَا مَشَى تَقَلَّعَ كَأَنَّمَا يَنْحَطُّ فِي صَبَبٍ، وَإِذَا التَفَتَ التَفَتَ مَعًا، بَيْنَ كَتِفَيْهِ خَاتَمُ النُّبُوَّةِ، وَهُوَ خَاتَمُ النَّبِيِّينَ، أَجْوَدُ النَّاسِ صَدْرًا، وَأَصْدَقُ النَّاسِ لَهْجَةً، وَأَلْيَنُهُمْ عَرِيكَةً، وَأَكْرَمُهُمْ عِشْرَةً، مَنْ رَآهُ بَدِيهَةً هَابَهُ، وَمَنْ خَالَطَهُ مَعْرِفَةً أَحَبَّهُ، يَقُولُ نَاعِتُهُ: لَمْ أَرَ قَبْلَهُ وَلَا بَعْدَهُ مِثْلَهُ».

قَالَ أَبُو عِيسَى: سَمِعْتُ أَبَا جَعْفَرٍ مُحَمَّدَ بْنَ الْحُسَيْنِ يَقُولُ: سَمِعْتُ الأَصْمَعِيَّ يَقُولُ فِي تَفْسِيرِ صِفَةِ النَّبِيِّ ﷺ: الـمُمَغَّطُ: الذَّاهِبُ طُولًا، وَقَالَ: سَمِعْتُ أَعْرَابِيًّا يَقُولُ فِي كَلامِهِ: تَمَغَّطَ فِي نُشَّابَتِهِ أَيْ: مَدَّهَا مَدًّا شَدِيدًا، وَالْمُتَرَدِّدُ: الدَّاخِلُ بَعْضُهُ فِي بَعْضٍ قِصَرًا، وَأَمَّا القَطَطُ: فَشَدِيدُ الجُعُودَةِ، وَالرَّجِلُ: الَّذِي فِي شَعْرِهِ حُجُونَةٌ: أَيْ: تَثَنٍّ قَلِيلٌ.

وَأَمَّا الْمُطَهَّمُ: فَالبَادِنُ الكَثِيرُ اللَّحْمِ، وَالـمُكَلْثَمُ: المدَوَّرُ الوَجْهِ، وَالـمُشْرَبُ: الَّذِي فِي بَيَاضِهِ حُمْرَةٌ.

وَالأَدْعَجُ: الشَّدِيدُ سَوَادِ العَيْنِ، وَالأَهْدَبُ: الطَّوِيلُ الأَشْفَارِ، وَالكَتَدُ: مُجْتَمَعُ الكَتِفَيْنِ، وَهُوَ الكَاهِلُ.

وَالمَسْرُبَةُ: هُوَ الشَّعْرُ الدَّقِيقُ الَّذِي كَأَنَّهُ قَضِيبٌ مِنَ الصَّدْرِ إِلَى السُّرَّةِ.

وَالشَّثْنُ: الغَلِيظُ الأَصَابعِ مِنَ الكَفَّيْنِ وَالقَدَمَيْنِ، وَالتَّقَلُّعُ: أَنْ يَمْشِيَ بِقُوَّةٍ، وَالصَّبَبُ: الحُدُورُ، يقالُ: انْحَدَرْنَا فِي صَبُوبٍ وَصَبَبٍ.

وَقَوْلُهُ: جَلِيلُ المُشَاشِ يُرِيدُ رُؤُوسَ المَنَاكِبِ، وَالعِشْرَةُ: الصُّحْبَةُ، وَالعَشِيرُ: الصَّاحِبُ، وَالبَدِيهَةُ: المُفَاجَأَةُ، يُقَالُ: بَدَهْتُهُ بِأَمْرٍ أَيْ فَجَأْتُهُ.

7. Aḥmad Ibn 'Abdah al-Ḍabbī al-Baṣrī narrated to us, as did 'Alī Ibn Ḥujr and Abū Jā'far Muḥammad Ibn al-Ḥusayn—Ibn Abī Ḥalīmah—with different wordings but the same meaning; 'Īsā Ibn Yūnus narrated to us; from 'Umar Ibn 'Abdullāh the servant of Ghufrah; Ibrāhīm Ibn Muḥammad—one of the sons of 'Alī Ibn Abū Ṭālib (*raḍiyAllāhu 'anhu*)—narrated to me that when 'Alī (*raḍiyAllāhu 'anhu*) described the Messenger of Allāh (ﷺ) he would say:

> "The Messenger of Allāh (ﷺ) was neither extremely tall nor extremely short, but of a medium stature among people. His hair was neither tightly curled nor completely straight, but had a slight wave in it. He was not overweight, nor was his face so fleshy as to be completely round; rather it was only slightly round.[7] He was fair skinned, having a reddish tinge. He had jet black eyes [pupils] with long eyelashes. He had big bone-joints and broad shoulders. Most of his body was hairless, though he had a long thin strip of hair extending from his chest to his navel. He had sturdily built hands and feet. When he walked, he moved briskly as if descending a slope. When he addressed a person he turned his entire body towards that person.[8] The Seal of Prophethood (*khātam al-nubuwah*) was situated between his shoulders. He was the Seal of the Prophets

[7] Meaning he did not have a fully round face nor a fully elongated face, but in between the two

[8] He did not only turn his face towards the person he addressed, as this is considered impolite, and sometimes, it even denotes pride.

(*khātam al-nabiyīn*). He was the most generous; he was the most truthful of people in speech, the best of them in temperament, and the most sociable amongst them. If someone saw him unexpectedly, he was awestruck by him, and if someone came to know him, he loved him. Those who described him would say, 'I have never seen anyone, before him nor after him, one who was comparable (*mithl*) to him.'"[9]

٨ـ حَدَّثَنَا سُفْيَانُ بْنُ وَكِيعٍ قَالَ: حَدَّثَنَا جُمَيْعُ بْنُ عُمَيْرِ بْنِ عَبْدِ الرَّحْمَنِ العِجْلِيُّ ـ إِمْلَاءً عَلَيْنَا مِنْ كِتَابِهِ ـ قَالَ: أَخْبَرَنِي رَجُلٌ مِنْ بَنِي تَمِيمٍ مِنْ وَلَدِ أَبِي هَالَةَ زَوْجِ خَدِيجَةَ، يُكْنَى أَبَا عَبْدِ اللهِ، عَنِ ابْنٍ لِأَبِي هَالَةَ، عَنِ الحَسَنِ بْنِ عَلِيٍّ ﵄ قَالَ: سَأَلْتُ خَالِي هِنْدَ بْنَ أَبِي هَالَةَ ـ وَكَانَ وَصَّافًا ـ عَنْ حِلْيَةِ النَّبِيِّ ﷺ، وَأَنَا أَشْتَهِي أَنْ يَصِفَ لِي مِنْهَا شَيْئًا أَتَعَلَّقُ بِهِ، فَقَالَ: «كَانَ النَّبِيُّ ﷺ فَخْمًا مُفَخَّمًا، يَتَلَأْلَأُ وَجْهُهُ تَلَأْلُؤَ القَمَرِ لَيْلَةَ البَدْرِ، أَطْوَلَ مِنَ المَرْبُوعِ، وَأَقْصَرَ مِنَ المُشَذَّبِ، عَظِيمَ الهَامَةِ، رَجِلَ الشَّعْرِ، إِنِ انْفَرَقَتْ عَقِيقَتُهُ فَرَقَهَا وَإِلَّا فَلَا يُجَاوِزُ شَعْرُهُ شَحْمَةَ أُذُنَيْهِ إِذَا هُوَ وَفَّرَهُ، أَزْهَرَ اللَّوْنِ، وَاسِعَ الجَبِينِ، أَزَجَّ الحَوَاجِبِ، سَوَابِغَ فِي غَيْرِ قَرَنٍ، بَيْنَهُمَا عِرْقٌ يُدِرُّهُ الغَضَبُ، أَقْنَى العِرْنِينِ، لَهُ نُورٌ يَعْلُوهُ، يَحْسَبُهُ مَنْ لَمْ يَتَأَمَّلْهُ أَشَمَّ، كَثَّ اللِّحْيَةِ، سَهْلَ الخَدَّيْنِ، ضَلِيعَ الفَمِ، مُفْلَجَ الأَسْنَانِ، دَقِيقَ المَسْرُبَةِ، كَأَنَّ عُنُقَهُ جِيدُ دُمْيَةٍ فِي صَفَاءِ الفِضَّةِ، مُعْتَدِلَ الخَلْقِ، بَادِنٌ مُتَمَاسِكٌ، سَوَاءُ البَطْنِ وَالصَّدْرُ، عَرِيضُ الصَّدْرِ، بَعِيدَ مَا بَيْنَ المَنْكِبَيْنِ، ضَخْمُ الكَرَادِيسِ، أَنْوَرُ المُتَجَرَّدِ، مَوْصُولُ مَا بَيْنَ اللَّبَّةِ وَالسُّرَّةِ بِشَعْرٍ يَجْرِي كَالخَطِّ، عَارِي الثَّدْيَيْنِ وَالبَطْنِ مِمَّا سِوَى ذَلِكَ، أَشْعَرُ الذِّرَاعَيْنِ وَالمَنْكِبَيْنِ وَأَعَالِي الصَّدْرِ،

[9] Tirmidhī, #3637. This ḥadīth has a weak chain although some of the wording has been established in other authentic narrations.

طَوِيلُ الزَّنْدَيْنِ، رَحْبُ الرَّاحَةِ، شَثْنُ الكَفَّيْنِ وَالقَدَمَيْنِ، سَائِلُ الأَطْرَافِ ـ أَوْ قَالَ: شَائِلُ الأَطْرَافِ ـ خُمْصَانُ الأَخْمَصَيْنِ، مَسِيحُ القَدَمَيْنِ، يَنْبُو عَنْهُمَا المَاءُ، إِذَا زَالَ زَالَ قَلَعًا[١]، يَخْطُو تَكَفِّيًا، وَيَمْشِي هَوْنًا، ذَرِيعُ المِشْيَةِ، إِذَا مَشَى كَأَنَّمَا يَنْحَطُّ مِنْ صَبَبٍ، وَإِذَا التَفَتَ التَفَتَ جَمِيعًا، خَافِضُ الطَّرْفِ، نَظَرُهُ إِلَى الأَرْضِ أَطْوَلُ مِنْ نَظَرِهِ إِلَى السَّمَاءِ، جُلُّ نَظَرِهِ المُلَاحَظَةُ، يَسُوقُ أَصْحَابَهُ، يَبْدُرُ مَنْ لَقِيَ بِالسَّلَامِ» .

8. Sufyān Ibn Wakīʿ narrated to us; Jumayʿ Ibn ʿUmayr Ibn ʿAbdu'l-Raḥmān al-ʿIjlī narrated to us: I was informed by a man from the Banu Tamīm, one of the children of Abū Ḥāla, the husband Khadījah, called Abū ʿAbdullāh; from Abū Ḥālah; al-Ḥasan Ibn ʿAlī (*raḍiyAllāhu ʿanhum*) who said: 'I inquired from my maternal uncle Hind Ibn Abī Ḥālah (*raḍiyAllāhu ʿanhā*) about the noble features of the Messenger of Allāh (ﷺ). He had often described the noble features of the Messenger of Allāh (ﷺ) in detail. I felt that I should hear from him personally, some of the noble appearance (*ḥilyah*) of the Messenger of Allāh (ﷺ), so that I could make his description a proof and testimony for myself and also memorise them, and, if possible, try to emulate and adopt them, so he said:

> "The Messenger of Allāh (ﷺ) was majestic and esteemed. His face would shine with the radiance of the moon on the moonlit night. He was slightly taller than a man of medium height, yet shorter than someone extremely tall. His head was grand [and impressive], with loosely curled hair. If his hair became parted naturally in the middle he left it so, otherwise he did not habitually make an effort to part his hair in the middle. If hair could be parted easily, he would part it, otherwise his hair would not exceed his earlobes, and he would let it grow plentiful and long (*wafrah*). He had a radiantly fair complexion and a wide forehead. His eyebrows were long and perfectly arched without being connected, with a vein between them

that used to throb when he became angry. His nose was prominent with a fine tip, slightly curved from the centre and shone so that any casual observer would think that he had an elevated bridge (*shamm*). He was thickly bearded, endowed with smooth cheeks, a [moderately] wide mouth, a gap between his [two upper front] teeth, and a long thin strip of hair extending from his chest to his navel. His neck was beautiful and thin, as if his neck were the neck of a statue shaped in pure silver. He was well proportioned in physique. His stomach and chest were perfectly aligned. He was wide-chested, broad-shouldered, endowed with large joints (denoting strength) and very shiny bare skin. He had a fine strand of hair like a thread running between the upper part of his chest and naval. His [lower] chest and stomach were hairless, while he had a lot of hair on his forearms, shoulders and upper part of his chest. His forearms were long and his palms were wide, sturdily built palms and feet, moderately-long fingers and toes. The soles of his feet were slender, and his feet were so smooth that water would bounce off them. When he walked, he lifted his legs with vigor, leaned slightly forward and placed his feet softly on the ground. He walked at a brisk pace, taking long strides. When he walked it seemed as if he was descending to a lower place. When he looked around, he turned completely. He would lower his gaze, and his gaze at the floor would be longer than his gaze at the sky. He would mostly gaze from the corner of his eyes. He would urge his Companions to proceed ahead of him, and he would rush to offer the greeting of peace to whomsoever he met."[10]

[10] Ṭabarānī in *al-Kabīr*, 22/155-159. This ḥadīth has a weak chain although some of the wording has been established in other authentic narrations.

٩ـ حَدَّثَنَا أَبُو مُوسَى مُحَمَّدُ بْنُ الْمُثَنَّى، حَدَّثَنَا مُحَمَّدُ بْنُ جَعْفَرٍ، قَالَ: حَدَّثَنَا شُعْبَةُ، عَنْ سِمَاكِ بْنِ حَرْبٍ، قَالَ: سَمِعْتُ جَابِرَ بْنَ سَمُرَةَ يَقُولُ: «كَانَ رَسُولُ اللهِ ﷺ ضَلِيعَ الفَمِ، أَشْكَلَ العَيْنِ، مَنْهُوسَ العَقِبِ».

قَالَ شُعْبَةُ: قُلتُ لِسِمَاكٍ: مَا ضَلِيعُ الفَمِ؟ قَالَ: عَظِيمُ الفَمِ، قُلتُ: مَا أَشْكَلُ العَيْنِ؟ قَالَ: طَوِيلُ شِقِّ العَيْنِ، قُلتُ: مَا مَنْهُوسُ العَقِبِ؟ قَالَ: قَلِيلُ لحمِ العَقِبِ .

9. Abū Mūsā Muḥammad Ibn al-Muthannā narrated to us; Muḥammad Ibn Jā'far narrated to us; Shu'bah narrated to us; from Simāk Ibn Ḥarb; who said that he heard Jābir Ibn Samurah (*raḍiyAllāhu 'anhu*) saying:

> 'The Messenger of Allāh (ﷺ) had a wide mouth, reddishness in the whites of his eyes, and lean heels.'

Shu'bah said: 'I asked Simāk: 'What is the meaning of *ḍalī' al-fam*?' To which he replied: 'A large mouth.' I asked: 'What is the meaning of *ashkal al-'ayn*?' To which he replied: 'Wide eyes.' I asked: 'What is the meaning of *manhūs al-'aqib*?' To which he replied: 'Of little flesh on the heels.'[11]

١٠ـ حَدَّثَنَا هَنَّادُ بْنُ السَّرِيِّ، قَالَ: حَدَّثَنَا عَبْثَرُ بْنُ القَاسِمِ، عَنْ أَشْعَثَ ـ يعني ابْنَ سَوَّارٍ ـ، عَنْ أَبِي إِسْحَاقَ، عَنْ جَابِرِ بْنِ سَمُرَةَ، قَالَ: «رَأَيْتُ رَسُولَ اللهِ ﷺ فِي لَيْلَةٍ إِضْحِيَانٍ، وَعَلَيْهِ حُلَّةٌ حَمْرَاءُ، فَجَعَلتُ أَنْظُرُ إِلَيْهِ وَإِلَى القَمَرِ، فَلَهُوَ عِنْدِي أَحْسَنُ مِنَ القَمَرِ» .

10. Hannād Ibn al-Sarrī narrated to us; 'Abthar Ibn al-Qāsim narrated to us; from Ash'āth—Ibn Sawwār—; from Abū Isḥāq; from

[11] Muslim, #2339 and Tirmidhī, #3646-3647

Jābir Ibn Samurah (*raḍiyAllāhu ʿanhu*) who said:

> "I [once] saw the Messenger of Allāh (ﷺ) on a clear, moonlit night wearing red clothing (*ḥullah*). I paused and gazed at him and then the moon and found that, in my estimation, he was more beautiful (*aḥsan*) than the moon."[12]

١١ـ حَدَّثَنَا سُفْيَانُ بْنُ وَكِيعٍ، قَالَ: حَدَّثَنَا حُمَيْدُ بْنُ عَبْدِ الرَّحْمَنِ الرُّؤَاسِيُّ، عَنْ زُهَيْرٍ، عَنْ أَبِي إِسْحَاقَ، قَالَ: سَأَلَ رَجُلٌ الْبَرَاءَ بْنَ عَازِبٍ رضي الله عنهما: «أَكَانَ وَجْهُ رَسُولِ اللهِ ﷺ مِثْلَ السَّيْفِ؟ قَالَ: لاَ، بَلْ مِثْلَ الْقَمَرِ».

11. Sufyān Ibn Wakīʿ narrated to us; Ḥumayd Ibn ʿAbdu'l-Raḥmān al-Ruwwāsī narrated to us; from Zuhayr; from Abū Isḥāq who said; a man asked Barā'a Ibn ʿĀzib (*raḍiyAllāhu ʿanhu*):

> "Was the face of the Messenger of Allāh (ﷺ) [shining] like a sword?' He replied: 'No, it was rather like the moon."[13]

١٢ـ حَدَّثَنَا أَبُو دَاوُدَ الْمَصَاحِفِيُّ سُلَيْمَانُ بْنُ سَلم قَالَ: حَدَّثَنَا النَّضْرُ ابْنُ شُمَيْلٍ، عَنْ صَالِحِ بْنِ أَبِي الأَخْضَرِ، عَنِ ابْنِ شِهَابٍ، عَنْ أَبِي سَلَمَةَ، عَنْ أَبِي هُرَيْرَةَ رضي الله عنه قَالَ: «كَانَ رَسُولُ اللهِ ﷺ أَبْيَضَ كَأَنَّمَا صِيغَ مِنْ فِضَّةٍ، رَجِلَ الشَّعْرِ».

12. Abū Dāwūd al-Maṣāḥifī—Sulaymān Ibn Salm—narrated to us; Naṣr Ibn Shumayl narrated to us; from Ṣāliḥ Ibn Abū'l-Akhdar;

[12] Tirmidhī, #2811, in the chain is Ashath Ibn Sawwar who is weak, although the similitude of the Prophet's (ﷺ) face with the moon and that he was more beautiful than the moon has other supporting narrations which will be mentioned later in this book.

[13] Tirmidhī, #3636, the chain has Sufyan Ibn Wakeeʿ who is weak, however Bukhārī has narrated this same ḥadith with a different chain, #3549.

from Ibn Shihāb; from Abū Salamah; from Abū Hurayrah (*raḍiyAllāhu ʿanhu*) that he said:

> "The Messenger of Allāh (ﷺ) was fair-complexioned, as if his body was fashioned and moulded from silver, with loosely curled hair."[14]

١٣ـ حَدَّثَنَا قُتَيْبَةُ بْنُ سَعِيدٍ قَالَ: أَخْبَرَنِي اللَّيْثُ بْنُ سَعْدٍ، عَنْ أَبِي الزُّبَيْرِ، عَنْ جَابِرِ بْنِ عَبْدِ اللهِ، أَنَّ رَسُولَ اللهِ ﷺ قَالَ: «عُرِضَ عَلَيَّ الأَنْبِيَاءُ؛ فَإِذَا مُوسَى عَلَيْهِ السَّلَام ضَرْبٌ مِنَ الرِّجَالِ، كَأَنَّهُ مِنْ رِجَالِ شَنُوءَةَ، وَرَأَيْتُ عِيسَى ابْنَ مَرْيَمَ عَلَيْهِ السَّلَام؛ فَإِذَا أَقْرَبُ مَنْ رَأَيْتُ بِهِ شَبَهًا عُرْوَةُ بنُ مَسْعُودٍ، وَرَأَيْتُ إِبْرَاهِيمَ عَلَيْهِ السَّلَام؛ فَإِذَا أَقْرَبُ مَنْ رَأَيْتُ بِهِ شَبَهًا صَاحِبُكُمْ ـ يَعْنِي نَفْسَهُ ـ، وَرَأَيْتُ جِبْرِيلَ عَلَيْهِ السَّلَام؛ فَإِذَا أَقْرَبُ مَنْ رَأَيْتُ بِهِ شَبَهًا دِحْيَةُ».

13. Qutaybah Ibn Saʿid narrated to us; Al-Layth Ibn Saʿd informed me; from Abū'l-Zubayr; from Jābir Ibn ʿAbdullāh (*raḍiyAllāhu ʿanhu*) that the Messenger of Allāh (ﷺ) said:

> "The Prophets were presented to me, and there was Mūsā (*ʿalayhis-salām*), a specimen of men of distinction, and his build and height were medium as if he was from the tribe of Shanu'ah. I also saw ʿIsā Ibn Maryam (*ʿalayhis-salām*), and the nearest I have seen in resembled to him is ʿUrwah Ibn Masʿud. I also saw Ibrahīm (*ʿalayhis-salām*), and the nearest I have seen in resembled to him is your Companion (namely, himself). I also saw Jibr'āl (*ʿalayhis-salām*) and nearest I have seen in resemblance to him is Dihyah [al-Kalbī]."[15]

---

[14] This chain has Ṣālih Ibn Al-Adhar about whom Ibn Hajr said: He is weak but can be used with supporting evidence. *Taqrīb al-Tahdhīb*, 2/271.

[15] Muslim,#167, Tirmidhī, #3649 and Aḥmad, 3/334.

١٤ـ حَدَّثَنَا سُفْيَانُ بْنُ وَكِيعٍ، وَمُحَمَّدُ بْنُ بَشَّارٍ ـ الـمَعْنَى وَاحِدٌ ـ قَالَا: أَخْبَرَنَا يَزِيدُ بْنُ هَارُونَ، عَنْ سَعِيدٍ الْجُرَيْرِيِّ قَالَ: سَمِعْتُ أَبَا الطُّفَيْلِ يَقُولُ: «رَأَيْتُ النَّبِيَّ ﷺ وَمَا بَقِيَ عَلَى وَجْهِ الأَرْضِ أَحَدٌ رَآهُ غَيْرِي»، قُلتُ: صِفْهُ لِي، قَالَ: «كَانَ أَبْيَضَ مَلِيحًا مُقَصَّدًا».

14. Sufyān Ibn Wakī' narrated to us, as did Muḥammad Ibn Bashshār (the meaning is one and the same); Yazīd Ibn Hārūn informed us that Sa'īd al-Jurayrī said: 'I heard Abū Ṭufayl (*raḍiyAllāhu 'anhu*) say:

> 'There is no one left on the face of the Earth, besides me who has seen the Prophet (ﷺ).' I said: 'Describe him for me!' He said: 'He had a fair-complexion, which was slightly reddish, of medium sized."[16]

١٥ـ حَدَّثَنَا عَبْدُ اللهِ بْنُ عَبْدِ الرَّحْمَنِ، قَالَ: حَدَّثَنَا إِبْرَاهِيمُ بْنُ الْمُنْذِرِ الْحِزَامِيُّ، قَالَ: حَدَّثَنَا عَبْدُ الْعَزِيزِ بْنُ أَبِي ثَابِتٍ الزُّهْرِيُّ، قَالَ: حَدَّثَنِي إِسْمَاعِيلُ بْنُ إِبْرَاهِيمَ ابْنُ أَخِي مُوسَى بْنِ عُقْبَةَ، عَنْ مُوسَى بْنِ عُقْبَةَ، عَنْ كُرَيْبٍ، عَنِ ابْنِ عَبَّاسٍ رضي الله عنهما قَالَ: «كَانَ رَسُولُ اللهِ ﷺ أَفْلَجَ الثَّنِيَّتَيْنِ، إِذَا تَكَلَّمَ رُئِيَ كَالنُّورِ يَخْرُجُ مِنْ بَيْنِ ثَنَايَاهُ».

15. 'Abdullāh Ibn 'Abdu'l-Raḥmān narrated to us; Ibrāhīm Ibn Mundhir al-Ḥizāmī narrated to us; 'Abdu'l-'Azīz Ibn Abī Thābit al-Zuhrī narrated to us; Ismā'īl Ibn Ibrahīm, the nephew of Mūsā Ibn 'Uqbah narrated to me; from Mūsā Ibn 'Uqbah; from Kurayb that Ibn 'Abbās (*raḍiyAllāhu 'anhumā*) said:

> "The Messenger of Allāh's two upper front teeth had a gap

[16] Muslim, #2340 and Abū Dāwūd, #4863.

between them. When he spoke, it was like light emerging from his two front teeth."[17]

[17] Ṭabarānī in *al-Kabīr*, 12181 and in *al-Awsaṭ*, #771. Chain has a narrator whose narrations are rejected.

CHAPTER TWO

بَابُ مَا جَاءَ فِي خَاتَمِ النُّبُوَّةِ

What has been narrated concerning the Seal of Prophethood (*Khātam al-Nubuwwa*)

١٦ـ حَدَّثَنَا أَبُو رَجَاءٍ قُتَيْبَةُ بْنُ سَعِيدٍ، قَالَ: حَدَّثَنَا حَاتِمُ بْنُ إِسْمَاعِيلَ، عَنِ الجَعْدِ بْنِ عَبْدِ الرَّحْمَنِ قَالَ: سَمِعْتُ السَّائِبَ بْنَ يَزِيدَ يَقُولُ: «ذَهَبَتْ بِي خَالَتِي إِلَى النَّبِيِّ ﷺ فَقَالَتْ: يَا رَسُولَ اللهِ! إِنَّ ابْنَ أُخْتِي وَجِعٌ؛ فَمَسَحَ رَأْسِي وَدَعَا لِي بِالبَرَكَةِ، وَتَوَضَّأَ، فَشَرِبْتُ مِنْ وَضُوئِهِ، وَقُمْتُ خَلْفَ ظَهْرِهِ، فَنَظَرْتُ إِلَى الخَاتَمِ بَيْنَ كَتِفَيْهِ، فَإِذَا هُوَ مِثْلُ زِرِّ الحَجَلَةِ»

16. Abū Rajā' Qutaybah Ibn Sa'īd narrated to us; Ḥātim Ibn Ismā'īl narrated to us; from al-Ja'd Ibn 'Abdu'l-Raḥmān that he heard al-Sā'ib Ibn Yazīd (*raḍiyAllāhu 'anhu*) saying:

> "My (maternal) aunt took me to the Prophet (ﷺ), and she said: 'O Messenger of Allāh, this nephew of mine is in pain.' So he (ﷺ) wiped his hand over my head and prayed for me to be blessed, and he performed ablution (wudu). I drank from his ablution and I stood behind his back, thereupon I saw the Seal of Prophethood (*Khātam al-Nubuwwa*) between his shoulders, it was like a button

on a curtain canopy."[18]

١٧ـ حَدَّثَنَا سَعِيدُ بْنُ يَعْقُوبَ الطَّالْقَانِيُّ قَالَ: حَدَّثَنَا أَيُّوبُ بْنُ جَابِرٍ، عَنْ سِمَاكِ بْنِ حَرْبٍ، عَنْ جَابِرِ بْنِ سَمُرَةَ قَالَ: «رَأَيْتُ الخَاتَمَ بَيْنَ كَتِفَيْ رَسُولِ اللهِ ﷺ غُدَّةً حَمْرَاءَ مِثْلَ بَيْضَةِ الحَمَامَةِ».

17. Sa'īd Ibn Ya'qūb al-Ṭāliqānī narrated to us; Ayyūb Ibn Jābir narrated to us; from Simāk Ibn Ḥarb that Jābir Ibn Samurah (*raḍiyAllāhu 'anhu*) said:

> "I saw the Seal (*khātam*) between the shoulders of the Messenger of Allāh (ﷺ) as a protruding red piece of red flesh similar to the size of a pigeon's egg."[19]

١٨ـ حَدَّثَنَا أَبُو مُصْعَبٍ المَدِينِيُّ قَالَ: حَدَّثَنَا يُوسُفُ بْنُ المَاجِشُونِ، عَنْ أَبِيهِ، عَنْ عَاصِمِ بْنِ عُمَرَ بْنِ قَتَادَةَ، عَنْ جَدَّتِهِ رُمَيْثَةَ ﵂ قَالَتْ: سَمِعْتُ رَسُولَ اللهِ ﷺ ـ وَلَوْ أَشَاءُ أَنْ أُقَبِّلَ الخَاتَمَ الَّذِي بَيْنَ كَتِفَيْهِ مِنْ قُرْبِهِ لَفَعَلْتُ ـ يَقُولُ لِسَعْدِ بْنِ مُعَاذٍ يَوْمَ مَاتَ: «اهْتَزَّ لَهُ عَرْشُ الرَّحْمَنِ»

18. Abū Muṣ'ab al-Madyanī narrated to us; Yūsuf Ibn al-Mājishūn narrated to us; from his father; from 'Āsim Ibn 'Umar Ibn Qatādah that his grandmother Rumaythah (*raḍiyAllāhu 'anhā*) said:

> "I heard from Messenger of Allāh (ﷺ) and at that time I was so near him, that if I wished to, I could have kissed the Seal between his shoulders - saying after the death of Sa'd Ibn Mu'adh, 'The Throne of the All-Merciful shook on account [of his death].'"[20]

[18] Bukhārī, #190, and Muslim, #2345 and Tirmidhī, #3643.
[19] Muslim, #2344 and Tirmidhī, #3644.
[20] Bukhārī, #3803, Muslim, #2466, Tirmidhī, #3848, Ibn Mājah, #158 and Aḥmad in his *Musnad*, #26793.

١٩ـ حَدَّثَنَا أَحْمَدُ بْنُ عَبْدَةَ الضَّبِّيُّ، وَعَلِيُّ بْنُ حُجْرٍ، وَغَيْرُ وَاحِدٍ، قَالُوا: حَدَّثَنَا عِيسَى بْنُ يُونُسَ، عَنْ عُمَرَ بْنِ عَبْدِ اللهِ مَوْلَى غُفْرَةَ قَالَ: حَدَّثَنِي إِبْرَاهِيمُ بْنُ مُحَمَّدٍ ـ مِنْ وَلَدِ عَلِيِّ بْنِ أَبِي طَالِبٍ ـ قَالَ: كَانَ عَلِيٌّ إِذَا وَصَفَ رَسُولَ اللهِ ﷺ ـ فَذَكَرَ الحَدِيثَ بِطُولِهِ ـ وَقَالَ: «بَيْنَ كَتِفَيْهِ خَاتَمُ النُّبُوَّةِ، وَهُوَ خَاتَمُ النَّبِيِّينَ»

19. Aḥmad Ibn ʿAbdah al-Dabbī as well as ʿAlī Ibn Ḥujr narrated to us; ʿIsā Ibn Yūnus narrated to us; from ʿUmar Ibn ʿAbdullāh, the freed slave of Ghufrah, said: Ibrāhīm Ibn Muḥammad, one of the sons of ʿAlī Ibn Abī Tālib (*raḍiyAllāhu ʿanhu*) narrated to me:

> "Whenever ʿAlī (*raḍiyAllāhu ʿanhu*) used to describe the noble attributes of the Messenger of Allāh (ﷺ), he used to mention the full tradition. He also used to say that the Seal of Prophethood was between his shoulders, and he is the Seal of the [all] Prophets."[21]

٢٠ـ حَدَّثَنَا مُحَمَّدُ بْنُ بَشَّارٍ، قَالَ: حَدَّثَنَا أَبُو عَاصِمٍ، قَالَ: حَدَّثَنَا عَزْرَةُ ابْنُ ثَابِتٍ، قَالَ: حَدَّثَنِي عِلْبَاءُ بْنُ أَحْمَرَ الْيَشْكُرِيُّ، قَالَ: حَدَّثَنِي أَبُو زَيْدٍ عَمْرُو ابْنُ أَخْطَبَ الأَنْصَارِيُّ، قَالَ: قَالَ لِي رَسُولُ اللهِ ﷺ: «يَا أَبَا زَيْدٍ، ادْنُ مِنِّي فَامْسَحْ ظَهْرِي»، فَمَسَحْتُ ظَهْرَهُ، فَوَقَعَتْ أَصَابِعِي عَلَى الخَاتَمِ، قُلْتُ: وَمَا الخَاتَمُ؟ قَالَ: شَعَرَاتٌ مُجْتَمِعَاتٌ.

20. Muḥammad Ibn Bashshār narrated to us; Abū ʿĀṣim narrated to us; Azrah Ibn Thābit narrated to us; ʿAlbāʾ Ibn Aḥmar al-Yashkūrī narrated to me; Abū Zayd ʿAmr Ibn Akhtab al-Anṣarī (*raḍiyAllāhu*

[21] Tirmidhī, #3638. This ḥadīth is weak because of two defects, although most of its wording is supported by other narrations.

'anhu) said: 'The Messenger of Allāh (ﷺ) said to me:

> "Abū Zayd, come close to me and wipe my back." I began wiping his back and my fingers touched the Seal [of Prophethood]. I said: 'What is the Seal?' He said: `It was a tuft of a few hairs.'"[22]

٢١ـ حَدَّثَنَا أَبُو عَمَّارٍ الْحُسَيْنُ بْنُ حُرَيْثٍ الْخُزَاعِيُّ، قَالَ: حَدَّثَنَا عَلِيُّ ابْنُ حُسَيْنِ بْنِ وَاقِدٍ، قَالَ حَدَّثَنِي أَبِي، قَالَ: حَدَّثَنِي عَبْدُ اللهِ بْنُ بُرَيْدَةَ، قَالَ: سَمِعْتُ أَبِي: بُرَيْدَةَ، يَقُولُ: جَاءَ سَلْمَانُ الْفَارِسِيُّ إِلَى رَسُولِ اللهِ ﷺ حِينَ قَدِمَ الْمَدِينَةَ بِمَائِدَةٍ عَلَيْهَا رُطَبٌ، فَوَضَعَهَا بَيْنَ يَدَيْ رَسُولِ اللهِ ﷺ، فَقَالَ: «يَا سَلْمَانُ! مَا هَذَا؟» فَقَالَ: صَدَقَةٌ عَلَيْكَ وَعَلَى أَصْحَابِكَ، فَقَالَ: «ارْفَعْهَا؛ فَإِنَّا لَا نَأْكُلُ الصَّدَقَةَ»، قَالَ: فَرَفَعَهَا، فَجَاءَ الْغَدَ بِمِثْلِهِ، فَوَضَعَهُ بَيْنَ يَدَيْ رَسُولِ اللهِ ﷺ، فَقَالَ: «مَا هَذَا يَا سَلْمَانُ؟!» فَقَالَ: هَدِيَّةٌ لَكَ، فَقَالَ رَسُولُ اللهِ ﷺ لِأَصْحَابِهِ: «ابْسُطُوا»، ثُمَّ نَظَرَ إِلَى الْخَاتَمِ عَلَى ظَهْرِ رَسُولِ اللهِ ﷺ فَآمَنَ بِهِ، وَكَانَ لِلْيَهُودِ؛ فَاشْتَرَاهُ رَسُولُ اللهِ ﷺ بِكَذَا وَكَذَا دِرْهَمًا عَلَى أَنْ يَغْرِسَ لَهُمْ نَخْلًا فَيَعْمَلَ سَلْمَانُ فِيهِ حَتَّى تُطْعِمَ، فَغَرَسَ رَسُولُ اللهِ ﷺ النَّخلَ إِلَّا نَخْلَةً وَاحِدَةً غَرَسَهَا عُمَرُ، فَحَمَلَتِ النَّخْلُ مِنْ عَامِهَا وَلَمْ تَحْمِلْ نَخْلَةٌ، فَقَالَ رَسُولُ اللهِ ﷺ: «مَا شَأْنُ هَذِهِ النَّخْلَةِ؟»، فَقَالَ عُمَرُ: يَا رَسُولَ اللهِ! أَنَا غَرَسْتُهَا، فَنَزَعَهَا رَسُولُ اللهِ ﷺ فَغَرَسَهَا، فَحَمَلَتْ مِنْ عَامِهَا.

21. Abū 'Ammar al-Ḥusayn Ibn Ḥurayth al-Khazā'ī narrated to us; 'Alī Ibn Ḥusayn Ibn Wāqid narrated to us; My father narrated to me; 'Abdullāh Ibn Buraydah narrated to me; I heard Abū Buraydah (*raḍiyAllāhu 'anhu*) say:

> 'When the Messenger of Allāh (ﷺ) came to Medīnah,

[22] Aḥmad in his *Musnad*, #20732.

Salmān al-Fārisī brought a tray which had fresh dates on it, and presented it before the Messenger of Allāh (ﷺ).' He said: "What is this, O Salmān?" He replied: 'A charitable gift (*ṣadaqah*) for you and your Companions.'

The Prophet (ﷺ) said: "Take it away, for we do not eat charity" He therefore took it away. Then he came next day with the like of it, and presented it before the Messenger of Allāh (ﷺ).' He said: "What is this, O Salmān?" He replied: 'A present (*hadiya*) for you.'

The Messenger of Allāh (ﷺ) told his Companions, "Extend [your hands to eat]." Then he saw the Seal [of Prophethood] on the back of the Messenger of Allāh (ﷺ), whereupon he came to believe in him [to be a Prophet]. He was a slave of the Jews; however, the Messenger of Allāh (ﷺ) purchased his freedom at such-and-such amount of silver coins (*dirham*), with the condition that he [the Prophet] would plant date palms for them on which Salmān would work until they bore fruit.

Then the Messenger of Allāh (ﷺ) planted [all] of the date palms, apart from one date that 'Umar planted. Then [all] the date palms bore their annual fruit, except one date palm that did not bear fruit. The Messenger of Allāh (ﷺ) said: "What is the matter with this date palm?" Whereupon 'Umar (*raḍiyAllāhu 'anhu*) said: 'O Messenger of Allāh, I planted it!' The Messenger of Allāh (ﷺ) then uprooted it and replanted it. Thereafter, it too bore it's annual fruit.'"[23]

[23] This chain of narration is weak although Aḥmad has narrated it with another chain in his *Musnad*, #22997 and was authenticated by Al-Busayrī.

٢٢ـ حَدَّثَنَا مُحَمَّدُ بْنُ بَشَّارٍ، قَالَ: حَدَّثَنَا بِشْرُ بْنُ الوَضَّاحِ، قَالَ: حَدَّثَنَا أَبُو عَقِيلٍ الدَّوْرَقِيُّ، عَنْ أَبِي نَضْرَةَ العَوَقِيِّ، قَالَ: سَأَلْتُ أَبَا سَعِيدٍ الخُدْرِيَّ عَنْ خَاتَمِ رَسُولِ اللهِ ﷺ ـ يَعْنِي خَاتَمَ النُّبُوَّةِ ـ فَقَالَ: كَانَ فِي ظَهْرِهِ بَضْعَةً نَاشِزَةً.

22. Muḥammad Ibn Bashshār narrated to us; Bishr Ibn al-Waḍḍāh narrated to us; Abū ʿAqīl al-Dawraqī narrated to us that Abū Naḍrah al-ʿAwaqī said:

> 'I asked Abū Saʿīd Khudrī (*raḍiyAllāhu ʿanhu*) about the Seal of the Messenger of Allāh (ﷺ)—meaning the Seal of Prophethood (*khātam al-nubuwwa*)—he said: "It was a protruding piece of flesh that was on his [upper] back."'

٢٣ـ حَدَّثَنَا أَحْمَدُ بْنُ المِقْدَامِ أَبُو الأَشْعَثِ العِجْلِيُّ البَصْرِيُّ، قَالَ: أَخْبَرَنَا حَمَّادُ ابْنُ زَيْدٍ، عَنْ عَاصِمٍ الأَحْوَلِ، عَنْ عَبْدِ اللهِ بْنِ سَرْجِسَ، قَالَ: أَتَيْتُ رَسُولَ اللهِ ﷺ وَهُوَ فِي نَاسٍ مِنْ أَصْحَابِهِ، فَدُرْتُ هَكَذَا مِنْ خَلْفِهِ، فَعَرَفَ الَّذِي أُرِيدُ، فَأَلْقَى الرِّدَاءَ عَنْ ظَهْرِهِ، فَرَأَيْتُ مَوْضِعَ الخَاتَمِ عَلَى كَتِفَيْهِ مِثْلَ الجُمْعِ حَوْلَهَا خِيلَانٌ كَأَنَّهَا ثَآلِيلُ، فَرَجَعْتُ حَتَّى اسْتَقْبَلْتُهُ، فَقُلْتُ: غَفَرَ اللهُ لَكَ يَا رَسُولَ اللهِ! فَقَالَ: «وَلَكَ» فَقَالَ القَوْمُ: أَسْتَغْفَرَ لَكَ رَسُولُ اللهِ ﷺ؟ فَقَالَ: نَعَمْ، وَلَكُمْ، ثُمَّ تَلَا هَذِهِ الآيَةَ: ﴿وَاسْتَغْفِرْ لِذَنْبِكَ وَلِلْمُؤْمِنِينَ وَالْمُؤْمِنَاتِ﴾ [محمد: ١٩].

23. Abū'l-Ashʿab Aḥmad Ibn al-Miqdām al-ʿIjlī al-Basrī narrated to us; Ḥammād Ibn Zayd informed us; from ʿĀṣim al-Aḥwal that ʿAbdullāh Ibn Sarjis (*raḍiyAllāhu ʿanhu*) said:

> "I came to the Messenger of Allāh (ﷺ), while he was among a group of his Companions and so I circled like

this from behind him. He understood what I wanted, and so threw his robe off behind his back. I saw the place of the Seal on his shoulders similar to a clenched fist surrounded by moles which appeared to be like warts. I came around to face him and said: 'May Allāh forgive you, O Messenger of Allāh (ﷺ)' He (ﷺ) said: "And you too." When the people asked: 'Did the Messenger of Allāh (ﷺ) ask forgiveness for you.' He said: 'Yes, and also for you!' Then he recited the following verse:

"And ask forgiveness for your sin[24], and for the believing men and the believing women." [*Muḥammad* (47): 19][25]

---

[24] This is in no way to suggest that the Messenger of Allāh (ﷺ) is sinful and therefore requires asking for forgiveness for his sins. This is only to raise and elevate him in his ranks of perfection and is similar to the many traditions that mention his habit of asking for forgiveness on a daily basis such as some traditions that mention 70 or 100 times a day.

Similarly it also shows the humility of the Messenger of Allāh (ﷺ) in doing so and in addition, it is a great blessing from Allāh for the believing men and the believing women to have the Messenger of Allāh (ﷺ) asking forgiveness for them. And Allāh knows best.

[25] Muslim, #2346.

CHAPTER THREE

بَابُ مَا جَاءَ فِي شَعْرِ رَسُولِ اللهِ ﷺ

What has been narrated concerning the Hair (*sha'r*) of the Messenger of Allāh (ﷺ)

٢٤ـ حَدَّثَنَا عَلِيُّ بْنُ حُجْرٍ قَالَ: أَخْبَرَنَا إِسْمَاعِيلُ بْنُ إِبْرَاهِيمَ، عَنْ حُمَيْدٍ، عَنْ أَنَسِ بْنِ مَالِكٍ، قَالَ: «كَانَ شَعْرُ رَسُولِ اللهِ ﷺ إِلَى نِصْفِ أُذُنَيْهِ».

24. 'Alī Ibn Ḥujr narrated to us; Ismā'īl Ibn Ibrāhīm informed to us; from Ḥumayd that Anas Ibn Mālik (*raḍiyAllāhu 'anhu*) said:

> "The hair (*sha'r*) of the Messenger of Allāh (ﷺ) reached down to the middle of his ears."[26]

٢٥ـ حَدَّثَنَا هَنَّادُ بْنُ السَّرِيِّ، قَالَ: أَخْبَرَنَا عَبْدُ الرَّحْمَنِ بْنُ أَبِي الزِّنَادِ، عَنْ هِشَامِ بْنِ عُرْوَةَ، عَنْ أَبِيهِ، عَنْ عَائِشَةَ، قَالَتْ: «كُنْتُ أَغْتَسِلُ أَنَا وَرَسُولُ اللهِ ﷺ مِنْ إِنَاءٍ وَاحِدٍ، وَكَانَ لَهُ شَعْرٌ فَوْقَ الجُمَّةِ وَدُونَ الوَفْرَةِ».

---

[26] Muslim, #2338.

25. Hannād Ibn al-Sari narrated to us; 'Abdu'l-Raḥmān Ibn al-Zinād informed us; from Hishām Ibn Urwah; from his father that 'A'ishah (*raḍiyAllāhu 'anhā*) said:

> "The Messenger of Allāh (ﷺ) and I used to perform the major ritual ablution from a single vessel; and he had hair above his shoulder level (*jummah*) and below the earlobes (*wafrah*)."[27, 28]

٢٦ـ حَدَّثنَا أَحْمَدُ بْنُ مَنِيعٍ، قَالَ: حَدَّثنَا أَبُو قَطَنٍ، قَالَ: حَدَّثنَا شُعْبَةُ، عَنْ أَبِي إِسْحَاقَ، عَنِ الْبَرَاءِ بْنِ عَازِبٍ، قَالَ: «كَانَ رَسُولُ اللهِ ﷺ مَرْبُوعًا، بَعِيدَ مَا بَيْنَ الْمَنْكِبَيْنِ، وَكَانَتْ جُمَّتُهُ تَضْرِبُ شَحْمَةَ أُذُنَيْهِ».

26. Aḥmad Ibn Manī' narrated to us; Abū Qaṭan narrated to us; Shu'bah narrated to us; from Abū Isḥāq that Barā'a Ibn 'Āzib (*raḍiyAllāhu 'anhu*) said:

> "The Messenger of Allāh (ﷺ) was of medium height, broad-shouldered, and his hair would fall to his earlobes."[29]

٢٧ـ حَدَّثنَا مُحَمَّدُ بْنُ بَشَّارٍ، قَالَ: حَدَّثنَا وَهْبُ بْنُ جَرِيرِ بْنِ حَازِمٍ، قَالَ: حَدَّثنِي أَبِي، عَنْ قَتَادَةَ، قَالَ: قُلتُ لأَنَسٍ: «كَيْفَ كَانَ شَعْرُ رَسُولِ اللهِ ﷺ؟ قَالَ: لَمْ يَكُنْ بِالْجَعْدِ وَلَا بِالسَّبْطِ، كَانَ يَبْلُغُ شَعْرُهُ شَحْمَةَ أُذُنَيْهِ».

27. Muḥammad Ibn Bashshār narrated to us; Wahab Ibn Jarīr Ibn Ḥāzim narrated to us; my father narrated to me; from Qatādah who

[27] It means that his (ﷺ) hair was neither very long nor short, but of a medium length

[28] Abū Dāwūd, #4187, Tirmidhī, #1755 and said it was ḥasan ṣaḥīḥ.

[29] Bukhārī, #3549, Muslim, #2337, Abū Dāwūd, #4184 and Tirmidhī, #1724.

said: I said to Anas (*raḍiyAllāhu ʿanhu*):

> 'How was the hair of the Messenger of Allāh (ﷺ)?' He replied: 'It was neither tightly curled nor completely straight [but slightly wavy]. His hair reached down to his ear-lobes."[30]

٢٨- حَدَّثَنَا مُحَمَّدُ بْنُ يَحْيَى بْنِ أَبِي عُمَرَ الْمَكِّيُّ، قَالَ: حَدَّثَنَا سُفْيَانُ بْنُ عُيَيْنَةَ، عَنِ ابْنِ أَبِي نَجِيحٍ، عَنْ مُجَاهِدٍ، عَنْ أُمِّ هَانِئٍ بِنْتِ أَبِي طَالِبٍ، قَالَتْ: «قَدِمَ رَسُولُ اللهِ ﷺ مَكَّةَ قَدْمَةً وَلَهُ أَرْبَعُ غَدَائِرَ».

28. Muḥammad Ibn Yaḥyā Ibn Abī ʿUmar al-Makkī narrated to us; Sufyān Ibn ʿUyaynah narrated to us; from Ibn Abī Najīḥ; from Mujāhid that Umm Hānī bint ʿAlī Ibn Abī Ṭālib (*raḍiyAllāhu ʿanhu*) said:

> "The Messenger of Allāh (ﷺ) arrived in Makkah [on the Day of the Conquest] and he had four braids [of hair]."[31]

٢٩- حَدَّثَنَا سُوَيْدُ بْنُ نَصْرٍ، قَالَ: حَدَّثَنَا عَبْدُ اللهِ بْنُ الْمُبَارَكِ، عَنْ مَعْمَرٍ، عَنْ ثَابِتٍ الْبُنَانِيِّ، عَنْ أَنَسٍ «أَنَّ شَعْرَ رَسُولِ اللهِ ﷺ كَانَ إِلَى أَنْصَافِ أُذُنَيْهِ».

29. Suwayd Ibn Naṣr narrated to us; ʿAbdullāh Ibn al-Mubārak narrated to us; from Maʿmar; from Thābit al-Banānī that Anas (*raḍiyAllāhu ʿanhu*) said:

> "The hair of the Messenger of Allāh (ﷺ) reached the

---

[30] Bukhārī, #5905 and Muslim, #2338.

[31] Abū Dāwūd, #4191, Tirmidhī, #1781 and Ibn Mājah, #3631. Imām Tirmdhī declared this ḥadīth as ḥasan, as well as other scholars such as Ibn al-Qayyim in Zad al-Maʿād, 1/177.

middle of his ears."[32]

٣٠ـ حَدَّثَنَا سُوَيْدُ بْنُ نَصْرٍ، حَدَّثَنَا عَبْدُ اللهِ بْنُ الْمُبَارَكِ، عَنْ يُونُسَ بْنِ يَزِيدَ، عَنِ الزُّهْرِيِّ قَالَ: حَدَّثَنَا عُبَيْدُ اللهِ بْنُ عَبْدِ اللهِ بْنِ عُتْبَةَ، عَنِ ابْنِ عَبَّاسٍ: «أَنَّ رَسُولَ اللهِ ﷺ كَانَ يَسْدِلُ شَعْرَهُ، وَكَانَ الْمُشْرِكُونَ يَفْرِقُونَ رُؤُوسَهُمْ، وَكَانَ أَهْلُ الْكِتَابِ يَسْدِلُونَ رُؤُوسَهُمْ، وَكَانَ يُحِبُّ مُوَافَقَةَ أَهْلِ الْكِتَابِ فِيمَا لَمْ يُؤْمَرْ فِيهِ بِشَيْءٍ، ثُمَّ فَرَقَ رَسُولُ اللهِ ﷺ رَأْسَهُ».

30. Suwayd Ibn Naṣr narrated to us; ʿAbdullāh Ibn al-Mubārak narrated to us; from Yūnus Ibn Yazīd; from al-Zuhrī; ʿUbaydullāh Ibn ʿAbdullāh Ibn ʿUtbah narrated to us that Ibn ʿAbbās (*raḍiyAllāhu ʿanhumā*) said:

> 'The Messenger of Allāh (ﷺ) used to let his hair hang in front, whereas the polytheists used to part the hair of their head. The People of the Scripture [on the other hand] would let their hair hang in front. He used to favour emulating the People of the Scripture in those matters for which he received no command, but then the Messenger of Allāh (ﷺ) began to part the hair of his head.'[33]

٣١ـ حَدَّثَنَا مُحَمَّدُ بْنُ بَشَّارٍ، قَالَ: حَدَّثَنَا عَبْدُ الرَّحْمَنِ بْنُ مَهْدِيٍّ، عَنْ إِبْرَاهِيمَ بْنِ نَافِعٍ الْمَكِّيِّ، عَنِ ابْنِ أَبِي نَجِيحٍ، عَنْ مُجَاهِدٍ، عَنْ أُمِّ هَانِئٍ، قَالَتْ: «رَأَيْتُ رَسُولَ اللهِ ﷺ ذَا ضَفَائِرَ أَرْبَعٍ».

31. Muḥammad Ibn Bashshār narrated to us; ʿAbdu'l-Raḥmān Ibn Mahdī narrated to us; from Ibrāhīm Ibn Nāfiʿ; from Ibn Abī Najīḥ;

[32] Muslim, #2338, Abū Dāwūd, #4186 and others.
[33] Bukhārī, #3588, Muslim, #2336, Abū Dāwūd, #4188 and others.

from Mujāhid that Umm Hanī (*raḍiyAllāhu ʿanhā*) said:

> "I saw the Messenger of Allāh (ﷺ) with four braids [of hair]."[34]

[34] Bukhārī, #3588 and Muslim, #2336.

CHAPTER FOUR

بَابُ مَا جَاءَ فِي تَرَجُّلِ رَسُولِ اللهِ ﷺ

What has been narrated concerning the Combing (*tarajjul*) of the Hair of the Messenger of Allāh (ﷺ)

٣٢ـ حَدَّثَنَا إِسْحَاقُ بْنُ مُوسَى الأَنْصَارِيُّ، قَالَ: حَدَّثَنَا مَعْنُ بْنُ عِيسَى، قَالَ: حَدَّثَنَا مَالِكُ بْنُ أَنَسٍ، عَنْ هِشَامِ بْنِ عُرْوَةَ، عَنْ أَبِيهِ، عَنْ عَائِشَةَ، قَالَتْ: «كُنْتُ أُرَجِّلُ رَأْسَ رَسُولِ اللهِ ﷺ وَأَنَا حَائِضٌ».

32. Isḥāq Ibn Mūsā al-Anṣarī narrated to us; Ma'an Ibn 'Isā narrated to us; Mālik Ibn Anas narrated to us; from Hishām Ibn 'Urwah that 'Ā'ishah (*raḍiyAllāhu 'anhā*) said:

> 'I used to comb the hair of the Messenger of Allāh (ﷺ), while I was in the state of menstruation.'[35]

٣٣ـ حَدَّثَنَا يُوسُفُ بْنُ عِيسَى، قَالَ: حَدَّثَنَا وَكِيعٌ، قَالَ: حَدَّثَنَا الرَّبِيعُ ابنُ صَبِيحٍ، عَنْ يَزِيدَ بْنِ أَبَانَ ـ هُوَ الرَّقَاشِيُّ ـ، عَنْ أَنَسِ بْنِ مَالِكٍ، قَالَ: «كَانَ

[35] Bukhārī, #295 and Muslim, #297.

رَسُولُ اللهِ ﷺ يُكْثِرُ دَهْنَ رَأْسِهِ، وَتَسْرِيحَ لِحْيَتِهِ، وَيُكْثِرُ القِنَاعَ حَتَّى كَأَنَّ ثَوْبَهُ ثَوْبُ زَيَّاتٍ».

33. Yūsuf Ibn ʿIsā narrated to us; Wakīʿ narrated to us; Al-Rabīʿ Ibn Sabīḥ narrated to us; from Yazīd Ibn Abān al-Raqāshī that Anas Ibn Mālik (*raḍiyAllāhu ʿanhu*) said:

> 'The Messenger of Allāh (ﷺ) used to frequently apply oil to his head and comb his beard. He would often wear a head cloth (*qinaʿ*), so much so that his clothing would resemble that of an oil seller."[36]

٣٤ـ حَدَّثَنَا هَنَّادُ بْنُ السَّرِيِّ، قَالَ: حَدَّثَنَا أَبُو الأَحْوَصِ، عَنْ أَشْعَثَ بْنِ أَبِي الشَّعْثَاءِ، عَنْ أَبِيهِ، عَنْ مَسْرُوقٍ، عَنْ عَائِشَةَ، قَالَتْ: «إِنْ كَانَ رَسُولُ اللهِ ﷺ لَيُحِبُّ التَّيَمُّنَ فِي طُهُورِهِ إِذَا تَطَهَّرَ، وَفِي تَرَجُّلِهِ إِذَا تَرَجَّلَ، وَفِي انْتِعَالِهِ إِذَا انْتَعَلَ».

34. Hannād Ibn al-Sarī narrated to us; Abū'l-Aḥwaṣ narrated to us; from Al-Ashʿath Ibn Abī al-Shaʿthā'; from his father; from Maṣrūq that ʿĀ'ishah (*raḍiyAllāhu ʿanhā*) said:

> "The Messenger of Allāh (ﷺ) used to love beginning with the right [side] while combing [his hair and beard]; while performing [ritual] ablution and when putting on his shoes."[37]

٣٥ـ حَدَّثَنَا مُحَمَّدُ بْنُ بَشَّارٍ قَالَ: حَدَّثَنَا يَحْيَى بْنُ سَعِيدٍ، عَنْ هِشَامِ بْنِ حَسَّانٍ،

[36] Bayhaqī in *al-Shuʿab*, 5/226. This ḥadīth is weak, due to a narrator having weak memory see Ibn Jawzī's *al-Ḍuʿafā' wa'l-Matrūkīn*, 1/281.
[37] Bukhārī, #168, Muslim, #268, Abū Dāwūd, #4140, Tirmidhī, #608 and others

عَنِ الحَسَنِ، عَنْ عَبْدِ اللهِ بْنِ مُغَفَّلٍ، قَالَ: «نَهَى رَسُولُ اللهِ ﷺ عنِ التَّرَجُّلِ إِلَّا غِبًّا».

35. Muḥammad Ibn Bashshār narrated to us; Yaḥyā Ibn Saʿīd narrated to us; from Hishām Ibn Ḥassān; from al-Ḥasan that ʿAbdullāh Mughaffal (*raḍiyAllāhu ʿanhu*) said:

> "The Messenger of Allāh (ﷺ) forbade combing [the hair] unless it is done occasionally."[38]

٣٦ـ حَدَّثَنَا الحَسَنُ بْنُ عَرَفَةَ قَالَ: حَدَّثَنَا عَبْدُ السَّلَامِ بْنُ حَرْبٍ، عَنْ يَزِيدَ ابْنِ أَبِي خَالِدٍ، عَنْ أَبِي العَلَاءِ الأَوْدِيِّ، عَنْ حُمَيْدِ بْنِ عَبْدِ الرَّحْمَنِ، عَنْ رَجُلٍ مِنْ أَصْحَابِ النَّبِيِّ ﷺ: «أَنَّ النَّبِيَّ ﷺ كَانَ يَتَرَجَّلُ غِبًّا».

36. Al-Ḥasan Ibn ʿArafah narrated to us; ʿAbdu'l-Salām Ibn Ḥarb narrated to us; from Yazīd Ibn Abī Khālid; from Abū'l-Aʿlā al-Awdī; from Ḥumayd Ibn ʿAbdu'l-Raḥmān; from a man among the Companions of the Prophet (ﷺ):

> "The Prophet (ﷺ) use to comb his hair occasionally."[39]

---

[38] Tirmidhī, #1756.

[39] In the chain is Yazīd Ibn Abī Khālid who is truthful but makes a lot of mistakes. The ḥadith is authentic due to supporting evidence.

CHAPTER FIVE

بَابُ مَا جَاءَ فِي شَيْبِ رَسُولِ اللهِ ﷺ

What has been narrated concerning the Greyness (*shayb*) of Hair of the Messenger of Allāh (ﷺ)

٣٧- حَدَّثَنَا مُحَمَّدُ بْنُ بَشَّارٍ، قَالَ: أَخْبَرَنَا أَبُو دَاوُدَ، قَالَ: أَخْبَرَنَا هَمَّامٌ، عَنْ قَتَادَةَ، قَالَ: قُلْتُ لأَنَسِ بْنِ مَالِكٍ: هَلْ خَضَبَ رَسُولُ اللهِ ﷺ؟ قَالَ: «لَمْ يَبْلُغْ ذَلِكَ، إِنَّمَا كَانَ شَيْبًا فِي صُدْغَيْهِ، وَلَكِنْ أَبُو بَكْرٍ رضي الله عنه خَضَبَ بِالحِنَّاءِ وَالكَتَمِ».

37. Muḥammad Ibn Bashshār narrated to us; Abū Dāwūd informed us; Hammām informed us; from Qatādah who said: 'I said to Anas Ibn Mālik (*raḍiyAllāhu 'anhu*):

> 'Did the Messenger of Allāh (ﷺ) dye his hair?' He replied: 'He did not reach such a stage where he would use a dye; however he did have greyness (*shayb*) on his temples, but Abū Bakr dyed his hair with [a combination of] henna and reddish dye (*katam*).'[40]

[40] Bukhārī, #3550 with a slightly different wording; similarly, it is also Muslim, #2341 with the addition of the name of 'Umar (*raḍiyAllāhu 'anhu*).

٣٨ـ حَدَّثَنَا إِسْحَاقُ بْنُ مَنْصُورٍ، وَيَحْيَى بْنُ مُوسَى، قَالاَ: حَدَّثَنَا عَبْدُ الرَّزَّاقِ، عَنْ مَعْمَرٍ، عَنْ ثَابِتٍ، عَنْ أَنَسٍ، قَالَ: «مَا عَدَدْتُ فِي رَأْسِ رَسُولِ اللهِ ﷺ وَلِحْيَتِهِ إِلَّا أَرْبَعَ عَشْرَةَ شَعْرَةً بَيْضَاءَ».

38. Isḥāq Ibn Manṣūr and Yaḥyā Ibn Mūsā narrated to us; Shuʿbah narrated to us; ʿAbdu'l-Razzāq narrated to us; from Maʿmar Ibn Thābit that Anas Ibn Mālik (*raḍiyAllāhu ʿanhu*) said:

> "I did not count more than fourteen white hairs on the head and beard of the Messenger of Allāh (ﷺ)."[41]

٣٩ـ حَدَّثَنَا مُحَمَّدُ بْنُ الْمُثَنَّى، قَالَ: أَخْبَرَنَا أَبُو دَاوُدَ، قَالَ: حَدَّثَنَا شُعْبَةُ، عَنْ سِمَاكِ ابْنِ حَرْبٍ، قَالَ: سَمِعْتُ جَابِرَ بْنَ سَمُرَةَ، وَقَدْ سُئِلَ عَنْ شَيْبِ رَسُولِ اللهِ ﷺ؟ فَقَالَ: «كَانَ إِذَا دَهَنَ رَأْسَهُ لَمْ يُرَ مِنْهُ شَيْبٌ، وَإِذَا لَمْ يَدْهَنْ رُئِيَ مِنْهُ».

39. Muḥammad Ibn al-Muthannā narrated to us; Abū Dāwūd informed us; Shuʿbah narrated to us; from Simāk Ibn Ḥarb who said: 'I heard Jābir Ibn Samurah, when asked about the greyness of the Messenger of Allāh (ﷺ), so he said:

> "When he would apply oil to his head, no greyness was visible, but when he did not apply oil [to his head] some were visible."[42]

٤٠ـ حَدَّثَنَا مُحَمَّدُ بْنُ عَمْرِو بْنِ الْوَلِيدِ الْكِنْدِيُّ الْكُوفِيُّ، قَالَ: حَدَّثَنَا يَحْيَى ابْنُ آدَمَ، عَنْ شَرِيكٍ، عَنْ عُبَيْدِ اللهِ بْنِ عُمَرَ، عَنْ نَافِعٍ، عَنْ عَبْدِ اللهِ بْنِ عُمَرَ، قَالَ: «إِنَّمَا

[41] Aḥmad in his Musnad, #12690.
[42] Muslim, #2344.

كَانَ شَيْبُ رَسُولِ اللهِ ﷺ نَحْوًا مِنْ عِشْرِينَ شَعْرَةً بَيْضَاءَ».

40. Muḥammad Ibn ʿUmar Ibn al-Walīd al-Kindī al-Kūfī narrated to us; Yaḥyā Ibn Adam narrated to us; from Sharīk; from ʿUbaydullāh Ibn ʿUmar; from Nāfiʿ that ʿAbdullāh Ibn ʿUmar (*raḍiyAllāhu ʿanhumā*) said:

> "The Messenger of Allāh (ﷺ) had merely twenty white hair."[43]

٤١- حَدَّثَنَا أَبُو كُرَيْبٍ مُحَمَّدُ بْنُ العَلَاءِ، قَالَ: حَدَّثَنَا مُعَاوِيَةُ بْنُ هِشَامٍ، عَنْ شَيْبَانَ، عَنْ أَبِي إِسْحَاقَ، عَنْ عِكْرِمَةَ، عَنِ ابْنِ عَبَّاسٍ، قَالَ: قَالَ أَبُو بَكْرٍ: يَا رَسُولَ اللهِ! قَدْ شِبْتَ، قَالَ: «شَيَّبَتْنِي هُودٌ، وَالوَاقِعَةُ، وَالْمُرْسَلَاتُ، وَعَمَّ يَتَسَاءَلُونَ، وَإِذَا الشَّمْسُ كُوِّرَتْ».

41. Abū Kurayb Muḥammad Ibn al-ʿAlā' narrated to us; Muʿāwiyah Ibn Hishām narrated to us; from Shaybān; from Abū Isḥāq; from ʿIkrimah that Ibn ʿAbbās (*raḍiyAllāhu ʿanhumā*) said:

> 'Abū Bakr (*raḍiyAllāhu ʿanhu*) once said: 'O Messenger of Allāh, you have greyed!' He (ﷺ) said: "I have been made grey-haired by [the following chapters of the Qur'ān] *Hūd*, *al-Wāqiʿah*, *al-Mursalāt*, *ʿAmma yastasā'alūn* and *Idhā al-shams kuwwirat*."[44]

٤٢- حَدَّثَنَا سُفْيَانُ بْنُ وَكِيعٍ، قَالَ: حَدَّثَنَا مُحَمَّدُ بْنُ بِشْرٍ، عَنْ عَلِيِّ بْنِ صَالِحٍ،

[43] Aḥmad and his Musnad, 2/90 and Ibn Mājah, #3630. One of the narrators in this chain has speech about his memorisation; however the ḥadīth is supported by the previous traditions from Bukhārī and Muslim.

[44] Tirmidhī, #3297 and Ḥākim, 2/343-476

عَنْ أَبِي إِسْحَاقَ، عَنْ أَبِي جُحَيْفَةَ، قَالَ: قَالُوا: يَا رَسُولَ اللهِ! نَرَاكَ قَدْ شِبْتَ، قَالَ: «قَدْ شَيَّبَتْنِي هُودٌ وَأَخَوَاتُهَا».

42. Sufyān Ibn Waki'narrated to us; Muḥammad Ibn Bashshār narrated to us; from 'Alī Ibn Ṣāliḥ; from Abū Isḥāq that Abū Juhayfah (*raḍiyAllāhu 'anhu*) said: 'They said:

> 'O Messenger of Allāh, we see that you have turned grey!' He (ﷺ) said: "[The chapters of] *Hūd* and its sisters have turned my hair grey."'[45]

٤٣- حَدَّثَنَا عَلِيُّ بْنُ حُجْرٍ، قَالَ: أَنْبَأَنَا شُعَيْبُ بْنُ صَفْوَانَ، عَنْ عَبْدِ الْمَلِكِ ابْنِ عُمَيْرٍ، عَنْ إِيَادِ بْنِ لَقِيطٍ الْعِجْلِيِّ، عَنْ أَبِي رِمْثَةَ التَّيمِيِّ تَيْمِ الرِّبَابِ، قَالَ: «أَتَيْتُ النَّبِيَّ ﷺ وَمَعِي ابْنٌ لِي، قَالَ: فَأُرِيتُهُ، فَقُلْتُ لَمَّا رَأَيْتُهُ: هَذَا نَبِيُّ اللهِ ﷺ وَعَلَيْهِ ثَوْبَانِ أَخْضَرَانِ، وَلَهُ شَعْرٌ قَدْ عَلَاهُ الشَّيْبُ، وَشَيْبُهُ أَحْمَرُ».

43. 'Alī Ibn Ḥujr narrated to us; Shu'ayb Ibn Ṣafwān narrated to us; from 'Abdu'l-Mālik Ibn 'Umayr; from Iyād Ibn Laqīṭ al-'Ijlī that Abū Rimthah al-Taymī (*raḍiyAllāhu 'anhu*) said: 'I came to the Prophet (ﷺ) with a son of mine, who said: 'When they showed him to me, I said when I saw him:

> 'This is the Prophet of Allāh!' He was wearing two pieces of green garments, and he had [a few] hairs that turned grey from the top, and its greyness [was dyed] red."[46]

[45] Tirmidhī, #3297 and declared weak by some scholars.

[46] In this chain is Shu'ayb Ibn Ṣafwān who is acceptable according to Ibn Ḥajr in *Al-Taqrīb*. However acceptable narrators (*maqbūl*) are only used as evidence when they have other supporting evidence. In this case there is not any, in fact there are narrations opposing this =

٤٤ـ حَدَّثَنَا أَحْمَدُ بْنُ مَنِيعٍ، قَالَ: حَدَّثَنَا سُرَيْجُ بْنُ النُّعْمَانِ، قَالَ: حَدَّثَنَا حَمَّادُ ابْنُ سَلَمَةَ، عَنْ سِمَاكِ بْنِ حَرْبٍ، قَالَ: قِيلَ لِجَابِرِ بْنِ سَمُرَةَ: «أَكَانَ فِي رَأْسِ رَسُولِ اللهِ ﷺ شَيْبٌ؟ قَالَ: لَمْ يَكُنْ فِي رَأْسِ رَسُولِ اللهِ ﷺ شَيْبٌ إِلَّا شَعَرَاتٌ فِي مَفْرِقِ رَأْسِهِ، إِذَا ادَّهَنَ وَارَاهُنَّ الدُّهْنُ».

44. Aḥmad Ibn Manīʿ narrated to us; Surayj Ibn al-Nuʿmān narrated to us; Ḥammād Ibn Salamah narrated to us; from Simāk Ibn Ḥarb who said: 'Jābir Ibn Samurah (*raḍiyAllāhu ʿanhu*) was asked:

> 'Was there greyness on the head of the Messenger of Allāh (ﷺ)?' He replied: 'There was no greyness, except a few hairs in the parting of his head, and when he applied oil to it, the oil would conceal [them].'[47]

=
one which do not contain the wording -"he had [a few] hairs that turned grey from the top." However, the first part of the ḥadīth, "He was wearing two pieces of green garments", have other supporting evidence, Abū Dāwūd, #4065, Tirmidhī, #2812 and Nasā'ī, #5319.

[47] Muslim, #2344, Aḥmad in his Musnad, 5/86-88 and Nasā'ī, #5114

CHAPTER SIX

بَابُ مَا جَاءَ فِي خِضَابِ رَسُولِ اللهِ ﷺ

What has been narrated concerning the Dye (*khiḍāb*) used by the Messenger of Allāh (ﷺ)

٤٥ـ حَدَّثَنَا أَحْمَدُ بْنُ مَنِيعٍ، قَالَ: حَدَّثَنَا هُشَيْمٌ، قَالَ: حَدَّثَنَا عَبْدُ المَلِكِ ابْنُ عُمَيْرٍ، عَنْ إِيَادِ بْنِ لَقِيطٍ، قَالَ: أَخْبَرَنِي أَبُو رِمْثَةَ، قَالَ: أَتَيْتُ رَسُولَ اللهِ ﷺ مَعَ ابْنٍ لِي، فَقَالَ: «ابْنُكَ هَذَا؟» فَقُلْتُ: نَعَمْ أَشْهَدُ بِهِ، قَالَ: «لَا يَجْنِي عَلَيْكَ، وَلَا تَجْنِي عَلَيْهِ» قَالَ: وَرَأَيْتُ الشَّيْبَ أَحْمَرَ.

45. Aḥmad Ibn Mani' narrated to us; Hushaym narrated to us; 'Abdu'l-Mālik Ibn 'Umayr narrated to us; from Iyād Ibn Laqīṭ who said: Abū Rimthah (*raḍiyAllāhu 'anhu*) informed me:

> 'I came to the Messenger of Allāh (ﷺ) with a son of mine. He asked: "Is this your son." I replied: 'Yes, be a witness to it.' He said: "You are not held accountable for his sins, nor is he held accountable for your sins."
>
> Abū Rimthah then remarked: 'I noticed that the greyness [of his hair] had been [dyed] red.'

قَالَ أَبُو عِيسَى: هَذَا أَحْسَنُ شَيْءٍ رُوِيَ فِي هَذَا البَابِ وَأَفْسَرُ؛ لأَنَّ الرِّوَايَاتِ الصَّحِيحَةَ أَنَّ النَّبِيَّ ﷺ لَمْ يَبْلُغِ الشَّيْبَ.

وَأَبُو رِمْثَةَ اسْمُهُ: رِفَاعَةُ بْنُ يَثْرِبِيٍّ التَّيمِيُّ.

Abū ʿIsā said: 'This tradition is very good and explanatory report on the subject of using a dye, because of the authentic reports that he (ﷺ) never greyed. Abū Rimthah name is Rifāʿa Ibn Yathribī al-Taimī.'[48]

٤٦ـ حَدَّثَنَا سُفْيَانُ بْنُ وَكِيعٍ، قَالَ: حَدَّثَنَا أَبِي، عَنْ شَرِيكٍ، عَنْ عُثْمَانَ ابْنِ مَوْهَبٍ، قَالَ: سُئِلَ أَبُو هُرَيْرَةَ: «هَلْ خَضَبَ رَسُولُ اللهِ ﷺ؟ قَالَ: نَعَمْ»

46. Sufyān Ibn Wakīʿ narrated to us; my father narrated to us; from Sharīk that ʿUthmān Ibn Mawhab said:

> 'Abū Hurayrah (*raḍiyAllāhu ʿanhu*) was asked: 'Did the Messenger of Allāh (ﷺ) dye his hair?' He said: 'Yes."

قَالَ أَبُو عِيسَى: وَرَوَى أَبُو عَوَانَةَ هَـذَا الحَدِيثَ عَنْ عُثْمَانَ بْنِ عَبْدِ اللهِ ابْنِ مَوْهَبٍ، فَقَالَ: عَنْ أُمِّ سَلَمَةَ .

Abū ʿIsā said: 'This tradition is also reported by Abū ʿAwānah by way of ʿUthmān Ibn ʿAbdullāh Ibn Mawhab, on the authority of Umm Salamah (*raḍiyAllāhu ʿanhā*).'[49]

---

[48] ʿAbdullāh Ibn Imām Aḥmad in his additions to the *Musnad*, #7113. There are supporting narrations in Abū Dāwūd, #4208 and Nasa'i, #5084.

[49] In this chain is Sharīk Al-Qaḍī who the scholars have said had a weak memory, and he has been opposed by those reliable, who said this tradition is of Umm Salamah (*raḍiyAllāhu ʿanhā*) and not of Abū Hurayrah (*raḍiyAllāhu ʿanhu*).

٤٧ـ حَدَّثَنَا إِبْرَاهِيمُ بْنُ هَارُونَ، قَالَ: أَنْبَأَنَا النَّضْرُ بْنُ زُرَارَةَ، عَنْ أَبِي جَنَابٍ، عَنْ إِيَادِ بْنِ لَقِيطٍ، عَنِ الْجَهْدَمَةِ، امْرَأَةِ بَشِيرِ ابْنِ الْخَصَاصِيَةِ، قَالَتْ: «أَنَا رَأَيْتُ رَسُولَ اللهِ ﷺ يَخْرُجُ مِنْ بَيْتِهِ يَنْفُضُ رَأْسَهُ، وَقَدِ اغْتَسَلَ، وَبِرَأْسِهِ رَدْعٌ مِنْ حِنَّاءٍ، أَوْ قَالَ: رَدْغٌ، شَكَّ فِي هَذَا الشَّيْخُ».

47. Ibrāhīm Ibn Hārun narrated to us; Al-Naḍr Ibn Zurārah informed us; from Abū Jināb; from Iyād Ibn Laqīṭ that al-Jahdamah, the wife of Bishr Ibn al-Khasāsiyyah (*raḍiyAllāhu ʿanhu*) said:

> 'I saw the Messenger of Allāh (ﷺ) coming out of his house with water dripping from his head, after taking a bath, and on his head there was trace of henna [or he said: 'saffron'].'[50]

٤٨ـ حَدَّثَنَا عَبْدُ اللهِ بْنُ عَبْدِ الرَّحْمَنِ، قَالَ: حَدَّثَنَا عَمْرُو بْنُ عَاصِمٍ، قَالَ: حَدَّثَنَا حَمَّادُ بْنُ سَلَمَةَ، قَالَ: حَدَّثَنَا حُمَيْدٌ، عَنْ أَنَسٍ، قَالَ: «رَأَيْتُ شَعْرَ رَسُولِ اللهِ ﷺ مَخْضُوبًا».

48. ʿAbdullāh Ibn ʿAbdu'l-Raḥmān narrated to us; ʿAmr Ibn ʿĀṣim narrated to us; Ḥammād Ibn Salamah narrated to us; Ḥumayd narrated to us that Anas (*raḍiyAllāhu ʿanhu*) said:

> 'I saw that the hair of the Messenger of Allāh (ﷺ) was dyed.'[51]

---

[50] Weak due to two narrators see Ibn Ḥajr in *Al-Taqrīb*, 2/562.

[51] In this ḥadīth is ʿAmr Ibn ʿĀṣim, about whom Ibn Ḥajr in *Al-Taqrīb*, 2/423, said is acceptable. So his narrations are not supported due to the opposition of the narrations of Muḥammed Ibn Sirīn, Thābit and Qatādah.

قَالَ حَمَّادٌ: وَأَخْبَرَنَا عَبْدُ اللهِ بْنُ مُحَمَّدِ بْنِ عَقِيلٍ قَالَ: رَأَيْتُ شَعْرَ رَسُولِ اللهِ ﷺ عِنْدَ أَنَسِ بْنِ مَالِكٍ مَخْضُوبًا .

Ḥammād said: 'Abdullāh Ibn Muḥammad Ibn 'Uqayl said: 'I saw that the hair of the Messenger of Allāh (ﷺ) was dyed in the presence of Anas Ibn Mālik (*raḍiyAllāhu 'anhu*)."

CHAPTER SEVEN

بَابُ مَا جَاءَ فِي كُحْلِ رَسُولِ اللهِ ﷺ

What has been narrated concerning the Kohl (*kuḥl*) Messenger of Allāh (ﷺ)

٤٩ـ حَدَّثَنَا مُحَمَّدُ بْنُ حُمَيْدٍ الرَّازِيُّ، قَالَ: حَدَّثَنَا أَبُو دَاوُدَ الطَّيَالِسِيُّ، عَنْ عَبَّادِ ابْنِ مَنْصُورٍ، عَنْ عِكْرِمَةَ، عَنِ ابْنِ عَبَّاسٍ، أَنَّ النَّبِيَّ ﷺ قَالَ: «اكْتَحِلُوا بِالإِثْمِدِ؛ فَإِنَّهُ يَجْلُو الْبَصَرَ، وَيُنْبِتُ الشَّعْرَ».

49. Muḥammad Ibn Ḥumayd al-Rāzī narrated to us; Abū Dāwūd al-Ṭāyālisī narrated to us; from ʿAbbād Ibn Manṣūr; from ʿIkrimah; from Ibn ʿAbbās (*raḍiyAllāhu ʿanhumā*) that the Prophet (ﷺ) said:

> "Use antimony (*ithmid*)[52] on the eye; for it strengthens the vision and nurtures the hair [eyelashes]."

وَزَعَمَ أَنَّ النَّبِيَّ ﷺ كَانَتْ لَهُ مُكْحُلَةٌ يَكْتَحِلُ مِنْهَا كُلَّ لَيْلَةٍ ثَلَاثَةً فِي هَذِهِ، وَثَلَاثَةً فِي هَذِهِ.

Ibn ʿAbbās (*raḍiyAllāhu ʿanhumā*) also used to say:

[52] *Ithmid* (isfahani antimony) is the best form among all types of kohl (*kuḥl*) and it is a black rock that has reddishness.

> 'The Prophet (ﷺ) had a small kohl pot, from which he applied kohl to his [eyelashes] every night, three times in this [eye], and three times in other [eye]."[53]

٥٠ـ حَدَّثَنَا عَبْدُاللهِ بْنُ الصَّبَّاحِ الـهَاشِمِيُّ البَصْرِيُّ، أَخْبَرَنَا عُبَيْدُ اللهِ ابْنُ مُوسَى، أَخْبَرَنَا إِسْرَائِيلُ بْنُ يُونُسَ، عَنْ عَبَّادِ بْنِ مَنْصُورٍ.

(ح) وَحَدَّثَنَا عَلِيُّ بْنُ حُجْرٍ، حَدَّثَنَا يَزِيدُ بْنُ هَارُونَ، حَدَّثَنَا عَبَّادُ بْنُ مَنْصُورٍ، عَنْ عِكْرِمَةَ، عَنِ ابْنِ عَبَّاسٍ، قَالَ: «كَانَ النَّبِيُّ ﷺ يَكْتَحِلُ قَبْلَ أَنْ يَنَامَ بِالإِثْمِدِ ثَلَاثًا فِي كُلِّ عَيْنٍ».

وَقَالَ يَزِيدُ بْنُ هَارُونَ فِي حَدِيثِهِ: «إِنَّ النَّبِيَّ ﷺ كَانَتْ لَهُ مُكْحُلَةٌ يَكْتَحِلُ مِنْهَا عِنْدَ النَّوْمِ ثَلَاثًا فِي كُلِّ عَيْنٍ».

50. 'Abdullāh Ibn al-Ṣabbāḥ al-Hāshimī al-Baṣrī narrated to us; 'Ubaydullāh Ibn Mūsā narrated to us; Isrā'īl narrated to us; from 'Abbād Ibn Manṣūr.

'Alī Ibn Ḥujr narrated to us; Yazīd Ibn Hārun narrated to us; from 'Ikrīmah that Ibn 'Abbās (*raḍiyAllāhu 'anhumā*) said:

> 'The Messenger of Allāh (ﷺ) used to apply ithmid before sleeping, three times in each eye.'

In a narration also from Ibn 'Abbās (*raḍiyAllāhu 'anhumā*):

> 'The Messenger of Allāh (ﷺ) had a small kohl pot, from which he applied kohl before sleeping, three times in each eye.'[54]

---

[53] Tirmidhī, #1757 and Ibn Mājah, #3499.

[54] This narration is weak although applying kohl is established in other authentic narrations, Tirmidhī, #1757, Nasā'ī, #5113 and Ibn Mājah, #3497.

٥١ـ حَدَّثَنَا أَحْمَدُ بْنُ مَنِيعٍ، قَالَ: حَدَّثَنَا مُحَمَّدُ بْنُ يَزِيدَ، عَنْ مُحَمَّدِ بْنِ إِسْحَاقَ، عَنْ مُحَمَّدِ بْنِ الْمُنْكَدِرِ، عَنْ جَابِرٍ ـ هُوَ ابْنُ عَبْدِ اللهِ ـ، قَالَ: قَالَ رَسُولُ اللهِ ﷺ: «عَلَيْكُمْ بِالإِثْمِدِ عِنْدَ النَّوْمِ؛ فَإِنَّهُ يَجْلُو الْبَصَرَ، وَيُنْبِتُ الشَّعْرَ».

51. Aḥmad Ibn Manīʿ narrated to us; Muḥammad Ibn Yazīd narrated to us; from Muḥammad Ibn Isḥāq; from Muḥammad Ibn al-Munkadir that Jābir Ibn ʿAbdullāh (*raḍiyAllāhu ʿanhu*) said:

> 'The Messenger of Allāh (ﷺ) said: "You should apply *ithmid* before going to sleep, for it strengthens the vision and nurtures the hair."'[55]

٥٢ـ حَدَّثَنَا قُتَيْبَةُ بْنُ سَعِيدٍ، قَالَ: حَدَّثَنَا بِشْرُ بْنُ الْمُفَضَّلِ، عَنْ عَبْدِ اللهِ بْنِ عُثْمَانَ بْنِ خُثَيْمٍ، عَنْ سَعِيدِ بْنِ جُبَيْرٍ، عَنِ ابْنِ عَبَّاسٍ، قَالَ: قَالَ رَسُولُ اللهِ ﷺ: «إِنَّ خَيْرَ أَكْحَالِكُمُ الإِثْمِدُ؛ يَجْلُو الْبَصَرَ، وَيُنْبِتُ الشَّعْرَ».

52. Qutaybah Ibn Saʿīd narrated to us; Bishr Ibn al-Mufaḍḍal narrated to us; from ʿAbdullāh Ibn ʿUthmān Ibn Khuthaym; Saʿīd Ibn Jubayr that Ibn ʿAbbās (*raḍiyAllāhu ʿanhumā*) said:

> 'The Messenger of Allāh (ﷺ) said: "The best type of kohl for you is [one made from] *ithmid*, for it strengthens the vision and nurtures the hair."'[56]

٥٣ـ حَدَّثَنَا إِبْرَاهِيمُ بْنُ الْمُسْتَمِرِّ الْبَصْرِيُّ، قَالَ: حَدَّثَنَا أَبُو عَاصِمٍ، عَنْ عُثْمَانَ بْنِ عَبْدِ الْمَلِكِ، عَنْ سَالِمٍ، عَنِ ابْنِ عُمَرَ، قَالَ: قَالَ رَسُولُ اللهِ ﷺ: «عَلَيْكُمْ

[55] Ibn Mājah, #3496.

[56] Abū Dāwūd, #3878, Ibn Mājah, #3497.

بِالإِثْمِدِ؛ فَإِنَّهُ يَجْلُو البَصَرَ، وَيُنْبِتُ الشَّعْرَ» .

53. Ibrāhīm Ibn al-Mustamir al-Baṣrī narrated to us; Abū ʿĀṣim narrated to us; from ʿUthmān Ibn ʿAbdu'l-Mālik; from Sālim that Ibn ʿUmar (*raḍiyAllāhu ʿanhumā*) said:

> ʿThe Messenger of Allāh (ﷺ) said: "You should apply *ith-mid*, for it strengthens the vision and nurtures the hair."'[57]

[57] Ibn Mājah, #3495, this tradition is supported by the previous two traditions.

CHAPTER EIGHT

بَابُ مَا جَاءَ فِي لِبَاسِ رَسُولِ اللهِ ﷺ

What has been narrated concerning the Clothing (*libās*) of the Messenger of Allāh (ﷺ)

٥٤ـ حَدَّثَنَا مُحَمَّدُ بْنُ حُمَيْدٍ الرَّازِيُّ، قَالَ: حَدَّثَنَا الفَضْلُ بْنُ مُوسَى، وَأَبُو تُمَيْلَةَ، وَزَيْدُ بْنُ حُبَابٍ، عَنْ عَبْدِ الْمُؤْمِنِ بْنِ خَالِدٍ، عَنْ عَبْدِ اللهِ بْنِ بُرَيْدَةَ، عَنْ أُمِّ سَلَمَةَ، قَالَتْ: «كَانَ أَحَبُّ الثِّيَابِ إِلَى رَسُولِ اللهِ ﷺ القَمِيصُ».

54. Muḥammad Ibn Ḥumayd al-Rāzī narrated to us; Al-Faḍl Ibn Mūsā, Abū Tumaylah and Zayd Ibn Ḥabbāb narrated to us; from ʿAbdu'l-Mu'min Ibn Khālid; from ʿAbdullāh Ibn Buraydah that Umm Salamah (*raḍiyAllāhu ʿanhā*) said:

> "The dearest of garments (*thiyāb*) to the Messenger of Allāh (ﷺ) was the shirt (*qamīṣ*)."[58]

٥٥ـ حَدَّثَنَا عَلِيُّ بْنُ حُجْرٍ، قَالَ: حَدَّثَنَا الفَضْلُ بْنُ مُوسَى، عَنْ عَبْدِ الْمُؤْمِنِ ابْنِ خَالِدٍ، عَنْ عَبْدِ اللهِ بْنِ بُرَيْدَةَ، عَنْ أُمِّ سَلَمَةَ، قَالَتْ: «كَانَ أَحَبُّ الثِّيَابِ إِلَى رَسُولِ اللهِ

---

[58] Abū Dāwūd, #4025, Tirmidhī, #1762 and Nasā'ī, #6968.

ﷺ القَمِيصَ».

55. 'Alī Ibn Ḥujr narrated to us; Al-Faḍl Ibn Mūsā narrated to us; from 'Abdu'l-Mu'min Ibn Khālid; from 'Abdullāh Ibn Buraydah that Umm Salamah (*raḍiyAllāhu 'anhā*) said:

> "The dearest of garments (*thiyāb*) to the Messenger of Allāh (ﷺ) was the shirt (*qamīṣ*)."[59]

٥٦ـ حَدَّثَنَا زِيَادُ بْنُ أَيُّوبَ البَغْدَادِيُّ، قَالَ: حَدَّثَنَا أَبُو تُمَيْلَةَ، عَنْ عَبْدِ المُؤْمِنِ ابنِ خَالِدٍ، عَنْ عَبْدِ الله بْنِ بُرَيْدَةَ، عَنْ أُمِّهِ، عَنْ أُمِّ سَلَمَةَ، قَالَتْ: «كَانَ أَحَبُّ الثِّيَابِ إِلَى رَسُولِ الله ﷺ يَلْبَسُهُ القَمِيصَ».

56. Ziyād Ibn Ayyūb al-Baghdādī narrated to us; Abū Tumaylah narrated to us; from 'Abdu'l-Mu'min Ibn Khālid; from 'Abdullāh Ibn Buraydah; from his mother that Umm Salamah (*raḍiyAllāhu 'anhā*) said:

> "The dearest of garments (*thiyāb*) to the Messenger of Allāh (ﷺ) was the shirt (*qamīṣ*) he used to wear"[60]

قَالَ: هَكَذَا قَالَ زِيَادُ بْنُ أَيُّوبَ، فِي حَدِيثِهِ: عَنْ عَبْدِ الله بْنِ بُرَيْدَةَ، عَنْ أُمِّهِ، عَنْ أُمِّ سَلَمَةَ، وَهَكَذَا رَوَى غَيْرُ وَاحِدٍ، عَنْ أَبِي تُمَيْلَةَ مِثْلَ رِوَايَةِ زِيَادِ بْنِ أَيُّوبَ، وَأَبُو تُمَيْلَةَ يَزِيدُ فِي هَذَا الحَدِيثِ «عَنْ أُمِّهِ» وَهُوَ أَصَحُّ.

He said: Ziyād Ibn Ayyub said in his tradition; from 'Abdullāh Ibn Buraydah; from his mother; from Umm Salamah (*raḍiyAllāhu 'anhā*).

---

[59] Abū Dāwūd, #4025, Tirmidhī, #1764and Nasā'ī, #6968.

[60] Abū Dāwūd, #4025, Tirmidhī, #1763 and Ibn Mājah, #3575.

Likewise, another tradition is by way of Abū Tumaylah, like the report of Ziyād Ibn Ayyūb and Abū Tumaylah which is more authentic.

٥٧- حَدَّثَنَا عَبْدُ اللهِ بْنُ مُحَمَّدِ بْنِ الحَجَّاجِ، قَالَ: حَدَّثَنَا مُعَاذُ بْنُ هِشَامٍ، قَالَ: حَدَّثَنِي أَبِي، عَنْ بُدَيْلٍ - يَعْنِي ابْنَ مَيْسَرَةَ العُقَيْلِيَّ -، عَنْ شَهْرِ بْنِ حَوْشَبٍ، عَنْ أَسْمَاءَ بِنْتِ يَزِيدَ، قَالَتْ: «كَانَ كُمُّ قَمِيصِ رَسُولِ اللهِ ﷺ إِلَى الرُّسْغِ».

57. ʿAbdullāh Ibn Muḥammad Ibn al-Ḥajjāj narrated to us; Muʿādh Ibn Hishām narrated to us; my father narrated to me; from Budayl Ibn Maysarah al-ʿUqaylī; from Shahr Ibn Ḥawshab that Asmā' bint Yazīd said:

> 'The sleeve of the shirt of the Messenger of Allāh (ﷺ) would reach up to the wrists.'[61]

٥٨- حَدَّثَنَا أَبُو عَمَّارٍ الحُسَيْنُ بْنُ حُرَيْثٍ، قَالَ: حَدَّثَنَا أَبُو نُعَيْمٍ، قَالَ: حَدَّثَنَا زُهَيْرٌ، عَنْ عُرْوَةَ بْنِ عَبْدِ اللهِ بْنِ قُشَيْرٍ، عَنْ مُعَاوِيَةَ بْنِ قُرَّةَ، عَنْ أَبِيهِ، قَالَ: «أَتَيْتُ رَسُولَ اللهِ ﷺ فِي رَهْطٍ مِنْ مُزَيْنَةَ لِنُبَايِعَهُ، وَإِنَّ قَمِيصَهُ لَمُطْلَقٌ، - أَوْ قَالَ: زِرُّ قَمِيصِهِ مُطْلَقٌ -، قَالَ: فَأَدْخَلْتُ يَدِي فِي جَيْبِ قَمِيصِهِ فَمَسَسْتُ الخَاتَمَ».

58. Abū ʿAmmaar al-Ḥusayn Ibn Ḥarithah narrated to us; Abū Nuʿaym narrated to us; Zuhayr narrated to us; from ʿUrwah Ibn ʿAbdullāh Ibn Qushayr; from Muʿāwiyyah Ibn Qurrah that his father said:

> 'I came to the Messenger of Allāh (ﷺ) with a small group from the tribe of Muzaynah to pledge allegiance to him, and [we found] his shirt to be unbuttoned or he

[61] Abū Dāwūd, #1765, Tirmidhī, #1765, and Abū Dāwūd, this ḥadīth is weak but is supported by other narrations.

said his shirt buttons were unfastened, and I inserted my hand in the collar of his shirt and I touched the Seal [of Prophethood].'[62]

٥٩ـ حَدَّثَنَا عَبْدُ بْنُ حُمَيْدٍ، قَالَ: حَدَّثَنَا مُحَمَّدُ بْنُ الفَضْلِ، قَالَ: حَدَّثَنَا حَمَّادُ ابْنُ سَلَمَةَ، عَنْ حَبِيبِ بْنِ الشَّهِيدِ، عَنِ الحَسَنِ، عَنْ أَنَسِ بْنِ مَالِكٍ، أَنَّ النَّبِيَّ ﷺ خَرَجَ وَهُوَ يَتَّكِئُ عَلَى أُسَامَةَ بْنِ زَيْدٍ، عَلَيْهِ ثَوْبٌ قِطْرِيٌّ قَدْ تَوَشَّحَ بِهِ، فَصَلَّى بِهِمْ.

59. 'Abd Ibn Ḥumayd narrated to us; Muḥammad Ibn al-Faḍl narrated to us; Ḥammād Ibn Salamah narrated to us; from Ḥabīb Ibn al-Shahīd; from al-Ḥasan that Anas Ibn Mālik (*raḍiyAllāhu 'anhu*) said:

> 'The Prophet (ﷺ) came out of his house leaning on Usāmah Ibn Zayd, wearing a garment of Yemeni sheet made of cotton (*qiṭrī*), which he had thrown on loosely, he then led them in the prayer.'[63]

٦٠ـ حَدَّثَنَا سُوَيْدُ بْنُ نَصْرٍ، قَالَ: حَدَّثَنَا عَبْدُ اللهِ بْنُ المُبَارَكِ، عَنْ سَعِيدِ ابْنِ إِيَاسٍ الجُرَيْرِيِّ، عَنْ أَبِي نَضْرَةَ، عَنْ أَبِي سَعِيدٍ الخُدْرِيِّ، قَالَ: كَانَ رَسُولُ اللهِ ﷺ إِذَا اسْتَجَدَّ ثَوْبًا سَمَّاهُ بِاسْمِهِ؛ عِمَامَةً أَوْ قَمِيصًا أَوْ رِدَاءً، ثُمَّ يَقُولُ: «اللَّهُمَّ لَكَ الحَمْدُ كَمَا كَسَوْتَنِيهِ، أَسْأَلُكَ خَيْرَهُ وَخَيْرَ مَا صُنِعَ لَهُ، وَأَعُوذُ بِكَ مِنْ شَرِّهِ، وَشَرِّ مَا صُنِعَ لَهُ».

60. Suwayd Ibn Naṣr narrated to us; 'Abdullāh Ibn al-Mubārak narrated to us; from Sa'īd Ibn Iyād al-Jariārī; from Abū Naḍrah that Abū Sa'īd al-Khudrī (*raḍiyAllāhu 'anhu*) said:

---

[62] Abū Dāwūd, #4082 and Ibn Mājah, #3578.

[63] Aḥmad in his *Musnad*, #13763 and Ibn Ḥibbān, #349.

> 'When the Messenger of Allāh (ﷺ) used to wear a new garment (*thowb*), he would mention it by its name, [for example], turban (*'imāmah*), or shirt (*qamīṣ*), or cloak (*ridā'*). He would then say: "O Allāh, all praise and thanks to You for clothing me with this [garment]. I ask You for the good of it and the good of what it was made for, and I ask Your protection from the evil of it and the evil of what it was made for."[64]

٦١ـ حَدَّثَنَا هِشَامُ بْنُ يُونُسَ الكُوفِيُّ قَالَ: حَدَّثَنَا القَاسِمُ بْنُ مَالِكٍ المُزَنِيُّ، عَنِ الجُرَيْرِيِّ، عَنْ أَبِي نَضْرَةَ، عَنْ أَبِي سَعِيدٍ الخُدْرِيِّ، عَنِ النَّبِيِّ ﷺ نَحْوَهُ.

61. Hishām Ibn Yūnus al-Kūfī narrated to us; Al-Qāsim Ibn Mālik al-Muzanī narrated to us; from Al-Jarīrī; from Abū Naḍrah; from Abū Sa'īd al-Khudrī (*raḍiyAllāhu 'anhu*) that the Prophet (ﷺ) mentioned this in a similar form.

٦٢ـ حَدَّثَنَا مُحَمَّدُ بْنُ بَشَّارٍ، قَالَ: حَدَّثَنَا مُعَاذُ بْنُ هِشَامٍ، قَالَ: حَدَّثَنِي أَبِي، عَنْ قَتَادَةَ، عَنْ أَنَسِ بْنِ مَالِكٍ، قَالَ: «كَانَ أَحَبُّ الثِّيَابِ إِلَى رَسُولِ اللهِ ﷺ يَلْبَسُهُ الحِبَرَةَ».

62. Muḥammad Ibn Bashshār narrated to us; 'Mu'ādh Ibn Hishām narrated to us; my father narrated to me; from Qatādah that Anas Ibn Mālik (*raḍiyAllāhu 'anhu*) said:

> "The dearest of garments to the Messenger of Allāh (ﷺ) was a Yemenite fabric with stripes (*ḥibarah*) that he used to wear"[65]

[64] Abū Dāwūd, #4020, Tirmidhī, #1767 and Nasā'ī, #309.

[65] Bukhārī, #5713, Muslim, #2079, Abū Dāwūd, #4060 and Tirmidhī, #1787.

٦٣- حَدَّثَنَا مَحْمُودُ بْنُ غَيْلَانَ، قَالَ: حَدَّثَنَا عَبْدُ الرَّزَّاقِ، قَالَ: حَدَّثَنَا سُفْيَانُ، عَنْ عَوْنِ بْنِ أَبِي جُحَيْفَةَ، عَنْ أَبِيهِ، قَالَ: «رَأَيْتُ النَّبِيَّ ﷺ وَعَلَيْهِ حُلَّةٌ حَمْرَاءُ، كَأَنِّي أَنْظُرُ إِلَى بَرِيقِ سَاقَيْهِ»، قَالَ سُفْيَانُ: أُرَاهَا حِبَرَةً.

63. Maḥmūd Ibn Ghaylān narrated to us; 'Abdu'l-Razzāq narrated to us; Sufyān al-Thawrī narrated to us; from 'Awn Ibn Abī Juhayfah that his father said:

> 'I saw the Messenger of Allāh (ﷺ) wearing red clothing (*ḥullah*), it is as if I am looking at the radiance of his shins.' Sufyān said: 'I think it is a Yemenite fabric with stripes (*ḥibarah*).'[66]

٦٤- حَدَّثَنَا عَلِيُّ بْنُ خَشْرَمٍ، قَالَ: حَدَّثَنَا عِيسَى بْنُ يُونُسَ، عَنْ إِسْرَائِيلَ، عَنْ أَبِي إِسْحَاقَ، عَنِ الْبَرَاءِ بْنِ عَازِبٍ، قَالَ: «مَا رَأَيْتُ أَحَدًا مِنَ النَّاسِ أَحْسَنَ فِي حُلَّةٍ حَمْرَاءَ مِنْ رَسُولِ اللهِ ﷺ، إِنْ كَانَتْ جُمَّتُهُ لَتَضْرِبُ قَرِيبًا مِنْ مَنْكِبَيْهِ».

64. 'Alī Ibn Khashram narrated to us; 'Isā Ibn Yūnus narrated to us; from Isrā'īl; from Abū Isḥāq that Barā'a Ibn 'Āzib (*raḍiyAllāhu 'anhu*) said:

> 'I have never seen anyone more handsome in red clothing (*ḥullah*) than the Messenger of Allāh (ﷺ), when the hair of his head reached his shoulders..'[67]

٦٥- حَدَّثَنَا مُحَمَّدُ بْنُ بَشَّارٍ، قَالَ: حَدَّثَنَا عَبْدُ الرَّحْمَنِ بْنُ مَهْدِيٍّ، قَالَ:

---

[66] Bukharī, #5859, Muslim, #503, Abū Dāwūd, #520 and Tirmidhī, #197.
[67] Bukhārī, #3549, Muslim, #2337, Abū Dāwūd, #1483 and Tirmidhī, #1724.

حَدَّثَنَا عُبَيْدُ اللهِ بْنُ إِيَادٍ، عَنْ أَبِيهِ، عَنْ أَبِي رِمْثَةَ، قَالَ: «رَأَيْتُ النَّبِيَّ ﷺ وَعَلَيْهِ بُرْدَانِ أَخْضَرَانِ».

65. Muḥammad Ibn Bashshār narrated to us; 'Abdu'l-Raḥmān Ibn Mahdī narrated to us; 'Ubaydullāh Ibn Iyād narrated to us; from his father that Abū Rimthah (*raḍiyAllāhu 'anhu*) said:

> 'I saw the Prophet (ﷺ) wearing two green [coloured] garments (*burdah*).'[68]

٦٦ـ حَدَّثَنَا عَبْدُ بْنُ حُمَيْدٍ، قَالَ: حَدَّثَنَا عَفَّانُ بْنُ مُسْلِمٍ، قَالَ: حَدَّثَنَا عَبْدُ اللهِ ابْنُ حَسَّانَ الْعَنْبَرِيُّ، عَنْ جَدَّتَيْهِ دُحَيْبَةَ وَعُلَيْبَةَ، عَنْ قَيْلَةَ بِنْتِ مَخْرَمَةَ، قَالَتْ: «رَأَيْتُ النَّبِيَّ ﷺ وَعَلَيْهِ أَسْمَالُ مُلَيَّتَيْنِ كَانَتَا بِزَعْفَرَانٍ، وَقَدْ نَفَضَتْهُ».

وَفِي الْحَدِيثِ قِصَّةٌ طَوِيلَةٌ.

66. 'Abd Ibn Ḥumayd narrated to us; 'Affān Ibn Muslim Ibn Muslim narrated to us; 'Abdullāh Ibn Ḥassān al-'Anbarī narrated to us; from his grandmothers, Duḥaybah and 'Ulaybah and Qaylah that Qayylah bint Makhramah (*raḍiyAllāhu 'anhumā*) said:

> 'I saw the Prophet (ﷺ) [in such a state that] he was wearing [two] unstitched worn-out garments dyed in saffron whose colour had faded away.'[69]

This tradition is part of a longer tradition.

---

[68] Abū Dāwūd, #4065, Tirmidhī, #2812 and Nasā'ī, #5319.

[69] Abū Dāwūd, #4065, Tirmidhī, #2814.

٦٧ـ حَدَّثَنَا قُتَيْبَةُ بْنُ سَعِيدٍ، قَالَ: حَدَّثَنَا بِشْرُ بْنُ الْمُفَضَّلِ، عَنْ عَبْدِ اللهِ ابْنِ عُثْمَانَ بْنِ خُثَيْمٍ، عَنْ سَعِيدِ بْنِ جُبَيْرٍ، عَنِ ابْنِ عَبَّاسٍ، قَالَ: قَالَ رَسُولُ اللهِ ﷺ: «عَلَيْكُمْ بِالْبَيَاضِ مِنَ الثِّيَابِ، لِيَلْبِسْهَا أَحْيَاؤُكُمْ، وَكَفِّنُوا فِيهَا مَوْتَاكُمْ؛ فَإِنَّهَا مِنْ خَيْرِ ثِيَابِكُمْ».

67. Qutaybah Ibn Sa'īd narrated to us; Bishr Ibn al-Mufaḍḍal narrated to us; from 'Abdullāh Ibn 'Uthmān Ibn Khuthaym; from Sa'īd Ibn Jubayr that Ibn 'Abbās (*raḍiyAllāhu 'anhumā*) said:

> 'You should [attain] white clothing, so that your living may wear them, and your deceased be shrouded in them, for they are [among] the best of your clothing.'[70]

٦٨ـ حَدَّثَنَا مُحَمَّدُ بْنُ بَشَّارٍ، قَالَ: حَدَّثَنَا عَبْدُ الرَّحْمَنِ بْنُ مَهْدِيٍّ، قَالَ: حَدَّثَنَا سُفْيَانُ، عَنْ حَبِيبِ بْنِ أَبِي ثَابِتٍ، عَنْ مَيْمُونِ بْنِ أَبِي شَبِيبٍ، عَنْ سَمُرَةَ بْنِ جُنْدُبٍ قَالَ: قَالَ رَسُولُ اللهِ ﷺ: «الْبَسُوا الْبَيَاضَ؛ فَإِنَّهَا أَطْهَرُ وَأَطْيَبُ، وَكَفِّنُوا فِيهَا مَوْتَاكُمْ».

68. Muḥammad Ibn Bashshār narrated to us; 'Abdu'l-Raḥmān Ibn Mahdī narrated to us; Sufyān narrated to us; from Ḥabīb Ibn Abī Thābit; from Maymūn Ibn Abī Shabīb that Samurah Ibn Jundub (*raḍiyAllāhu 'anhu*) said: 'The Messenger of Allāh (ﷺ) said:

> "Wear white clothing for it is more pure and pleasant, and you must shroud your deceased in it."[71]

[70] Abū Dāwūd, #3878, Tirmidhī, #2810 and Ibn Mājah, #3566.
[71] Tirmidhī, #2810 and Ibn Mājah, #3567.

٦٩ـ حَدَّثَنَا أَحْمَدُ بْنُ مَنِيعٍ، قَالَ حَدَّثَنَا يَحْيَى بْنُ زَكَرِيَّا بْنِ أَبِي زَائِدَةَ، قَالَ: حَدَّثَنَا أَبِي، عَنْ مُصْعَبِ بْنِ شَيْبَةَ، عَنْ صَفِيَّةَ بِنْتِ شَيْبَةَ، عَنْ عَائِشَةَ، قَالَتْ: «خَرَجَ رَسُولُ اللهِ ﷺ ذَاتَ غَدَاةٍ وَعَلَيْهِ مِرْطٌ مِنْ شَعَرٍ أَسْوَدَ».

69. Aḥmad Ibn Manīʿ narrated to us; Yaḥyā Ibn Zakariyyāh Ibn Abī Zā'idah narrated to us; my father narrated to me; from Muṣʿab Ibn Shaybah; from Ṣafiyyah bint Shaybah that ʿAishah (*raḍiyAllāhu ʿanhā*) said:

> 'The Messenger of Allāh (ﷺ) once left the house early morning, wearing a sheet (*mirṭ*) made of black strands of [camel] hair.'[72]

٧٠ـ حَدَّثَنَا يُوسُفُ بْنُ عِيسَى، قَالَ: حَدَّثَنَا وَكِيعٌ، قَالَ: حَدَّثَنَا يُونُسُ بْنُ أَبِي إِسْحَاقَ، عَنْ أَبِيهِ، عَنِ الشَّعْبِيِّ، عَنْ عُرْوَةَ بْنِ الْمُغِيرَةِ بْنِ شُعْبَةَ، عَنْ أَبِيهِ، «أَنَّ النَّبِيَّ ﷺ لَبِسَ جُبَّةً رُومِيَّةً ضَيِّقَةَ الْكُمَّيْنِ».

70. Yūsuf Ibn ʿIsā narrated to us; Wakīʿ narrated to us; Yūnus Ibn Abī Isḥāq narrated to us; from his father; from Al-Shaʿbī; from ʿUrwah Ibn al-Mughīrah Ibn Shuʿbah (*raḍiyAllāhu ʿanhu*) that his father said:

> 'The Prophet (ﷺ) wore a tight-sleeved Byzantine robe (*jubbah*).'[73]

[72] Muslim, #2082, Abū Dāwūd, #4032 and Tirmidhī, #2813.
[73] Muslim, #274 and Tirmidhī, #1768.

CHAPTER NINE

بَابُ مَا جَاءَ فِي عَيْشِ رَسُولِ اللهِ ﷺ

What has been narrated concerning the Living (*'aish*) of the Messenger of Allāh (ﷺ)

٧١ـ حَدَّثَنَا قُتَيْبَةُ بْنُ سَعِيدٍ، قَالَ: حَدَّثَنَا حَمَّادُ بْنُ زَيْدٍ، عَنْ أَيُّوبَ، عَنْ مُحَمَّدِ ابْنِ سِيرِينَ، قَالَ: كُنَّا عِنْدَ أَبِي هُرَيْرَةَ، وَعَلَيْهِ ثَوْبَانِ مُمَشَّقَانِ مِنْ كَتَّانٍ فَتَمَخَّطَ فِي أَحَدِهِمَا، فَقَالَ: «بَخٍ بَخٍ؛ يَتَمَخَّطُ أَبُو هُرَيْرَةَ فِي الكَتَّانِ، لَقَدْ رَأَيْتُنِي وَإِنِّي لأَخِرُّ فِيمَا بَيْنَ مِنْبَرِ رَسُولِ اللهِ ﷺ وَحُجْرَةِ عَائِشَةَ مَغْشِيًّا عَلَيَّ، فَيَجِيءُ الجَائِي فَيَضَعُ رِجْلَهُ عَلَى عُنُقِي يَرَى أَنَّ بِي جُنُونًا، وَمَا بِي جُنُونٌ، وَمَا هُوَ إِلَّا الجُوعُ».

71. Qutaybah Ibn Sa'id narrated to us; Ḥammād Ibn Zayd narrated to us; from Ayyūb that Muḥammad Ibn Sirīn said:

> 'We were in the company of Abū Hurayrah, who happened to be wearing two linen garments dyed in red clay. He blew his nose in one of them and said: 'Bravo! Bravo! [Is] Abū Hurayrah blowing his nose in the linen? I have found myself falling down unconscious between the pulpit of the Messenger of Allāh (ﷺ) and the apartment of 'Ā'ishah until someone would come along and place their foot on my neck assuming that I am insane, when in reality

I was not insane; it is merely due to [extreme] hunger."[74]

٧٢ـ حَدَّثَنَا قُتَيْبَةُ، قَالَ: حَدَّثَنَا جَعْفَرُ بْنُ سُلَيْمَانَ الضُّبَعِيُّ، عَنْ مَالِكِ بْنِ دِينَارٍ قَالَ: «مَا شَبِعَ رَسُولُ اللهِ ﷺ مِنْ خُبْزٍ قَطُّ وَلَا لَحْمٍ، إِلَّا عَلَى ضَفَفٍ»، قَالَ مَالِكٌ: «سَأَلْتُ رَجُلًا مِنْ أَهْلِ الْبَادِيَةِ: مَا الضَّفَفُ؟ قَالَ: أَنْ يَتَنَاوَلَ مَعَ النَّاسِ».

72. Qutaybah narrated to us; Jā'far Ibn Sulaymān al-Ḍab'ī narrated to us that Mālik Ibn Dinār said:

> 'The Messenger of Allāh (ﷺ) never had his fill of bread or meat except when he had guests (*ḍafaf*).' I asked a Bedouin man: 'What is meant by *ḍafaf*.' He replied: 'That he would eat with the people.'[75]

[74] Bukhārī, #7324 and Tirmidhī, #2367.

[75] Ibn Ḥibbān, #6359. This ḥadīth is mursal—the name of the companion is missing.

CHAPTER TEN

بَابُ مَا جَاءَ فِي خُفِّ رَسُولِ اللهِ ﷺ

What has been narrated concerning the Socks (*khuff*) of the Messenger of Allāh (ﷺ)

٧٣ـ حَدَّثَنَا هَنَّادُ بْنُ السَّرِيِّ، قَالَ: حَدَّثَنَا وَكِيعٌ، عَنْ دَلْهَمِ بْنِ صَالِحٍ، عَنْ حُجَيْرِ بْنِ عَبْدِ اللهِ، عَنِ ابْنِ بُرَيْدَةَ، عَنْ أَبِيهِ، أَنَّ النَّجَاشِيَّ أَهْدَى لِلنَّبِيِّ ﷺ خُفَّيْنِ أَسْوَدَيْنِ سَاذَجَيْنِ، «فَلَبِسَهُمَا ثُمَّ تَوَضَّأَ وَمَسَحَ عَلَيْهِمَا».

73. Hannād Ibn al-Sarī narrated to us; Wakī' narrated to us; from Dalham Ibn Ṣāliḥ; from Ḥujayr Ibn 'Abdullāh; from Ibn Buraydah that his father said:

> 'The Negus (Najāshī) gifted the Prophet (ﷺ) a pair of plain black *khuffs*. He wore them and then wiped over them after performing ablution.'[76]

٧٤ـ حَدَّثَنَا قُتَيْبَةُ بْنُ سَعِيدٍ، قَالَ: حَدَّثَنَا يَحْيَى بْنُ زَكَرِيَّا بْنِ أَبِي زَائِدَةَ، عَنِ الْحَسَنِ بْنِ عَيَّاشٍ، عَنْ أَبِي إِسْحَاقَ، عَنِ الشَّعْبِيِّ، قَالَ: قَالَ الْمُغِيرَةُ بْنُ شُعْبَةَ: «أَهْدَى

[76] Abū Dāwūd, #155, Tirmidhī, #2820 and Ibn Mājah, #549.

٧٤ـ حَدَّثَنَا قُتَيْبَةُ بْنُ سَعِيدٍ، قَالَ: حَدَّثَنَا يَحْيَى بْنُ زَكَرِيَّا بْنِ أَبِي زَائِدَةَ، عَنِ الحَسَنِ بْنِ عَيَّاشٍ، عَنْ أَبِي إِسْحَاقَ، عَنِ الشَّعْبِيِّ، قَالَ: قَالَ المُغِيرَةُ بْنُ شُعْبَةَ: «أَهْدَى دِحْيَةُ لِلنَّبِيِّ ﷺ خُفَّيْنِ، فَلَبِسَهُمَا ـ وَقَالَ إِسْرَائِيلُ: عَنْ جَابِرٍ، عَنْ عَامِرٍ: وَجُبَّةً فَلَبِسَهُمَا ـ حَتَّى تَخَرَّقَا لَا يَدْرِي النَّبِيُّ ﷺ أَذَكِيٌّ هُمَا أَمْ لَا، قَالَ أَبُو عِيسَى: وَأَبُو إِسْحَاقَ هَذَا هُوَ أَبُو إِسْحَاقَ الشَّيْبَانِيُّ، وَاسْمُهُ سُلَيْمَانُ.

74. Qutaybah Ibn Saʿīd narrated to us; Yaḥyā Ibn Zakariyyāh Ibn Abī Zā'idah narrated to us; from Al-Ḥasan Ibn ʿAyyāsh; Abū Isḥāq; from Al-Shaʿbī that al-Mughīrah Ibn Shuʿbah (*raḍiyAllāhu ʿanhu*) said:

> 'Dihyah [al-Kalbī] gifted the Prophet (ﷺ) a pair of socks (*khuffs*) which he then wore.' Isrā'īl said: 'From Jābir on the authority of ʿAmir: '[He was also gifted] a gown (*jubbah*). He continued to wear them until they had holes in them, without the Prophet (ﷺ) knowing whether or not they were slaughtered lawfully."[77]

Abū ʿIsā said: 'The Abū Isḥāq [mentioned] is Abū Isḥāq al-Shaybānī and his name is Sulaymān.'

[77] Tirmidhī, #1769 and is classed as weak.

CHAPTER ELEVEN

بَابُ مَا جَاءَ فِي نَعْلِ رَسُولِ اللهِ ﷺ

What has been narrated concerning the Sandals (*na'l*) of the Messenger of Allāh (ﷺ)

٧٥ـ حَدَّثَنَا مُحَمَّدُ بْنُ بَشَّارٍ، قَالَ: حَدَّثَنَا أَبُو دَاوُدَ الطَّيَالِسِيُّ، قَالَ: حَدَّثَنَا هَمَّامٌ، عَنْ قَتَادَةَ، قَالَ: قُلْتُ لأَنَسِ بْنِ مَالِكٍ: «كَيْفَ كَانَ نَعْلُ رَسُولِ اللهِ ﷺ؟ قَالَ: لَهُمَا قِبَالَانِ».

75. Muḥammad Ibn Bashshār narrated to us; Abū Dāwūd al-Ṭayālisī narrated to us; Hammām narrated to us that Qatādah said:

> 'I asked Anas Ibn Mālik (*raḍiyAllāhu 'anhu*): 'How were the sandals (*na'l*) of the Messenger of Allāh (ﷺ).' He said: 'Each sandal had two straps.'[78]

٧٦ـ حَدَّثَنَا أَبُو كُرَيْبٍ مُحَمَّدُ بْنُ العَلَاءِ، قَالَ: حَدَّثَنَا وَكِيعٌ، عَنْ سُفْيَانَ، عَنْ خَالِدٍ الحَذَّاءِ، عَنْ عَبْدِ اللهِ بْنِ الحَارِثِ، عَنِ ابْنِ عَبَّاسٍ، قَالَ: «كَانَ لِنَعْلِ رَسُولِ اللهِ ﷺ قِبَالَانِ مَثْنِيٌّ شِرَاكُهُمَا».

[78] Bukhārī, #5858, Abū Dāwūd, #4134, Tirmidhī, #1772 and Ibn Mājah, #3615.

76. Abū Kurayb Muḥammad Ibn al-ʿAlā' narrated to us; Wakīʿ narrated to us; from Sufyān; from Khālid al-Ḥadhdhā'; from ʿAbdullāh Ibn al-Ḥārith that Ibn ʿAbbās (*raḍiyAllāhu ʿanhumā*) said:

> 'The Messenger of Allāh's (ﷺ) had (*naʿl*) sandals, [each] had two double straps.'[79]

٧٧ـ حَدَّثَنَا أَحْمَدُ بْنُ مَنِيعٍ، قَالَ: حَدَّثَنَا أَبُو أَحْمَدَ الزُّبَيْرِيُّ، قَالَ: حَدَّثَنَا عِيسَى ابْنُ طَهْمَانَ، قَالَ: أَخْرَجَ إِلَيْنَا أَنَسُ بْنُ مَالِكٍ نَعْلَيْنِ جَرْدَاوَيْنِ لَهُمَا قِبَالَانِ، قَالَ: فَحَدَّثَنِي ثَابِتٌ بَعْدُ عَنْ أَنَسٍ أَنَّهُمَا كَانَتَا نَعْلَيِ النَّبِيِّ ﷺ.

77. Aḥmad Ibn Manīʿ narrated to us; Abū Aḥmad al-Zubayrī narrated to us that ʿIsā Ibn Ṭahmān said:

> 'Anas Ibn Mālik (*raḍiyAllāhu ʿanhu*) brought out for us a pair of hairless sandals with double straps. Then Thābit narrated to me afterwards; from Anas that they were the sandals of the Prophet (ﷺ).'[80]

٧٨ـ حَدَّثَنَا إِسْحَاقُ بْنُ مُوسَى الأَنْصَارِيُّ قَالَ: حَدَّثَنَا مَعْنٌ، قَالَ: حَدَّثَنَا مَالِكٌ، قَالَ: حَدَّثَنَا سَعِيدُ بْنُ أَبِي سَعِيدٍ الْمَقْبُرِيُّ، عَنْ عُبَيْدِ بْنِ جُرَيْجٍ، أَنَّهُ قَالَ لابْنِ عُمَرَ: رَأَيْتُكَ تَلْبَسُ النِّعَالَ السِّبْتِيَّةَ، قَالَ: «إِنِّي رَأَيْتُ رَسُولَ اللهِ ﷺ يَلْبَسُ النِّعَالَ الَّتِي لَيْسَ فِيهَا شَعْرٌ، وَيَتَوَضَّأُ فِيهَا، فَأَنَا أُحِبُّ أَنْ أَلْبَسَهَا».

78. Isḥāq Ibn Mūsā al-Anṣārī narrated to us; Maʿan narrated to us; Mālik narrated to us; Saʿīd Ibn Abī Saʿīd al-Maqburī narrated to us that ʿUbayd Ibn Jurayj said to Ibn ʿUmar (*raḍiyAllāhu ʿanhumā*):

[79] Ibn Mājah, #3614.

[80] Bukhārī, #5858 without the word *"hairless"*.

'I saw you wearing tanned [leather] hairless (*sibti*) sandals.' He said: 'I had seen the Messenger of Allāh (ﷺ) wear hairless sandals and he performed ritual ablution (*wūḍu'*) in them, and therefore I love to wear them."[81]

٧٩ـ حَدَّثَنَا إِسْحَاقُ بْنُ مَنْصُورٍ، قَالَ: حَدَّثَنَا عَبْدُ الرَّزَّاقِ، عَنْ مَعْمَرٍ، عَنِ ابْنِ أَبِي ذِئْبٍ، عَنْ صَالِحٍ مَوْلَى التَّوْأَمَةِ، عَنْ أَبِي هُرَيْرَةَ، قَالَ: «كَانَ لِنَعْلِ رَسُولِ اللهِ ﷺ قِبَالَانِ».

79. Isḥāq Ibn Manṣūr narrated to us; 'Abdu'l-Razzāq narrated to us; from Ma'mar; from Ibn Abī Dhi'b; from Sālih Mawlah al-Taw'āma that Abū Hurayrah (*raḍiyAllāhu 'anhu*) said:

'The sandals (*na'l*) of the Messenger of Allāh (ﷺ) had two straps.'[82]

٨٠ـ حَدَّثَنَا أَحْمَدُ بْنُ مَنِيعٍ، قَالَ: حَدَّثَنَا أَبُو أَحْمَدَ، قَالَ: حَدَّثَنَا سُفْيَانُ، عَنِ السُّدِّيِّ، قَالَ: حَدَّثَنِي مَنْ سَمِعَ عَمْرَو بْنَ حُرَيْثٍ يَقُولُ: «رَأَيْتُ رَسُولَ اللهِ ﷺ يُصَلِّي فِي نَعْلَيْنِ مَخْصُوفَتَيْنِ».

80. Aḥmad Ibn Manī' narrated to us; Abū Aḥmad narrated to us; Sufyān narrated to us that Al-Suddī said: ' Someone narrated to me that he heard 'Amr Ibn Ḥurayth (*raḍiyAllāhu 'anhu*) saying:

'I saw the Messenger of Allāh (ﷺ) performing the prayer while wearing the sandals [that had another leather] sole sewn onto them.'[83]

[81] Bukhārī, #5851, Muslim, #1187 and Abū Dāwūd, #1772

[82] *Al-'Ilal al-Kabīr* of al-Bukhārī, #291

[83] Nasā'ī in *al-Kubrah*, #9179, it is weak but supported by a narration in the *Musnad*, #21587.

٨١ـ حَدَّثَنَا إِسْحَاقُ بْنُ مُوسَى الأَنْصَارِيُّ، قَالَ: حَدَّثَنَا مَعْنٌ، قَالَ: حَدَّثَنَا مَالِكٌ، عَنْ أَبِي الزِّنَادِ، عَنِ الأَعْرَجِ، عَنْ أَبِي هُرَيْرَةَ، أَنَّ رَسُولَ اللهِ ﷺ قَالَ: «لَا يَمْشِيَنَّ أَحَدُكُمْ فِي نَعْلٍ وَاحِدَةٍ، لِيُنْعِلْهُمَا جَمِيعًا، أَوْ لِيُحْفِهِمَا جَمِيعًا».

81. Isḥāq Ibn Mūsā al-Anṣārī narrated to us; Maʿan narrated to us; Mālik narrated to us; from Abū'l-Zinād; from Al-Aʿraj that Abū Hurayrah (*raḍiyAllāhu ʿanhu*) said: 'The Messenger of Allāh (ﷺ) said:

> "Let none of you walk in a single sandal, let him either wear both sandals or take both of them off."[84]

٨٢ـ حَدَّثَنَا قُتَيْبَةُ، عَنْ مَالِكِ بْنِ أَنَسٍ، عَنْ أَبِي الزِّنَادِ نَحْوَهُ.

82. Qutaybah narrated to us; from Mālik Ibn Anas that Abū'l-Zinād reported something similar.

٨٣ـ حَدَّثَنَا إِسْحَاقُ بْنُ مُوسَى، قَالَ: حَدَّثَنَا مَعْنٌ، قَالَ: حَدَّثَنَا مَالِكٌ، عَنْ أَبِي الزُّبَيْرِ، عَنْ جَابِرٍ، «أَنَّ النَّبِيَّ ﷺ نَهَى أَنْ يَأْكُلَ ـ يَعْنِي الرَّجُلَ ـ بِشِمَالِهِ، أَوْ يَمْشِيَ فِي نَعْلٍ وَاحِدَةٍ».

83. Isḥāq Ibn Mūsā narrated to us; Maʿan narrated to us; Mālik narrated to us; from Abu'l-Zubayr that Jābir (*raḍiyAllāhu ʿanhu*) said:

> 'The Prophet (ﷺ) forbade [a man] to eat with the left hand, or walk in a single sandal.[85]

---

[84] Bukhārī, #5855, Muslim, #2097, Abū Dāwūd, #4136 and Tirmidhī, #1774.

[85] Muslim, #2099, Abū Dāwūd, #4137 and Nasā'ī, #5369.

٨٤ـ حَدَّثَنَا قُتَيْبَةُ، عَنْ مَالِكٍ، (ح) وَحَدَّثَنَا إِسْحَاقُ بْنُ مُوسَى، قَالَ: حَدَّثَنَا مَعْنٌ، قَالَ: حَدَّثَنَا مَالِكٌ، عَنْ أَبِي الزِّنَادِ، عَنِ الأَعْرَجِ، عَنْ أَبِي هُرَيْرَةَ، أَنَّ النَّبِيَّ ﷺ قَالَ: «إِذَا انْتَعَلَ أَحَدُكُمْ فَلْيَبْدَأْ بِالْيَمِينِ، وَإِذَا نَزَعَ فَلْيَبْدَأْ بِالشِّمَالِ، فَلْتَكُنِ الْيُمْنَى أَوَّلَـهُمَا تُنْعَلُ، وَآخِرَهُمَا تُنْزَعُ».

84. Qutaybah narrated to us; from Mālik; and Isḥāq Ibn Mūsā narrated to us; Maʿan narrated to us; Mālik narrated to us; from Abū'l-Zinād; from Al-Aʿraj that Abū Hurayrah (*raḍiyAllāhu ʿanhu*) said: 'The Prophet (ﷺ) said:

> "When one of you wants to wear his sandals, let him begin with the right [foot], and when he takes them off, let him begin with the left [foot]. The right [foot] should be first of the two for the sandal to be worn and the last of the two when taken off."[86]

٨٥ـ حَدَّثَنَا أَبُو مُوسَى مُحَمَّدُ بْنُ الْمُثَنَّى، قَالَ: حَدَّثَنَا مُحَمَّدُ بْنُ جَعْفَرٍ، قَالَ: حَدَّثَنَا شُعْبَةُ، قَالَ: حَدَّثَنَا أَشْعَثُ ـ وَهُوَ ابْنُ أَبِي الشَّعْثَاءِ ـ، عَنْ أَبِيهِ، عَنْ مَسْرُوقٍ، عَنْ عَائِشَةَ، قَالَتْ: «كَانَ رَسُولُ اللهِ ﷺ يُحِبُّ التَّيَمُّنَ مَا اسْتَطَاعَ: فِي تَرَجُّلِهِ وَتَنَعُّلِهِ وَطُهُورِهِ».

85. Abū Mūsā Muḥammad Ibn al-Muthannā narrated to us; Muḥammad Ibn Jāʿfar narrated to us; Shuʿbah narrated to us; Ashʿath narrated to us; Ibn Abī al-Shaʿthā' narrated to us; from his father; from Maṣrūq that ʿĀ'ishah (*raḍiyAllāhu ʿanhā*) said:

> 'The Messenger of Allāh (ﷺ) would love to begin on the right side as much as he could, in his combing, in wearing

[86] Bukhārī, #5856, Muslim, #2097, and Tirmidhī, #1779.

his sandals and in his purification.'[87]

٨٦ـ حَدَّثَنَا مُحَمَّدُ بْنُ مَرْزُوقٍ أَبُو عَبْدِ اللهِ، قَالَ: حَدَّثَنَا عَبْدُ الرَّحْمَنِ بْنُ قَيْسٍ أَبُو مُعَاوِيَةَ، قَالَ: حَدَّثَنَا هِشَامٌ، عَنْ مُحَمَّدٍ، عَنْ أَبِي هُرَيْرَةَ، قَالَ: «كَانَ لِنَعْلِ رَسُولِ اللهِ ﷺ قِبَالَانِ، وَأَبِي بَكْرٍ وَعُمَرَ، وَأَوَّلُ مَنْ عَقَدَ عَقْدًا وَاحِدًا عُثْمَانُ».

86. Muḥammad Ibn Maṣrūq, Abū 'Abdullāh narrated to us; 'Abdu'l-Raḥmān Ibn Qays, Abū Mu'āwiyyah narrated to us; Hishām narrated to us; from Muḥammad [Ibn Sirīn] that Abū Hurayrah (*raḍiyAllāhu 'anhu*) said:

> 'The sandals of the Messenger of Allāh (ﷺ) had two straps, as did Abū Bakr and 'Umar (*raḍiyAllāhu 'anhumā*). The first person to tie a single strap was 'Uthmān (*raḍiyAllāhu 'anhu*).'[88]

[87] Bukhārī, #5854, Muslim, #268, Abū Dāwūd, #4140, Tirmidhī, #608 and others

[88] *Majma' al-Zawā'id wa-Maba' al-Fawā'id*, 5/141.This chain of narration is weak.

CHAPTER TWELVE

بَابٌ مَا جَاءَ فِي ذِكْرِ خَاتَمِ رَسُولِ اللهِ ﷺ

What has been narrated concerning the Ring (*khātam*) of the Messenger of Allāh (ﷺ)

٨٧ـ حَدَّثَنَا قُتَيْبَةُ بْنُ سَعِيدٍ، وَغَيْرُ وَاحِدٍ، عَنْ عَبْدِ اللهِ بْنِ وَهْبٍ، عَنْ يُونُسَ، عَنِ ابْنِ شِهَابٍ، عَنْ أَنَسِ بْنِ مَالِكٍ، قَالَ: «كَانَ خَاتَمُ النَّبِيِّ ﷺ مِنْ وَرِقٍ، وَكَانَ فَصُّهُ حَبَشِيًّا».

87. Qutaybah Ibn Sa'īd narrated to us; from 'Abdullāh Ibn Wahb; from Yūnus; from Ibn Shihāb that Anas Ibn Mālik (*raḍiyAllāhu 'anhu*) said:

> "The ring (*khātam*) of the Prophet (ﷺ) was made of silver, and its gem stone was Abyssinian (*ḥabashī*)."[89]

٨٨ـ حَدَّثَنَا قُتَيْبَةُ، قَالَ: حَدَّثَنَا أَبُو عَوَانَةَ، عَنْ أَبِي بِشْرٍ، عَنْ نَافِعٍ، عَنِ ابْنِ عُمَرَ، «أَنَّ النَّبِيَّ ﷺ اتَّخَذَ خَاتَمًا مِنْ فِضَّةٍ، فَكَانَ يَخْتِمُ بِهِ، وَلَا يَلْبَسُهُ».

قَالَ أَبُو عِيسَى: أَبُو بِشْرٍ اسْمُهُ: جَعْفَرُ بْنُ أَبِي وَحْشِيَّةَ.

88. Qutaybah narrated to us; Abū 'Awānah narrated to us; from

[89] Bukhārī, #5870, Muslim, #2094, Abū Dāwūd, #4216, Tirmidhī, #1739 and others.

Abū Bishr; from Nafīʿ that Ibn ʿUmar (*raḍiyAllāhu ʿanhumā*) said:

> "The Prophet (ﷺ) kept a ring made of silver, he used it [as a signet] to seal [his letters], yet did not wear it."[90]

Abū ʿIsā said: 'The name of Abū Bishr is Jāʿfar Ibn Abī Wahshī.'

٨٩ـ حَدَّثَنَا مَحْمُودُ بْنُ غَيْلَانَ، قَالَ: حَدَّثَنَا حَفْصُ بْنُ عُمَرَ بْنِ عُبَيْدٍ ـ هُوَ الطَّنَافِسِيُّ ـ قَالَ: حَدَّثَنَا زُهَيْرٌ أَبُو خَيْثَمَةَ، عَنْ حُمَيْدٍ، عَنْ أَنَسِ بْنِ مَالِكٍ قَالَ: «كَانَ خَاتَمُ النَّبِيِّ ﷺ مِنْ فِضَّةٍ فَصُّهُ مِنْهُ».

89. Maḥmūd Ibn Ghaylān narrated to us; Ḥafs Ibn ʿUmar Ibn ʿUbayd al-Ṭanāfisi narrated to us; Zuhayr Abū Khaythamah narrated to us; from Ḥumayd that Anas Ibn Mālik (*raḍiyAllāhu ʿanhu*) said:

> "The ring of the Messenger of Allāh (ﷺ) was made of silver, and its stone (*faṣṣ*) [was also of silver]."[91]

٩٠ـ حَدَّثَنَا إِسْحَاقُ بْنُ مَنْصُورٍ، قَالَ: حَدَّثَنَا مُعَاذُ بْنُ هِشَامٍ، قَالَ: حَدَّثَنِي أَبِي، عَنْ قَتَادَةَ، عَنْ أَنَسِ بْنِ مَالِكٍ، قَالَ: «لَـمَّا أَرَادَ رَسُولُ اللهِ ﷺ أَنْ يَكْتُبَ إِلَى العَجَمِ قِيلَ لَهُ: إِنَّ العَجَمَ لَا يَقْبَلُونَ إِلَّا كِتَابًا عَلَيْهِ خَاتَمٌ؛ فَاصْطَنَعَ خَاتَمًا، فَكَأَنِّي أَنْظُرُ إِلَى بَيَاضِهِ فِي كَفِّهِ».

90. Isḥāq Ibn Manṣūr narrated to us; Muʿādh Ibn Hishām narrated to us; my father narrated to me; from Qatādah that Anas Ibn Mālik (*raḍiyAllāhu ʿanhu*) said:

[90] Bukhārī, #5865, Muslim, #2091, and Tirmidhī, #1741.
[91] Bukhārī, #5870, Abū Dāwūd, #4217and Tirmidhī, #1740.

> 'When the Messenger of Allāh (ﷺ) wanted to write letters to [the kings of] the non-Arabs, he was told: 'The non-Arabs do not accept [letters] unless it has a seal.' He therefore created a signet ring, and it is as if I am looking at its whiteness in his palms."[92]

٩١- حَدَّثَنَا مُحَمَّدُ بْنُ يَحْيَى، قَالَ: حَدَّثَنَا مُحَمَّدُ بْنُ عَبْدِ اللهِ الأَنْصَارِيُّ، قَالَ: حَدَّثَنِي أَبِي، عَنْ ثُمَامَةَ، عَنْ أَنَسِ بْنِ مَالِكٍ، قَالَ: «كَانَ نَقْشُ خَاتَمِ رَسُولِ اللهِ ﷺ: مُحَمَّدٌ: سَطْرٌ، وَرَسُولُ: سَطْرٌ، وَاللهُ: سَطْرٌ» .

91. Muḥammad Ibn Yaḥyā narrated to us; Muḥammad Ibn 'Abdullāh al-Anṣārī narrated to us; my father narrated to me; from Thumāmah that Anas Ibn Mālik (*raḍiyAllāhu 'anhu*) said:

> "The inscription engraved on the signet ring of the Messenger of Allāh (ﷺ) was: *'Muḥammad'* on a line, *'Rasul'* on a line, and *'Allāh'* on a line.'[93]

٩٢- حَدَّثَنَا نَصْرُ بْنُ عَلِيٍّ الجَهْضَمِيُّ أَبُو عَمْرٍو، قَالَ: حَدَّثَنَا نُوحُ بْنُ قَيْسٍ، عَنْ خَالِدِ بْنِ قَيْسٍ، عَنْ قَتَادَةَ، عَنْ أَنَسِ بْنِ مَالِكٍ، «أَنَّ النَّبِيَّ ﷺ كَتَبَ إِلَى كِسْرَى وَقَيْصَرَ وَالنَّجَاشِيِّ، فَقِيلَ لَهُ: إِنَّهُمْ لَا يَقْبَلُونَ كِتَابًا إِلَّا بِخَاتَمٍ؛ فَصَاغَ رَسُولُ اللهِ ﷺ خَاتَمًا حَلْقَتُهُ فِضَّةٌ، وَنُقِشَ فِيهِ: مُحَمَّدٌ رَسُولُ اللهِ» .

92. Abū 'Amr Naṣr Ibn 'Alī al Jahḍamī narrated to us; Nūḥ Ibn Qays narrated to us; from Khālid Ibn Qays; from Qatādah that Anas Ibn Mālik (*raḍiyAllāhu 'anhu*) said:

> 'The Prophet (ﷺ) wrote letters to Chosroes, Caesar and the

[92] Bukhārī, #5875, Muslim, #2092, and Tirmidhī, #1747.
[93] Bukhārī, #3104, and Tirmidhī, #1747.

> Negus, he was told: 'They do not accept letters unless they are sealed.' Therefore, the Messenger of Allāh (ﷺ) had a signet ring produced for him, made from silver and had engraved on it, 'Muḥammad is the Messenger of Allāh.'"[94]

٩٣- حَدَّثَنَا إِسْحَاقُ بْنُ مَنْصُورٍ، قَالَ: حَدَّثَنَا سَعِيدُ بْنُ عَامِرٍ، وَالحَجَّاجُ ابْنُ مِنْهَالٍ، عَنْ هَمَّامٍ، عَنِ ابْنِ جُرَيْجٍ، عَنِ الزُّهْرِيِّ، عَنْ أَنَسٍ، «أَنَّ النَّبِيَّ ﷺ كَانَ إِذَا دَخَلَ الخَلَاءَ نَزَعَ خَاتَمَهُ».

93. Isḥāq Ibn Manṣūr narrated to us; Sa'īd Ibn 'Āmir and Al-Ḥajjāj Ibn Minhāl narrated to us; from Hammām; from Ibn Jurayj; from Al-Zuhrī that Anas Ibn Mālik (*raḍiyAllāhu 'anhu*) said:

> "When the Prophet (ﷺ) entered the toilet, he used to remove his ring."[95]

٩٤- حَدَّثَنَا إِسْحَاقُ بْنُ مَنْصُورٍ، قَالَ: حَدَّثَنَا عَبْدُ اللهِ بْنُ نُمَيْرٍ، قَالَ: حَدَّثَنَا عُبَيْدُ اللهِ بْنُ عُمَرَ، عَنْ نَافِعٍ، عَنِ ابْنِ عُمَرَ، قَالَ: «اتَّخَذَ رَسُولُ اللهِ ﷺ خَاتَمًا مِنْ وَرِقٍ، فَكَانَ فِي يَدِهِ، ثُمَّ كَانَ فِي يَدِ أَبِي بَكْرٍ، وَيَدِ عُمَرَ، ثُمَّ كَانَ فِي يَدِ عُثْمَانَ، حَتَّى وَقَعَ فِي بِئْرِ أَرِيسٍ؛ نَقْشُهُ: مُحَمَّدٌ رَسُولُ اللهِ» .

94. Isḥāq Ibn Manṣūr narrated to us; 'Abdullāh Ibn Numayr narrated to us; 'Ubaydullāh Ibn 'Umar narrated to us; from Nāfi' that Ibn 'Umar (*raḍiyAllāhu 'anhumā*) said:

> "The Messenger of Allāh (ﷺ) kept a ring made of silver,

[94] Bukhārī, #5865, Muslim, #2091, and Tirmidhī, #1741.

[95] Tirmidhī, #1742, and he said the ḥadīth is ḥasan gharīb. Abū Dāwūd reported in his Sunan, #19 and said the ḥadīth is rejected.

and hence it used to be in his possession (*yad*) [until his demise]. Then it was in the possession of Abū Bakr and [then after him] it was in the possession of 'Umar. Then [after him] it was in the possession of 'Uthmān, until it fell into the well of Arīs. The inscription on this ring was "Muḥammad is the Messenger of Allāh.'"[96]

[96] Bukhārī, #5873, Muslim, #2091 and Abū Dāwūd, #4218

CHAPTER THIRTEEN

بَابُ مَا جَاءَ فِي أَنَّ النَّبِيَّ ﷺ كَانَ يَتَخَتَّمُ فِي يَمِينِهِ

What has been narrated concerning the Messenger of Allāh (ﷺ) wearing a [Signet] Ring on his Right Hand (*yamīn*)

٩٥ـ حَدَّثَنَا مُحَمَّدُ بْنُ سَهْلِ بْنِ عَسْكَرٍ الْبَغْدَادِيُّ، وَعَبْدُ اللهِ بْنُ عَبْدِ الرَّحْمَنِ، قَالَا: أَخْبَرَنَا يَحْيَى بْنُ حَسَّانَ، قَالَ: حَدَّثَنَا سُلَيْمَانُ بْنُ بِلَالٍ، عَنْ شَرِيكِ بْنِ عَبْدِ اللهِ ابْنِ أَبِي نَمِرٍ، عَنْ إِبْرَاهِيمَ بْنِ عَبْدِ اللهِ بْنِ حُنَيْنٍ، عَنْ أَبِيهِ، عَنْ عَلِيِّ بْنِ أَبِي طَالِبٍ: «أَنَّ النَّبِيَّ ﷺ كَانَ يَلْبَسُ خَاتَمَهُ فِي يَمِينِهِ».

95. Muḥammad Ibn Sahl Ibn ʿAskar al-Baghdādī and ʿAbdullāh Ibn ʿAbdu'l-Raḥmān narrated to us; Yaḥyā Ibn Ḥassān informed us; Sulaymān Ibn Bilāl narrated to us; from Sarīk Ibn ʿAbdullāh Ibn Abī Namir; from Ibrāhīm Ibn ʿAbdullāh Ibn Ḥunayn; from his father that ʿAlī Ibn Abī Ṭālib (*raḍiyAllāhu ʿanhu*) said:

> "The Prophet (ﷺ) would wear his ring on the right hand (*yamīn*)."[97]

---

[97] Abū Dāwūd, #4226 and Nasā'ī, #5203, although the chain has a weakness, it is supported by other texts as will come later.

٩٦ـ حَدَّثَنَا مُحَمَّدُ بْنُ يَحْيَى، قَالَ: حَدَّثَنَا أَحْمَدُ بْنُ صَالِحٍ، قَالَ: حَدَّثَنَا عَبْدُ اللهِ ابْنُ وَهْبٍ، عَنْ سُلَيْمَانَ بْنِ بِلَالٍ، عَنْ شَرِيكِ بْنِ عَبْدِ اللهِ بْنِ أَبِي نَمِرٍ، نَحْوَهُ.

96. Muḥammad Ibn Yaḥyā narrated to us; Aḥmad Ibn Ṣāliḥ narrated to us; 'Abdullāh Ibn Wahb narrated to us; from Sulaymān Ibn Bilāl; from Sarīk Ibn 'Abdullāh Ibn Abī Namir said something similar.

٩٧ـ حَدَّثَنَا أَحْمَدُ بْنُ مَنِيعٍ، قَالَ: حَدَّثَنَا يَزِيدُ بْنُ هَارُونَ، عَنْ حَمَّادِ بْنِ سَلَمَةَ، قَالَ: رَأَيْتُ ابْنَ أَبِي رَافِعٍ يَتَخَتَّمُ فِي يَمِينِهِ، فَسَأَلْتُهُ عَنْ ذَلِكَ، فَقَالَ: رَأَيْتُ عَبْدَ اللهِ بْنَ جَعْفَرٍ يَتَخَتَّمُ فِي يَمِينِهِ، وَقَالَ عَبْدُ اللهِ بْنُ جَعْفَرٍ: «كَانَ رَسُولُ اللهِ ﷺ يَتَخَتَّمُ فِي يَمِينِهِ».

97. Aḥmad Ibn Manī' narrated to us; Yazīd Ibn Hārun narrated to us that Ḥammād Ibn Salamah said: 'I saw Ibn Abī Rāfi' wearing a [signet] ring on his right hand, so I asked him [the reason for] that and he said:

> 'I saw 'Abdullāh Ibn Jā'far wearing a [signet] ring on his right hand, and he said: "The Messenger of Allāh (ﷺ) used to wear the [signet] ring on his right [hand]."'[98]

٩٨ـ حَدَّثَنَا يَحْيَى بْنُ مُوسَى، قَالَ: حَدَّثَنَا عَبْدُ اللهِ بْنُ نُمَيْرٍ، قَالَ: حَدَّثَنَا إِبْرَاهِيمُ بْنُ الفَضْلِ، عَنْ عَبْدِ اللهِ بْنِ مُحَمَّدِ بْنِ عَقِيلٍ، عَنْ عَبْدِ اللهِ بْنِ جَعْفَرٍ: «أَنَّ النَّبِيَّ ﷺ كَانَ يَتَخَتَّمُ فِي يَمِينِهِ».

98. Yaḥyā Ibn Mūsā narrated to us; 'Abdullāh Ibn Abī Numayr nar-

[98] Tirmidhī, #1744.

rated to us; Ibrāhīm Ibn Al-Faḍl narrated to us; from ʿAbdullāh Ibn Muḥammad Ibn ʿAqīl that ʿAbdullāh Ibn Jāʿfar (*raḍiyAllāhu ʿanhu*) said:

> "He (ﷺ) used to wear the [signet] ring on his right [hand]."[99]

٩٩ـ حَدَّثَنَا أَبُو الخَطَّابِ زِيَادُ بْنُ يَحْيَى، قَالَ: حَدَّثَنَا عَبْدُ اللهِ بْنُ مَيْمُونٍ، عَنْ جَعْفَرِ ابنِ مُحَمَّدٍ، عَنْ أَبِيهِ، عَنْ جَابِرِ بْنِ عَبْدِ اللهِ: «أَنَّ النَّبِيَّ ﷺ كَانَ يَتَخَتَّمُ فِي يَمِينِهِ» .

99. Abū'l-Khaṭṭāb Ziyād Ibn Yaḥyā narrated to us; ʿAbdullāh Ibn Maymūn narrated to us; from Jāʿfar Ibn Muḥammad; from his father that Jābir Ibn ʿAbdullāh (*raḍiyAllāhu ʿanhu*) said:

> "The Prophet of Allāh (ﷺ) used to wear the [signet] ring on his right [hand]."[100]

١٠٠ـ حَدَّثَنَا مُحَمَّدُ بْنُ حُمَيْدٍ الرَّازِيُّ، قَالَ: حَدَّثَنَا جَرِيرٌ، عَنْ مُحَمَّدِ ابنِ إِسْحَاقَ، عَنِ الصَّلتِ بْنِ عَبْدِ اللهِ، قَالَ: كَانَ ابْنُ عَبَّاسٍ يَتَخَتَّمُ فِي يَمِينِهِ وَلَا إِخَالُهُ إِلَّا قَالَ: «كَانَ رَسُولُ اللهِ ﷺ يَتَخَتَّمُ فِي يَمِينِهِ».

100. Muḥammad Ibn Ḥumayd al-Rāzī narrated to us; Jarīr narrated to us; from Muḥammad Ibn Isḥāq that Ṣalt Ibn ʿAbdullāh said:

> ʿIbn ʿAbbās (*raḍiyAllāhu ʿanhumā*) used to wear a [signet] ring on his right [hand], without adornment and he said: "The Messenger of Allāh (ﷺ) used to wear the [signet] ring on his right [hand]."[101]

---

[99] Ibn Mājah, #3647, Aḥmad in his *Musnad*, 3/195 and this ḥadith is weak.

[100] *Al-ʿIlal al-Kabīr* of al-Bukhārī, #287 who said this report from Jabir (*raḍiyAllāhu ʿanhu*) through this chain is not authentic.

[101] Tirmidhī, #1742, and Abū Dāwūd, #4229. This tradition is supported by other authentic narrations.

١٠١ـ حَدَّثَنَا مُحَمَّدُ بْنُ أَبِي عُمَرَ، قَالَ: حَدَّثَنَا سُفْيَانُ، عَنْ أَيُّوبَ بْنِ مُوسَى، عَنْ نَافِعٍ، عَنِ ابْنِ عُمَرَ: «أَنَّ النَّبِيَّ ﷺ اتَّخَذَ خَاتَمًا مِنْ فِضَّةٍ، وَجَعَلَ فَصَّهُ مِمَّا يَلِي كَفَّهُ، وَنَقَشَ فِيهِ (مُحَمَّدٌ رَسُولُ اللهِ)، وَنَهَى أَنْ يَنْقُشَ أَحَدٌ عَلَيْهِ، وَهُوَ الَّذِي سَقَطَ مِنْ مُعَيْقِيبٍ فِي بِئْرِ أَرِيسَ».

101. Muḥammad Ibn Abī ʿUmar narrated to us; Sufyān narrated to us; from Ayyūb Ibn Mūsā; from Nāfiʿ that Ibn ʿUmar (*raḍiyAllāhu ʿanhumā*) said:

> "The Prophet of Allāh (ﷺ) kept a [signet] ring made of silver and puts its stone in the part facing his palm, he engraved on it, 'Muḥammad the Messenger of Allāh' and he forbade anyone to engrave on it. It is [the same ring] which fell from [the hands of] Muʿayqib into the well of Arīs [during the reign of ʿUthmān]."[102]

١٠٢ـ حَدَّثَنَا قُتَيْبَةُ بْنُ سَعِيدٍ، قَالَ: حَدَّثَنَا حَاتِمُ بْنُ إِسْمَاعِيلَ، عَنْ جَعْفَرِ ابْنِ مُحَمَّدٍ، عَنْ أَبِيهِ، قَالَ: «كَانَ الْحَسَنُ وَالْحُسَيْنُ يَتَخَتَّمَانِ فِي يَسَارِهِمَا».

102. Qutaybah Ibn Saʿīd narrated to us; Ḥātim Ibn Ismāʿīl narrated to us; from Jāʿfar Ibn Muḥammad that his father said:

> "Al-Ḥasan and Ḥusayn both used to wear their [signet] ring on their left hand (*yasār*)."[103]

١٠٣ـ حَدَّثَنَا عَبْدُ اللهِ بْنُ عَبْدِ الرَّحْمَنِ، قَالَ: حَدَّثَنَا مُحَمَّدُ بْنُ عِيسَى ـ وَهُوَ ابْنُ الطَّبَّاعِ ـ، قَالَ: حَدَّثَنَا عَبَّادُ بْنُ الْعَوَّامِ، عَنْ سَعِيدِ بْنِ أَبِي عَرُوبَةَ، عَنْ قَتَادَةَ، عَنْ

[102] Muslim, #2091 and Abū Dāwūd, #4219.

[103] Tirmidhī, #1743, this tradition has a broken chain of narration.

أَنَسِ بْنِ مَالِكٍ: «أَنَّهُ ﷺ كَانَ يَتَخَتَّمُ فِي يَمِينِهِ».

103. ʿAbdullāh Ibn ʿAbdu'l-Raḥmān narrated to us; Muḥammad Ibn ʿIsā Ibn al-Ṭabbāʿ narrated to us; ʿAbbād Ibn al-ʿAwwām narrated to us; from Saʿid Ibn Abī ʿArūbah; from Qatādah that Anas Ibn Mālik (*raḍiyAllāhu ʿanhu*) said:

"He (ﷺ) used to wear the [signet] ring on his right hand."[104]

١٠٤ـ حَدَّثَنَا مُحَمَّدُ بْنُ عُبَيْدِ اللهِ الْمُحَارِبِيُّ، قَالَ: حَدَّثَنَا عَبْدُ الْعَزِيزِ بْنُ أَبِي حَازِمٍ، عَنْ مُوسَى بْنِ عُقْبَةَ، عَنْ نَافِعٍ، عَنِ ابْنِ عُمَرَ، قَالَ: «اتَّخَذَ رَسُولُ اللهِ ﷺ خَاتَمًا مِنْ ذَهَبٍ، فَكَانَ يَلْبَسُهُ فِي يَمِينِهِ، فَاتَّخَذَ النَّاسُ خَوَاتِيمَ مِنْ ذَهَبٍ فَطَرَحَهُ ﷺ، وَقَالَ: «لَا أَلْبَسُهُ أَبَدًا» فَطَرَحَ النَّاسُ خَوَاتِيمَهُمْ».

104. Muḥammad Ibn ʿUbayd al-Muḥāribī narrated to us; ʿAbdu'l-ʿAzīz Ibn Abī Ḥāzim narrated to us; from Mūsā Ibn ʿUqbah; from Nāfiʿ that Ibn ʿUmar (*raḍiyAllāhu ʿanhumā*) said:

"The Messenger of Allāh (ﷺ) kept a [signet] ring of gold and he used to wear it on his right [hand]. The people [also] began to keep gold rings, so he (ﷺ) threw it away and said: "I will never wear it again!" Thereafter, the people threw their rings away [also].'[105]

---

[104] Nasāʾī, #5204.

[105] Bukhārī, #5865, Muslim, #209, Abū Dāwūd, #4218 and Tirmidhī, #1741.

CHAPTER FOURTEEN

بَابٌ مَا جَاءَ فِي صِفَةِ سَيْفِ رَسُولِ اللهِ ﷺ

What has been narrated concerning the Description of the Sword (*sayf*) of the Messenger of Allāh (ﷺ)

١٠٥ـ حَدَّثَنَا مُحَمَّدُ بْنُ بَشَّارٍ، قَالَ: حَدَّثَنَا وَهْبُ بْنُ جَرِيرٍ، قَالَ: حَدَّثَنَا أَبِي، عَنْ قَتَادَةَ، عَنْ أَنَسٍ، قَالَ: «كَانَتْ قَبِيعَةُ سَيْفِ رَسُولِ اللهِ ﷺ مِنْ فِضَّةٍ».

105. Muḥammad Ibn Bashshār narrated to us; Wahb Ibn Jarīr narrated to us; my father narrated to us; from Qatādah that Anas (*raḍiyAllāhu ʿanhu*) said:

> "The pommel [handel] of the sword (*sayf*) of the Messenger (ﷺ) of was made of silver (*fiḍḍah*)."[106]

١٠٦ـ حَدَّثَنَا مُحَمَّدُ بْنُ بَشَّارٍ، قَالَ: حَدَّثَنَا مُعَاذُ بْنُ هِشَامٍ، قَالَ: حَدَّثَنِي أَبِي، عَنْ قَتَادَةَ، عَنْ سَعِيدِ بْنِ أَبِي الحَسَنِ، قَالَ: «كَانَتْ قَبِيعَةُ سَيْفِ رَسُولِ اللهِ ﷺ مِنْ فِضَّةٍ».

106. Muḥammad Ibn Bashshār narrated to us; Muʿādh Ibn Hishām narrated to us; my father narrated to us; from Qatādah that Saʿīd Ibn

[106] Abū Dāwūd, #2583 and Tirmidhī, #1691.

Abī al-Ḥasan (*raḍiyAllāhu ʿanhu*) said:

> "The pommel of the sword (*sayf*) of the Messenger (ﷺ) was made of silver."[107]

١٠٧ـ حَدَّثَنَا أَبُو جَعْفَرٍ مُحَمَّدُ بْنُ صُدْرَانَ الْبَصْرِيُّ، قَالَ: حَدَّثَنَا طَالِبُ ابْنُ حُجَيْرٍ، عَنْ هُودٍ ـ وَهُوَ ابْنُ عَبْدِ اللهِ بْنِ سَعْدٍ ـ عَنْ جَدِّهِ، قَالَ: «دَخَلَ رَسُولُ اللهِ ﷺ مَكَّةَ يَوْمَ الْفَتْحِ وَعَلَى سَيْفِهِ ذَهَبٌ وَفِضَّةٌ».

قَالَ طَالِبٌ: فَسَأَلْتُهُ عَنِ الْفِضَّةِ فَقَالَ: «كَانَتْ قَبِيعَةُ السَّيْفِ فِضَّةً».

107. Abū Jāʿfar Muḥammad Ibn Ṣudrān al-Baṣrī narrated to us; Ṭālib Ibn Ḥujayr narrated to us; from Hūd Ibn ʿAbdullāh Ibn Saʿd that his grandfather [Mazyadah Ibn Mālik (*raḍiyAllāhu ʿanhu*)] said:

> "The Messenger of Allāh (ﷺ) entered Makkah on the Day of Conquest (*yawm al-fatḥ*) with a sword that had gold and silver on it."

Ṭālib [Ibn Ḥujayr] said: 'I asked [my teacher] about the silver, and he said:

> 'The pommel of the sword was made of silver."[108]

١٠٨ـ حَدَّثَنَا مُحَمَّدُ بْنُ شُجَاعٍ الْبَغْدَادِيُّ، قَالَ: حَدَّثَنَا أَبُو عُبَيْدَةَ الْحَدَّادُ، عَنْ عُثْمَانَ ابْنِ سَعْدٍ، عَنِ ابْنِ سِيرِينَ، قَالَ: «صَنَعْتُ سَيْفِي عَلَى سَيْفِ سَمُرَةَ بْنِ جُنْدُبٍ، وَزَعَمَ سَمُرَةُ أَنَّهُ صَنَعَ سَيْفَهُ عَلَى سَيْفِ رَسُولِ اللهِ ﷺ وَكَانَ حَنَفِيًّا».

[107] Abū Dāwūd, #2584, Tirmidhī, #1691 and Nasāʾī, #5375.

[108] Tirmidhī, #1690, this tradition is not established, as it is not known that the Messenger of Allah (ﷺ) had or used gold on his sword.

108. Muḥammad Ibn Shujāʿ al-Baghdādī narrated to us; Abū ʿUbadah al-Ḥaddād narrated to us; from ʿUthmān Ibn Saʿd that Ibn Sirīn said:

> 'I made my sword [a replica of] to the sword of Samurah Ibn Jundub (*raḍiyAllāhu ʿanhu*). Samurah also said that his sword was [a replicate] to the sword of the Messenger of Allāh (ﷺ), and it was [a high quality sword manufactured by the tribe] of Banu Ḥanīfah.[109]

١٠٩ـ حَدَّثَنَا عُقْبَةُ بْنُ مُكْرَمٍ الْبَصْرِيُّ، قَالَ: حَدَّثَنَا مُحَمَّدُ بْنُ بَكْرٍ، عَنْ عُثْمَانَ بْنِ سَعْدٍ، بِهَذَا الإِسْنَادِ نَحْوَهُ.

109. ʿUqbah Ibn Mukhrim al-Baṣrī narrated to us; Muḥammad Ibn Bakr narrated to us; from ʿUthmān Ibn Saʿd, with this chain of narration.

[109] Tirmidhī, #1683—this chain of narration is weak.

CHAPTER FIFTEEN

بَابُ مَا جَاءَ فِي صِفَةِ دِرْعِ رَسُولِ اللهِ ﷺ

What has been narrated concerning the Description of the Body Armour (*dir'*) of the Messenger of Allāh (ﷺ)

١١٠ـ حَدَّثَنَا أَبُو سَعِيدٍ عَبْدُ اللهِ بْنُ سَعِيدٍ الأَشَجُّ، قَالَ: حَدَّثَنَا يُونُسُ ابْنُ بُكَيْرٍ، عَنْ مُحَمَّدِ بْنِ إِسْحَاقَ، عَنْ يَحْيَى بْنِ عَبَّادِ بْنِ عَبْدِ اللهِ بْنِ الزُّبَيْرِ، عَنْ أَبِيهِ، عَنْ جَدِّهِ عَبْدِ اللهِ بْنِ الزُّبَيْرِ، عَنِ الزُّبَيْرِ بْنِ العَوَّامِ، قَالَ: «كَانَ عَلَى النَّبِيِّ ﷺ يَوْمَ أُحُدٍ دِرْعَانِ، فَنَهَضَ إِلَى الصَّخْرَةِ فَلَمْ يَسْتَطِعْ، فَأَقْعَدَ طَلْحَةَ تَحْتَهُ، وَصَعِدَ النَّبِيُّ ﷺ حَتَّى اسْتَوَى عَلَى الصَّخْرَةِ» قَالَ: سَمِعْتُ النَّبِيَّ ﷺ يَقُولُ: «أَوْجَبَ طَلْحَةُ».

110. Abū Sa'īd 'Abdullāh Ibn Sa'īd al-Ashajj narrated to us; Yūnus Ibn Bukayr narrated to us; from Muḥammad Ibn Isḥāq; Yaḥyā Ibn 'Abbād Ibn 'Abdullāh Ibn al-Zubayr; from his father; from his grandfather 'Abdullāh Ibn al-Zubayr that Al-Zubayr Ibn al-'Awwām said:

> 'The Prophet of Allāh (ﷺ) wore two coats of armour [on his body] on the Day of Uhud, so he tried to jump on to the rock but was not able.[110] He therefore requested

[110] Due to the heavy weight of the two armors and the wounds he received on his noble head which resulted in losing a lot of blood.

> Ṭalḥah (*raḍiyAllāhu 'anhu*) to sit beneath him [with his aid], the Prophet (ﷺ), climbed up the rock until he rose on it.' He (*raḍiyAllāhu 'anhu*) said: 'I heard the Prophet of Allāh (ﷺ) say: "Ṭalḥah has made [it] incumbent."'[111]

١١١ـ حَدَّثَنَا مُحَمَّدُ بْنُ أَبِي عُمَرَ، قَالَ: حَدَّثَنَا سُفْيَانُ بْنُ عُيَيْنَةَ، عَنْ يَزِيدَ ابْنِ خُصَيْفَةَ، عَنِ السَّائِبِ بنِ يَزِيدَ، «أَنَّ رَسُولَ الله ﷺ كَانَ عَلَيْهِ يَوْمَ أُحُدٍ دِرْعَانِ، قَدْ ظَاهَرَ بَيْنَهُمَا».

111. Ibn Abī 'Umar narrated to us; Sufyān Ibn 'Uyaynah narrated to us; from Yazīd Ibn Khuṣayfah that Al-Sā'ib Ibn Yazīd (*raḍiyAllāhu 'anhu*) said:

> "The Messenger of Allāh (ﷺ) on the Day of Uhud was wearing two coats armour, one on top of the other."[112]

[111] Tirmidhī, #1692—this is weak but the same tradition has been narrated in the *Musnad* of Imam Aḥmad, #1417.

[112] Abū Dāwūd, #2590 and Ibn Mājah, #2806.

CHAPTER SIXTEEN

بَابُ مَا جَاءَ فِي صِفَةِ مِغْفَرِ رَسُولِ اللهِ ﷺ

What has been narrated concerning the Description of the Helmet (*mighfar*) of the Messenger of Allāh (ﷺ)

١١٢ـ حَدَّثَنَا قُتَيْبَةُ بْنُ سَعِيدٍ، قَالَ: حَدَّثَنَا مَالِكُ بْنُ أَنَسٍ، عَنِ ابْنِ شِهَابٍ، عَنْ أَنَسِ بْنِ مَالِكٍ: أَنَّ النَّبِيَّ ﷺ دَخَلَ مَكَّةَ وَعَلَيْهِ مِغْفَرٌ، فَقِيلَ لَهُ: هَذَا ابْنُ خَطَلٍ مُتَعَلِّقٌ بِأَسْتَارِ الكَعْبَةِ، فَقَالَ: «اقْتُلُوهُ».

112. Qutaybah Ibn Sa'īd narrated to us; Mālik Ibn Anas narrated to us; from Ibn Shihāb that Anas Ibn Mālik (*raḍiyAllāhu 'anhu*) said:

> 'The Prophet (ﷺ) entered Makkah wearing a helmet (*maghfar*).' He was told: 'Ibn Khaṭal is clinging to the curtains of the Ka'bah.' So he (ﷺ) said: "[Regardless] kill him."'[113]

[113] Bukhārī, #3044, Muslim, #1357, Abū Dāwūd, #2685 and Tirmidhī, #1693.

١١٣ـ حَدَّثَنَا عِيسَى بْنُ أَحْمَدَ، قَالَ: حَدَّثَنَا عَبْدُ اللهِ بْنُ وَهْبٍ، قَالَ: حَدَّثَنِي مَالِكُ بْنُ أَنَسٍ، عَنِ ابْنِ شِهَابٍ، عَنْ أَنَسِ بْنِ مَالِكٍ، أَنَّ رَسُولَ اللهِ ﷺ دَخَلَ مَكَّةَ عَامَ الفَتْحِ، وَعَلَى رَأْسِهِ المِغْفَرُ، قَالَ: فَلَمَّا نَزَعَهُ جَاءَهُ رَجُلٌ، فَقَالَ لَهُ: ابْنُ خَطَلٍ مُتَعَلِّقٌ بِأَسْتَارِ الكَعْبَةِ، فَقَالَ: «اقْتُلُوهُ».

قَالَ ابْنُ شِهَابٍ: وَبَلَغَنِي أَنَّ رَسُولَ اللهِ ﷺ لَمْ يَكُنْ يَوْمَئِذٍ مُحْرِمًا.

113. ʿIsā Ibn Aḥmad narrated to us; ʿAbdullāh Ibn Wahb narrated to us; Mālik Ibn Anas narrated to me; from Ibn Shihāb that Anas Ibn Mālik (*raḍiyAllāhu ʿanhu*) said:

> 'The Prophet (ﷺ) entered Makkah in the Year of the Conquest (*ʿām al-fatḥ*) wearing on his head a helmet (*mighfar*).' When he took it off, a man came up to him and said: 'Ibn Khaṭal is clinging to the curtains of the Kaʿbah.' So he (ﷺ) said: "[Regardless] kill him."'

Ibn Shihāb Zuhrī said: 'It has also reached me that the Messenger of Allāh (ﷺ) was not in the state of *Iḥrām* (*muḥrim*) on that day.'[114]

[114] Bukhārī, #3044, Muslim, #1357, Abū Dāwūd, #2685, Tirmidhī, #1693 and Muwaṭṭā' Imām Mālik, #1271.

CHAPTER SEVENTEEN

بَابُ مَا جَاءَ فِي عِمَامَةِ رَسُولِ اللهِ ﷺ

What has been narrated concerning the Description of the Turban (*ʿimāmah*) of the Messenger of Allāh (ﷺ)

١١٤ـ حَدَّثَنَا مُحَمَّدُ بْنُ بَشَّارٍ، قَالَ: حَدَّثَنَا عَبْدُ الرَّحْمَنِ بْنُ مَهْدِيٍّ، عَنْ حَمَّادِ ابْنِ سَلَمَةَ، (ح) وَحَدَّثَنَا مَحْمُودُ بْنُ غَيْلَانَ، قَالَ: حَدَّثَنَا وَكِيعٌ، عَنْ حَمَّادِ بْنِ سَلَمَةَ، عَنْ أَبِي الزُّبَيْرِ، عَنْ جَابِرٍ، قَالَ: «دَخَلَ النَّبِيُّ ﷺ مَكَّةَ يَوْمَ الْفَتْحِ وَعَلَيْهِ عِمَامَةٌ سَوْدَاءُ».

114. Muḥammad Ibn Bashshār narrated to us; ʿAbdu'l-Raḥmān Ibn Mahdī narrated to us; from Ḥammād Ibn Salamah, and Maḥmūd Ibn Ghaylān narrated to us; Wakīʿ narrated to us; from Ḥammād Ibn Salamah narrated to us; from Ibn Abī al-Zubayr that Jābir (*raḍiyAllāhu ʿanhu*) said:

> "The Prophet (ﷺ) entered Makkah in the Year of the Conquest wearing a black turban (*ʿimāmah suwdāʾ*)."[115]

115. Ibn Abī ʿUmar narrated to us; Sufyān narrated to us; from Musāwir al-Warrāq; Jāʿfar Ibn ʿAmr Ibn Ḥurayth that his father said:

---

[115] Muslim, #1358, Abū Dāwūd, #4076 and Tirmidhī, #1735.

"I saw the Prophet (ﷺ) addressing the people from the pulpit while wearing a black turban."[116]

١١٦ـ حَدَّثَنَا مَحْمُودُ بْنُ غَيْلَانَ، وَيُوسُفُ بْنُ عِيسَى، قَالَا: حَدَّثَنَا وَكِيعٌ، عَنْ مُسَاوِرٍ الْوَرَّاقِ، عَنْ جَعْفَرِ بْنِ عَمْرِو بْنِ حُرَيْثٍ، عَنْ أَبِيهِ، «أَنَّ النَّبِيَّ ﷺ خَطَبَ النَّاسَ وَعَلَيْهِ عِمَامَةٌ سَوْدَاءُ».

116. Maḥmūd Ibn Ghaylān and Yūsuf Ibn ʿIsā narrated to us; Wakīʿ narrated to us; from Musāwir al-Warrāq; Jāʿfar Ibn ʿAmr Ibn Ḥurayth that his father said:

"The Prophet (ﷺ) addressed the people whilst wearing a black turban."[117]

١١٧ـ حَدَّثَنَا هَارُونُ بْنُ إِسْحَاقَ الْهَمْدَانِيُّ، قَالَ: حَدَّثَنَا يَحْيَى بْنُ مُحَمَّدٍ الْمَدَنِيُّ، عَنْ عَبْدِ الْعَزِيزِ بْنِ مُحَمَّدٍ، عَنْ عُبَيْدِ اللهِ بنِ عُمَرَ، عَنْ نَافِعٍ، عَنِ ابْنِ عُمَرَ، قَالَ: «كَانَ النَّبِيُّ ﷺ إِذَا اعْتَمَّ سَدَلَ عِمَامَتَهُ بَيْنَ كَتِفَيْهِ».

قَالَ نَافِعٌ: وَكَانَ ابْنُ عُمَرَ يَفْعَلُ ذَلِكَ؛ قَالَ عُبَيْدُ اللهِ: وَرَأَيْتُ الْقَاسِمَ ابْنَ مُحَمَّدٍ، وَسَالِمًا يَفْعَلَانِ ذَلِكَ .

117. Hārun Ibn Isḥāq al-Hamdānī narrated to us; Yaḥyā Ibn Muḥammad al-Madanī narrated to us; from ʿAbdu'l-ʿAzīz Ibn Muḥammad; from ʿUbaydullāh Ibn ʿUmar; from Nāfiʿ that Ibn ʿUmar (*raḍiyAllāhu ʿanhumā*) said:

"When the Prophet (ﷺ) wrapped a turban around his

[116] Muslim, #359 and Abū Dāwūd, #4077.
[117] Muslim, #359, Abū Dāwūd, #4077 and Ibn Mājah, #1104.

> head, he would let [the tail of] his turban hang between his shoulders."

Nāfi' said: 'I saw Ibn 'Umar (*raḍiyAllāhu 'anhumā*) do it in the same manner.'

'Ubaydullāh said: 'I saw Qāsim Ibn Muḥammad and Sālim Ibn 'Abdullāh do it in the same manner.'[118]

١١٨ـ حَدَّثَنَا يُوسُفُ بْنُ عِيسَى، قَالَ: حَدَّثَنَا وَكِيعٌ، قَالَ: حَدَّثَنَا أَبُو سُلَيْمَانَ ـ وَهُوَ عَبْدُ الرَّحْمَنِ بْنُ الغَسِيلِ ـ، عَنْ عِكْرِمَةَ، عَنِ ابْنِ عَبَّاسٍ: «أَنَّ النَّبِيَّ ﷺ خَطَبَ النَّاسَ وَعَلَيْهِ عِصَابَةٌ دَسْمَاءُ».

118. Yūsuf Ibn 'Isā narrated to us; Wakī' narrated to us; Abū Sulaymān 'Abdu'l-Raḥmān Ibn Ghasīl narrated to us; from 'Ikrimah that Ibn 'Abbās (*raḍiyAllāhu 'anhumā*) said:

> "The Prophet (ﷺ) addressed the people whilst wearing a turban that was [stained with oil from his hair]."[119]

[118] Tirmidhī, #1736, this is tradition is weak but does have other supporting evidence.
[119] Bukhārī, #927.

CHAPTER EIGHTEEN

بَابُ مَا جَاءَ فِي صِفَةِ إِزَارِ رَسُولِ اللهِ ﷺ

What has been narrated concerning the Description of the Loincloth(*izār*) of the Messenger of Allāh (ﷺ)

١١٩ـ حَدَّثَنَا أَحْمَدُ بْنُ مَنِيعٍ، قَالَ: حَدَّثَنَا إِسْمَاعِيلُ بْنُ إِبْرَاهِيمَ، قَالَ: حَدَّثَنَا أَيُّوبُ، عَنْ حُمَيْدِ بْنِ هِلَالٍ، عَنْ أَبِي بُرْدَةَ، قَالَ: «أَخْرَجَتْ إِلَيْنَا عَائِشَةُ كِسَاءً مُلَبَّدًا، وَإِزَارًا غَلِيظًا، فَقَالَتْ: قُبِضَ رُوحُ رَسُولِ اللهِ ﷺ فِي هَذَيْنِ».

119. Aḥmad Ibn Manīʿ narrated to us; Ismāʿīl Ibn Ibrāhīm narrated to us; Abū Ayyūb narrated to us; from Ḥumayd Ibn Hilāl; from Abū Burdah that his father said:

> "Ā'ishah (*raḍiyAllāhu ʿanhā*) took out for us a patched (*mulabbad*) upper garment (*kisā'*) and a [thick] coarse loincloth (*izār*), then she said: "The soul of the Messenger of Allāh (ﷺ) was taken in these two."[120]

١٢٠ـ حَدَّثَنَا مَحْمُودُ بْنُ غَيْلَانَ، قَالَ: حَدَّثَنَا أَبُو دَاوُدَ، عَنْ شُعْبَةَ، عَنِ

[120] Bukhārī, #3108, Muslim, #2080, and Abū Dāwūd, #4036 and Tirmidhī, #1733.

الأَشْعَثِ بْنِ سُلَيْمٍ، قَالَ: سَمِعْتُ عَمَّتِي تُحَدِّثُ عَنْ عَمِّهَا، قَالَ: «بَيْنَا أَنَا أَمْشِي بِالْمَدِينَةِ، إِذَا إِنْسَانٌ خَلْفِي يَقُولُ: «ارْفَعْ إِزَارَكَ؛ فَإِنَّهُ أَتْقَى وَأَبْقَى»، فَإِذَا هُوَ رَسُولُ اللهِ ﷺ، فَقُلْتُ: يَا رَسُولَ اللهِ! إِنَّمَا هِيَ بُرْدَةٌ مَلْحَاءُ، قَالَ: «أَمَا لَكَ فِيَّ أُسْوَةٌ»؟ فَنَظَرْتُ فَإِذَا إِزَارُهُ إِلَى نِصْفِ سَاقَيْهِ.

120. Maḥmūd Ibn Ghaylān narrated to us; Abū Dāwūd narrated to us; from Shuʿbah that Al-Ashʿath Ibn Sulaym said: 'I heard my maternal aunt narrate from her paternal uncle:

> 'While I was walking in Medīnah, someone behind me said: 'Raise your loincloth (*izār*) as it is closer to piety (*atqā*) and makes it last longer.' Lo and behold, it was the Messenger of Allāh (ﷺ), so I said: 'O Messenger of Allāh, it is merely a black mantle with white stripes.' He said: "Do you not have an example in me?" I looked at him and I noticed that his loincloth (*izār*) reached the middle of his shins.'"[121]

١٢١ـ حَدَّثَنَا سُوَيْدُ بْنُ نَصْرٍ، قَالَ: حَدَّثَنَا عَبْدُ اللهِ بْنُ الْمُبَارَكِ، عَنْ مُوسَى ابْنِ عُبَيْدَةَ، عَنْ إِيَاسِ بْنِ سَلَمَةَ بْنِ الأَكْوَعِ، عَنْ أَبِيهِ، قَالَ: «كَانَ عُثْمَانُ بْنُ عَفَّانَ يَأْتَزِرُ إِلَى أَنْصَافِ سَاقَيْهِ، وَقَالَ: هَكَذَا كَانَتْ إِزْرَةُ صَاحِبِي ـ يَعْنِي النَّبِيَّ ﷺ ـ».

121. Suwayd Ibn Naṣr narrated to us; 'Abdullāh Ibn al-Mubārak narrated to us; from Mūsā Ibn 'Ubaydah; from Iyās Ibn Salamah Ibn Akwaʿ (*raḍiyAllāhu ʿanhu*) that his father said:

> "Uthmān Ibn 'Affān used to wear a loincloth (*izār*) reaching the middle parts of his shins and he said: "Thus was the manner in which my companion—meaning, the Prophet

[121] Aḥmad in his *Musnad*, #23086, # 23087 and #19472.

(ﷺ) wore his loincloth (*izār*).'"[122]

١٢٢ـ حَدَّثَنَا قُتَيْبَةُ بْنُ سَعِيدٍ، قَالَ: حَدَّثَنَا أَبُو الأَحْوَصِ، عَنْ أَبِي إِسْحَاقَ، عَنْ مُسْلِمِ بْنِ نَذِيرٍ، عَنْ حُذَيْفَةَ بْنِ اليَمَانِ، قَالَ: «أَخَذَ رَسُولُ اللهِ ﷺ بِعَضَلَةِ سَاقِي أَوْ سَاقِهِ، فَقَالَ: هَذَا مَوْضِعُ الإِزَارِ، فَإِنْ أَبَيْتَ فَأَسْفَلُ، فَإِنْ أَبَيْتَ فَلَا حَقَّ لِلإِزَارِ فِي الكَعْبَيْنِ».

122. Qutaybah Ibn Sa'īd narrated to us; Abū'l-Aḥwaṣ narrated to us; from Abū Isḥāq; from Muslim Ibn Nadhīr that Hudhayfah Ibn Al-Yamān (*raḍiyAllāhu 'anhumā*) said:

> 'The Messenger of Allāh (ﷺ) grabbed hold of the calf muscle of my shin or his shin and said: "This is where the loincloth should reach. But if you object [to that], then let it hang lower, and if you even object [to that], then [realise] that the loincloth has no right on the ankles."[123]

[122] This chain is weak due to Mūsā Ibn 'Ubaydah.

[123] Tirmidhī, #1783 and Ibn Mājah, #3574 and this ḥadīth has a weak chain.

CHAPTER NINETEEN

بَابُ مَا جَاءَ فِي مِشْيَةِ رَسُولِ اللهِ ﷺ

What has been narrated concerning the Description of the Walking (*mishya*) of the Messenger of Allāh (ﷺ)

١٢٣ـ حَدَّثَنَا قُتَيْبَةُ بْنُ سَعِيدٍ، قَالَ: حَدَّثَنَا ابْنُ لَهِيعَةَ، عَنْ أَبِي يُونُسَ، عَنْ أَبِي هُرَيْرَةَ، قَالَ: «وَلَا رَأَيْتُ شَيْئًا أَحْسَنَ مِنْ رَسُولِ اللهِ ﷺ؛ كَأَنَّ الشَّمْسَ تَجْرِي فِي وَجْهِهِ، وَمَا رَأَيْتُ أَحَدًا أَسْرَعَ فِي مِشْيَتِهِ مِنْ رَسُولِ اللهِ ﷺ؛ كَأَنَّمَا الأَرْضُ تُطْوَى لَهُ، إِنَّا لَنُجْهِدُ أَنْفُسَنَا وَإِنَّهُ لَغَيْرُ مُكْتَرِثٍ!».

123. Qutaybah Ibn Saʿid narrated to us; Abū Lahīʿah narrated to us; from Abū Yūnus that Abū Hurayrah (*raḍiyAllāhu ʿanhu*) said:

> "I have not seen anyone more handsome (*aḥsan*) than the Messenger of Allāh (ﷺ); it was as if [the rays of] the sun permeated his face. Nor have I seen anyone walk faster than the Messenger of Allāh (ﷺ), it was as if the earth was folded up for him; we would exert ourselves [and found it difficult to keep up with him], while he would walk at a normal pace."[124]

[124] Tirmidhī, #3648 and Ibn Ḥibbān, 14/216.

١٢٤ـ حَدَّثَنَا عَلِيُّ بْنُ حُجْرٍ، وَغَيْرُ وَاحِدٍ، قَالُوا: حَدَّثَنَا عِيسَى بْنُ يُونُسَ، عَنْ عُمَرَ بْنِ عَبْدِ اللهِ مَوْلَى غُفْرَةَ، قَالَ: أَخْبَرَنِي إِبْرَاهِيمُ بْنُ مُحَمَّدٍ، مِنْ وَلَدِ عَلِيِّ ابْنِ أَبِي طَالِبٍ، قَالَ: كَانَ عَلِيٌّ إِذَا وَصَفَ النَّبِيَّ ﷺ قَالَ: «كَانَ إِذَا مَشَى تَقَلَّعَ كَأَنَّمَا يَنْحَطُّ مِنْ صَبَبٍ».

124. ʿAlī Ibn Ḥujr narrated to us; ʿIsā Ibn Yūnus narrated to us; from ʿUmar Ibn ʿAbdullāh, the Mawlā of Ghufrah; Ibrāhīm Ibn Muḥammad one of the sons of ʿAlī Ibn Abī Ṭālib (*raḍiyAllāhu ʿanhu*) told me:

> 'When ʿAlī (*raḍiyAllāhu ʿanhu*) described the Prophet (ﷺ), he used to say: "When he walked, he moved as if he were descending a downward slope."'[125]

١٢٥ـ حَدَّثَنَا سُفْيَانُ بْنُ وَكِيعٍ، قَالَ: حَدَّثَنَا أَبِي، عَنِ الْمَسْعُودِيِّ، عَنْ عُثْمَانَ ابْنِ مُسْلِمِ بْنِ هُرْمُزَ، عَنْ نَافِعِ بْنِ جُبَيْرِ بْنِ مُطْعِمٍ، عَنْ عَلِيِّ بْنِ أَبِي طَالِبٍ قَالَ: «كَانَ النَّبِيُّ ﷺ إِذَا مَشَى تَكَفَّأَ تَكَفُّؤًا، كَأَنَّمَا يَنْحَطُّ مِنْ صَبَبٍ».

125. Sufyān Ibn Wakīʿ narrated to us; my father narrated to us; from al-Masʿūdī; from ʿUthmān Ibn Muslim Ibn Hurmuz; from Nāfiʿ Ibn Jubayr Ibn Muṭʿim that ʿAlī Ibn Abī Ṭālib (*raḍiyAllāhu ʿanhu*) said:

> "When the Prophet (ﷺ) walked, he leant forward as if descending a downward slope."[126]

[125] Tirmidhī, #3637. This ḥadīth has a weak chain although some of the wording has been established in other authentic narrations.

[126] Tirmidhī, #3637, Ibn Ḥibbān, #6311, Ḥākim, 2/605-606 and Tirmdhī said this ḥadīth is ḥasan saḥīḥ.

CHAPTER TWENTY

بَابُ مَا جَاءَ فِي تَقَنُّعِ رَسُولِ اللهِ ﷺ

What has been narrated concerning the Description of the Head Covering (*taqannu'*) of the Messenger of Allāh (ﷺ)

١٢٦ـ حَدَّثَنَا يُوسُفُ بْنُ عِيسَى، قَالَ: حَدَّثَنَا وَكِيعٌ، قَالَ: حَدَّثَنَا الرَّبِيعُ ابْنُ صَبِيحٍ، عَنْ يَزِيدَ بْنِ أَبَانَ، عَنْ أَنَسِ بْنِ مَالِكٍ، قَالَ: «كَانَ رَسُولُ اللهِ ﷺ يُكْثِرُ القِنَاعَ كَأَنَّ ثَوْبَهُ ثَوْبُ زَيَّاتٍ».

126. Yūsuf Ibn 'Isā narrated to us; Wakī' narrated to us; Al-Rabī' Ibn Ṣabīḥ narrated to us; from Yazīd Ibn Abān that Anas Ibn Mālik (*raḍiyAllāhu 'anhu*) said:

> "The Messenger of Allāh (ﷺ) would often wear a head cloth (*qinā'*), so much so that his clothing would resemble that of an oil seller."[127]

[127] Bayhaqī in *al-Shu'ab*, 5/226. This ḥadīth is weak, due to a narrator having weak memory see Ibn Jawzī's *al-Ḍu'afā' wa'l-Matrūkīn*, 1/281.

CHAPTER TWENTY-ONE

بَابُ مَا جَاءَ فِي جِلْسَةِ رَسُولِ اللهِ ﷺ

What has been narrated concerning the Nature of Sitting *(jilsah)* of the Messenger of Allāh (ﷺ)

١٢٧ـ حَدَّثَنَا عَبْدُ بْنُ حُمَيْدٍ، قَالَ: حَدَّثَنَا عَفَّانُ بْنُ مُسْلِمٍ، قَالَ: حَدَّثَنَا عَبْدُ اللهِ ابْنُ حَسَّانَ، عَنْ جَدَّتَيْهِ، عَنْ قَيْلَةَ بِنْتِ مَخْرَمَةَ، «أَنَّهَا رَأَتْ رَسُولَ اللهِ ﷺ فِي الْمَسْجِدِ وَهُوَ قَاعِدٌ الْقُرْفُصَاءَ، قَالَتْ: فَلَمَّا رَأَيْتُ رَسُولَ اللهِ ﷺ الْمُتَخَشِّعَ فِي الْجِلْسَةِ أُرْعِدْتُ مِنَ الْفَرَقِ» .

127. ʿAbd Ibn Ḥumayd narrated to us; ʿAffān Ibn Muslim narrated to us; ʿAbdullāh Ibn Ḥassān narrated to us; from his grandmother that Qaylah bint Makhramah (*raḍiyAllāhu ʿanhā*) said:

> "That she saw the Messenger of Allāh (ﷺ) in the *masjid* squatting on his heels (*qurfaṣā'*). She said: 'When I saw the Messenger of Allāh (ﷺ) sitting humbly (*mutakhashiʿ*), I began trembling in fear [due to immense awe of him].'"[128]

[128] Abū Dāwūd, #4847 and Tirmidhī, #2814.

١٢٨ـ حَدَّثَنَا سَعِيدُ بْنُ عَبْدِ الرَّحْمَنِ الْمَخْزُومِيُّ، وَغَيْرُ وَاحِدٍ قَالُوا: حَدَّثَنَا سُفْيَانُ، عَنِ الزُّهْرِيِّ، عَنْ عَبَّادِ بْنِ تَمِيمٍ، عَنْ عَمِّهِ، «أَنَّهُ رَأَى النَّبِيَّ ﷺ مُسْتَلْقِيًا فِي الْمَسْجِدِ وَاضِعًا إِحْدَى رِجْلَيْهِ عَلَى الأُخْرَى» .

128. Sa'īd Ibn 'Abdu'l-Raḥmān al-Makhzūmī and others narrated to us; Sufyān narrated to us; from Zuhrī; from 'Abbād Ibn Tamīmī that his paternal uncle said:

> "That he saw the Prophet (ﷺ) lying [flat] on his back (*mustalq*) in the *masjid*, placing one of his legs over the other.[129]

١٢٩ـ حَدَّثَنَا سَلَمَةُ بْنُ شَبِيبٍ، قَالَ: حَدَّثَنَا عَبْدُ اللهِ بْنُ إِبْرَاهِيمَ الْمَدَنِيُّ، قَالَ: حَدَّثَنَا إِسْحَاقُ بْنُ مُحَمَّدٍ الأَنْصَارِيُّ، عَنْ رُبَيْحِ بْنِ عَبْدِ الرَّحْمَنِ بْنِ أَبِي سَعِيدٍ، عَنْ أَبِيهِ، عَنْ جَدِّهِ أَبِي سَعِيدٍ الْخُدْرِيِّ، قَالَ: «كَانَ رَسُولُ اللهِ ﷺ إِذَا جَلَسَ فِي الْمَسْجِدِ احْتَبَى بِيَدَيْهِ».

129. Salmah Ibn Shayb narrated to us; 'Abdullāh Ibn Ibrāhīm al-Madanī narrated to us; Isḥāq Ibn Muḥammad al-Anṣārī narrated to us; from Rabīḥ Ibn 'Abdu'l-Raḥmān Ibn Abī Sa'īd; from his father that his grandfather Abū Sa'īd al-Khudrī (*raḍiyAllāhu 'anhu*) said:

> "When the Messenger of Allāh (ﷺ) would sit in the *masjid*, he would do so by bringing his legs tightly against his stomach (*iḥtibā'*) with his hands."[130]

[129] Bukhārī, #6287, Muslim, #2100 and Tirmidhī, #2765.
[130] Abū Dāwūd, #4846

CHAPTER TWENTY-TWO

بَابُ مَا جَاءَ فِي تُكَأَةِ رَسُولِ اللهِ ﷺ

What has been narrated concerning the Reclining (*tukā'a*) of the Messenger of Allāh (ﷺ)

١٣٠ـ حَدَّثَنَا عَبَّاسُ بْنُ مُحَمَّدٍ الدُّورِيُّ الْبَغْدَادِيُّ، قَالَ: حَدَّثَنَا إِسْحَاقُ ابْنُ مَنْصُورٍ، عَنْ إِسْرَائِيلَ، عَنْ سِمَاكِ بْنِ حَرْبٍ، عَنْ جَابِرِ بْنِ سَمُرَةَ، قَالَ: «رَأَيْتُ رَسُولَ اللهِ ﷺ مُتَّكِئًا عَلَى وِسَادَةٍ عَلَى يَسَارِهِ».

130. ʿAbbās Ibn Muḥammad al-Dūrī al-Baghdādī narrated to us; Isḥāq Ibn Manṣūr narrated to us; from Isrā'īl; from Simāk Ibn Ḥarb that Jābir Ibn Samurah (*raḍiyAllāhu ʿanhu*) said:

> "I saw the Messenger of Allāh (ﷺ) reclining on a cushion on his left side."[131]

١٣١ـ حَدَّثَنَا حُمَيْدُ بْنُ مَسْعَدَةَ، قَالَ: حَدَّثَنَا بِشْرُ بْنُ الْمُفَضَّلِ، قَالَ: حَدَّثَنَا الْجُرَيْرِيُّ، عَنْ عَبْدِ الرَّحْمَنِ بْنِ أَبِي بَكْرَةَ، عَنْ أَبِيهِ، قَالَ: قَالَ رَسُولُ اللهِ ﷺ: «أَلَا أُحَدِّثُكُمْ بِأَكْبَرِ الْكَبَائِرِ؟» قَالُوا: بَلَى يَا رَسُولَ اللهِ! قَالَ: «الإِشْرَاكُ بِاللهِ، وَعُقُوقُ

[131] Abū Dāwūd, #4143 and Tirmidhī, #2770.

الوَالِدَيْنِ»، قَالَ: وَجَلَسَ رَسُولُ اللهِ ﷺ وَكَانَ مُتَّكِئًا قَالَ: «وَشَهَادَةُ الزُّورِ»، أَوْ «قَوْلُ الزُّورِ» قَالَ: فَمَا زَالَ رَسُولُ اللهِ ﷺ يَقُولُهَا حَتَّى قُلْنَا: لَيْتَهُ سَكَتَ!.

131. Ḥumayd Ibn Musʿadah narrated to us; Bishr Ibn Al-Mufaḍḍal narrated to us; Al-Jarīrī narrated to us; from ʿAbdu'l-Raḥmān Ibn Abī Bakrah that his father [Abū Bakrah (*raḍiyAllāhu ʿanhu*)] said: 'The Messenger of Allāh (ﷺ) said:

> "Should I tell you about the greatest of the major sins (*akbar al-kabā'ir*)?" They said: 'Certainly, O Messenger of Allāh.' He said: "Associating partners with Allāh (*ishrāk billāh*), and defiance against parents (*ʿuqūq al-walaydain*)." The Messenger of Allāh (ﷺ) sat up as he was reclining and added: "and false testimony (*shahadah al-zūr*) or false speech (*qawl al-zūr*)." The Messenger of Allāh (ﷺ) kept saying it so much that we said: 'If only he would keep silent."'[132]

١٣٢ـ حَدَّثَنَا قُتَيْبَةُ بْنُ سَعِيدٍ، قَالَ: حَدَّثَنَا شَرِيكٌ، عَنْ عَلِيِّ بْنِ الأَقْمَرِ، عَنْ أَبِي جُحَيْفَةَ قَالَ: قَالَ رَسُولُ اللهِ ﷺ: «أَمَّا أَنَا فَلَا آكُلُ مُتَّكِئًا».

132. Qutaybah Ibn Saʿīd narrated to us; Sharīk narrated to us; from ʿAlī Ibn al-Aqmar that Abū Juḥayfah (*raḍiyAllāhu ʿanhu*) said:

> 'The Messenger of Allāh (ﷺ) said: "As for me, I do not eat while reclining."'[133]

١٣٣ـ حَدَّثَنَا مُحَمَّدُ بْنُ بَشَّارٍ، قَالَ: حَدَّثَنَا عَبْدُ الرَّحْمَنِ بْنُ مَهْدِيٍّ، قَالَ: حَدَّثَنَا سُفْيَانُ، عَنْ عَلِيِّ بْنِ الأَقْمَرِ، قَالَ: سَمِعْتُ أَبَا جُحَيْفَةَ، يَقُولُ: قَالَ رَسُولُ اللهِ ﷺ:

---

[132] Bukhārī, #2653 and Muslim, #87.

[133] Bukhārī, #5398, Abū Dāwūd, #3769 and Tirmidhī, #1830.

«لَا آكُلُ مُتَّكِئًا».

133. Muḥammad Ibn Bashshār narrated to us; 'Abdu'l-Raḥmān Ibn Mahdī narrated to us; Sufyān narrated to us that 'Alī Ibn al-Aqmar said: 'I heard Abū Juḥayfah (*raḍiyAllāhu 'anhu*) say:

> 'The Messenger of Allāh (ﷺ) said: "I do not eat while reclining."'[134]

١٣٤ـ حَدَّثَنَا يُوسُفُ بْنُ عِيسَى، قَالَ: حَدَّثَنَا وَكِيعٌ، قَالَ: حَدَّثَنَا إِسْرَائِيلُ، عَنْ سِمَاكِ بْنِ حَرْبٍ، عَنْ جَابِرِ بْنِ سَمُرَةَ، قَالَ: «رَأَيْتُ النَّبِيَّ ﷺ مُتَّكِئًا عَلَى وِسَادَةٍ».

قَالَ أَبُو عِيسَى: لَمْ يَذْكُرْ وَكِيعٌ «عَلَى يَسَارِهِ»، وَهَكَذَا رَوَى غَيْرُ وَاحِدٍ عَنْ إِسْرَائِيلَ نَحْوَ رِوَايَةِ وَكِيعٍ، وَلَا نَعْلَمُ أَحَدًا رَوَى فِيهِ «عَلَى يَسَارِهِ» إِلَّا مَا رَوَاهُ إِسْحَاقُ ابْنُ مَنْصُورٍ، عَنْ إِسْرَائِيلَ.

134. Yūsuf Ibn 'Isā narrated to us; Wakī' narrated to us; Isrā'īl narrated to us; from Simāk Ibn Ḥarb that Jābir Ibn Samurah (*raḍiyAllāhu 'anhu*) said:

> "I saw the Messenger of Allāh (ﷺ) reclining on a cushion."[135]

Abū 'Isā said: 'Wakī' did not mention: *"...on his left side."* Similarly, others have reported similar to the narration of Wakī' such as the report of Isrā'īl, and we do not know of any narration that mentions: *"...on his left side,"* except what has been reported by Isḥāq Ibn Mansur from Isrā'īl.'

[134] Bukhārī, #5398, Abū Dāwūd, #3769 and Tirmidhī, #1830.
[135] Abū Dāwūd, #4143 and Tirmidhī, #2771.

CHAPTER TWENTY-THREE

بَابُ مَا جَاءَ فِي اتِّكَاءِ رَسُولِ اللهِ ﷺ

What has been narrated concerning the Leaning (*ittikā'*) of the Messenger of Allāh (ﷺ)

١٣٥ـ حَدَّثَنَا عَبْدُ اللهِ بْنُ عَبْدِ الرَّحْمَنِ، قَالَ: حَدَّثَنَا عَمْرُو بْنُ عَاصِمٍ، قَالَ: حَدَّثَنَا حَمَّادُ بْنُ سَلَمَةَ، عَنْ حُمَيْدٍ، عَنْ أَنَسٍ: «أَنَّ النَّبِيَّ ﷺ كَانَ شَاكِيًا فَخَرَجَ يَتَوَكَّأُ عَلَى أُسَامَةَ بْنِ زَيْدٍ، وَعَلَيْهِ ثَوْبٌ قِطْرِيٌّ قَدْ تَوَشَّحَ بِهِ فَصَلَّى بِهِمْ».

135. ʿAbdullāh Ibn ʿAbdu'l-Raḥmān narrated to us; ʿAmr Ibn ʿĀṣim narrated to us; Ḥammād Ibn Salamah narrated to us; from Ḥumayd that Anas (*raḍiyAllāhu ʿanhu*) said:

> "The Prophet (ﷺ) was feeling ill, so he came out leaning on Usāmah Ibn Zayd, wearing a garment of Yemenī sheet made of cotton (*qiṭrī*), which he had thrown on loosely, he then led them in the prayer."[136]

١٣٦ـ حَدَّثَنَا عَبْدُ اللهِ بْنُ عَبْدِ الرَّحْمَنِ، قَالَ: حَدَّثَنَا مُحَمَّدُ بْنُ الْمُبَارَكِ، قَالَ:

---

[136] Aḥmad in his *Musnad*, #13763 and Ibn Ḥibbān, #349.

حَدَّثَنَا عَطَاءُ بْنُ مُسْلِمٍ الخَفَّافُ الحَلَبِيُّ، قَالَ: حَدَّثَنَا جَعْفَرُ بْنُ بُرْقَانَ، عَنْ عَطَاءِ ابْنِ أَبِي رَبَاحٍ، عَنِ الفَضْلِ بْنِ عَبَّاسٍ، قَالَ: دَخَلتُ عَلَى رَسُولِ اللهِ ﷺ فِي مَرَضِهِ الَّذِي تُوُفِّيَ فِيهِ، وَعَلَى رَأْسِهِ عِصَابَةٌ صَفْرَاءُ، فَسَلَّمْتُ عَلَيْهِ، فَقَالَ: «يَا فَضْلُ!»، قُلتُ: لَبَّيْكَ يَا رَسُولَ اللهِ! قَالَ: «اُشْدُدْ بِهَذِهِ العِصَابَةِ رَأْسِي»، قَالَ: فَفَعَلتُ، ثُمَّ قَعَدَ، فَوَضَعَ كَفَّهُ عَلَى مَنْكِبِي، ثُمَّ قَامَ فَدَخَلَ فِي المَسْجِدِ، وَفِي الحَدِيثِ قِصَّةٌ.

136. ʿAbdullāh Ibn ʿAbdu'l-Raḥmān narrated to us; Muḥammad Ibn al-Mubārak narrated to us; ʿAṭā' Ibn Muslim al-Khaffāf al-Ḥalabī narrated to us; Jāʿfar Ibn Burqān narrated to us; from ʿAṭā' Ibn Abī Rabāḥ that Faḍl Ibn ʿAbbās (*raḍiyAllāhu ʿanhumā*) said:

> 'I visited the Messenger of Allāh (ﷺ) during his illness in which he passed away, on his head was a yellow band. I greeted him and he said: "O Faḍl!" I said: 'At your service, O Messenger of Allāh!' He said: "Fasten firmly this band on my head." So I did. He then sat up and placed the palm of his hand on my shoulder. Then he stood up and entered the *masjid*."'[137]

This tradition is part of a lengthier story.

[137] Ṭabarānī in *al-Kabīr*, 18/280. This ḥadīth is weak.

CHAPTER TWENTY-FOUR

بَابُ مَا جَاءَ فِي صِفَةِ أَكْلِ رَسُولِ اللهِ ﷺ

What has been narrated concerning the Manner of the Eating (*akl*) of the Messenger of Allāh (ﷺ)

١٣٧ـ حَدَّثَنَا مُحَمَّدُ بْنُ بَشَّارٍ، قَالَ: حَدَّثَنَا عَبْدُ الرَّحْمَنِ بْنُ مَهْدِيٍّ، عَنْ سُفْيَانَ، عَنْ سَعْدِ بْنِ إِبْرَاهِيمَ، عَنِ ابْنٍ لِكَعْبِ بْنِ مَالِكٍ، عَنْ أَبِيهِ، «أَنَّ النَّبِيَّ ﷺ كَانَ يَلْعَقُ أَصَابِعَهُ ثَلَاثًا».

قَالَ أَبُو عِيسَى: وَرَوَى غَيْرُ مُحَمَّدِ بنِ بَشَّارٍ هَذَا الْحَدِيثَ قَالَ: «يَلْعَقُ أَصَابِعَهُ الثَّلَاثَ».

137. Muḥammad Ibn Bashshār narrated to us; 'Abdu'l-Raḥmān Ibn Mahdī narrated to us; from Sufyān; from Sa'd Ibn Ibrāhīm; Ibn al-Ka'b Ibn Mālik that his father (*raḍiyAllāhu 'anhu*) said:

> "The Prophet (ﷺ) used to lick his fingers clean three times [after eating]."[138]

Abū 'Isā said: 'This tradition has been narrated by other than Muḥammad Ibn Bashshār.' He said: 'He used to lick his three fingers.'

---

[138] Muslim, #2032 and Abū Dāwūd, #3848.

١٣٨ـ حَدَّثَنَا الحَسَنُ بْنُ عَلِيٍّ الخَلَّالُ، قَالَ: حَدَّثَنَا عَفَّانُ، قَالَ: حَدَّثَنَا حَمَّادُ ابْنُ سَلَمَةَ، عَنْ ثَابِتٍ، عَنْ أَنَسٍ، قَالَ: «كَانَ النَّبِيُّ ﷺ إِذَا أَكَلَ طَعَامًا لَعِقَ أَصَابِعَهُ الثَّلَاثَ».

138. Al-Ḥasan Ibn 'Alī al-Khallāl narrated to us; 'Affān narrated to us; Ḥammād Ibn Salamah narrated to us; from Thābit that Anas (*raḍiyAllāhu 'anhu*) said:

> "When the Prophet (ﷺ) ate a meal, he used to lick his three fingers [clean after eating]."[139]

١٣٩ـ حَدَّثَنَا الحُسَيْنُ بْنُ عَلِيِّ بْنِ يَزِيدَ الصُّدَائِيُّ البَغْدَادِيُّ، قَالَ: حَدَّثَنَا يَعْقُوبُ بْنُ إِسْحَاقَ ـ يَعْنِي: الحَضْرَمِيَّ ـ قَالَ: حَدَّثَنَا شُعْبَةُ، عَنْ سُفْيَانَ الثَّوْرِيِّ، عَنْ عَلِيِّ بْنِ الأَقْمَرِ، عَنْ أَبِي جُحَيْفَةَ، قَالَ: قَالَ النَّبِيُّ ﷺ: «أَمَّا أَنَا فَلَا آكُلُ مُتَّكِئًا».

139. Al-Ḥusayn Ibn 'Alī Ibn Zayd al-Ṣudā'ī al-Baghdādī narrated to us; Ya'qūb Ibn Isḥāq al-Ḥaḍramī narrated to us; Shu'bah narrated to us; from Sufyān al-Thawrī; 'Alī Ibn Al-Aqmar that Abū Juḥayfah (*raḍiyAllāhu 'anhu*) said:

> 'The Prophet (ﷺ) said: "As for me, I do not eat while reclining."'[140]

١٤٠ـ حَدَّثَنَا مُحَمَّدُ بْنُ بَشَّارٍ، قَالَ: حَدَّثَنَا عَبْدُ الرَّحْمَنِ بْنُ مَهْدِيٍّ، قَالَ: حَدَّثَنَا سُفْيَانُ، عَنْ عَلِيِّ بْنِ الأَقْمَرِ نَحْوَهُ.

140. Muḥammad Ibn Bashshār narrated to us; 'Abdu'l-Raḥmān

[139] Muslim, #2034 and Abū Dāwūd, #3845.
[140] Bukhārī, #5398, Abū Dāwūd, #3769 and Tirmidhī, #1830.

Ibn Mahdī narrated to us; Sufyān narrated to us; from ʿAlī Ibn Al-Aqmar, who narrated the same tradition with a different chain of narration.

١٤١ـ حَدَّثَنَا هَارُونُ بْنُ إِسْحَاقَ الْهَمْدَانِيُّ، قَالَ: حَدَّثَنَا عَبْدَةُ بْنُ سُلَيْمَانَ، عَنْ هِشَامِ بْنِ عُرْوَةَ، عَنِ ابْنٍ لِكَعْبِ بْنِ مَالِكٍ، عَنْ أَبِيهِ، قَالَ: «كَانَ رَسُولُ اللهِ ﷺ يَأْكُلُ بِأَصَابِعِهِ الثَّلَاثِ وَيَلْعَقُهُنَّ».

141. Hārun Ibn Isḥāq al-Hamdānī narrated to us; ʿAbdah Ibn Sulaymān narrated to us; from Hishām Ibn ʿUrwah; Ibn al-Kaʿb Ibn Mālik that his father (*raḍiyAllāhu ʿanhu*) said:

> "The Messenger of Allāh (ﷺ) would eat with his three fingers and would clean them [after eating]."[141]

١٤٢ـ حَدَّثَنَا أَحْمَدُ بْنُ مَنِيعٍ، قَالَ: حَدَّثَنَا الْفَضْلُ بْنُ دُكَيْنٍ، قَالَ: حَدَّثَنَا مُصْعَبُ بْنُ سُلَيْمٍ، قَالَ: سَمِعْتُ أَنَسَ بْنَ مَالِكٍ يَقُولُ: «أُتِيَ رَسُولُ اللهِ ﷺ بِتَمْرٍ فَرَأَيْتُهُ يَأْكُلُ وَهُوَ مُقْعٍ مِنَ الْجُوعِ».

142. Aḥmad Ibn Manīʿ narrated to us; Al-Faḍl Ibn Dukayn narrated to us that Muṣʿab Ibn Sulaym said: 'I heard Anas Ibn Mālik (*raḍiyAllāhu ʿanhu*) say:

> "The Messenger of Allāh (ﷺ) was gifted [some] dates. I saw him eat them while he was hunched over, due to hunger (*jūʿ*)."[142]

[141] Muslim, #2032 and Abū Dāwūd, #3848.
[142] Muslim, #2044 and Abū Dāwūd, #3771.

CHAPTER TWENTY-FIVE

بَابُ مَا جَاءَ فِي صِفَةِ خُبْزِ رَسُولِ اللهِ ﷺ

What has been narrated concerning the Description of the Bread (*khubz*) of the Messenger of Allāh (ﷺ)

١٤٣ـ حَدَّثَنَا مُحَمَّدُ بْنُ الْمُثَنَّى، وَمُحَمَّدُ بْنُ بَشَّارٍ، قَالَا: حَدَّثَنَا مُحَمَّدُ بْنُ جَعْفَرٍ، قَالَ: حَدَّثَنَا شُعْبَةُ، عَنْ أَبِي إِسْحَاقَ، قَالَ: سَمِعْتُ عَبْدَ الرَّحْمَنِ بْنَ يَزِيدَ، يُحَدِّثُ عَنِ الأَسْوَدِ بْنِ يَزِيدَ، عَنْ عَائِشَةَ، أَنَّهَا قَالَتْ: «مَا شَبِعَ آلُ مُحَمَّدٍ ﷺ مِنْ خُبْزِ الشَّعِيرِ يَوْمَيْنِ مُتَتَابِعَيْنِ حَتَّى قُبِضَ رَسُولُ اللهِ ﷺ».

143. Muḥammad Ibn al-Muthannā and Muḥammad Ibn Bashshār narrated to me; Muḥammad Ibn Jā'far narrated to us; Shu'bah narrated to us that Abū Isḥāq said: 'I heard 'Abdu'l-Raḥmān Ibn Yazīd narrate from Al-Aswad Ibn Yazīd that 'Ā'ishah (*raḍiyAllāhu 'anhā*) said:

> "The family of Muḥammad (ﷺ) never satiated on barley-bread (*khubz al-sha'īr*) for two consecutive days, until the Messenger of Allāh (ﷺ) was taken from this world."[143]

[143] Muslim, #2970, Tirmidhī, #2357 and Ibn Mājah, #2346.

١٤٤ـ حَدَّثَنَا عَبَّاسُ بْنُ مُحَمَّدٍ الدُّورِيُّ، قَالَ: حَدَّثَنَا يَحْيَى بْنُ أَبِي بُكَيْرٍ، قَالَ: حَدَّثَنَا حَرِيزُ بْنُ عُثْمَانَ، عَنْ سُلَيْمِ بْنِ عَامِرٍ، قَالَ: سَمِعْتُ أَبَا أُمَامَةَ الْبَاهِلِيَّ، يَقُولُ: «مَا كَانَ يَفْضُلُ عَنْ أَهْلِ بَيْتِ رَسُولِ اللهِ ﷺ خُبْزُ الشَّعِيرِ».

144. ʿAbbās Ibn Muḥammad al-Dawrī narrated to us; Yaḥyā Ibn Abī Bukayr narrated to us; Ḥarīz Ibn ʿUthmān narrated to us that Sulaym Ibn ʿĀmir said: ʿI heard Abū Umāmah al-Bāhilī (*raḍiyAllāhu ʿanhu*) say:

> "There was never sufficient barley-bread for the people of the household (*Ahlul-bayt*) of the Messenger of Allāh (ﷺ)."[144]

١٤٥ـ حَدَّثَنَا عَبْدُ اللهِ بنُ مُعَاوِيَةَ الْجُمَحِيُّ، قَالَ: حَدَّثَنَا ثَابِتُ بْنُ زَيْدٍ، عَنْ هِلَالِ ابْنِ خَبَّابٍ، عَنْ عِكْرِمَةَ، عَنِ ابنِ عَبَّاسٍ، قَالَ: «كَانَ رَسُولُ اللهِ ﷺ يَبِيتُ اللَّيَالِيَ الْمُتَتَابِعَةَ طَاوِيًا هُوَ وَأَهْلُهُ، لَا يَجِدُونَ عَشَاءً، وَكَانَ أَكْثَرُ خُبْزِهِمْ خُبْزَ الشَّعِيرِ».

145. ʿAbdullāh Ibn Muʿāwiyah al-Jumanhī narrated to us; Thābit Ibn Yazīd narrated to us; from Hilāl Ibn Khabbāb; from ʿIkrimah that lbn ʿAbbās (*raḍiyAllāhu ʿanhumā*) said:

> "The Messenger of Allāh (ﷺ) and his family would spend consecutive nights starving, not finding any supper; and most of their bread was barley-bread."[145]

---

[144] Tirmidhī, #2359.

[145] Tirmidhī, #2359. This ḥadīth is supported by other narration which will come later in this book.

١٤٦ـ حَدَّثَنَا عَبْدُ اللهِ بْنُ عَبْدِ الرَّحْمَنِ، قَالَ: حَدَّثَنَا عُبَيْدُ اللهِ بْنُ عَبْدِ الْمَجِيدِ الْحَنَفِيُّ، حَدَّثَنَا عَبْدُ الرَّحْمَنِ بْنُ عَبْدِ اللهِ بْنِ دِينَارٍ، قَالَ: حَدَّثَنَا أَبُو حَازِمٍ، عَنْ سَهْلِ ابْنِ سَعْدٍ، أَنَّهُ قِيلَ لَهُ: «أَكَلَ رَسُولُ اللهِ ﷺ النَّقِيَّ؟ - يَعْنِي الْحُوَّارَى - فَقَالَ سَهْلٌ: مَا رَأَى رَسُولُ اللهِ ﷺ النَّقِيَّ حَتَّى لَقِيَ اللهَ ﷻ؛ فَقِيلَ لَهُ: هَلْ كَانَتْ لَكُمْ مَنَاخِلُ عَلَى عَهْدِ رَسُولِ اللهِ ﷺ؟ قَالَ: مَا كَانَتْ لَنَا مَنَاخِلُ؛ قِيلَ: كَيْفَ كُنْتُمْ تَصْنَعُونَ بِالشَّعِيرِ؟ قَالَ: كُنَّا نَنْفُخُهُ فَيَطِيرُ مِنْهُ مَا طَارَ ثُمَّ نَعْجِنُهُ».

146. ʿAbdullāh Ibn ʿAbdu'l-Raḥmān narrated to us; ʿUbaydullāh Ibn ʿAbdu'l-Majid al-Hanafi narrated to us; ʿAbdu'l-Raḥmān Ibn ʿAbdullāh Ibn Dinār narrated to us; Abū Hāzim narrated to us; from Sahl Ibn Saʿd (*raḍiyAllāhu ʿanhu*) that he was asked:

> 'Did the Messenger of Allāh (ﷺ) eat the finest flour, meaning white bread?' Sahl said: 'The Messenger of Allāh (ﷺ) never saw the finest flour up until he met Allāh, the Mighty and Masjestic.' Then he was asked: 'Did you have sieves in the time of the Messenger of Allāh (ﷺ)?' He said: 'We did not have sieves.' He was then asked: 'How did you prepare barely?' He said: 'We used to blow on it, so whatever [husks] on it would fly off, and then we would knead it into dough."[146]

١٤٧ـ حَدَّثَنَا مُحَمَّدُ بْنُ بَشَّارٍ، قَالَ: حَدَّثَنَا مُعَاذُ بْنُ هِشَامٍ، قَالَ: حَدَّثَنِي أَبِي، عَنْ يُونُسَ، عَنْ قَتَادَةَ، عَنْ أَنَسِ بْنِ مَالِكٍ، قَالَ: «مَا أَكَلَ نَبِيُّ اللهِ ﷺ عَلَى خِوَانٍ، وَلَا فِي سُكُرَّجَةٍ، وَلَا خُبِزَ لَهُ مُرَقَّقٌ».

147. Muḥammad Ibn Bashshār narrated to us; Muʿādh Ibn Hishām

[146] Bukhārī, #5413 and Tirmidhī, #2364.

narrated to us; My father narrated to me; from Qatādah that Anas Ibn Mālik (*raḍiyAllāhu ʿanhu*) said:

> 'The Prophet of Allāh (ﷺ) did not eat food on a table, nor in a bowl, and nor did he have refined bread.' Yūnus said: 'I asked Qatādah: 'Then what did they eat on?' He said: 'On these leather mats (*sufur*).'"[147]

Muḥammad Ibn Bashshār said: 'This Yūnus, who narrated from Qatādah, is Yūnus al-Iskāf.'

١٤٨ـ حَدَّثَنَا أَحْمَدُ بْنُ مَنِيعٍ، قَالَ: حَدَّثَنَا عَبَّادُ بْنُ عَبَّادٍ الْمُهَلَّبِيُّ، عَنْ مُجَالِدٍ، عَنِ الشَّعْبِيِّ، عَنْ مَسْرُوقٍ، قَالَ: دَخَلْتُ عَلَى عَائِشَةَ، فَدَعَتْ لِي بِطَعَامٍ، وَقَالَتْ: «مَا أَشْبَعُ مِنْ طَعَامٍ فَأَشَاءُ أَنْ أَبْكِيَ إِلَّا بَكَيْتُ؛ قَالَ: قُلْتُ: لِمَ؟ قَالَتْ: أَذْكُرُ الْحَالَ الَّتِي فَارَقَ عَلَيْهَا رَسُولُ اللهِ ﷺ الدُّنْيَا، وَاللهِ مَا شَبِعَ مِنْ خُبْزٍ وَلَحْمٍ مَرَّتَيْنِ فِي يَوْمٍ».

148. Aḥmad Ibn Manīʿ narrated to us; 'Abbād Ibn 'Abbād al-Muhallabī narrated to us; from Mujālid; from Al-Shaʿbī that Masrūq said:

> 'I went to see 'Ā'ishah (*raḍiyAllāhu ʿanhā*), so she ordered food for me and said: 'I never have my fill of food, and then want to cry, except I start crying!' I said: 'Why?' She said: 'I remember the state in which the Messenger of Allāh (ﷺ) departed from this world. By Allāh, he never had his fill of bread and meat twice in one day!'"[148]

---

[147] Bukhārī, #5415 and Tirmidhī, #1788.

[148] Tirmidhī, #2356, this ḥadīth is weak.

١٤٩ـ حَدَّثَنَا مَحْمُودُ بْنُ غَيْلَانَ، قَالَ: حَدَّثَنَا أَبُو دَاوُدَ، قَالَ: حَدَّثَنَا شُعْبَةُ، عَنْ أَبِي إِسْحَاقَ، قَالَ: سَمِعْتُ عَبْدَ الرَّحْمَنِ بْنَ يَزِيدَ، يُحَدِّثُ عَنِ الأَسْوَدِ بْنِ يَزِيدَ، عَنْ عَائِشَةَ، قَالَتْ: «مَا شَبِعَ رَسُولُ اللهِ ﷺ مِنْ خُبْزِ الشَّعِيرِ يَوْمَيْنِ مُتَتَابِعَيْنِ حَتَّى قُبِضَ».

149. Maḥmūd Ibn Ghaylān narrated to us; Abū Dāwūd narrated to us; Shuʿbah narrated to us that Abū Isḥāq said: 'I heard ʿAbdu'l-Raḥmān Ibn Yazīd narrate from Al-Aswad Ibn Yazīd that ʿĀ'ishah (*raḍiyAllāhu ʿanhā*) said:

> "The Messenger of Allāh (ﷺ) never had his fill of barley-bread two consecutive days until he passed away."[149]

١٥٠ـ حَدَّثَنَا عَبْدُ اللهِ بْنُ عَبْدِ الرَّحْمَنِ، قَالَ: حَدَّثَنَا عَبْدُ اللهِ بْنُ عَمْرٍو أَبُو مَعْمَرٍ، حَدَّثَنَا عَبْدُ الوَارِثِ، عَنْ سَعِيدِ بْنِ أَبِي عَرُوبَةَ، عَنْ قَتَادَةَ، عَنْ أَنَسٍ، قَالَ: «مَا أَكَلَ رَسُولُ اللهِ ﷺ عَلَى خِوَانٍ، وَلَا أَكَلَ خُبْزًا مُرَقَّقًا حَتَّى مَاتَ».

150. ʿAbdullāh Ibn ʿAbdu'l-Raḥmān narrated to us; Abū Maʿmar ʿAbdullāh Ibn ʿAmr narrated to us; ʿAbdu'l-Wārith narrated to us; from Saʿīd Ibn Abī ʿArūbah; from Qatādah that Anas (*raḍiyAllāhu ʿanhu*) said:

> "The Messenger of Allāh (ﷺ) did not eat food on a table, and nor did he eat refined bread, until he passed away.'[150]

[149] Bukhārī, #5416, Muslim, #2970 and Tirmidhī, #2357.
[150] Bukhārī, #5415 and Tirmidhī, #2363.

CHAPTER TWENTY-SIX

بَابُ مَا جَاءَ فِي صِفَةِ إِدَامِ رَسُولِ اللهِ ﷺ

What has been narrated concerning the Condiments (*idām*) of the Messenger of Allāh (ﷺ)

١٥١ - حَدَّثَنَا مُحَمَّدُ بْنُ سَهْلِ بْنِ عَسْكَرٍ، وَعَبْدُ اللهِ بْنُ عَبْدِ الرَّحْمَنِ، قَالَا: حَدَّثَنَا يَحْيَى بْنُ حَسَّانَ، قَالَ: حَدَّثَنَا سُلَيْمَانُ بْنُ بِلَالٍ، عَنْ هِشَامِ بْنِ عُرْوَةَ، عَنْ أَبِيهِ، عَنْ عَائِشَةَ، أَنَّ رَسُولَ اللهِ ﷺ قَالَ: «نِعْمَ الإِدَامُ الخَلُّ»، قَالَ عَبْدُ اللهِ بْنُ عَبْدِ الرَّحْمَنِ فِي حَدِيثِهِ: «نِعْمَ الإِدَامُ - أَوِ الأُدْمُ - الخَلُّ».

151. Muḥammad Ibn Sahl al-ʿAskar and ʿAbdullāh Ibn ʿAbdu'l-Raḥmān narrated to us; Yaḥyā Ibn Ḥassān narrated to us; Sulaymān Ibn Bilāl narrated to us; from Hisham Ibn ʿUrwah; from his father that ʿĀ'ishah (*raḍiyAllāhu ʿanhā*) said:

> 'The Messenger of Allāh (ﷺ) said: "What an excellent condiment (*idām*) vinegar (*khal*) is!"[151]

ʿAbdullāh Ibn ʿAbdu'l-Raḥmān in his tradition said: "How excellent is the condiment," or "the condiment, vinegar!"

[151] Muslim, #2051 and Tirmidhī, #1840.

١٥٢ـ حَدَّثَنَا قُتَيْبَةُ، قَالَ: حَدَّثَنَا أَبُو الأَحْوَصِ، عَنْ سِمَاكِ بْنِ حَرْبٍ، قَالَ: سَمِعْتُ النُّعْمَانَ بْنَ بَشِيرٍ، يَقُولُ: «أَلَسْتُمْ فِي طَعَامٍ وَشَرَابٍ مَا شِئْتُمْ؟ لَقَدْ رَأَيْتُ نَبِيَّكُمْ ﷺ وَمَا يَجِدُ مِنَ الدَّقَلِ مَا يَمْلأُ بَطْنَهُ».

152. Qutaybah narrated to us; Abū'l-Aḥwaṣ narrated to us that Simāk Ibn Ḥarb said: 'I heard al-Nu'mān Ibn Bashīr (*raḍiyAllāhu 'anhu*) say:

> 'Do you not indulge in whatever food and drink you wish?' I saw that your Prophet (ﷺ) was unable to find poor-quality dates (*daqal*) with which to fill his stomach.'''[152]

١٥٣ـ حَدَّثَنَا عَبْدَةُ بْنُ عَبْدِ اللهِ الْخُزَاعِيُّ، قَالَ: حَدَّثَنَا مُعَاوِيَةُ بْنُ هِشَامٍ، عَنْ سُفْيَانَ، عَنْ مُحَارِبِ بْنِ دِثَارٍ، عَنْ جَابِرِ بْنِ عَبْدِ اللهِ، قَالَ: قَالَ رَسُولُ اللهِ ﷺ: «نِعْمَ الإِدَامُ الْخَلُّ».

153. 'Abdah Ibn 'Abdullāh al-Khuzā'ī narrated to us; Mu'āwiyah Ibn Hāshim narrated to us; from Sufyān; from Muḥārib Ibn Dithār that Jābir Ibn 'Abdullāh (*raḍiyAllāhu 'anhu*) said:

> 'The Messenger of Allāh (ﷺ) said: "What an excellent condiment vinegar is!"'[153]

١٥٤ـ حَدَّثَنَا هَنَّادٌ، قَالَ: حَدَّثَنَا وَكِيعٌ، عَنْ سُفْيَانَ، عَنْ أَيُّوبَ، عَنْ أَبِي قِلَابَةَ، عَنْ زَهْدَمٍ الْجَرْمِيِّ، قَالَ: «كُنَّا عِنْدَ أَبِي مُوسَى الأَشْعَرِيِّ، فَأُتِيَ بِلَحْمِ دَجَاجٍ فَتَنَحَّى

[152] Muslim, #2977 and Tirmidhī, #2372.
[153] Muslim, #2052, Abū Dāwūd, #3820 and Tirmidhī, #1839.

رَجُلٌ مِنَ الْقَوْمِ، فَقَالَ: مَا لَكَ؟ فَقَالَ: إِنِّي رَأَيْتُهَا تَأْكُلُ شَيْئًا فَحَلَفْتُ أَنْ لَا آكُلَهَا، قَالَ: ادْنُ؛ فَإِنِّي رَأَيْتُ رَسُولَ اللهِ ﷺ يَأْكُلُ لَحْمَ دَجَاجٍ».

154. Hannạd narrated to us; Wakīʿ narrated to us; from Sufyān; from Ayyūb; from Abū Qilābah that Zahdam Al-Jarmī (*raḍiyAllāhu ʿanhu*) said:

> 'We were in the presence of Abū Mūsā Ashʿarī when he was served chicken. [Upon seeing the dish] one of the men in the group withdrew, so he asked him: "What is the matter with you?" He replied: 'I saw it eat something, so I swore that I would not eat it.' Abū Mūsā Ashʿarī (*raḍiyAllāhu ʿanhu*) said: "Come close, for I have seen the Messenger of Allāh (ﷺ) eating the meat of chickens!"'"[154]

١٥٥ـ حَدَّثَنَا الْفَضْلُ بْنُ سَهْلٍ الْأَعْرَجُ الْبَغْدَادِيُّ، قَالَ: حَدَّثَنَا إِبْرَاهِيمُ ابْنُ عَبْدِ الرَّحْمَنِ بْنِ مَهْدِيٍّ، عَنْ إِبْرَاهِيمَ بْنِ عُمَرَ بْنِ سَفِينَةَ، عَنْ أَبِيهِ، عَنْ جَدِّهِ، قَالَ: «أَكَلْتُ مَعَ رَسُولِ اللهِ ﷺ لَحْمَ حُبَارَى».

155. Al-Faḍl Ibn Sahl Al-Aʿraj al-Baghdādī narrated to us; Ibrāhīm Ibn ʿAbdu'l-Raḥmān Ibn Mahdī narrated to us; from Ibrāhīm Ibn ʿUmar Ibn Safīnah; from his father that his grandfather said:

> "I ate meat of a bustard (*ḥubārah*) together with the Messenger of Allāh (ﷺ)."[155]

---

[154] Bukhārī, #5517 and Muslim, #1649.

[155] Abū Dāwūd, #3797 and Tirmidhī, #1728, this ḥadīth is weak.

١٥٦ـ حَدَّثَنَا عَلِيُّ بْنُ حُجْرٍ، قَالَ: حَدَّثَنَا إِسْمَاعِيلُ بْنُ إِبْرَاهِيمَ، عَنْ أَيُّوبَ، عَنِ الْقَاسِمِ التَّمِيمِيِّ، عَنْ زَهْدَمٍ الْجَرْمِيِّ، قَالَ: كُنَّا عِنْدَ أَبِي مُوسَى الأَشْعَرِيِّ، قَالَ: فَقَدَّمَ طَعَامَهُ وَقَدَّمَ فِي طَعَامِهِ لَحْمَ دَجَاجٍ؛ وَفِي الْقَوْمِ رَجُلٌ مِنْ بَنِي تَيْمِ اللهِ أَحْمَرُ كَأَنَّهُ مَوْلًى، قَالَ: فَلَمْ يَدْنُ، فَقَالَ لَهُ أَبُو مُوسَى: ادْنُ، فَإِنِّي قَدْ رَأَيْتُ رَسُولَ اللهِ ﷺ أَكَلَ مِنْهُ، فَقَالَ: إِنِّي رَأَيْتُهُ يَأْكُلُ شَيْئًا فَقَذِرْتُهُ فَحَلَفْتُ أَنْ لَا أَطْعَمَهُ أَبَدًا.

156. ʿAlī Ibn Ḥujr narrated to us; Ismāʿīl Ibn Ibrāhīm narrated to us; from Ayyūb; from Al-Qāsim al-Tamīmī that Zahdam al-Jarmī (*raḍiyAllāhu ʿanhu*) said:

> 'We were in the presence of Abū Mūsā Al-Ashʿarī, when we were served food that had chicken meat in it. Among those present, was a man from the tribe Banu Taymullah, ruddy as if he were a freed slave, and he did not come close [to the food], so Abū Mūsā said: "Come closer, for I have seen the Messenger of Allāh (ﷺ) eat it." The man said: 'I saw it eat something unclean, so I swore that I would never eat it.'"[156]

١٥٧ـ حَدَّثَنَا مَحْمُودُ بْنُ غَيْلَانَ، قَالَ: حَدَّثَنَا أَبُو أَحْمَدَ الزُّبَيْرِيُّ، وَأَبُو نُعَيْمٍ، قَالَا: حَدَّثَنَا سُفْيَانُ، عَنْ عَبْدِ اللهِ بْنِ عِيسَى، عَنْ رَجُلٍ مِنْ أَهْلِ الشَّامِ يُقَالُ لَهُ: عَطَاءٌ، عَنْ أَبِي أَسِيدٍ قَالَ: قَالَ رَسُولُ اللهِ ﷺ: «كُلُوا الزَّيْتَ وَادَّهِنُوا بِهِ؛ فَإِنَّهُ مِنْ شَجَرَةٍ مُبَارَكَةٍ».

157. Maḥmūd Ibn Ghaylān narrated to us; Abū Aḥmad al-Zubayrī and Abū Nuʿaym narrated to us; Sufyān narrated to us; from ʿAbdullāh Ibn ʿIsā that a man from the people of Syria, named ʿAṭā' Ibn Abī Asid (*raḍiyAllāhu ʿanhu*) said:

[156] Bukhārī, #5517, Muslim, #1649 and Tirmidhī, #1827.

> 'The Messenger of Allāh (ﷺ) said: "Eat olive oil (*zayt*), and apply it, for indeed it is from a blessed tree (*shajra mubārakah*).'"[157]

١٥٨ـ حَدَّثَنَا يَحْيَى بْنُ مُوسَى، قَالَ: حَدَّثَنَا عَبْدُ الرَّزَّاقِ، قَالَ: حَدَّثَنَا مَعْمَرٌ، عَنْ زَيْدِ بْنِ أَسْلَمَ، عَنْ أَبِيهِ، عَنْ عُمَرَ بْنِ الخَطَّابِ، قَالَ: قَالَ رَسُولُ الله ﷺ: «كُلُوا الزَّيْتَ وَادَّهِنُوا بِهِ؛ فَإِنَّهُ مِنْ شَجَرَةٍ مُبَارَكَةٍ».

قَالَ أَبُو عِيسَى: وَعَبْدُ الرَّزَّاقِ كَانَ يَضْطَرِبُ فِي هَذَا الحَدِيثِ فَرُبَّمَا أَسْنَدَهُ، وَرُبَّمَا أَرْسَلَهُ.

158. Yaḥyā Ibn Mūsā narrated to us; 'Abdu'l-Razzāq narrated to us; Ma'mar narrated to us; from Zayd Ibn Aslam; from his father that 'Umar Ibn al-Khaṭṭāb (*raḍiyAllāhu 'anhu*) said 'The Messenger of Allāh (ﷺ) said:

> "Eat olive oil, and apply it, for indeed it is from a blessed tree.'"[158]

Abū 'Isā said: "Abdu'l-Razzāq was confused in his ascribing of this tradition, he may have provided a complete chain of transmission, and may not have.'

١٥٩ـ حَدَّثَنَا السِّنْجِيُّ ـ وَهُوَ أَبُو دَاوُدَ سُلَيْمَانُ بْنُ مَعْبَدٍ السِّنْجِيُّ ـ، قَالَ: حَدَّثَنَا عَبْدُ الرَّزَّاقِ، عَنْ مَعْمَرٍ، عَنْ زَيْدِ بْنِ أَسْلَمَ، عَنْ أَبِيهِ، عَنِ النَّبِيِّ ﷺ نَحْوَهُ، وَلَمْ يَذْكُرْ فِيهِ عَنْ عُمَرَ.

[157] Tirmidhī, #1852, this ḥadīth is accepted due to supporting narrations such as the following ḥadīth.
[158] Tirmidhī, #1851 and Ibn Ḥibbān, #3319.

159. Abū Dāwūd Sulaymān Ibn Maʿbad al-Marwazī al-Sanjī narrated to us; ʿAbdu'l-Razzāq narrated to us; from Maʿmar; from Zayd Ibn Aslam; from his father that the Prophet (ﷺ) said something similar but did not mention ʿUmar in the chain.[159]

١٦٠ـ حَدَّثَنَا مُحَمَّدُ بْنُ بَشَّارٍ، قَالَ: حَدَّثَنَا مُحَمَّدُ بْنُ جَعْفَرٍ، وَعَبْدُ الرَّحْمَنِ ابْنُ مَهْدِيٍّ، قَالَا: حَدَّثَنَا شُعْبَةُ، عَنْ قَتَادَةَ، عَنْ أَنَسِ بْنِ مَالِكٍ، قَالَ: «كَانَ النَّبِيُّ ﷺ يُعْجِبُهُ الدُّبَّاءُ، فَأُتِيَ بِطَعَامٍ، أَوْ دُعِيَ لَهُ، فَجَعَلْتُ أَتَتَبَّعُهُ فَأَضَعُهُ بَيْنَ يَدَيْهِ لِمَا أَعْلَمُ أَنَّهُ يُحِبُّهُ».

160. Muḥammad Ibn Bashshār narrated to us; Muḥammad Ibn Jāʿfar and ʿAbdu'l-Razzāq Ibn Mahdī narrated to us; Shuʿbah narrated to us; from Qatādah that Anas Ibn Mālik (*raḍiyAllāhu ʿanhu*) said:

> "The Prophet (ﷺ) loved gourd (*dubbāʾ*), and upon one occasion food was presented to him or he was invited by someone to partake of it, so I sought to seek out [the pieces in the dish and present them to him]; as I knew of his love for it."[160]

١٦١ـ حَدَّثَنَا قُتَيْبَةُ بْنُ سَعِيدٍ، قَالَ: حَدَّثَنَا حَفْصُ بْنُ غِيَاثٍ، عَنْ إِسْمَاعِيلَ ابْنِ أَبِي خَالِدٍ، عَنْ حَكِيمِ بْنِ جَابِرٍ، عَنْ أَبِيهِ، قَالَ: دَخَلْتُ عَلَى النَّبِيِّ ﷺ فَرَأَيْتُ عِنْدَهُ دُبَّاءً يُقَطَّعُ، فَقُلْتُ: مَا هَذَا؟ قَالَ: «نُكَثِّرُ بِهِ طَعَامَنَا».

قَالَ أَبُو عِيسَى: وجَابِرٌ هَذَا: هُوَ جَابِرُ بْنُ طَارِقٍ، وَيُقَالُ: ابْنُ أَبِي طَارِقٍ، وَهُوَ رَجُلٌ مِنْ أَصْحَابِ رَسُولِ اللهِ ﷺ، وَلَا نَعْرِفُ لَهُ إِلَّا هَذَا الحَدِيثَ الوَاحِدَ، وَأَبُو خَالِدٍ اسْمُهُ: سَعْدٌ.

[159] ʿAbdu'l-Razzāq in his *Musannaf*, #19568.
[160] Aḥmad in his Musnad, #12911.

161. Qutaybah Ibn Saʿid narrated to us; Ḥafs Ibn Ghiyāth narrated to us; from Ismāʿīl Ibn Abī Khālid; from Ḥākim Ibn Jābir that his father (*raḍiyAllāhu ʿanhu*) said:

> 'I came to visit the Prophet (ﷺ) and saw that he had gourd sliced into pieces, so I asked: 'What is this?' He replied: "We increase our food with it."'[161]

Abū 'Isā said: 'This Jābir is Jābir Ibn Ṭāriq and it is also said that he is Ibn Abī Ṭāriq. He is a man among the Companions of the Messnger of Allāh (ﷺ), and we know of no other tradition attributes to him. Abū Khālid named him Saʿd.'

١٦٢ـ حَدَّثَنَا قُتَيْبَةُ بْنُ سَعِيدٍ، عَنْ مَالِكِ بْنِ أَنَسٍ، عَنِ إِسْحَاقَ بْنِ عَبْدِ اللهِ ابْنِ أَبِي طَلحَةَ، أَنَّهُ سَمِعَ أَنَسَ بْنَ مَالِكٍ يَقُولُ: إِنَّ خَيَّاطًا دَعَا رَسُولَ اللهِ ﷺ لِطَعَامٍ صَنَعَهُ، قَالَ أَنَسٌ: فَذَهَبْتُ مَعَ رَسُولِ اللهِ ﷺ إِلَى ذَلِكَ الطَّعَامِ، فَقَرَّبَ إِلَى رَسُولِ اللهِ ﷺ خُبْزًا مِنْ شَعِيرٍ وَمَرَقًا فِيهِ دُبَّاءٌ وَقَدِيدٌ، قَالَ أَنَسٌ: فَرَأَيْتُ النَّبِيَّ ﷺ يَتَتَبَّعُ الدُّبَّاءَ حَوَالَيِ القَصْعَةِ فَلَمْ أَزَلْ أُحِبُّ الدُّبَّاءَ مِنْ يَوْمِئِذٍ .

162. Qutaybah Ibn Saʿīd narrated to us; from Mālik Ibn Anas; from Isḥāq Ibn ʿAbdullāh Ibn Abī Ṭalḥah, that he heard Anas Ibn Mālik (*raḍiyAllāhu ʿanhu*) say:

> 'A tailor once invited the Messenger of Allāh (ﷺ) for a meal he had prepared. So I also attended the invitation with the Messenger of Allāh (ﷺ) to that meal. He presented the Messenger of Allāh (ﷺ) with some barley-bread and broth containing dried meat and gourd (pumpkin). Then I saw the Prophet (ﷺ) seek out the gourd around the sides of the bowl, thereafter, I never stopped loving

[161] Ibn Mājah, #3304.
[162] Bukhārī, #5379, Muslim, #2041, and Tirmidhī, #1850.

gourd.'[162]

١٦٣ـ حَدَّثَنَا أَحْمَدُ بْنُ إِبْرَاهِيمَ الدَّوْرَقِيُّ، وَسَلَمَةُ بْنُ شَبِيبٍ، وَمَحْمُودُ ابْنُ غَيْلَانَ، قَالُوا: حَدَّثَنَا أَبُو أُسَامَةَ، عَنْ هِشَامِ بْنِ عُرْوَةَ، عَنْ أَبِيهِ، عَنْ عَائِشَةَ قَالَتْ: «كَانَ النَّبِيُّ ﷺ يُحِبُّ الْحَلْوَاءَ وَالْعَسَلَ».

163. Aḥmad Ibn Ibrāhīm al-Dawraqī, Salamah Ibn Shabīb and Maḥmud Ibn Ghaylān narrated to us; Abū Umāmah narrated to us; from Hisham Ibn 'Urwah; from his father that 'Ā'ishah (*raḍiyAllāhu 'anhā*) said:

> "The Prophet (ﷺ) used to love sweets (*ḥalwa*) and honey (*'asl*)."[163]

١٦٤ـ حَدَّثَنَا الْحَسَنُ بْنُ مُحَمَّدٍ الزَّعْفَرَانِيُّ، قَالَ: حَدَّثَنَا الْحَجَّاجُ بْنُ مُحَمَّدٍ، قَالَ: قَالَ ابْنُ جُرَيْجٍ: أَخْبَرَنِي مُحَمَّدُ بْنُ يُوسُفَ، أَنَّ عَطَاءَ بْنَ يَسَارٍ، أَخْبَرَهُ أَنَّ أُمَّ سَلَمَةَ، أَخْبَرَتْهُ «أَنَّهَا قَرَّبَتْ إِلَى رَسُولِ اللهِ ﷺ جَنْبًا مَشْوِيًّا فَأَكَلَ مِنْهُ، ثُمَّ قَامَ إِلَى الصَّلَاةِ وَمَا تَوَضَّأَ».

164. Al-Ḥasan Ibn Muḥammad al-Za'farānī narrated to us; Al-Ḥajjāj Ibn Muḥammad narrated to us that Ibn Jurayj said:

> 'Muḥammad Ibn Yūsuf informed me that 'Aṭā' Ibn Yasar informed him that Umm Salamah (*raḍiyAllāhu 'anhā*) informed him that she served a grilled flank to the Messenger of Allāh (ﷺ) and he ate it. He then stood up to pray without performing ritual abultion.'[164]

---

[163] Bukhārī, #5431, Muslim, #1473, and Tirmidhī, #1831.
[164] Tirmidhī, #1829.

١٦٥ـ حَدَّثَنَا قُتَيْبَةُ، قَالَ: حَدَّثَنَا ابْنُ لَهِيعَةَ، عَنْ سُلَيْمَانَ بْنِ زِيَادٍ، عَنْ عَبْدِ اللهِ ابْنِ الحَارِثِ، قَالَ: «أَكَلْنَا مَعَ رَسُولِ اللهِ ﷺ شِوَاءً فِي المَسْجِدِ».

165. Qutaybah narrated to us; Ibn Lahī'ah narrated to us; from Sulaymān Ibn Ziyād that 'Abdullāh Ibn Ḥārith (*raḍiyAllāhu 'anhu*) said:

> "We partook of grilled meat with the Messenger of Allāh (ﷺ) in the *masjid*."[165]

١٦٦ـ حَدَّثَنَا مَحْمُودُ بْنُ غَيْلَانَ، قَالَ: حَدَّثَنَا وَكِيعٌ، قَالَ: حَدَّثَنَا مِسْعَرٌ، عَنْ أَبِي صَخْرَةَ جَامِعِ بْنِ شَدَّادٍ، عَنِ المُغِيرَةِ بْنِ عَبْدِ اللهِ، عَنِ المُغِيرَةِ بْنِ شُعْبَةَ، قَالَ: ضِفْتُ مَعَ رَسُولِ اللهِ ﷺ ذَاتَ لَيْلَةٍ فَأُتِيَ بِجَنْبٍ مَشْوِيٍّ، ثُمَّ أَخَذَ الشَّفْرَةَ فَجَعَلَ يَحُزُّ، فَحَزَّ لِي بِهَا مِنْهُ، قَالَ: فَجَاءَ بِلَالٌ يُؤْذِنُهُ بِالصَّلَاةِ فَأَلْقَى الشَّفْرَةَ، فَقَالَ: «مَا لَهُ تَرِبَتْ يَدَاهُ؟»، قَالَ: وَكَانَ شَارِبُهُ قَدْ وَفَى، فَقَالَ لَهُ: «أَقُصُّهُ لَكَ عَلَى سِوَاكٍ»، أَوْ «قُصَّهُ عَلَى سِوَاكٍ».

166. Maḥmūd Ibn Ghaylān narrated to us; Wakī' narrated to us; Mis'ar narrated to us; from Abū Ṣakhrah Jāmi' Ibn Shaddād; from Al-Mughīrah Ibn 'Abdullāh that Al-Mughīrah Ibn Shu'bah (*raḍiyAllāhu 'anhu*) said:

> "I was a guest with the Messenger of Allāh (ﷺ) one night when a grilled flank was brought to him. He then took a knife and began to carve it into pieces, and he carved some of it for me. Bilāl arrived calling him to prayer, so he dropped the knife and said: "What is wrong with him? May his hands be struck to the ground!" His moustache hung down close to his mouth, so he said to him: "Shall

[165] Ibn Mājah, #3311, in the chain is Ibn Lahī'ah who is trustworthy but became confused after his books were burnt.

I trim it for you over a tooth-stick (*siwak*)?" or he said: "Trim it over a tooth-stick.'"[166]

١٦٧ـ حَدَّثَنَا وَاصِلُ بْنُ عَبْدِ الأَعْلَى، قَالَ: حَدَّثَنَا مُحَمَّدُ بْنُ فُضَيْلٍ، عَنْ أَبِي حَيَّانَ التَّيمِيِّ، عَنْ أَبِي زُرْعَةَ، عَنْ أَبِي هُرَيْرَةَ، قَالَ: «أُتِيَ النَّبِيُّ ﷺ بِلَحْمٍ فَرُفِعَ إِلَيْهِ الذِّرَاعُ، وَكَانَتْ تُعْجِبُهُ فَنَهَسَ مِنْهَا».

167. Wisāl Ibn ʿAbdu'l-Aʿlā narrated to us; Muḥammad Ibn Fuḍayl narrated to us; from Abū Ḥayyān al-Taymī; from Abū Zurʿah that Abū Hurayrah (*raḍiyAllāhu ʿanhu*) said:

"Some meat was brought to the Prophet (ﷺ), so the foreleg was given to him, and he liked it, so he took a bite of it [and ate it]."[167]

١٦٨ـ حَدَّثَنَا مُحَمَّدُ بْنُ بَشَّارٍ، قَالَ: حَدَّثَنَا أَبُو دَاوُدَ، عَنْ زُهَيْرٍ ـ يَعْنِي ابْنَ مُحَمَّدٍ ـ عَنْ أَبِي إِسْحَاقَ، عَنْ سَعْدِ بْنِ عِيَاضٍ، عَنِ ابْنِ مَسْعُودٍ، قَالَ: «كَانَ النَّبِيُّ ﷺ يُعْجِبُهُ الذِّرَاعُ، قَالَ: وَسُمَّ فِي الذِّرَاعِ، وَكَانَ يَرَى أَنَّ اليَهُودَ سَمُّوهُ».

168. Muḥammad Ibn Bashshār narrated to us; Abū Dāwūd narrated to us; from Zuhayr Ibn Muḥammad; Abū Isḥāq; from Saʿd Ibn ʿIyaḍ that Ibn Masʿūd (*raḍiyAllāhu ʿanhu*) said:

"The Prophet (ﷺ) used to like [the meat of] the foreleg." He also added: 'He was poisoned with a foreleg,' as he used to believe that the Jews had poisoned him."[168]

[166] Abū Dāwūd, #188

[167] Bukhārī, #4712, Muslim, #194, and Tirmidhī, #1837.

[168] Abū Dāwūd, #3780, this ḥadīth has other supporting narrations which make it hasan.

١٦٩ـ حَدَّثَنَا مُحَمَّدُ بْنُ بَشَّارٍ، قَالَ: حَدَّثَنَا مُسْلِمُ بْنُ إِبْرَاهِيمَ، قَالَ: حَدَّثَنَا أَبَانُ بْنُ يَزِيدَ، عَنْ قَتَادَةَ، عَنْ شَهْرِ بْنِ حَوْشَبٍ، عَنْ أَبِي عُبَيْدٍ، قَالَ: طَبَخْتُ لِلنَّبِيِّ ﷺ قِدْرًا وَقَدْ كَانَ يُعْجِبُهُ الذِّرَاعُ فَنَاوَلْتُهُ الذِّرَاعَ، ثُمَّ قَالَ: «نَاوِلْنِي الذِّرَاعَ»، فَنَاوَلْتُهُ، ثُمَّ قَالَ: «نَاوِلْنِي الذِّرَاعَ»، فَقُلْتُ: يَا رَسُولَ اللهِ! وَكَمْ لِلشَّاةِ مِنْ ذِرَاعٍ، فَقَالَ: «وَالَّذِي نَفْسِي بِيَدِهِ لَوْ سَكَتَّ لَنَاوَلْتَنِي الذِّرَاعَ مَا دَعَوْتُ».

169. Muḥammad Ibn Bashshar narrated to us; Muslim Ibn Ibrāhīm narrated to us; Abān Ibn Yazīd narrated to us; from Qatādah; from Shahr Ibn Ḥawshab that Abū 'Ubayd (*raḍiyAllāhu 'anhu*) said:

> 'I cooked a pot [of meat] for the Prophet (ﷺ), and he used to enjoy the foreleg, so I passed him the foreleg. Then he said: "Pass me the foreleg." So I passed it to him. Then he said: "Pass me the foreleg." So I passed it to him. Then he said: "Pass me the foreleg." So I said: 'O Messenger of Allāh, how many forelegs does a sheep have?' He said: "By the One in whose Hand is my soul, had you remained silent, you would have kept passing me foreleg as long I asked for it."'[169]

١٧٠ـ حَدَّثَنَا الحَسَنُ بْنُ مُحَمَّدٍ الزَّعْفَرَانِيُّ، قَالَ: حَدَّثَنَا يَحْيَى بْنُ عَبَّادٍ، عَنْ فُلَيْحِ ابنِ سُلَيْمَانَ، قَالَ: حَدَّثَنِي رَجُلٌ مِنْ بَنِي عَبَّادٍ، يُقَالُ لَهُ: عَبْدُ الوَهَّابِ بْنُ يَحْيَى ابنِ عَبَّادٍ، عَنْ عَبْدِ اللهِ بْنِ الزُّبَيْرِ، عَنْ عَائِشَةَ، قَالَتْ: مَا كَانَتِ الذِّرَاعُ أَحَبَّ اللَّحْمِ إِلَى رَسُولِ اللهِ ﷺ وَلَكِنَّهُ كَانَ لَا يَجِدُ اللَّحْمَ إِلَّا غِبًّا، وَكَانَ يَعْجَلُ إِلَيْهَا؛ لِأَنَّهَا أَعْجَلُهَا نُضْجًا.

[169] Aḥmad, 3/484-5, this ḥadīth has a weak chain although al-Albānī has mentioned other supporting evidence and declared it authentic in *Mukhtaṣir Shamā'il*, p.96.

170. Al-Ḥasan Ibn Muḥammad al-Za'farānī narrated to us; Yaḥyā Ibn 'Abbād narrated to us that Fulayh Ibn Sulaymān said: 'A man from Banu 'Abbād named 'Abdu'l-Wahhab Ibn Yaḥyā Ibn 'Abbād narrated to me; from 'Abdullāh Ibn al-Zubayr (*raḍiyAllāhu 'anhumā*) that 'Ā'ishah (*raḍiyAllāhu 'anhā*) said:

> "The foreleg was not the meat dearest to the Messenger of Allāh (ﷺ), but he only got to consume meat occasionally, so he would take to the foreleg; because it was the quickest portion of meat to prepare."[170]

١٧١ـ حَدَّثَنَا مَحْمُودُ بْنُ غَيْلَانَ، قَالَ: حَدَّثَنَا أَبُو أَحْمَدَ، قَالَ: حَدَّثَنَا مِسْعَرٌ، قَالَ: سَمِعْتُ شَيْخًا مِنْ فَهْمٍ، قَالَ: سَمِعْتُ عَبْدَ اللهِ بْنَ جَعْفَرٍ، يَقُولُ: سَمِعْتُ رَسُولَ اللهِ ﷺ يَقُولُ: «إِنَّ أَطْيَبَ اللَّحْمِ لَحْمُ الظَّهْرِ».

171. Maḥmūd Ibn Ghaylān narrated to us; Abū Aḥmad narrated to us; Mis'ar narrated to us: 'I heard a Shaikh from Fahm say: "Abdullāh Ibn Jā'far (*raḍiyAllāhu 'anhu*) say:

> 'I heard the Messenger of Allāh (ﷺ) say: "The best meat is the meat of the back."[171]

١٧٢ـ حَدَّثَنَا سُفْيَانُ بْنُ وَكِيعٍ، قَالَ: حَدَّثَنَا زَيْدُ بْنُ الْحُبَابِ، عَنْ عَبْدِ اللهِ ابْنِ الْمُؤَمَّلِ، عَنِ ابْنِ أَبِي مُلَيْكَةَ، عَنْ عَائِشَةَ: أَنَّ النَّبِيَّ ﷺ قَالَ: «نِعْمَ الإِدَامُ الْخَلُّ».

172. Sufyān Ibn Wakī' narrated to us; Zayd Ibn al-Ḥubāb narrated to us; from 'Abdullāh Ibn al-Mu'ammal; from Ibn Abī Mulaykah that 'Ā'ishah (*raḍiyAllāhu 'anhā*) said:

[170] Tirmidhī, #1838, this ḥadīth is weak.
[171] Ibn Mājah, #3308, this ḥadīth is weak.

'The Prophet (ﷺ) said: "What an excellent condiment vinegar is!"'[172]

١٧٣ـ حَدَّثَنَا أَبُو كُرَيْبٍ مُحَمَّدُ بْنُ الْعَلَاءِ، قَالَ: حَدَّثَنَا أَبُو بَكْرِ بْنُ عَيَّاشٍ، عَنْ ثَابِتٍ أَبِي حَمْزَةَ الثُّمَالِيِّ، عَنِ الشَّعْبِيِّ، عَنْ أُمِّ هَانِئٍ، قَالَتْ: دَخَلَ عَلَيَّ النَّبِيُّ ﷺ فَقَالَ: «أَعِنْدَكِ شَيْءٌ؟» فَقُلْتُ: لَا إِلَّا خُبْزٌ يَابِسٌ وَخَلٌّ، فَقَالَ: «هَاتِي، مَا أَقْفَرَ بَيْتٌ مِنْ أُدْمٍ فِيهِ خَلٌّ».

173. Abū Kurayb Muḥammad Ibn al-'Alā' narrated to us; Aby Bakr Ibn 'Ayyāsh narrated to us; from Thābit Ibn Ḥamzah al-Thumāli; from Al-Sha'bī that Umm Hānī' (*raḍiyAllāhu 'anha*) said:

'The Prophet (ﷺ) came in to visit me and said: "Do you have anything [to eat]." I said: 'No, other than some dry bread and vinegar.' So he said: "Bring it! For no household in which there is vinegar is devoid of seasoning!"'[173]

١٧٤ـ حَدَّثَنَا مُحَمَّدُ بْنُ الْمُثَنَّى، قَالَ: حَدَّثَنَا مُحَمَّدُ بْنُ جَعْفَرٍ، قَالَ: حَدَّثَنَا شُعْبَةُ، عَنْ عَمْرِو بْنِ مُرَّةَ، عَنْ مُرَّةَ الْهَمْدَانِيِّ، عَنْ أَبِي مُوسَى الْأَشْعَرِيِّ، عَنِ النَّبِيِّ ﷺ قَالَ: «فَضْلُ عَائِشَةَ عَلَى النِّسَاءِ كَفَضْلِ الثَّرِيدِ عَلَى سَائِرِ الطَّعَامِ».

174. Muḥammad Ibn al-Muthannā narrated to us; Muḥammad Ibn Jā'far narrated to us; Shu'bah narrated to us; from 'Amr Ibn Murrah; from Murrah al-Hamdānī that Abū Mūsā Ash'arī (*raḍiyAllāhu 'anhu*) said that the Prophet (ﷺ) said:

"The superiority of 'Ā'ishah over all other women is like

---

[172] Muslim, #2051 and Tirmidhī, #1840.

[173] Tirmidhī, #1841, this ḥadīth is authentic with supporting evidence.

the superiority of *tharīd*[174] over all other food."[175]

١٧٥ـ حَدَّثَنَا عَلِيُّ بْنُ حُجْرٍ، قَالَ: حَدَّثَنَا إِسْمَاعِيلُ بْنُ جَعْفَرٍ، قَالَ: حَدَّثَنَا عَبْدُ اللهِ ابْنُ عَبْدِ الرَّحْمَنِ بْنِ مَعْمَرٍ الأَنْصَارِيُّ أَبُو طُوَالَةَ، أَنَّهُ سَمِعَ أَنَسَ بْنَ مَالِكٍ، يَقُولُ: قَالَ رَسُولُ اللهِ ﷺ: «فَضْلُ عَائِشَةَ عَلَى النِّسَاءِ كَفَضْلِ الثَّرِيدِ عَلَى سَائِرِ الطَّعَامِ».

175. 'Alī Ibn Ḥujr narrated to us; Ismā'īl Ibn Jā'far narrated to us; Abū Ṭuwāla 'Abdullāh Ibn 'Abdu'l-Raḥmān Ibn Ma'mar al-Anṣārī narrated to us that he heard Anas Ibn Mālik (*raḍiyAllāhu 'anhu*) say: 'The Messenger of Allāh (ﷺ) said:

> "The superiority of 'Ā'ishah over all other women is like the superiority of *tharīd* over all other food.'"[176]

١٧٦ـ حَدَّثَنَا قُتَيْبَةُ بْنُ سَعِيدٍ، قَالَ: حَدَّثَنَا عَبْدُ العَزِيزِ بْنُ مُحَمَّدٍ، عَنْ سُهَيْلِ ابْنِ أَبِي صَالِحٍ، عَنْ أَبِيهِ، عَنْ أَبِي هُرَيْرَةَ، «أَنَّهُ رَأَى رَسُولَ اللهِ ﷺ تَوَضَّأَ مِنْ أَكْلِ ثَوْرِ أَقِطٍ، ثُمَّ رَآهُ أَكَلَ مِنْ كَتِفِ شَاةٍ، ثُمَّ صَلَّى وَلَمْ يَتَوَضَّأْ».

176. Qutaybah Ibn Sa'īd narrated to us; 'Abdu'l-'Azīz Ibn Muḥammad narrated to us; from Suhayl Ibn Abī Sāliḥ that his father said: 'Abū Hurayrah (*raḍiyAllāhu 'anhu*) said:

> "He saw the Messenger of Allāh (ﷺ) perform ritual ablution after eating some pieces of cheese. Then he saw him eat from the flank of a sheep, and then perform the prayer without performing ritual ablution.'"[177]

[174] *Tharīd*: this is bread shredded in broth, usually containing meat.

[175] Bukhārī, #5418, Muslim, #2431, and Tirmidhī, #1834.

[176] Bukhārī, #5428, Muslim, #2446, and Tirmidhī, #3887.

[177] Aḥmad in his *Musnad*, #9049 and #9050.

١٧٧ـ حَدَّثَنَا ابْنُ أَبِي عُمَرَ، قَالَ: حَدَّثَنَا سُفْيَانُ بْنُ عُيَيْنَةَ، عَنْ وَائِلِ ابْنِ دَاوُدَ، عَنِ ابْنِهِ ـ وَهُوَ بَكْرُ بْنُ وَائِلٍ ـ، عَنِ الزُّهْرِيِّ، عَنْ أَنَسِ بْنِ مَالِكٍ قَالَ: «أَوْلَمَ رَسُولُ اللهِ ﷺ عَلَى صَفِيَّةَ بِتَمْرٍ وَسَوِيقٍ».

177. Ibn Abī 'Umar narrated to us; Sufyān Ibn 'Uyaynah narrated to us; from Wā'il Ibn Dāwūd; from Bakr Ibn Wā'il from Al-Zuhrī that Anas Ibn Mālik (*raḍiyAllāhu 'anhu*) said:

> "The Messenger of Allāh (ﷺ) gave a wedding banquet for [his marriage with] Ṣafiyyah with dates (*tamr*) and a drink made from barley (*sawīq*)."[178]

١٧٨ـ حَدَّثَنَا الْحُسَيْنُ بْنُ مُحَمَّدٍ الْبَصْرِيُّ، قَالَ: حَدَّثَنَا الْفُضَيْلُ بْنُ سُلَيْمَانَ، قَالَ: حَدَّثَنِي فَائِدٌ مَوْلَى عُبَيْدِ اللهِ بْنِ عَلِيِّ بْنِ أَبِي رَافِعٍ مَوْلَى رَسُولِ اللهِ ﷺ، قَالَ: حَدَّثَنِي عُبَيْدُ اللهِ بْنُ عَلِيٍّ، عَنْ جَدَّتِهِ سَلْمَى، أَنَّ الْحَسَنَ بْنَ عَلِيٍّ، وَابْنَ عَبَّاسٍ، وَابْنَ جَعْفَرٍ أَتَوْهَا فَقَالُوا لَهَا: «اصْنَعِي لَنَا طَعَامًا مِمَّا كَانَ يُعْجِبُ رَسُولَ اللهِ ﷺ وَيُحْسِنُ أَكْلَهُ، فَقَالَتْ: يَا بُنَيَّ! لَا تَشْتَهِيهِ الْيَوْمَ، قَالَ: بَلَى اصْنَعِيهِ لَنَا؛ قَالَ: فَقَامَتْ فَأَخَذَتْ شَيْئًا مِنْ شَعِيرٍ فَطَحَنَتْهُ، ثُمَّ جَعَلَتْهُ فِي قِدْرٍ، وَصَبَّتْ عَلَيْهِ شَيْئًا مِنْ زَيْتٍ وَدَقَّتِ الْفُلْفُلَ وَالتَّوَابِلَ فَقَرَّبَتْهُ إِلَيْهِمْ، فَقَالَتْ: هَذَا مِمَّا كَانَ يُعْجِبُ رَسُولَ اللهِ ﷺ وَيُحْسِنُ أَكْلَهُ».

178. Al-Ḥusayn Ibn Muḥammad al-Baṣrī narrated to us; Al-Fuḍayl Ibn Sulaymān narrated to us; from Fā'id, the freed slave of 'Ubaydullāh Ibn 'Alī Ibn Abī Rāfi', the freed slave of the Messenger of Allāh (ﷺ) narrated to me; 'Ubaydullāh Ibn 'Alī narrated to me; from his grandmother Salmāh that Al-Ḥasan Ibn 'Alī, Ibn 'Abbās

[178] Abū Dāwūd, #3744, Tirmidhī, #1090 and Ibn Mājah, #1909.

and Ibn Jā'far (*raḍiyAllāhu 'anhum*) came to her and said:

> 'Prepare for us a meal which the Messenger of Allāh (ﷺ) used to like and enjoy eating.' She said: 'O my dear sons, you will not enjoy [such food] today.' They said: 'Surely we will, prepare it for us.' She stood up, took some barley and ground it; then place it in a pot and poured olive oil over it, crushed the pepper and the spices, and presented it to them, and said: 'This is what the Messenger of Allāh (ﷺ) used to like and enjoy eating.'"[179]

١٧٩ـ حَدَّثَنَا مَحْمُودُ بْنُ غَيْلَانَ، قَالَ: حَدَّثَنَا أَبُو أَحْمَدَ، قَالَ: حَدَّثَنَا سُفْيَانُ، عَنِ الأَسْوَدِ بْنِ قَيْسٍ، عَنْ نُبَيْحٍ العَنَزِيِّ، عَنْ جَابِرِ بْنِ عَبْدِ اللهِ، قَالَ: «أَتَانَا النَّبِيُّ ﷺ فِي مَنْزِلِنَا فَذَبَحْنَا لَهُ شَاةً، فَقَالَ: كَأَنَّهُمْ عَلِمُوا أَنَّا نُحِبُّ اللَّحْمَ» وَفِي الحَدِيثِ قِصَّةٌ.

179. Maḥmūd Ibn Ghaylān narrated to us; Abū Aḥmad narrated to us; Sufyān narrated to us: from Al-Aswad Ibn Qays; from Nubayḥ al-'Anazī that Jābir Ibn 'Abdullāh (*raḍiyAllāhu 'anhu*) said:

> 'The Prophet (ﷺ) came to us in our house, so we slaughtered a sheep for him. He (ﷺ) said: "It is as if they knew that we love meat."' This ḥadīth is part of a longer incident.[180]

١٨٠ـ حَدَّثَنَا ابْنُ أَبِي عُمَرَ، قَالَ: حَدَّثَنَا سُفْيَانُ، قَالَ: حَدَّثَنَا عَبْدُ اللهِ بْنُ مُحَمَّدِ ابْنِ عَقِيلٍ، أَنَّهُ سمعَ جَابِرًا، قَالَ سُفْيَانُ: وَحَدَّثَنَا مُحَمَّدُ بْنُ الْمُنْكَدِرِ، عَنْ جَابِرٍ قَالَ: «خَرَجَ رَسُولُ اللهِ ﷺ وَأَنَا مَعَهُ فَدَخَلَ عَلَى امْرَأَةٍ مِنَ الأَنْصَارِ، فَذَبَحَتْ لَهُ شَاةً فَأَكَلَ

[179] Ṭabarānī in *al-Kabīr*, 24/299, this chain of narration is weak.
[180] Aḥmad in his *Musnad*, #14245.

مِنْهَا، وَأَتَتْهُ بِقِنَاعٍ مِنْ رُطَبٍ، فَأَكَلَ مِنْهُ، ثُمَّ تَوَضَّأَ لِلظُّهْرِ وَصَلَّى ﷺ، ثُمَّ انْصَرَفَ، فَأَتَتْهُ بِعُلَالَةٍ مِنْ عُلَالَةِ الشَّاةِ، فَأَكَلَ ثُمَّ صَلَّى العَصْرَ وَلَمْ يَتَوَضَّأْ» .

180. Ibn Abī ʿUmar narrated to us; Sufyān narrated to us; ʿAbdullāh Ibn Muḥammad Ibn ʿAqīl narrated to us that he heard Jābir, Sufyān said: ʿMuḥammad Ibn al-Munkadir narrated to us that Jābir (*raḍiyAllāhu ʿanhu*) said:

> "The Messenger of Allāh (ﷺ) once went out together with me to visit one of the women from among the Ansar. She slaughtered for him a sheep for and he ate some of it. She then served him a dish of fresh dates, and he ate some of them also. He then performed ablution for the noon prayer (*ẓuhr*) and performed the prayer. After praying, he returned and she served him with the remaining meat from the sheep, and he ate it. He then performed the afternoon prayer (*ʿaṣr*) without performing ablution."[181]

١٨١ـ حَدَّثَنَا العَبَّاسُ بْنُ مُحَمَّدٍ الدُّورِيُّ، قَالَ: حَدَّثَنَا يُونُسُ بْنُ مُحَمَّدٍ، قَالَ: حَدَّثَنَا فُلَيْحُ بْنُ سُلَيْمَانَ، عَنْ عُثْمَانَ بْنِ عَبْدِ الرَّحْمَنِ، عَنْ يَعْقُوبَ بْنِ أَبِي يَعْقُوبَ، عَنْ أُمِّ المُنْذِرِ، قَالَتْ: «دَخَلَ عَلَيَّ رَسُولُ اللهِ ﷺ وَمَعَهُ عَلِيٌّ، وَلَنَا دَوَالٍ مُعَلَّقَةٌ، قَالَتْ: فَجَعَلَ رَسُولُ اللهِ ﷺ يَأْكُلُ وَعَلِيٌّ مَعَهُ يَأْكُلُ، فَقَالَ رَسُولُ اللهِ ﷺ لِعَلِيٍّ: مَهْ يَا عَلِيُّ! فَإِنَّكَ نَاقِهٌ، قَالَتْ: فَجَلَسَ عَلِيٌّ وَالنَّبِيُّ ﷺ يَأْكُلُ، قَالَتْ: فَجَعَلْتُ لَهُمْ سِلْقًا وَشَعِيرًا، فَقَالَ النَّبِيُّ ﷺ لِعَلِيٍّ: مِنْ هَذَا فَأَصِبْ؛ فَإِنَّ هَذَا أَوْفَقُ لَكَ» .

181. Al-ʿAbbās Ibn Muḥammad al-Durī narrated to us; Yūnus Ibn Muḥammad narrated to us; Fulayḥ Ibn Sulaymān narrated to us;

[181] Abū Dāwūd, #191 and Tirmidhī, #80.

from ʿUthmān Ibn ʿAbdu'l-Raḥmān; from Yaʿqūb Ibn Abī Yaʿqūb that Umm al-Mundhir (*raḍiyAllāhu ʿanhā*) said:

> 'The Messenger of Allāh (ﷺ) came to visit me together with ʿAlī. We had some dates hanging, so the Messenger of Allāh (ﷺ) began to eat them. When ʿAlī (*raḍiyAllāhu ʿanhu*) also began to eat with him, the Messenger of Allāh (saw) said to ʿAli: "Stop, O ʿAlī as you have just recovered from an illness." ʿAlī then sat down while the Prophet (ﷺ) continued to eat, I then prepared for them some chards (*silq*) and barley (*shaʿīr*). The Prophet (ﷺ) said to ʿAlī: "Eat of this, for indeed it is more suitable for you."'[182]

١٨٢ـ حَدَّثَنَا مَحْمُودُ بْنُ غَيْلَانَ، قَالَ: حَدَّثَنَا بِشْرُ بْنُ السَّرِيِّ، عَنْ سُفْيَانَ، عَنْ طَلحَةَ بْنِ يَحْيَى، عَنْ عَائِشَةَ بِنْتِ طَلحَةَ، عَنْ عَائِشَةَ أُمِّ الْمُؤْمِنِينَ، قَالَتْ: «كَانَ النَّبِيُّ ﷺ يَأْتِينِي فَيَقُولُ: أَعِنْدَكِ غَدَاءٌ؟ فَأَقُولُ: لَا، قَالَتْ: فَيَقُولُ: إِنِّي صَائِمٌ، قَالَتْ: فَأَتَانِي يَوْمًا، فَقُلْتُ: يَا رَسُولَ اللهِ! إِنَّهُ أُهْدِيَتْ لَنَا هَدِيَّةٌ، قَالَ: وَمَا هِيَ؟ قُلْتُ: حَيْسٌ، قَالَ: أَمَا إِنِّي أَصْبَحْتُ صَائِمًا قَالَتْ: ثُمَّ أَكَلَ» .

182. Maḥmūd Ibn Ghaylān narrated to us; Bishr Ibn al-Sarī narrated to us; from Sufyān; from Ṭalḥah Ibn Yaḥyā; from ʿĀ'ishah bint Ṭalḥah that ʿĀ'ishah, the Mother of the Believers (*raḍiyAllāhu ʿanhā*) said:

> 'The Prophet (ﷺ) used to come to me and say: "Do you have any breakfast?" I would say: "No." He would then say: "I shall fast." One day, when he came to me, I said: 'O Messenger of Allāh, we have been given a gift!' He said:

[182] Tirmidhī, #2037, and he said: 'This tradition is ḥasan gharīb. We only know this tradition from Fulayh.

> "What is it?" I said: 'It is a dish of dates mixed with butter and cheese (*hays*).' He said: "As for me, I began fasting in the morning," and [then] he ate it.'[183]

١٨٣ـ حَدَّثَنَا عَبْدُ اللهِ بْنُ عَبْدِ الرَّحْمَنِ، قَالَ: حَدَّثَنَا عُمَرُ بْنُ حَفْصِ بْنِ غِيَاثٍ، قَالَ: حَدَّثَنَا أَبِي، عَنْ مُحَمَّدِ بْنِ أَبِي يَحْيَى الأَسْلَمِيِّ، عَنْ يَزِيدَ بْنِ أَبِي أُمَيَّةَ الأَعْوَرِ، عَنْ يُوسُفَ بْنِ عَبْدِ اللهِ بْنِ سَلَامٍ، قَالَ: رَأَيْتُ النَّبِيَّ ﷺ أَخَذَ كِسْرَةً مِنْ خُبْزِ الشَّعِيرِ فَوَضَعَ عَلَيْهَا تَمْرَةً، وَقَالَ: «هَذِهِ إِدَامُ هَذِهِ» وَأَكَلَ .

183. 'Abdullāh Ibn 'Abdu'l-Raḥmān narrated to us; 'Umar Ibn Ḥafs Ibn Ghiyāth narrated to us; my father narrated to us; from Muḥammad Ibn Abī Yaḥyā al-Aslamī; from Yazīd Ibn Abī Umayyah al-A'war that Yūsuf Ibn 'Abdullāh Ibn Salām (*raḍiyAllāhu 'anhu*) said:

> 'I saw the Prophet (ﷺ) take a slice of barley-bread, then placed dates upon it and said: "This compliments this." He then ate it.'[184]

١٨٤ ـ حَدَّثَنَا عَبْدُ اللهِ بْنُ عَبْدِ الرَّحْمَنِ، قَالَ: حَدَّثَنَا سَعِيدُ بْنُ سُلَيْمَانَ، عَنْ عَبَّادِ ابْنِ الْعَوَّامِ، عَنْ حُمَيْدٍ، عَنْ أَنَسٍ: «أَنَّ رَسُولَ اللهِ ﷺ كَانَ يُعْجِبُهُ الثُّفْلُ» ، قَالَ عَبْدُ اللهِ: يَعْنِي مَا بَقِيَ مِنَ الطَّعَامِ.

184. 'Abdullāh Ibn 'Abdu'l-Raḥmān narrated to us; Sa'īd Ibn Sulaymān narrated to us; from 'Abbād Ibn al-'Awwām; from Ḥumayd that Anas (*raḍiyAllāhu 'anhu*) said about the Messenger of Allāh (ﷺ):

---

183 Muslim, #1154, and Tirmidhī, #734.
184 Abū Dāwūd, #3260, this ḥadīth is weak.

"He used to like the food left over (*al-thufl*)."

'Abdullāh said: 'That means what is left over from the meal.'[185]

[185] Aḥmad in his *Musnad*, #13300.

CHAPTER TWENTY-SEVEN

بَابُ مَا جَاءَ فِي صِفَةِ وُضُوءِ رَسُولِ اللهِ ﷺ عِنْدَ الطَّعَامِ

What has been narrated concerning the Description of the Ablution (*wūḍu'*) of the Messenger of Allāh (ﷺ) at Mealtime

١٨٥ـ حَدَّثَنَا أَحْمَدُ بْنُ مَنِيعٍ، قَالَ: حَدَّثَنَا إِسْمَاعِيلُ بْنُ إِبْرَاهِيمَ، عَنْ أَيُّوبَ، عَنِ ابْنِ أَبِي مُلَيْكَةَ، عَنِ ابْنِ عَبَّاسٍ، أَنَّ رَسُولَ اللهِ ﷺ خَرَجَ مِنَ الخَلَاءِ فَقُرِّبَ إِلَيْهِ الطَّعَامُ، فَقَالُوا: أَلَا نَأْتِيكَ بِوَضُوءٍ؟ قَالَ: «إِنَّمَا أُمِرْتُ بِالوُضُوءِ إِذَا قُمْتُ إِلَى الصَّلَاةِ».

185. Aḥmad Ibn Manī‘ narrated to us; Ismā‘īl Ibn Ibrāhīm narrated to us; from Ayyub; from Ibn Abū Mulaykah that Ibn ‘Abbās (*raḍiyAllāhu ‘anhumā*) said:

> "The Messenger of Allāh (ﷺ) came out of the toilet, a meal was brought to him and they asked: 'Shall we not bring you water for ablution?' He replied: "I have only been ordered to perform ablution (*wūḍu'*) when I stand up for prayer."[186]

[186] Abū Dāwūd, #3760 and Tirmidhī, #1847.

ablution is only for prayer.

١٨٦ـ حَدَّثَنَا سَعِيدُ بْنُ عَبْدِ الرَّحْمَنِ الْمَخْزُومِيُّ، قَالَ: حَدَّثَنَا سُفْيَانُ بْنُ عُيَيْنَةَ، عَنْ عَمْرِو بْنِ دِينَارٍ، عَنْ سَعِيدِ بْنِ الْحُوَيْرِثِ، عَنِ ابْنِ عَبَّاسٍ قَالَ: «خَرَجَ رَسُولُ اللهِ ﷺ مِنَ الْغَائِطِ فَأُتِيَ بِطَعَامٍ، فَقِيلَ لَهُ: أَلَا تَتَوَضَّأُ؟ فَقَالَ: أَأُصَلِّي فَأَتَوَضَّأَ؟!».

186. Sa'id Ibn 'Abdu'l-Raḥmān al-Makhzūmī narrated to us; Sufyān Ibn 'Uyaynah narrated to us; from 'Amr Ibn Dinār; Sa'īd Ibn al-Huwayrith that Ibn 'Abbās (*raḍiyAllāhu 'anhumā*) said:

> 'The Messenger of Allāh (ﷺ) came out after relieving himself from the call of nature and he was brought a meal, so he was asked: 'Will you not perform ablution?' He replied: "Am I going to perform the prayer, so that I need to perform ablution!?"'[187]

١٨٧ـ حَدَّثَنَا يَحْيَى بْنُ مُوسَى، قَالَ: حَدَّثَنَا عَبْدُ اللهِ بْنُ نُمَيْرٍ، قَالَ: حَدَّثَنَا قَيْسُ ابْنُ الرَّبِيعِ، (ح) وَحَدَّثَنَا قُتَيْبَةُ، قَالَ: حَدَّثَنَا عَبْدُ الْكَرِيمِ الْجُرْجَانِيُّ، عَنْ قَيْسِ ابْنِ الرَّبِيعِ، عَنْ أَبِي هَاشِمٍ، عَنْ زَاذَانَ، عَنْ سَلْمَانَ، قَالَ: قَرَأْتُ فِي التَّوْرَاةِ أَنَّ بَرَكَةَ الطَّعَامِ الْوُضُوءُ بَعْدَهُ، فَذَكَرْتُ ذَلِكَ لِلنَّبِيِّ ﷺ، وَأَخْبَرْتُهُ بِمَا قَرَأْتُ فِي التَّوْرَاةِ، فَقَالَ رَسُولُ اللهِ ﷺ: «بَرَكَةُ الطَّعَامِ الْوُضُوءُ قَبْلَهُ وَالْوُضُوءُ بَعْدَهُ».

187. Yaḥyā Ibn Mūsā narrated to us; 'Abdulllāh Ibn Numayr narrated to us; Qays Ibn Al-Rabī' and Qutaybah narrated to us; 'Abdu'l-Karīm al-Jurjānī narrated to us; from Qays Ibn Al-Rabī'; from Abū Hāshim; from Zādhān that Salmān [al-Farsī] (*raḍiyAllāhu 'anhu*) said:

> 'I read in the Torah, that the blessings of food are [attained] by performing ablution [washing the hands and

[187] Muslim, #374, Abū Dāwūd, #3760 and Tirmidhī, 1847

rinsing the mouth] after it, so I mentioned this to the Prophet (ﷺ), and I informed him what I read in the Torah.' The Messenger of Allāh (ﷺ) said: "The blessing of food are [attained] by performing ablution [washing the hands and rinsing the mouth] before it and ablution after it.'"[188]

[188] Abū Dāwūd, #3761 and Tirmidhī, #1846, this ḥadīth is weak.

CHAPTER TWENTY-EIGHT

بَابُ مَا جَاءَ فِي قَوْلِ رَسُولِ اللهِ ﷺ قَبْلَ الطَّعَامِ وَبَعْدَمَا يَفْرُغُ مِنْهُ

What has been narrated concerning the Saying (*qawl*) of the Messenger of Allāh (ﷺ) Before and after Eating

١٨٨ـ حَدَّثَنَا قُتَيْبَةُ، قَالَ: حَدَّثَنَا ابْنُ لَهِيعَةَ، عَنْ يَزِيدَ بْنِ أَبِي حَبِيبٍ، عَنْ رَاشِدِ ابْنِ جَنْدَلٍ الْيَافِعِيِّ، عَنْ حَبِيبِ بْنِ أَوْسٍ، عَنْ أَبِي أَيُّوبَ الأَنْصَارِيِّ، قَالَ: كُنَّا عِنْدَ النَّبِيِّ ﷺ يَوْمًا، فَقُرِّبَ إِلَيْهِ طَعَامٌ، فَلَمْ أَرَ طَعَامًا كَانَ أَعْظَمَ بَرَكَةً مِنْهُ أَوَّلَ مَا أَكَلْنَا، وَلَا أَقَلَّ بَرَكَةً فِي آخِرِهِ، فَقُلْنَا: يَا رَسُولَ اللهِ! كَيْفَ هَذَا؟ قَالَ: «إِنَّا ذَكَرْنَا اسْمَ اللهِ حِينَ أَكَلْنَا، ثُمَّ قَعَدَ مَنْ أَكَلَ وَلَمْ يُسَمِّ اللهَ تَعَالَى فَأَكَلَ مَعَهُ الشَّيْطَانُ» .

188. Qutaybah narrated to us; Ibn Lahī'ah narrated to us; from Yazīd Ibn Abī Ḥabīb; from Rashīd Ibn Jandal al-Yāfi'ī; from Ḥabīb Ibn Aws that Abū Ayyūb al-Anṣārī (*raḍiyAllāhu 'anhu*) said:

> 'We were with the Prophet (ﷺ) one day, when a meal was brought to him. I had never seen a meal that possessed greater blessing (*barakah*) at the beginning of our eating, nor possessing less blessing at the end of it. We said: 'O Messenger of Allāh, how is this?' He said: "We mentioned

> the name of Allāh when we began to eat. Then sat someone who ate and failed to mention the name of Allāh, the Exalted, so Satan ate with him.'"[189]

١٨٩ـ حَدَّثَنَا يَحْيَى بْنُ مُوسَى، قَالَ: حَدَّثَنَا أَبُو دَاوُدَ، قَالَ: حَدَّثَنَا هِشَامٌ الدَّسْتَوائِيُّ، عَنْ بُدَيْلٍ الْعُقَيْلِيِّ، عَنْ عَبْدِ اللهِ بْنِ عُبَيْدِ بْنِ عُمَيْرٍ، عَنْ أُمِّ كُلْثُومٍ، عَنْ عَائِشَةَ، قَالَتْ: قَالَ رَسُولُ اللهِ ﷺ: «إِذَا أَكَلَ أَحَدُكُمْ فَنَسِيَ أَنْ يَذْكُرَ اللهَ تَعَالَى عَلَى طَعَامِهِ؛ فَلْيَقُلْ: بِاسْمِ اللهِ أَوَّلَهُ وَآخِرَهُ».

189. Yaḥyā Ibn Mūsā narrated to us; Abū Dāwūd narrated to us; Hisham Al-Dastuwā'ī narrated to us; from Budayl al-'Uqaylī; from 'Abdullāh Ibn 'Ubayd Ibn 'Umayr; from Umm Kulthum that 'Ā'ishah (*raḍiyAllāhu 'anhumā*) said:

> 'The Messenger of Allāh (ﷺ) said: "If one of you eats but forgets to mention the name of Allāh, the Exalted during his meal, let him say: *"Bismillāhi awwalahu wa ākhirahu"*—"I began with name of Allāh at its beginning and at its end."'"[190]

١٩٠ـ حَدَّثَنَا عَبْدُ اللهِ بْنُ الصَّبَّاحِ الْهَاشِمِيُّ الْبَصْرِيُّ، قَالَ: حَدَّثَنَا عَبْدُ الأَعْلَى، عَنْ مَعْمَرٍ، عَنْ هِشَامِ بْنِ عُرْوَةَ، عَنْ أَبِيهِ، عَنْ عُمَرَ بْنِ أَبِي سَلَمَةَ، أَنَّهُ دَخَلَ عَلَى رَسُولِ اللهِ ﷺ وَعِنْدَهُ طَعَامٌ، فَقَالَ: «ادْنُ يَا بُنَيَّ! فَسَمِّ اللهَ تَعَالَى، وَكُلْ بِيَمِينِكَ، وَكُلْ مِمَّا يَلِيكَ».

---

[189] Aḥmad in his *Musnad*, #23522, this ḥadīth is weak but the meaning is authentic because of other supporting evidences.

[190] Abū Dāwūd, #3767 and Tirmidhī, #1858, this ḥadīth is supported by other evidence in the *Musnad* of Abū Ya'lā, #7153 with slightly different wording.

190. ʿAbdullāh Ibn al-Sabbāḥ al-Hashimī al-Baṣrī narrated to us; ʿAbdu'l-Aʿlā narrated to us; from Maʿmar; from Hisham Ibn ʿUrwah; from his father that ʿUmar Ibn Abī Salamah (*raḍiyAllāhu ʿanhu*) said:

> 'He went to see the Messenger of Allāh (ﷺ) who had a meal before him, so he said: "Come close, dear son, mention the name of Allāh, the Exalted, eat with your right hand, and eat what is directly in front of you."'[191]

١٩١ـ حَدَّثَنَا مَحْمُودُ بْنُ غَيْلَانَ، قَالَ: حَدَّثَنَا أَبُو أَحْمَدَ الزُّبَيْرِيُّ، قَالَ: حَدَّثَنَا سُفْيَانُ الثَّوْرِيُّ، عَنْ أَبِي هَاشِمٍ، عَنْ إِسْمَاعِيلَ بْنِ رِيَاحٍ، عَنْ أَبِيهِ رِيَاحِ بْنِ عَبِيدَةَ، عَنْ أَبِي سَعِيدٍ الْخُدْرِيِّ، قَالَ: كَانَ رَسُولُ اللهِ ﷺ إِذَا فَرَغَ مِنْ طَعَامِهِ، قَالَ: «الْحَمْدُ للهِ الَّذِي أَطْعَمَنَا، وَسَقَانَا، وَجَعَلَنَا مُسْلِمِينَ».

191. Maḥmūd Ibn Ghaylān narrated to us; Abū Aḥmad al-Zubayrī narrated to us; Sufyān Ibn al-Thawrī narrated to us; from Abū Hishām; from Ismāʿīl Ibn Riyāḥ; from his father Riyāḥ that Abū Saʿīd al-Khudrī (*raḍiyAllāhu ʿanhu*) said:

> 'The Messenger of Allāh (ﷺ) used to say when he finished his meal: "*Al-ḥamdulillāhi-aladhi atʿamanā wa-saqā-nā wa-jaʿalanā muslimīn*"—"Praise be to Allāh, who fed us and quenched our thirst, and has made us Muslims."'[192]

١٩٢ـ حَدَّثَنَا مُحَمَّدُ بْنُ بَشَّارٍ، قَالَ: حَدَّثَنَا يَحْيَى بْنُ سَعِيدٍ، قَالَ: حَدَّثَنَا ثَوْرُ ابْنُ يَزِيدَ، عَنْ خَالِدِ بْنِ مَعْدَانَ، عَنْ أَبِي أُمَامَةَ، قَالَ: كَانَ رَسُولُ اللهِ ﷺ إِذَا رُفِعَتِ الْمَائِدَةُ

[191] Tirmidhī, #1857, and Ibn Mājah, #3265.

[192] Abū Dāwūd, #3850, and Tirmidhī, #3457, there is an unknown narrator in the chain.

مِنْ بَيْنِ يَدَيْهِ يَقُولُ: «الحَمْدُ لله حَمْدًا كَثِيرًا طَيِّبًا مُبَارَكًا فِيهِ، غَيْرَ مُوَدَّعٍ، وَلَا مُسْتَغْنًى عَنْهُ رَبَّنَا».

192. Muḥammad Ibn Bashshār narrated to us; Yaḥyā Ibn Saʿīd narrated to us; Thawr Ibn Yazīd narrated to us; from Khālid Ibn Maʿdān that Abū Umāmah (*raḍiyAllāhu ʿanhu*) said:

> 'When the table [mat] was removed from in front of him [after finishing his meal] the Messenger of Allāh (ﷺ) used to say:
>
> *"Al-ḥamdulillāhi ḥamdan kathiran ṭayyiban mubarakan fihi-ghayra muwaddaʿin wa-laa mus-taghnan ʿanhu rabbanā."* —"Praise be to Allāh, praise which is abundant, good and blessed that is neither insufficient, nor abandoned, nor from our Lord"[193]

١٩٣ـ حَدَّثَنَا أَبُو بَكْرٍ مُحَمَّدُ بْنُ أَبَانَ، قَالَ: حَدَّثَنَا وَكِيعٌ، عَنْ هِشَامٍ الدَّسْتُوائِيِّ، عَنْ بُدَيْلِ بْنِ مَيْسَرَةَ العُقَيْلِيِّ، عَنْ عَبْدِ الله بْنِ عُبَيْدِ بْنِ عُمَيْرٍ، عَنْ أُمِّ كُلْثُومٍ، عَنْ عَائِشَةَ، قَالَتْ: كَانَ النَّبِيُّ ﷺ يَأْكُلُ الطَّعَامَ فِي سِتَّةٍ مِنْ أَصْحَابِهِ، فَجَاءَ أَعْرَابِيٌّ فَأَكَلَهُ بِلُقْمَتَيْنِ، فَقَالَ رَسُولُ الله ﷺ: «لَوْ سَمَّى لَكَفَاكُمْ».

193. Abū Bakr Muḥammad Ibn Abān narrated to us; Wakīʿ narrated to us; from Hishām Al-Dastuwā'ī; from Budayl Ibn Maysarah al-ʿUqaylī; from ʿAbdullāh Ibn ʿUbayd Ibn ʿUmayr; from Umm Kulthum that ʿĀ'ishah (*raḍiyAllāhu ʿanhumā*) said:

> 'The Prophet (ﷺ) was eating with six of his Companions, when a Bedouin came and finished the meal in two mor-

[193] Bukhārī, #5358, and Tirmidhī, #3456.

sels. The Messenger of Allāh (ﷺ) said: "Had he begun with the name of Allāh, it would have been enough for you all.'"[194]

١٩٤ـ حَدَّثَنَا هَنَّادٌ، وَمَحْمُودُ بْنُ غَيْلَانَ، قَالَا: حَدَّثَنَا أَبُو أُسَامَةَ، عَنْ زَكَرِيَّا ابْنِ أَبِي زَائِدَةَ، عَنْ سَعِيدِ بْنِ أَبِي بُرْدَةَ، عَنْ أَنَسِ بْنِ مَالِكٍ قَالَ: قَالَ رَسُولُ اللهِ ﷺ: «إِنَّ اللهَ لَيَرْضَى عَنِ العَبْدِ أَنْ يَأْكُلَ الأَكْلَةَ، أَوْ يَشْرَبَ الشَّرْبَةَ فَيَحْمَدَهُ عَلَيْهَا».

194. Hannād and Maḥmūd Ibn Ghaylān narrated to us; Abū Usāmah narrated to us; from Zakariyyāh Ibn Abī Zā'idah; from Sa'īd Ibn Abī Burdah that Anas Ibn Mālik (*raḍiyAllāhu 'anhu*) said:

'The Messenger of Allāh (ﷺ) said: "Allāh is pleased with a servant who eats a morsel and thereafter praises Him for it, or has a drink and thereafter praises Him for it.'"[195]

[194] Tirmidhī, #1858, this ḥadīth is supported by other evidence in the *Musnad* of Abū Ya'la, #7153 with slightly different wording.
[195] Muslim, #2734, and Tirmidhī, #1816.

CHAPTER TWENTY-NINE

بَابُ مَا جَاءَ فِي قَدَحِ رَسُولِ اللهِ ﷺ

What has been narrated concerning the Drinking Vessel (*qadaḥ*) of the Messenger of Allāh (ﷺ)

١٩٥ـ حَدَّثَنَا الْحُسَيْنُ بْنُ الأَسْوَدِ الْبَغْدَادِيُّ، قَالَ: حَدَّثَنَا عَمْرُو بْنُ مُحَمَّدٍ، قَالَ: حَدَّثَنَا عِيسَى بْنُ طَهْمَانَ، عَنْ ثَابِتٍ، قَالَ: «أَخْرَجَ إِلَيْنَا أَنَسُ بْنُ مَالِكٍ، قَدَحَ خَشَبٍ غَلِيظًا مُضَبَّبًا بِحَدِيدٍ، فَقَالَ: يَا ثَابِتُ! هَذَا قَدَحُ رَسُولِ اللهِ ﷺ».

195. Al-Ḥusayn Ibn al-Aswad al-Baghdādī narrated to us; ʿAmr Ibn Muḥammad narrated to us; ʿIsā Ibn Ṭahmān narrated to us that Thābit said: ʿAnas Ibn Mālik (*raḍiyAllāhu ʿanhu*) brought out to us a wooden drinking vessel (*qadaḥ*), clamped with iron, and said:

> "O Thābit, this is the drinking vessel of the Messenger of Allāh (ﷺ).'"[196]

١٩٦ـ حَدَّثَنَا عَبْدُ اللهِ بْنُ عَبْدِ الرَّحْمَنِ، قَالَ: أَنْبَأَنَا عَمْرُو بْنُ عَاصِمٍ، قَالَ: أَنْبَأَنَا حَمَّادُ بْنُ سَلَمَةَ، قَالَ: أَنْبَأَنَا حُمَيْدٌ، وَثَابِتٌ، عَنْ أَنَسٍ، قَالَ: «لَقَدْ سَقَيْتُ رَسُولَ اللهِ ﷺ

---

[196] This is a weak ḥadīth. Although Bukhārī does report something similar, #5638.

بِهَذَا الْقَدَحِ الشَّرَابَ كُلَّهُ؛ الْمَاءَ وَالنَّبِيذَ وَالْعَسَلَ وَاللَّبَنَ» .

196. 'Abdullāh Ibn 'Abdu'l-Raḥmān narrated to us; 'Amr Ibn 'Āṣim informed us; Ḥammād Ibn Salamah informed us; Ḥumayd and Thābit informed us that Anas (*raḍiyAllāhu 'anhu*) said:

> 'I gave the Messenger of Allāh (ﷺ) all types of drinks from this vessel, water, drink made from dates or grapes (*nabīdh*), honey and milk.'[197]

[197] Muslim, #2008.

CHAPTER THIRTY

بَابُ مَا جَاءَ فِي فَاكِهَةِ رَسُولِ اللهِ ﷺ

What has been narrated concerning the Description of the Fruits (*fākihah*) Eaten by the Messenger of Allāh (ﷺ)

١٩٧ـ حَدَّثَنَا إِسْمَاعِيلُ بْنُ مُوسَى الفَزَارِيُّ، قَالَ: حَدَّثَنَا إِبْرَاهِيمُ بْنُ سَعْدٍ، عَنْ أَبِيهِ، عَنْ عَبْدِ اللهِ، قَالَ: «كَانَ النَّبِيُّ ﷺ يَأْكُلُ القِثَّاءَ بِالرُّطَبِ» .

197. Ismāʿīl Ibn Mūsā al-Fazārī narrated to us; Ibrāhīm Ibn Saʿd narrated to us; from his father that ʿAbdullāh Ibn Jāʿfar (*raḍiyAllāhu ʿanhu*) said:

> "The Prophet (ﷺ) used to eat cucumber (*qithā'*) with fresh ripe dates (*ruṭab*)."[198]

١٩٨ـ حَدَّثَنَا عَبْدَةُ بْنُ عَبْدِ اللهِ الخُزَاعِيُّ البَصْرِيُّ، قَالَ: حَدَّثَنَا مُعَاوِيَةُ ابْنُ هِشَامٍ، عَنْ سُفْيَانَ، عَنْ هِشَامِ بْنِ عُرْوَةَ، عَنْ أَبِيهِ، عَنْ عَائِشَةَ: «أَنَّ النَّبِيَّ ﷺ كَانَ يَأْكُلُ البِطِّيخَ بِالرُّطَبِ» .

[198] Bukhārī, #5440, Muslim, #2043, and Tirmidhī, #1844.

198. ʿAbdah Ibn ʿAbdullāh al-Khuzāʿī al-Baṣrī narrated to us; Muʿāwiyah Ibn Hishām narrated to us; from Sufyān; from Hishām Ibn ʿUrwah; from his father that ʿĀ'ishah (*raḍiyAllāhu ʿanhā*) said:

> "The Prophet (ﷺ) used to eat watermelon (*biṭṭīkh*) with fresh ripe dates (*ruṭab*)."[199]

١٩٩ـ حَدَّثَنَا إِبْرَاهِيمُ بْنُ يَعْقُوبَ، قَالَ: حَدَّثَنَا وَهْبُ بْنُ جَرِيرٍ، قَالَ: حَدَّثَنَا أَبِي قَالَ: سَمِعْتُ حُمَيْدًا ـ أَوْ قَالَ: حَدَّثَنِي حُمَيْدٌ ـ قَالَ وَهْبٌ: وَكَانَ صَدِيقًا لَهُ، عَنْ أَنَسِ بْنِ مَالِكٍ قَالَ: «رَأَيْتُ رَسُولَ اللهِ ﷺ يَجْمَعُ بَيْنَ الخِرْبِزِ وَالرُّطَبِ».

199. Ibrāhīm Ibn Yaʿqūb narrated to us; Wahb Ibn Jarīr narrated to us; my father narrated to—he heard Ḥumayd say or Ḥumayd narrated to me—Wahb a friend of his, said:

> ʿAnas Ibn Mālik (*raḍiyAllāhu ʿanhu*) said: "I saw the Messenger of Allāh (ﷺ) combined between watermelon (*khirbiz*) and fresh ripe dates."[200]

٢٠٠ـ حَدَّثَنَا مُحَمَّدُ بْنُ يَحْيَى، قَالَ: حَدَّثَنَا مُحَمَّدُ بْنُ عَبْدِ العَزِيزِ الرَّمْلِيُّ، قَالَ: حَدَّثَنَا عَبْدُ اللهِ بْنُ يَزِيدَ بْنِ الصَّلْتِ، عَنْ مُحَمَّدِ بْنِ إِسْحَاقَ، عَنْ يَزِيدَ بْنِ رُومَانَ، عَنْ عُرْوَةَ، عَنْ عَائِشَةَ: «أَنَّ النَّبِيَّ ﷺ أَكَلَ البِطِّيخَ بِالرُّطَبِ».

200. Muḥammad Ibn Yaḥyā narrated to us; Muḥammad Ibn ʿAbdu'l-ʿAzīz al-Ramlī narrated to us; ʿAbdullāh Ibn Yazīd Ibn Ṣalt narrated to us; from Muḥammad Ibn Isḥāq; from Yazīd Ibn Rūmān; from ʿUrwah that ʿĀ'ishah (*raḍiyAllāhu ʿanhā*) said:

[199] Abū Dāwūd, #3836, and Tirmidhī, #1834.

[200] Aḥmad in his *Musnad*, #12449, #12460.

"The Prophet (ﷺ) ate watermelon with fresh ripe dates."[201]

٢٠١ـ حَدَّثَنَا قُتَيْبَةُ بْنُ سَعِيدٍ، عَنْ مَالِكِ بْنِ أَنَسٍ، (ح) وَحَدَّثَنَا إِسْحَاقُ ابْنُ مُوسَى، قَالَ: حَدَّثَنَا مَعْنٌ، قَالَ: حَدَّثَنَا مَالِكٌ، عَنْ سُهَيْلِ بْنِ أَبِي صَالِحٍ، عَنْ أَبِيهِ، عَنْ أَبِي هُرَيْرَةَ، قَالَ: كَانَ النَّاسُ إِذَا رَأَوْا أَوَّلَ الثَّمَرِ جَاءُوا بِهِ إِلَى رَسُولِ اللهِ ﷺ، فَإِذَا أَخَذَهُ رَسُولُ اللهِ ﷺ قَالَ: «اللَّهُمَّ بَارِكْ لَنَا فِي ثِمَارِنَا، وَبَارِكْ لَنَا فِي مَدِينَتِنَا، وَبَارِكْ لَنَا فِي صَاعِنَا، وَفِي مُدِّنَا، اللَّهُمَّ إِنَّ إِبْرَاهِيمَ عَبْدُكَ وَخَلِيلُكَ وَنَبِيُّكَ، وَإِنِّي عَبْدُكَ وَنَبِيُّكَ، وَإِنَّهُ دَعَاكَ لِمَكَّةَ، وَإِنِّي أَدْعُوكَ لِلْمَدِينَةِ بِمِثْلِ مَا دَعَاكَ بِهِ لِمَكَّةَ وَمِثْلِهِ مَعَهُ» قَالَ: ثُمَّ يَدْعُو أَصْغَرَ وَلِيدٍ يَرَاهُ فَيُعْطِيهِ ذَلِكَ الثَّمَرَ .

201. Qutaybah Ibn Sa'īd narrated to us; from Mālik Ibn Anas and Isḥāq Ibn Mūsā narrated to us; Mālik narrated to us; Ma'an narrated to us; from Suhayl Ibn Abī Ṣāliḥ; from his father that Abū Hurayrah (*raḍiyAllāhu 'anhu*) said:

> 'When the people saw the first fruits [of the harvest], they would bring it to the Messenger of Allāh (ﷺ), and when the Messenger of Allāh (ﷺ) would take them, he said:
>
> *"Allāhummā barik lanā fī thimārrinā, wa barik lanā fī madīnatinā, wa barik lanā fī sā'inaa wa fī muddinā.*
>
> *Allāhummā inna Ibrāhīma 'abduka wa khalīluka wa nabiyyuka, wa innī 'abduka wa nabiyyuka wa innahu da'āka li-makkah, wa innī ad'ūka lil-madīnah bimithli mā da'āka bihi li-makkah wa mithlihi ma'ahu."*
>
> "O Allāh, grant us blessing in our fruits, grant us blessing in our city, grant us blessing in our [measures of grain of]

[201] Abū Dāwūd, #3836, and Tirmidhī, #1834.

ṣāʿ and *mudd*.[202]

O Allāh, Ibrāhīm is Your servant (*ʿabd*), Your intimate friend (*khalīl*) and Your Prophet (*nabi*), I am Your servant (*ʿabd*) and Your Prophet (*nabi*).[203] He supplicated to You for Makkah, and I supplicate to You for Medīnah as he supplicated to You Makkah and more like it." He then would call the youngest child he could see and give him that fruit.'[204]

٢٠٢ـ حَدَّثَنَا مُحَمَّدُ بْنُ حُمَيْدٍ الرَّازِيُّ، قَالَ: حَدَّثَنَا إِبْرَاهِيمُ بْنُ الْمُخْتَارِ، عَنْ مُحَمَّدِ بْنِ إِسْحَاقَ، عَنْ أَبِي عُبَيْدَةَ بْنِ مُحَمَّدِ بْنِ عَمَّارِ بْنِ يَاسِرٍ، عَنِ الرُّبَيِّعِ بِنْتِ مُعَوِّذِ ابْنِ عَفْرَاءَ، قَالَتْ: «بَعَثَنِي مُعَاذُ بْنُ عَفْرَاءَ بِقِنَاعٍ مِنْ رُطَبٍ وَعَلَيْهِ أَجْرٍ مِنْ قِثَّاءٍ زُغْبٍ، وَكَانَ النَّبِيُّ ﷺ يُحِبُّ الْقِثَّاءَ، فَأَتَيْتُهُ بِهِ وَعِنْدَهُ حِلْيَةٌ قَدْ قَدِمَتْ عَلَيْهِ مِنَ الْبَحْرَيْنِ، فَمَلأَ يَدَهُ مِنْهَا فَأَعْطَانِيهِ».

202. Muḥammad Ibn Ḥumayd al-Rāzī narrated to us; Ibrāhīm Ibn al-Mukhtār narrated to us; from Muḥammad Ibn Isḥāq; from Abū ʿUbaydah Ibn Muḥammad Ibn ʿAmmār Ibn Yāsir that Al-Rabīʿ bint Muʿawwidh Ibn ʿAfrā' (*raḍiyAllāhu ʿanhā*) said:

'[My uncle] Muʿādh Ibn ʿAfrā' sent me with a tray of fresh ripe dates, on which there were pieces of cucumbers, as he [the Prophet (ﷺ)] used to love cucumbers, so I brought them to him. He has some jewellery that had been sent to

[202] These are two units of measurement: *Ṣāʿ* is equal to four *mudds* and each *mudd* is two handfuls.

[203] The Prophet (ﷺ) due to his great humility and humbleness did not say: *"wa khalīluka"*—"and Your intimate friend" when describing himself, even though his own rank is more distinguished and higher than that Prophet Ibrāhīm (*ʿalayhis-salām*) and Allāh knows best.

[204] Muslim, #2037, and Tirmidhī, #3454.

> him from Bahrain. He took hold of a handful and gave it to me.'[205]

٢٠٣ـ حَدَّثَنَا عَلِيُّ بْنُ حُجْرٍ، قَالَ: حَدَّثَنَا شَرِيكٌ، عَنْ عَبْدِ اللهِ بْنِ مُحَمَّدِ ابْنِ عَقِيلٍ، عَنِ الرُّبَيِّعِ بِنْتِ مُعَوِّذِ بْنِ عَفْرَاءَ، قَالَتْ: «أَتيتُ النَّبِيَّ ﷺ بِقِنَاعٍ مِنْ رُطَبٍ وَأَجْرٍ زُغْبٍ، فَأَعْطَانِي مِلءَ كَفِّهِ حُلِيًّا، أَوْ قَالَتْ: ذَهَبًا» .

203. 'Alī Ibn Ḥujr narrated to us; Sharīk narrated to us; from 'Abdullāh Ibn Muḥammad Ibn 'Aqīl that Al-Rabī' bint Mu'awwidh Ibn 'Afrā' (*raḍiyAllāhu 'anha*) said:

> 'I came to the Prophet (ﷺ) with a tray of fresh ripe dates and pieces of cucumber. He gave me a handful of jewellery or she said gold.'[206]

[205] *Sharh al-Sunnah* of al-Baghawi, #2897, this ḥadīth is weak.
[206] Aḥmad in his *Musnad*, #27020.

CHAPTER THIRTY-ONE

بَابُ مَا جَاءَ فِي صِفَةِ شَرَابِ رَسُولِ اللهِ ﷺ

What has been narrated concerning the Description of the Drinks (*sharāb*) of the Messenger of Allāh (ﷺ)

٢٠٤ـ حَدَّثَنَا ابْنُ أَبِي عُمَرَ، قَالَ: حَدَّثَنَا سُفْيَانُ، عَنْ مَعْمَرٍ، عَنِ الزُّهْرِيِّ، عَنْ عُرْوَةَ، عَنْ عَائِشَةَ، قَالَتْ: «كَانَ أَحَبَّ الشَّرَابِ إِلَى رَسُولِ اللهِ ﷺ الْحُلْوُ الْبَارِدُ».

204. Ibn Abī ʿUmar narrated to us; Sufyān narrated to us; from Maʿmar; from Al-Zuhrī; from ʿUrwah that ʿĀ'ishah (*raḍiyAllāhu ʿanhā*) said:

> 'The drink (*sharāb*) dearest to the Messenger of Allāh (ﷺ) was sweet and cold.'[207]

٢٠٥ـ حَدَّثَنَا أَحْمَدُ بْنُ مَنِيعٍ، قَالَ: حَدَّثَنَا إِسْمَاعِيلُ بْنُ إِبْرَاهِيمَ، قَالَ: حَدَّثَنَا عَلِيُّ ابْنُ زَيْدٍ، عَنْ عُمَرَ هُوَ ابْنُ أَبِي حَرْمَلَةَ، عَنِ ابْنِ عَبَّاسٍ، قَالَ: دَخَلْتُ مَعَ رَسُولِ اللهِ ﷺ أَنَا وَخَالِدُ بْنُ الْوَلِيدِ عَلَى مَيْمُونَةَ، فَجَاءَتْنَا بِإِنَاءٍ مِنْ لَبَنٍ، فَشَرِبَ رَسُولُ اللهِ ﷺ

---

[207] Tirmidhī, #1895.

وَأَنَا عَلَى يَمِينِهِ وَخَالِدٌ عَلَى شِمَالِهِ، فَقَالَ لِي: «الشَّرْبَةُ لَكَ؛ فَإِنْ شِئْتَ آثَرْتَ بِهَا خَالِدًا» فَقُلْتُ: مَا كُنْتُ لأُوثِرَ عَلَى سُؤْرِكَ أَحدًا، ثُمَّ قَالَ رَسُولُ اللهِ ﷺ: «مَنْ أَطْعَمَهُ اللهُ طَعَامًا، فَلْيَقُلْ: اللَّهُمَّ بَارِكْ لَنَا فِيهِ، وَأَطْعِمْنَا خَيْرًا مِنْهُ، وَمَنْ سَقَاهُ اللهُ ﷻ لَبَنًا، فَلْيَقُلْ: اللَّهُمَّ بَارِكْ لَنَا فِيهِ، وَزِدْنَا مِنْهُ»، ثُمَّ قَالَ: قَالَ رَسُولُ اللهِ ﷺ: «لَيْسَ شَيْءٌ يُجْزِئُ مَكَانَ الطَّعَامِ وَالشَّرَابِ غَيْرُ اللَّبَنِ».

205. Aḥmad Ibn Manīʿ narrated to us; Ismāʿīl Ibn Ibrāhīm narrated to us; ʿAlī Ibn Zayd narrated to us; from ʿUmar Ibn Abī Harmala that Ibn ʿAbbās (*raḍiyAllāhu ʿanhumā*) said:

> 'Together with the Messenger of Allāh (ﷺ), Khālid Ibn al-Walīd and I, visited Maymūnah. She brought for us a vessel filled with milk and the Messenger of Allāh (ﷺ) drank. I was on his right side while Khālid was on his left. So he said to me: "The drink is yours, but if you wish, you can prefer Khālid have it." I said: 'I would not give up your [blessed] leftover drink for anyone.' Then the Messenger of Allāh (ﷺ) said: "If Allāh feeds someone a meal, let him say: 'O Allāh, grant us blessing in it, and feed us something better than it.' If Allāh gives someone milk to drink, let him say: 'O Allāh grant us blessings in it and increase it for us.' Then the Messenger of Allāh (ﷺ) said: "There is nothing that suffices in place of food and drink other than milk."'[208]

Abū ʿIsā said: 'Maymūnah bint al-Ḥārithah is the wife of the Prophet (ﷺ) as well as the maternal aunt of Khālid Ibn al-Walīd, the maternal aunt of Ibn ʿAbbās and the maternal aunt of Yazīd Ibn al-Asamm (*raḍiyAllāhu ʿanhum*).

---

[208] Abū Dāwūd, #3730, and Tirmidhī, #2455, this ḥadīth is weak but does have supporting evidence refer to *Silsilah al-Saḥiḥah*, #2320.

CHAPTER THIRTY-TWO

بَابُ مَا جَاءَ فِي صِفَةِ شَرَابِ رَسُولِ اللهِ ﷺ

What has been narrated concerning the Manner of Drinking (*shurb*) of the Messenger of Allāh (ﷺ)

٢٠٦ـ حَدَّثَنَا أَحْمَدُ بْنُ مَنِيعٍ، قَالَ: حَدَّثَنَا هُشَيْمٌ، قَالَ: حَدَّثَنَا عَاصِمٌ الأَحْوَلُ، وَمُغِيرَةُ، عَنِ الشَّعْبِيِّ، عَنِ ابْنِ عَبَّاسٍ: «أَنَّ النَّبِيَّ ﷺ شَرِبَ مِنْ زَمْزَمَ وَهُوَ قَائِمٌ».

206. Aḥmad Ibn Manīʿ narrated to us; Hushīm narrated to us; ʿĀṣim al-Aḥwal and Mughīrah narrated to us; from Al-Shaʿbī that Ibn ʿAbbās (*raḍiyAllāhu ʿanhumā*) said:

"The Prophet (ﷺ) drank *Zamzam* [water] while standing."[209]

٢٠٧ـ حَدَّثَنَا قُتَيْبَةُ بْنُ سَعِيدٍ، قَالَ: حَدَّثَنَا مُحَمَّدُ بْنُ جَعْفَرٍ، عَنْ حُسَيْنٍ الْمُعَلِّمِ، عَنْ عَمْرِو بْنِ شُعَيْبٍ، عَنْ أَبِيهِ، عَنْ جَدِّهِ قَالَ: «رَأَيْتُ رَسُولَ اللهِ ﷺ يَشْرَبُ قَائِمًا وَقَاعِدًا».

---

[209] Bukhārī, #5617, Muslim, #2027, and Tirmidhī, #1882.

207. Qutaybah Ibn Sa'īd narrated to us; Muḥammad Ibn Jā'far narrated to us; from Ḥusayn al-Mu'allim; from 'Amr Ibn Shu'ayb; from his father that his grandfather said:

> "I saw the Messenger of Allāh (ﷺ) drink while standing and sitting."[210]

٢٠٨ـ حَدَّثَنَا عَلِيُّ بْنُ حُجْرٍ، قَالَ: حَدَّثَنَا ابْنُ الْمُبَارِكِ، عَنْ عَاصِمٍ الأَحْوَلِ، عَنِ الشَّعْبِيِّ، عَنِ ابْنِ عَبَّاسٍ، قَالَ: «سَقَيْتُ النَّبِيَّ ﷺ مِنْ زَمْزَمَ فَشَرِبَ وَهُوَ قَائِمٌ».

208. 'Alī Ibn Ḥujr narrated to us; Ibn al-Mubārak narrated to us; from 'Aṣim al-Aḥwal; from Al-Sha'bī that Ibn 'Abbās (*raḍiyAllāhu 'anhumā*) said:

> "I gave the Prophet (ﷺ) *Zamzam* water, and he drank it while standing."[211]

٢٠٩ـ حَدَّثَنَا أَبُو كُرَيْبٍ مُحَمَّدُ بْنُ العَلَاءِ، وَمُحَمَّدُ بْنُ طَرِيفٍ الكُوفِيُّ، قَالَا: حَدَّثَنَا ابْنُ الفُضَيْلِ، عَنِ الأَعْمَشِ، عَنْ عَبْدِ المَلِكِ بْنِ مَيْسَرَةَ، عَنِ النَّزَّالِ بْنِ سَبْرَةَ قَالَ: أَتَى عَلِيٌّ بِكُوزٍ مِنْ مَاءٍ وَهُوَ فِي الرَّحْبَةِ، فَأَخَذَ مِنْهُ كَفًّا فَغَسَلَ يَدَيْهِ، وَمَضْمَضَ وَاسْتَنْشَقَ، وَمَسَحَ وَجْهَهُ، وَذِرَاعَيْهِ، وَرَأْسَهُ، ثُمَّ شَرِبَ وَهُوَ قَائِمٌ، ثُمَّ قَالَ: هَذَا وُضُوءُ مَنْ لَمْ يُحْدِثْ، هَكَذَا رَأَيْتُ رَسُولَ اللهِ ﷺ فَعَلَ.

209. Abū Kurayb Muḥammad Ibn al-'Alā' and Muḥammad Ibn Tarif al-Kufi narrated to us; Ibn Al-Fuḍayl narrated to us; from Al-A'mash; 'Abdu'l-Mālik Ibn al-Maysarah that Al-Nazzāl Ibn Sabrah said:

---

[210] Abū Dāwūd, #653, Tirmidhī, #1883, and Ibn Mājah, #931.
[211] Bukhārī, #5617, Muslim, #2027, and Tirmidhī, #1882

> "Alī was presented with a jug of water while he was in al-Rahbah. He took a handful of it and washed his hands, gargled, sniffed water up the nose, and then wiped his face, forearms and head. He then drank from it while standing. Then he said: 'This is the ablution of one who is not ritually impure. This is how I saw the Messenger of Allāh (ﷺ) perform it."[212]

٢١٠ـ حَدَّثَنَا قُتَيْبَةُ بْنُ سَعِيدٍ، وَيُوسُفُ بْنُ حَمَّادٍ، قَالَا: حَدَّثَنَا عَبْدُ الوَارِثِ ابْنُ سَعِيدٍ، عَنْ أَبِي عِصَامٍ، عَنْ أَنَسِ بْنِ مَالِكٍ، أَنَّ النَّبِيَّ ﷺ: «كَانَ يَتَنَفَّسُ فِي الإِنَاءِ ثَلَاثًا إِذَا شَرِبَ، وَيَقُولُ: هُوَ أَمْرَأُ وَأَرْوَى».

210. Qutaybah Ibn Sa'īd and Yūsuf Ibn Ḥammād narrated to us; 'Abdu'l-Wārith Ibn Sa'īd narrated to us; from Abū 'Aṣām that Anas Ibn Mālik (*raḍiyAllāhu 'anhu*) said:

> 'The Prophet (ﷺ) used to take three breaths in a vessel when he drank, and would say: "It is more palatable and thirst-quenching."'[213]

٢١١ـ حَدَّثَنَا عَلِيُّ بْنُ خَشْرَمٍ، قَالَ: حَدَّثَنَا عِيسَى بْنُ يُونُسَ، عَنْ رِشْدِينَ ابْنِ كُرَيْبٍ، عَنْ أَبِيهِ، عَنِ ابْنِ عَبَّاسٍ: «أَنَّ النَّبِيَّ ﷺ كَانَ إِذَا شَرِبَ تَنَفَّسَ مَرَّتَيْنِ».

211. 'Alī Ibn Khasham narrated to us; 'Isā Ibn Yūnus narrated to us; from Rishdayn Ibn Kurayb; from his father that Ibn Abbās (*raḍiyAllāhu 'anhumā*) said:

> 'When the Prophet (ﷺ) drank, he used to take two

[212] Bukhārī, #5615 and Abū Dāwūd, #3718.
[213] Muslim, #2028, and Tirmidhī, #1884.

breaths.'[214]

٢١٢ـ حَدَّثَنَا ابْنُ أَبِي عُمَرَ، قَالَ: حَدَّثَنَا سُفْيَانُ، عَنْ يَزِيدَ بْنِ يَزِيدَ بْنِ جَابِرٍ، عَنْ عَبْدِ الرَّحْمَنِ بْنِ أَبِي عَمْرَةَ، عَنْ جَدَّتِهِ كَبْشَةَ، قَالَتْ: «دَخَلَ عَلَيَّ النَّبِيُّ ﷺ فَشَرِبَ مِنْ فِي قِرْبَةٍ مُعَلَّقَةٍ قَائِمًا»، فَقُمْتُ إِلَى فِيهَا فَقَطَعْتُهُ.

212. Ibn Abī 'Umar narrated to us; Sufyān narrated to us; from Yazīd Ibn Yazīd Ibn Jābir; from 'Abdu'l-Raḥmān Ibn Abī 'Amrah that his grandmother Kabshah [bint Thabit] (*raḍiyAllāhu 'anhā*) said:

> 'The Prophet (ﷺ) entered my house, then he drank from the mouth of a hanging waterskin while standing, so I stood up and and cut it off [in order to preserve where he placed his mouth upon and keep it for blessings].'[215]

٢١٣ـ حَدَّثَنَا مُحَمَّدُ بْنُ بَشَّارٍ، قَالَ: حَدَّثَنَا عَبْدُ الرَّحْمَنِ بْنُ مَهْدِيٍّ، قَالَ: حَدَّثَنَا عَزْرَةُ بْنُ ثَابِتٍ الأَنْصَارِيُّ، عَنْ ثُمَامَةَ بْنِ عَبْدِ اللهِ، قَالَ: كَانَ أَنَسُ بْنُ مَالِكٍ، يَتَنَفَّسُ فِي الإِنَاءِ ثَلَاثًا، وَزَعَمَ أَنَسٌ «أَنَّ النَّبِيَّ ﷺ كَانَ يَتَنَفَّسُ فِي الإِنَاءِ ثَلَاثًا».

213. Muḥammad Ibn Bashshār narrated to us; 'Abdu'l-Raḥmān Ibn Mahdī narrated to us; 'Urwah Ibn Thābit al-Anṣārī that Thumāmah Ibn 'Abdullāh (*raḍiyAllāhu 'anhu*) said:

> 'Anas Ibn Mālik used to take three breaths in a vessel when he drank, and Anas Ibn Mālik asserted that the Prophet (ﷺ) also used to take three breaths in a vessel.'[216]

[214] Tirmidhī, #1886 and Ibn Mājah, #3417, this ḥadith is weak.
[215] Tirmidhī, #1892 and Ibn Mājah, #3423.
[216] Bukhārī, #5631, Muslim, #2028, and Tirmidhī, #1884.

٢١٤ـ حَدَّثَنَا عَبْدُ اللهِ بْنُ عَبْدِ الرَّحْمَنِ، قَالَ: حَدَّثَنَا أَبُو عَاصِمٍ، عَنِ ابْنِ جُرَيْجٍ، عَنْ عَبْدِ الكَرِيمِ، عَنِ البَرَاءِ بْنِ زَيْدٍ ـ ابْنِ ابْنَةِ أَنَسِ بْنِ مَالِكٍ ـ عَنْ أَنَسِ ابْنِ مَالِكٍ: «أَنَّ النَّبِيَّ ﷺ دَخَلَ عَلَى أُمِّ سُلَيْمٍ وَقِرْبَةٌ مُعَلَّقَةٌ، فَشَرِبَ مِنْ فَمِ القِرْبَةِ وَهُوَ قَائِمٌ، فَقَامَتْ أُمُّ سُلَيْمٍ إِلَى رَأْسِ القِرْبَةِ فَقَطَعَتْهَا».

214. 'Abdullāh Ibn 'Abdu'l-Raḥmān narrated to us; Abū 'Āṣim narrated to us; from Ibn Jurayj; from 'Abdu'l-Karīm; from Al-Barā' Ibn Zayd, the son of Anas Ibn Mālik's daughter that Anas Ibn Mālik (*raḍiyAllāhu 'anhu*) said:

> 'The Prophet (ﷺ) entered the house of Umm Sulaym, and a waterskin was hanging there, so he drank from the mouth of the waterskin while standing. Umm Sulaym stood up and cut off the mouth of the waterskin.'[217]

٢١٥ـ حَدَّثَنَا أَحْمَدُ بْنُ نَصْرٍ النَّيْسَابُورِيُّ، قَالَ: حَدَّثَنَا إِسْحَاقُ بْنُ مُحَمَّدٍ الفَرْوِيُّ، قَالَ: حَدَّثَتْنَا عُبَيْدَةُ بِنْتُ نَائِلٍ، عَنْ عَائِشَةَ بِنْتِ سَعْدِ بْنِ أَبِي وَقَّاصٍ، عَنْ أَبِيهَا «أَنَّ النَّبِيَّ ﷺ كَانَ يَشْرَبُ قَائِمًا»، قَالَ أَبُو عِيسَى: وَقَالَ بَعْضُهُمْ: عُبَيْدَةُ بِنْتُ نَابِلٍ.

215. Aḥmad Ibn Naṣr al-Naysābūrī narrated to us; Isḥāq Ibn Muḥammad al-Farwī narrated to us; 'Ubaydah bint Nā'il narrated to us; from 'Ā'ishah bint Sa'd Ibn Ibn Abī Waqqāṣ that her father (*raḍiyAllāhu 'anhu*) said:

> 'The Prophet (ﷺ) drank water while standing.'[218]

Abū 'Isā said: 'Some of them said 'Ubaydah bint Nābil.'

---

[217] Aḥmad in his *Musnad*, #12188.

[218] In this chain there is an unknown narrator which makes the ḥadīh weak.

CHAPTER THIRTY-THREE

بَابُ مَا جَاءَ فِي تَعَطُّرِ رَسُولِ اللهِ ﷺ

What has been narrated concerning the Perfuming (*taʿaṭṭur*) of the Messenger of Allāh (ﷺ)

٢١٦ـ حَدَّثَنَا مُحَمَّدُ بْنُ رَافِعٍ، وَغَيْرُ وَاحِدٍ، قَالُوا: حَدَّثَنَا أَبُو أَحْمَدَ الزُّبَيْرِيُّ قَالَ: حَدَّثَنَا شَيْبَانُ، عَنْ عَبْدِ اللهِ بْنِ الْمُخْتَارِ، عَنْ مُوسَى بْنِ أَنَسِ بْنِ مَالِكٍ، عَنْ أَبِيهِ، قَالَ: «كَانَ لِرَسُولِ اللهِ ﷺ سُكَّةٌ يَتَطَيَّبُ مِنْهَا».

216. Muḥammad Ibn Rāfiʿ and others narrated to us; Abū Aḥmad al-Zubayrī narrated to us; Shaybān narrated to us; from ʿAbdullāh Ibn al-Mukhtār; from Mūsā Ibn Anas Ibn Mālik that his father (*raḍiyAllāhu ʿanhu*) said:

> 'The Messenger of Allāh (ﷺ) used to have a vial of perfume blend (*sukkah*) from which he used to perfume himself.'[219]

٢١٧ـ حَدَّثَنَا مُحَمَّدُ بْنُ بَشَّارٍ، قَالَ: حَدَّثَنَا عَبْدُ الرَّحْمَنِ بْنُ مَهْدِيٍّ، قَالَ: حَدَّثَنَا عَزْرَةُ بْنُ ثَابِتٍ، عَنْ ثُمَامَةَ بْنِ عَبْدِ اللهِ، قَالَ: كَانَ أَنَسُ بْنُ مَالِكٍ لَا يَرُدُّ الطِّيبَ، وَقَالَ أَنَسٌ: «إِنَّ النَّبِيَّ ﷺ كَانَ لَا يَرُدُّ الطِّيبَ».

[219] Tirmidhī, #991, Nasā'ī, #1905, and Aḥmad, #11311.

217. Muḥammad Ibn Bashshār narrated to us; 'Abdu'l-Raḥmān Ibn Mahdī narrated to us; 'Urwah Ibn Thābit al-Anṣārī that Thumāmah Ibn 'Abdullāh (*raḍiyAllāhu 'anhu*) said:

> 'Anas Ibn Mālik never refused perfume (*ṭayyib*), and he would say: 'The Prophet (ﷺ) never refused perfume (*ṭayyib*).'[220]

٢١٨ـ حَدَّثَنَا قُتَيْبَةُ بْنُ سَعِيدٍ، قَالَ: حَدَّثَنَا ابْنُ أَبِي فُدَيْكٍ، عَنْ عَبْدِ اللهِ ابْنِ مُسْلِمِ بْنِ جُنْدُبٍ، عَنْ أَبِيهِ، عَنِ ابْنِ عُمَرَ، قَالَ: قَالَ رَسُولُ اللهِ ﷺ: «ثَلَاثٌ لَا تُرَدُّ: الوَسَائِدُ، وَالدُّهْنُ، وَاللَّبَنُ» .

218. Qutaybah Ibn Sa'īd narrated to us; Ibn Abī Fudayk narrated to us; from 'Abdullāh Ibn Muslim Ibn Jundub; from his father that Ibn 'Umar (*raḍiyAllāhu 'anhuma*) said:

> 'The Messenger of Allāh (ﷺ) said: "Three things should not be rejected: a cushion [to lean upon], [fragrant] oils (*duhn*) and milk."'[221]

٢١٩ـ حَدَّثَنَا مَحْمُودُ بْنُ غَيْلَانَ، قَالَ: حَدَّثَنَا أَبُو دَاوُدَ الحَفَرِيُّ، عَنْ سُفْيَانَ، عَنِ الجُرَيْرِيِّ، عَنْ أَبِي نَضْرَةَ، عَنْ رَجُلٍ، عَنْ أَبِي هُرَيْرَةَ، قَالَ: قَالَ رَسُولُ اللهِ ﷺ: «طِيبُ الرِّجَالِ: مَا ظَهَرَ رِيحُهُ وَخَفِيَ لَوْنُهُ، وَطِيبُ النِّسَاءِ: مَا ظَهَرَ لَوْنُهُ وَخَفِيَ رِيحُهُ» .

219. Maḥmūd Ibn Ghaylān narrated to us; Abū Dāwūd al-Ḥafarī narrated to us; from Sufyān; from Al-Jarīrī; from Abū Naḍrah; from a man from Al-Tafāwī that Abū Hurayrah (*raḍiyAllāhu 'anhu*) said:

> 'The Messenger of Allāh (ﷺ) said: "The perfume of men

[220] Bukhārī, #5929, and Tirmidhī, #2789.
[221] Tirmidhī, #2890.

is such that its fragrance is apparent, yet its colour is hidden, and the perfume of women is such that its colour is apparent, yet its fragrance is hidden.'"[222]

٢٢٠ـ حَدَّثَنَا عَلِيُّ بْنُ حُجْرٍ، قَالَ: أَنْبَأَنَا إِسْمَاعِيلُ بْنُ إِبْرَاهِيمَ، عَنِ الْجُرَيْرِيِّ، عَنْ أَبِي نَضْرَةَ، عَنِ الطُّفَاوِيِّ، عَنْ أَبِي هُرَيْرَةَ، عَنِ النَّبِيِّ ﷺ مِثْلَهُ بِمَعْنَاهُ .

220. ʿAlī Ibn Ḥujr narrated to us; Ismāʿīl Ibn Ibrāhīm informed us; from Al-Jarīrī; from Abū Naḍrah; from Al-Tafāwī; from Abū Hurayrah (*raḍiyAllāhu ʿanhu*) that the Prophet (ﷺ) made similar statement with the same meaning.[223]

٢٢١ـ حَدَّثَنَا مُحَمَّدُ بْنُ خَلِيفَةَ، وَعَمْرُو بْنُ عَلِيٍّ، قَالَا: حَدَّثَنَا يَزِيدُ ابْنُ زُرَيْعٍ، قَالَ: حَدَّثَنَا حَجَّاجٌ الصَّوَّافُ، عَنْ حَنَانٍ، عَنْ أَبِي عُثْمَانَ النَّهْدِيِّ، قَالَ: قَالَ رَسُولُ اللهِ ﷺ: «إِذَا أُعْطِيَ أَحَدُكُمُ الرَّيْحَانَ فَلَا يَرُدَّهُ؛ فَإِنَّهُ خَرَجَ مِنَ الْجَنَّةِ» .

قَالَ أَبُو عِيسَى: وَلَا نَعْرِفُ لِحَنَانٍ غَيْرَ هَذَا الْحَدِيثِ.

221. Muḥammad Ibn Khalīfah and ʿAmr Ibn ʿAlī narrated to us; Yazīd Ibn Zurayʿ narrated to us; Ḥajjāj al-Ṣawwāf narrated to us; from Hannān that Abū ʿUthmān al-Nahdī said:

> 'The Messenger of Allāh (ﷺ) said: "If anyone of you is offered a flower (*rayḥān*), he should not refuse it, for it comes from Paradise."'[224]

Abū ʿIsā said: 'We do not know of any other tradition narrated

---

[222] Abū Dāwūd, #2174, and Tirmidhī, #2787.

[223] Tirmdhī, this ḥadith is weak due to an unknown narrator.

[224] Tirmidhī, #2791, this ḥadith does not necessitates that the perfume itself is from Paradise but that pure fragrances and pleasant smells come from Paradise and Allah knows best.

by Hannān other than this.'

٢٢٢ـ حَدَّثَنَا عُمَرُ بْنُ إِسْمَاعِيلَ بْنِ مُجَالِدِ بْنِ سَعِيدٍ الهَمْدَانِيُّ، قَالَ: حَدَّثَنَا أَبِي، عَنْ بَيَانٍ، عَنْ قَيْسِ بْنِ أَبِي حَازِمٍ، عَنْ جَرِيرِ بْنِ عَبْدِ اللهِ، قَالَ: عُرِضْتُ بَيْنَ يَدَيْ عُمَرَ بْنِ الخَطَّابِ، فَأَلْقَى جَرِيرٌ رِدَاءَهُ وَمَشَى فِي إِزَارٍ، فَقَالَ لَهُ: خُذْ رِدَاءَكَ؛ فَقَالَ عُمَرُ لِلْقَوْمِ: مَا رَأَيْتُ رَجُلًا أَحْسَنَ إِلَّا مَا بَلَغَنَا مِنْ صُورَةِ يُوسُفَ عليه السلام.

222. 'Umar Ibn Ismā'īl Ibn Mujālid Ibn Sa'īd al-Hamdānī narrated to us; my father narrated to me; from Bayān; from Qays Ibn Abī Hāzim that Jarīr Ibn 'Abdullāh (*raḍiyAllāhu 'anhu*) said:

> 'I was brought before 'Umar Ibn al-Khaṭṭāb (*raḍiyAllāhu 'anhu*), whereupon Jarir removed his upper garment and walked only in his loincloth (*izār*), he said to him: 'Take your upper garment.' Then 'Umar said to the people: 'I have not seen a man with a more handsome form than Jarīr, except for what has reached us regarding the [handsome] form of [Prophet] Yūsuf (*'alayhis-salām*).'"[225]

[225] *Musnad al-Farūq* of Ibn Kathīr, 2/682, this is a weak ḥadīth. However this narration has no relevance to this chapter. Some of the scholars have given their explanations to why this narration is in this chapter; from them is that it was added mistakenly by the transcribers or that a handsome form necessitates a pleasant smell and Allah knows best.

CHAPTER THIRTY-FOUR

بَابُ كَيْفَ كَانَ كَلَامُ رَسُولِ اللهِ ﷺ

What has been narrated concerning the Manner of Speech (*kalām*) of the Messenger of Allāh (ﷺ)

٢٢٣ـ حَدَّثَنَا حُمَيْدُ بْنُ مَسْعَدَةَ الْبَصْرِيُّ، قَالَ: حَدَّثَنَا حُمَيْدُ بْنُ الأَسْوَدِ، عَنْ أُسَامَةَ بْنِ زَيْدٍ، عَنِ الزُّهْرِيِّ، عَنْ عُرْوَةَ، عَنْ عَائِشَةَ قَالَتْ: «مَا كَانَ رَسُولُ اللهِ ﷺ يَسْرُدُ سَرْدَكُمْ هَذَا، وَلَكِنَّهُ كَانَ يَتَكَلَّمُ بِكَلَامٍ بَيِّنٍ فَصْلٍ، يَحْفَظُهُ مَنْ جَلَسَ إِلَيْهِ».

223. Ḥumayd Ibn Masʿadah al-Baṣrī narrated to us; Ḥumayd Ibn al-Aswad narrated to us; from Usāmah Ibn Zayd; from Al-Zuhrī; from ʿUrwah that ʿĀ'ishah (*raḍiyAllāhu ʿanhā*) said:

> 'The Messenger of Allāh (ﷺ) would not hasten [or speak relentlessly in] his speech as you do. Rather, he would speak clearly and distinctly (*faṣl*), so that those who sat with him would remember what he said.'[226]

٢٢٤ـ حَدَّثَنَا مُحَمَّدُ بْنُ يَحْيَى، قَالَ: حَدَّثَنَا أَبُو قُتَيْبَةَ سَلْمُ بْنُ قُتَيْبَةَ، عَنْ عَبْدِ اللهِ بْنِ الْمُثَنَّى، عَنْ ثُمَامَةَ، عَنْ أَنَسِ بْنِ مَالِكٍ، قَالَ: «كَانَ رَسُولُ اللهِ ﷺ يُعِيدُ

[226] Tirmidhī, #3639, the source of this ḥadīth is found in Bukhārī, #3568 and Muslim, #2493 with a slightly different wording.

الكَلِمَةَ ثَلَاثًا لِتُعْقَلَ عَنْهُ».

224. Muḥammad Ibn Yaḥyā narrated to us; Abū Qutaybah Salm Ibn Qutaybah narrated to us; from 'Abdullāh Ibn Muthannā; from Thumāmah that Anas Ibn Mālik (*raḍiyAllāhu 'anhu*) said:

> 'The Messenger of Allāh (ﷺ) used to repeat each expression (*kalimah*) three times, so that it may be understood from him.'[227]

٢٢٥ـ حَدَّثَنَا سُفْيَانُ بْنُ وَكِيعٍ، قَالَ: حَدَّثَنَا جُمَيْعُ بْنُ عُمَيْرِ بْنِ عَبْدِ الرَّحْمَنِ العِجْلِيُّ، قَالَ: حَدَّثَنِي رَجُلٌ مِنْ بَنِي تَمِيمٍ مِنْ وَلَدِ أَبِي هَالَةَ زَوْجِ خَدِيجَةَ يُكْنَى أَبَا عَبْدِ اللهِ، عَنِ ابْنٍ لأَبِي هَالَةَ، عَنِ الحَسَنِ بْنِ عَلِيٍّ، قَالَ: سَأَلْتُ خَالِي هِنْدَ بْنَ أَبِي هَالَةَ، وَكَانَ وَصَّافًا، فَقُلْتُ: صِفْ لِي مَنْطِقَ رَسُولِ اللهِ ﷺ قَالَ: «كَانَ رَسُولُ اللهِ ﷺ مُتَوَاصِلَ الأَحْزَانِ، دَائِمَ الفِكْرَةِ، لَيْسَتْ لَهُ رَاحَةٌ، طَوِيلَ السَّكْتِ، لَا يَتَكَلَّمُ فِي غَيْرِ حَاجَةٍ، يَفْتَتِحُ الكَلَامَ وَيَخْتِمُهُ بِاسْمِ اللهِ تَعَالَى، وَيَتَكَلَّمُ بِجَوَامِعِ الكَلِمِ، كَلَامُهُ فَصْلٌ، لَا فُضُولَ وَلَا تَقْصِيرَ، لَيْسَ بِالجَافِي وَلَا المَهِينِ، يُعَظِّمُ النِّعْمَةَ وَإِنْ دَقَّتْ، لَا يَذُمُّ مِنْهَا شَيْئًا، غَيْرَ أَنَّهُ لَمْ يَكُنْ يَذُمُّ ذَوَاقًا وَلَا يَمْدَحُهُ، وَلَا تُغْضِبُهُ الدُّنْيَا، وَلَا مَا كَانَ لَهَا، فَإِذَا تُعُدِّيَ الحَقُّ لَمْ يَقُمْ لِغَضَبِهِ شَيْءٌ حَتَّى يَنْتَصِرَ لَهُ، وَلَا يَغْضَبُ لِنَفْسِهِ، وَلَا يَنْتَصِرُ لَهَا، إِذَا أَشَارَ أَشَارَ بِكَفِّهِ كُلِّهَا، وَإِذَا تَعَجَّبَ قَلَبَهَا، وَإِذَا تَحَدَّثَ اتَّصَلَ بِهَا، وَضَرَبَ بِرَاحَتِهِ اليُمْنَى بَطْنَ إِبْهَامِهِ اليُسْرَى، وَإِذَا غَضِبَ أَعْرَضَ وَأَشَاحَ، وَإِذَا فَرِحَ غَضَّ طَرْفَهُ، جُلُّ ضَحِكِهِ التَّبَسُّمُ، يَفْتَرُّ عَنْ مِثْلِ حَبِّ الغَمَامِ».

225. Sufyān Ibn Waki'narrated to us; Jumay' Ibn 'Umar Ibn 'Abdu'l-Raḥmān al-'Ijlī narrated to us; a man from Banu Tamīm, one

[227] Bukhārī, #6244, and Tirmidhī, #3640.

of the sons of Abū Ḥālah, the husband of Khadījah, Abū ʿAbdullāh narrated to me; from Ibn Abī Ḥālah that Ḥasan Ibn ʿAlī (*raḍiyAllāhu ʿanhumā*) said:

> 'I asked my maternal uncle, Hind Ibn Abī Ḥālah, who was skilled at describing [the Prophet (ﷺ)]. I said: 'Describe for me the manner in which the Messenger of Allāh (ﷺ) would speak.' He said: 'The Messenger of Allāh was constantly sympathetic with sorrows (*mutawāsil al-ahzān*), and always in deep thought, and he never found a moment in which he was free of thought. He would remain silent for prolonged periods, and would not speak unnecessarily (*ghayr ḥājah*). He would begin and conclude his speech with the name of Allāh, the Most High. He would speak using simple words bearing profound meanings (*jawāmiʿ al-kalim*), his words would be distinct (*faṣl*), neither excessive (*fuḍūl*) nor inadequate (*taqsīr*). He was neither harsh (*jāfī*) nor one to shame others (*muhīn*). He would appreciate a blessing (*niʿma*), however small, and he wound not find fault with any aspect of it. He neither condemned nor praised food and drink, and he would not be angered by this world [and what was for it]. If, however, a right was violated, then nothing could stand in the way of his anger until he defended it. He would not be angry for his own sake, nor come to his own defence. When he pointed towards something, he would do so with his entire hand, and when he was astonished, he turned it over, and when spoke, he gestured with his hands, and placed his right palm over the base of his left thumb. When he was angered, he would direct his attention away [from that person], and when he was happy, he lowered his gaze. Most of his laughter was but a smile, beautifully revealing [his teeth] as white as hailstones.'[228]

[228] Ṭabarānī in *al-Kabīr*, 22/155-159. This ḥadith has a weak chain although some of the wording has been established in other authentic narrations.

CHAPTER THIRTY-FIVE

بَابُ مَا جَاءَ فِي ضَحِكِ رَسُولِ اللهِ ﷺ

What has been narrated concerning the Laughter (*ḍaḥik*) of the Messenger of Allāh (ﷺ)

٢٢٦ـ حَدَّثَنَا أَحْمَدُ بْنُ مَنِيعٍ، قَالَ حَدَّثَنَا عَبَّادُ بْنُ العَوَّامِ، قَالَ أَخْبَرَنَا الحَجَّاجُ وَهُوَ ابْنُ أَرْطَاةَ، عَنْ سِمَاكِ بْنِ حَرْبٍ، عَنْ جَابِرِ بْنِ سَمُرَةَ، قَالَ: «كَانَ فِي سَاقَيْ رَسُولِ اللهِ ﷺ حُمُوشَةٌ، وَكَانَ لَا يَضْحَكُ إِلَّا تَبَسُّمًا، فَكُنْتُ إِذَا نَظَرْتُ إِلَيْهِ قُلْتُ: أَكْحَلُ العَيْنَيْنِ، وَلَيْسَ بِأَكْحَلَ» .

226. Aḥmad Ibn Manīʿ narrated to us; ʿAbbad Ibn ʿAwwām narrated to us; Al-Ḥajjāj Ibn Arṭā'a informed us; from Simāk Ibn Ḥarb that Jābir Ibn Samurah (*raḍiyAllāhu ʿanhu*) said:

> 'The shins of the Messenger of Allāh (ﷺ) were slender, and his laugher would only consist of a joyful smile, so when I looked at him, I would say to myself: 'His eyes were applied with kohl (*kuḥl*), when in fact they were not."[229]

[229] Tirmidhī, #3645 and this ḥadīth is weak.

٢٢٧ـ حَدَّثَنَا قُتَيْبَةُ بْنُ سَعِيدٍ، قَالَ: أَخْبَرَنَا ابْنُ لَهِيعَةَ، عَنْ عُبَيْدِ اللهِ ابْنِ الْمُغِيرَةِ، عَنْ عَبْدِ اللهِ بنِ الحَارِثِ بنِ جَزْءٍ، أَنَّهُ قَالَ: «مَا رَأَيْتُ أَحَدًا أَكْثَرَ تَبَسُّمًا مِنْ رَسُولِ اللهِ ﷺ».

227. Qutaybah Ibn Sa'id narrated to us; Ibn Lahī'ah informed us; from 'Ubaydullāh Ibn al-Mughīrah that 'Abdullāh Ibn Ḥārith Ibn Jaz' (*raḍiyAllāhu 'anhu*) said:

> 'I never saw anyone who smiled more abundantly than the Messenger of Allāh (ﷺ).'[230]

٢٢٨ـ حَدَّثَنَا أَحْمَدُ بْنُ خَالِدٍ الخَلَّالُ، قَالَ: حَدَّثَنَا يَحْيَى بْنُ إِسْحَاقَ السَّيْلَحَانِيُّ، قَالَ: حَدَّثَنَا لَيْثُ بْنُ سَعْدٍ، عَنْ يَزِيدَ بْنِ أَبِي حَبِيبٍ، عَنْ عَبْدِ اللهِ بْنِ الحَارِثِ، قَالَ: «مَا كَانَ ضَحِكُ رَسُولِ اللهِ ﷺ إِلَّا تَبَسُّمًا».

228. Aḥmad Ibn Khālid al-Khallāl narrated to us; Yaḥyā Ibn Isḥāq al-Saylahānī narrated to us; Layth Ibn Sa'd narrated to us; from Yazīd Ibn Abī Ḥabīb that 'Abdullāh Ibn Ḥārith (*raḍiyAllāhu 'anhu*) said:

> 'The laughter of the Messenger of Allāh (ﷺ) was nothing but a smile.'[231]

٢٢٩ـ حَدَّثَنَا أَبُو عَمَّارٍ الْحُسَيْنُ بْنُ حُرَيْثٍ، قَالَ: حَدَّثَنَا وَكِيعٌ، قَالَ: حَدَّثَنَا الأَعْمَشُ، عَنِ المَعْرُورِ بْنِ سُوَيْدٍ، عَنْ أَبِي ذَرٍّ، قَالَ: قَالَ رَسُولُ اللهِ ﷺ: «إِنِّي لأَعْلَمُ

[230] Tirmidhī, #3641 and Bayhaqī in *Shu'ab al-Īmān*, 6/251.
[231] Tirmidhī, #3642, and he said this ḥadith is ṣaḥīḥ gharīb.

أَوَّلَ رَجُلٍ يَدْخُلُ الْجَنَّةَ، وَآخِرَ رَجُلٍ يَخْرُجُ مِنَ النَّارِ، يُؤْتَى بِالرَّجُلِ يَوْمَ الْقِيَامَةِ فَيُقَالُ: اعْرِضُوا عَلَيْهِ صِغَارَ ذُنُوبِهِ، وَيُخَبَّأُ عَنْهُ كِبَارُهَا، فَيُقَالُ لَهُ: عَمِلتَ يَوْمَ كَذَا وَكَذَا كَذَا، وَهُوَ مُقِرٌّ لَا يُنْكِرُ، وَهُوَ مُشْفِقٌ مِنْ كِبَارِهَا، فَيُقَالُ: أَعْطُوهُ مَكَانَ كُلِّ سَيِّئَةٍ عَمِلَهَا حَسَنَةً، فَيَقُولُ: إِنَّ لِي ذُنُوبًا مَا أَرَاهَا هَهُنَا!»، قَالَ أَبُو ذَرٍّ: «فَلَقَدْ رَأَيْتُ رَسُولَ اللهِ ﷺ ضَحِكَ حَتَّى بَدَتْ نَوَاجِذُهُ».

229. Abū 'Ammar al-Ḥusayn Ibn Ḥārith narrated to us; Waki' narrated to us; Al-A'mash narrated to us; from Al-Ma'rūr Ibn Suwayd that Abū Dhārr (*raḍiyAllāhu 'anhu*) said:

> 'The Messenger of Allāh (ﷺ) said: "I know the first man who will enter Paradise and the last man who will exit from the Fire of Hell. The man will be brought on Day of Resurrection and it will be said to him: 'Present to him his minor sins and let his major sins be hidden from him!' He will be told: 'On such-and-such a day, you committed such-and-such sins.' He will acknowledge it and will not deny, while being fearful of those sins that are major. Then it will be said: 'Give him in place of every bad deed he committed a good deed.' He will then say: 'I have sins [greater] that I do not see here."'
>
> Abū Dharr (*raḍiyAllāhu 'anhu*) said: 'I saw the Messenger of Allāh (ﷺ) laugh until his molar teeth were visible.'[232]

٢٣٠ـ حَدَّثَنَا أَحْمَدُ بْنُ مَنِيعٍ، قَالَ: حَدَّثَنَا مُعَاوِيَةُ بْنُ عَمْرٍو، قَالَ: حَدَّثَنَا زَائِدَةُ،

[232] Muslim, #190 and Tirmidhī, #2596.

عَنْ بَيَانٍ، عَنْ قَيْسِ بْنِ أَبِي حَازِمٍ، عَنْ جَرِيرِ بْنِ عَبْدِ اللهِ قَالَ: «مَا حَجَبَنِي رَسُولُ اللهِ ﷺ مُنْذُ أَسْلَمْتُ، وَلَا رَآنِي إِلَّا ضَحِكَ» .

230. Aḥmad Ibn Manīʿ narrated to us; Muʿāwiyyah Ibn ʿAmr narrated to us; Zā'idah narrated to us; from Bayān; from Qays Ibn Abī Ḥāzim that Jarīr Ibn ʿAbdullāh (*raḍiyAllāhu ʿanhu*) said:

> 'The Messenger of Allāh (ﷺ) never shunned me after I embraced Islām, nor did he ever see me except he would laugh (*ḍaḥik*).'[233]

٢٣١ـ حَدَّثَنَا أَحْمَدُ بْنُ مَنِيعٍ، قَالَ: حَدَّثَنَا مُعَاوِيَةُ بْنُ عَمْرٍو، قَالَ: حَدَّثَنَا زَائِدَةُ، عَنِ إِسْمَاعِيلَ بْنِ أَبِي خَالِدٍ، عَنْ قَيْسٍ، عَنْ جَرِيرٍ، قَالَ: «مَا حَجَبَنِي رَسُولُ اللهِ ﷺ وَلَا رَآنِي مُنْذُ أَسْلَمْتُ إِلَّا تَبَسَّمَ» .

231. Aḥmad Ibn Manīʿ narrated to us; Muʿāwiyyah Ibn ʿAmr narrated to us; Zā'idah narrated to us; from Ismāʿīl Ibn Abī Khālid; from Qays that Jarīr (*raḍiyAllāhu ʿanhu*) said:

> 'The Messenger of Allāh (ﷺ) never shunned me after I embraced Islām, nor did he ever see me except he would smile (*tabassam*).'[234]

٢٣٢ـ حَدَّثَنَا هَنَّادُ بْنُ السَّرِيِّ، قَالَ: حَدَّثَنَا أَبُو مُعَاوِيَةَ، عَنِ الأَعْمَشِ، عَنِ إِبْرَاهِيمَ، عَنْ عَبِيدَةَ السَّلْمَانِيِّ، عَنْ عَبْدِ اللهِ بْنِ مَسْعُودٍ، قَالَ: قَالَ رَسُولُ اللهِ ﷺ: «إِنِّي لَأَعْرِفُ آخِرَ أَهْلِ النَّارِ خُرُوجًا، رَجُلٌ يَخْرُجُ مِنْهَا زَحْفًا، فَيُقَالُ لَهُ: انْطَلِقْ فَادْخُلِ الجَنَّةَ،

[233] Bukhārī #3035, Muslim, #2475, and Tirmidhī, #3820.
[234] Tirmidhī, #3821.

قَالَ: فَيَذْهَبُ لِيَدْخُلَ الجَنَّةَ، فَيَجِدُ النَّاسَ قَدْ أَخَذُوا المَنَازِلَ، فَيَرْجِعُ، فَيَقُولُ: يَا رَبِّ! قَدْ أَخَذَ النَّاسُ المَنَازِلَ، فَيُقَالُ لَهُ: أَتَذْكُرُ الزَّمَانَ الَّذِي كُنْتَ فِيهِ، فَيَقُولُ: نَعَمْ، قَالَ: فَيُقَالُ لَهُ: تَمَنَّ، قَالَ: فَيَتَمَنَّى، فَيُقَالُ لَهُ: فَإِنَّ لَكَ الَّذِي تَمَنَّيْتَ وَعَشَرَةَ أَضْعَافِ الدُّنْيَا، قَالَ: فَيَقُولُ: تَسْخَرُ بِي وَأَنْتَ المَلِكُ! قَالَ: فَلَقَدْ رَأَيْتُ رَسُولَ اللهِ ﷺ ضَحِكَ حَتَّى بَدَتْ نَوَاجِذُهُ».

232. Hannād Ibn al-Sarī narrated to us; Abū Mu'āwiyyah narrated to us; from Al-A'mash; from Ibrāhīm; from 'Ubaydah al-Salmānī that 'Abdullāh Ibn Mas'ūd (*raḍiyAllāhu 'anhu*) said:

> 'The Messenger of Allāh (ﷺ) said: "I surely know of the last person to exit the Hellfire, a man who will exit crawling, and it will be said to him: 'Go and enter Paradise!' He will go to enter only to find that the people have taken their places of residence, so he will return and say: 'O my Lord, the people have taken their places of residence!' Then he will be asked: 'Do you remember the time you were in?' He will say: 'Yes.' It will be said to him: 'Make a wish!' So he will make a wish. Then it will be said to him: 'You have what you wished for, the world and ten times over.' He will say: 'Are You mocking me and You are the King?'"
>
> He (*raḍiyAllāhu 'anhu*) said: 'I saw the Messenger of Allāh (ﷺ) laugh until his molar teeth became visible.'[235]

٢٣٣ـ حَدَّثَنَا قُتَيْبَةُ بْنُ سَعِيدٍ، قَالَ: حَدَّثَنَا أَبُو الأَحْوَصِ، عَنْ أَبِي إِسْحَاقَ، عَنْ عَلِيِّ بْنِ رَبِيعَةَ، قَالَ: شَهِدْتُ عَلِيًّا، أُتِيَ بِدَابَّةٍ لِيَرْكَبَهَا فَلَمَّا وَضَعَ رِجْلَهُ فِي الرِّكَابِ قَالَ: بِاسْمِ اللهِ! فَلَمَّا اسْتَوَى عَلَى ظَهْرِهَا، قَالَ: الحَمْدُ للهِ، ثُمَّ قَالَ: ﴿سُبْحَٰنَ ٱلَّذِى سَخَّرَ لَنَا

[235] Bukhārī, #6571, Muslim, #186, and Tirmidhī, #2595.

هَٰذَا وَمَا كُنَّا لَهُۥ مُقۡرِنِينَ ﴿١٣﴾ [سورة الزخرف]، ثُمَّ قَالَ: الحَمْدُ لله ثَلَاثًا، وَاللهُ أَكْبَرُ ثَلَاثًا، سُبْحَانَكَ إِنِّي ظَلَمْتُ نَفْسِي، فَاغْفِرْ لِي، فَإِنَّهُ لَا يَغْفِرُ الذُّنُوبَ إِلَّا أَنْتَ، ثُمَّ ضَحِكَ، فَقُلْتُ لَهُ: مِنْ أَيِّ شَيْءٍ ضَحِكْتَ يَا أَمِيرَ المُؤْمِنِينَ؟! قَالَ: رَأَيْتُ رَسُولَ اللهِ ﷺ صَنَعَ كَمَا صَنَعْتُ، ثُمَّ ضَحِكَ، فَقُلْتُ: مِنْ أَيِّ شَيْءٍ ضَحِكْتَ يَا رَسُولَ اللهِ؟! قَالَ: إِنَّ رَبَّكَ لَيَعْجَبُ مِنْ عَبْدِهِ إِذَا قَالَ: رَبِّ اغْفِرْ لِي ذُنُوبِي، إِنَّهُ لَا يَغْفِرُ الذُّنُوبَ غَيْرُكَ .

233. Qutaybah Ibn Sa'id narrated to us; Abū'l-Aḥwas narrated to us; from Abū Isḥāq that 'Alī Ibn Rabī'ah (*raḍiyAllāhu 'anhu*) said:

> I was present with 'Alī (*raḍiyAllāhu 'anhu*) when a [riding] beast was brought for him to ride on. When he placed his foot in the stirrup, he said: "*Bismillah*"—"In the Name of Allāh." Then, when he sat up straight on its back, he said:
>
> *"Subḥāna lladhī sakhkhara lana hādha wa mā kunnālahu muqrinīn wa innā ilā Rabbinā la-munqalibūn"*
>
> "Glory to Him who has subjected this [beast] for [to ride on], for we could never have accomplished this [by ourselves]. And to our Lord, surely, we will return."[236]
>
> Then he said:
>
> *"Alḥamdulillah"*—"Praise be to Allāh," three times, and: *"Allāhu Akbar"*—"Allāh is Supremely Great," three times, then:
>
> *"Subḥānaka innī ẓalamku nafsī faghfirlī fa-inna-hu lā yaghfiru*

[236] *Al-Zukhruf* (43): 13-14

al-dhunub illā anta"

"Glory be to You! I have wronged myself, so forgive me, for no one forgives sins but You." Then he laughed, so I said to him: 'What has made you laugh, O Leader of the Believers?' He said: 'I saw the Messenger of Allāh (ﷺ) do as I did and then laughed, so I said: 'What has made you laugh, O Messenger of Allāh?' He (ﷺ) said: "Your Lord is pleased at His servant when he says: 'My Lord forgive me my sins,' knowing that none other than Him forgives sins."'[237]

٢٣٤- حَدَّثَنَا مُحَمَّدُ بْنُ بَشَّارٍ، قَالَ: حَدَّثَنَا مُحَمَّدُ بْنُ عَبْدِ اللهِ الأَنْصَارِيُّ، قَالَ: حَدَّثَنَا عَبْدُ اللهِ بْنُ عَوْنٍ، عَنْ مُحَمَّدِ بْنِ مُحَمَّدِ بْنِ الأَسْوَدِ، عَنْ عَامِرِ بْنِ سَعْدٍ، قَالَ: قَالَ سَعْدٌ: «لَقَدْ رَأَيْتُ النَّبِيَّ ﷺ ضَحِكَ يَوْمَ الخَنْدَقِ حَتَّى بَدَتْ نَوَاجِذُهُ؛ قَالَ: قُلْتُ: كَيْفَ كَانَ؟ قَالَ: كَانَ رَجُلٌ مَعَهُ تُرْسٌ، وَكَانَ سَعْدٌ رَامِيًا، وَكَانَ يَقُولُ كَذَا وَكَذَا بِالتُّرْسِ يُغَطِّي جَبْهَتَهُ، فَنَزَعَ لَهُ سَعْدٌ بِسَهْمٍ، فَلَمَّا رَفَعَ رَأْسَهُ رَمَاهُ فَلَمْ يُخْطِئْ هَذِهِ مِنْهُ - يَعْنِي جَبْهَتَهُ - وَانْقَلَبَ الرَّجُلُ، وَشَالَ بِرِجْلِهِ، فَضَحِكَ النَّبِيُّ ﷺ حَتَّى بَدَتْ نَوَاجِذُهُ؛ قَالَ: قُلْتُ: مِنْ أَيِّ شَيْءٍ ضَحِكَ؟ قَالَ: مِنْ فِعْلِهِ بِالرَّجُلِ».

234. Muḥammad Ibn Bashshār narrated to us; Muḥammad Ibn 'Abdullāh al-Anṣārī narrated to us; 'Abdullāh Ibn 'Awn narrated to us; from Muḥammad Ibn Muḥammad Ibn al-Aswad that 'Āmir Ibn Sa'd said: 'Sa'd [Ibn Abī Waqqāṣ] (*raḍiyAllāhu 'anhu*) said:

'I saw the Prophet (ﷺ) laugh on the Day of the Battle of of the Trench (*al-Khandaq*) until his molar teeth became visible.' I said: 'What made him laugh.' He said: 'There was a man holding a shield and Sa'd was an archer, and the

[237] Abū Dāwūd, #2602 and Tirmidhī, #3446.

man was saying such-and-such with the shield covering his forehead. So Sa'd aimed an arrow at him and shot it when he raised his head, and did not miss his forehead. The man fell to the ground and his feet were raised upwards. The Prophet (ﷺ) then laughed until his molar teeth were visible. He said: 'I asked: 'What made him laugh?' He replied: 'What he did to the man.'"[238]

[238] Aḥmad in his *Musnad*, #1620, and the chain has an unknown narrator in it which makes this ḥadīth weak.

CHAPTER THIRTY-SIX

بَابُ مَا جَاءَ فِي صِفَةِ مِزَاحِ رَسُولِ اللهِ ﷺ

What has been narrated concerning the Jesting (*muzāḥ*) of the Messenger of Allāh (ﷺ)

٢٣٥- حَدَّثَنَا مَحْمُودُ بْنُ غَيْلَانَ، قَالَ: حَدَّثَنَا أَبُو أُسَامَةَ، عَنْ شَرِيكٍ، عَنْ عَاصِمٍ الأَحْوَلِ، عَنْ أَنَسِ بْنِ مَالِكٍ أَنَّ النَّبِيَّ ﷺ قَالَ لَهُ: «يَا ذَا الأُذُنَيْنِ!».

قَالَ مَحْمُودٌ: قَالَ أَبُو أُسَامَةَ: يَعْنِي يُمَازِحُهُ.

235. Maḥmūd Ibn Ghaylān narrated to us; Abū Usāmah narrated to us; from Sharīk; from ʿĀṣim al-Aḥwal that Anas Ibn Mālik (*raḍiyAllāhu ʿanhu*) said:

> 'The Prophet (ﷺ) said to him: "O one with the two ears."'[239]

Maḥmūd said: 'Abū Usāmah said: 'It means that he was jesting with him.'

٢٣٦- حَدَّثَنَا هَنَّادُ بْنُ السَّرِيِّ، قَالَ: حَدَّثَنَا وَكِيعٌ، عَنْ شُعْبَةَ، عَنْ أَبِي التَّيَّاحِ،

[239] Abū Dāwūd, #5002 and Tirmidhī, #1992, the chain is weak.

عَنْ أَنَسِ بْنِ مَالِكٍ، قَالَ: إِنْ كَانَ رَسُولُ اللهِ ﷺ لَيُخَالِطُنَا حَتَّى يَقُولَ لأَخٍ لِي صَغِيرٍ: «يَا أَبَا عُمَيْرٍ! مَا فَعَلَ النُّغَيْرُ؟».

236. Hannād Ibn al-Sarī narrated to us; Wakī' narrated to us; from Shu'bah; from Abū'l-Tayyāh that Anas Ibn Mālik (*radiyAllāhu 'anhu*) said:

> 'The Messenger of Allāh (ﷺ) used to interact with us that he said to my younger brother: "O Abū Umayr, what happened to the little red-beaked sparrow (*al-nughayr*)?"'[240]

قَالَ أَبُو عِيسَى: وَفِقْهُ هَذَا الحَدِيثِ أَنَّ النَّبِيَّ ﷺ كَانَ يُمَازِحُ، وَفِيهِ أَنَّهُ كَنَّى غُلَامًا صَغِيرًا، فَقَالَ لَهُ: «يَا أَبَا عُمَيْرٍ!»، وَفِيهِ أَنَّهُ لَا بَأْسَ أَنْ يُعْطَى الصَّبِيُّ الطَّيْرَ لِيَلْعَبَ بِهِ، وَإِنَّمَا قَالَ لَهُ النَّبِيُّ ﷺ: «يَا أَبَا عُمَيْرٍ! مَا فَعَلَ النُّغَيْرُ؟»؛ لأَنَّهُ كَانَ لَهُ نُغَيْرٌ يَلْعَبُ بِهِ فَمَاتَ، فَحَزِنَ الغُلَامُ عَلَيْهِ، فَمَازَحَهُ النَّبِيُّ ﷺ فَقَالَ: «يَا أَبَا عُمَيْرٍ! مَا فَعَلَ النُّغَيْرُ».

Abū 'Isā said: 'What is understood from this tradition is that the Prophet (ﷺ) used to joke, and that he nicknamed a young boy, for he said to him: 'Abū Umayr!' It also proves that there is no harm in a young child playing with a bird, since the Prophet (ﷺ) said to him: "O Abū Umayr, what happened to the little red-beaked sparrow?" for the boy had a little bird that he would play with, but died which saddened him, so the Prophet (ﷺ) joked with him [in order to cheer him up] and said: "O Abū Umayr, what happened to the little red-beaked sparrow?"

[240] Bukhārī, #6129, Muslim, #2150, and Tirmidhī, #1989.

٢٣٧ـ حَدَّثَنَا عَبَّاسُ بْنُ مُحَمَّدٍ الدُّورِيُّ، قَالَ: حَدَّثَنَا عَلِيُّ بنُ الحَسَنِ بنِ شَقِيقٍ، قَالَ: أَنْبَأَنَا عَبْدُ الله بْنُ المُبَارِكِ، عَنِ أُسَامَةَ بْنِ زَيْدٍ، عَنْ سَعِيدٍ المَقْبُرِيِّ، عَنْ أَبِي هُرَيْرَةَ، قَالَ: قَالُوا: يَا رَسُولَ الله! إِنَّكَ تُدَاعِبُنَا؟! قَالَ: «إِنِّي لَا أَقُولُ إِلَّا حَقًّا».

237. ʿAbbās Ibn Muḥammad al-Durī narrated to us; ʿAlī Ibn Al-Ḥasan Ibn Shaqīq narrated to us; ʿAbdullāh Ibn al-Mubārak informed us; from Usāmah Ibn Zayd; from Saʿīd al-Maqburī that Abū Hurayrah (*raḍiyAllāhu ʿanhu*) said:

> 'They [the Companions] said: 'O Messenger of Allāh, you joke with us?' He (ﷺ) said: "Yes, but I only speak the truth."'[241]

٢٣٨ـ حَدَّثَنَا قُتَيْبَةُ بْنُ سَعِيدٍ، قَالَ: حَدَّثَنَا خَالِدُ بْنُ عَبْدِ الله، عَنْ حُمَيْدٍ، عَنْ أَنَسِ ابنِ مَالِكٍ، أَنَّ رَجُلًا اسْتَحْمَلَ رَسُولَ الله ﷺ فَقَالَ: «إِنِّي حَامِلُكَ عَلَى وَلَدِ نَاقَةٍ»، فَقَالَ: يَا رَسُولَ الله! مَا أَصْنَعُ بِوَلَدِ النَّاقَةِ؟ فَقَالَ ﷺ: «وَهَلْ تَلِدُ الإِبِلَ إِلَّا النُّوقُ».

238. Qutaybah Ibn Saʿīd narrated to us; Khālid Ibn ʿAbdullāh narrated to us; from Ḥumayd that Anas Ibn Mālik (*raḍiyAllāhu ʿanhu*) said:

> 'A man asked the Messenger of Allāh (ﷺ) to give him a mount, so he said: "I will give you an offspring of a she-camel." The man said: 'O Messenger of Allāh, what am I supposed to do with an offspring of a she-camel.' He (ﷺ) said: "Do other than she-camels give birth to camels?"[242]

---

[241] Tirmidhī, #1990 and Aḥmad in his *Musnad*, 2/360.
[242] Abū Dāwūd, #3998 and Tirmidhī, #1991.

٢٣٩ـ حَدَّثَنَا إِسْحَاقُ بْنُ مَنْصُورٍ، قَالَ: حَدَّثَنَا عَبْدُ الرَّزَّاقِ، قَالَ: حَدَّثَنَا مَعْمَرٌ، عَنْ ثَابِتٍ، عَنْ أَنَسِ بْنِ مَالِكٍ، أَنَّ رَجُلًا مِنْ أَهْلِ البَادِيَةِ كَانَ اسْمُهُ زَاهِرًا وَكَانَ يُهْدِي إِلَى النَّبِيِّ ﷺ هَدِيَّةً مِنَ البَادِيَةِ، فَيُجَهِّزُهُ النَّبِيُّ ﷺ إِذَا أَرَادَ أَنْ يَخْرُجَ، فَقَالَ النَّبِيُّ ﷺ: إِنَّ زَاهِرًا بَادِيَتُنَا وَنَحْنُ حَاضِرُوهُ، وَكَانَ ﷺ يُحِبُّهُ، وَكَانَ رَجُلًا دَمِيمًا، فَأَتَاهُ النَّبِيُّ ﷺ يَوْمًا وَهُوَ يَبِيعُ مَتَاعَهُ فَاحْتَضَنَهُ مِنْ خَلْفِهِ وَهُوَ لَا يُبْصِرُهُ، فَقَالَ: مَنْ هَذَا؟ أَرْسِلْنِي، فَالْتَفَتَ فَعَرَفَ النَّبِيَّ ﷺ فَجَعَلَ لَا يَأْلُو مَا أَلْصَقَ ظَهْرَهُ بِصَدْرِ النَّبِيِّ ﷺ حِينَ عَرَفَهُ، فَجَعَلَ النَّبِيُّ ﷺ يَقُولُ: «مَنْ يَشْتَرِي هَذَا العَبْدَ؟» فَقَالَ: يَا رَسُولَ اللهِ! إِذًا وَاللهِ تَجِدُنِي كَاسِدًا، فَقَالَ النَّبِيُّ ﷺ: «لَكِنْ عِنْدَ اللهِ لَسْتَ بِكَاسِدٍ»، أَوْ قَالَ: «أَنْتَ عِنْدَ اللهِ غَالٍ».

239. Isḥāq Ibn Mansūr narrated to us; ʻAbdu'l-Razzāq narrated to us; Maʻmar narrated to us; from Thābit that Anas Ibn Mālik (*raḍiyAllāhu ʻanhu*) said:

> 'There was a man from the people of the desert, his name was *Zāhir*, and he used to bring the Prophet (ﷺ) a gift from the desert, and the Prophet (ﷺ) would equip him [with provisions of the city] when he wanted to return [to his family]. The Prophet (ﷺ) said: "*Zāhir* is our desert, and we are his valleys." He (ﷺ) used to love him [dearly], though he was an unattractive man (*damim*). One day, while he was selling his merchandise, the Prophet (ﷺ) came up to him and embraced him from behind so that he could not see who it was. He asked: 'Who is this? Let go of me!' Then, when he turned around and recognised it was the Prophet (ﷺ), he began to press his back against the Prophet's chest, so the Prophet (ﷺ) began to say: "Who will purchase this slave (*'abd*)." He said: 'O Messenger of Allāh, in that case, by Allāh, you will find me to be unsellable (*kāsid*).' The

> Prophet (ﷺ) said: "But with Allāh you are not unsellable." Or he said: "You are valuable to Allāh!'"[243]

٢٤٠ـ حَدَّثَنَا عَبْدُ بْنُ حُمَيْدٍ، قَالَ: حَدَّثَنَا مُصْعَبُ بْنُ المِقْدَامِ، قَالَ: حَدَّثَنَا المُبَارِكُ بْنُ فَضَالَةَ، عَنِ الحَسَنِ، قَالَ: أَتَتْ عَجُوزٌ إِلَى النَّبِيِّ ﷺ، فَقَالَتْ: يَا رَسُولَ اللهِ! ادْعُ اللهَ أَنْ يُدْخِلَنِي الجَنَّةَ، فَقَالَ: «يَا أُمَّ فُلَانٍ! إِنَّ الجَنَّةَ لَا تَدْخُلُهَا عَجُوزٌ»، قَالَ: فَوَلَّتْ تَبْكِي، فَقَالَ: «أَخْبِرُوهَا أَنَّهَا لَا تَدْخُلُهَا وَهِيَ عَجُوزٌ، إِنَّ اللهَ تَعَالَى يَقُولُ: ﴿إِنَّآ أَنشَأْنَٰهُنَّ إِنشَآءً ﴿٣٥﴾ فَجَعَلْنَٰهُنَّ أَبْكَارًا ﴿٣٦﴾ عُرُبًا أَتْرَابًا﴾ [سورة الواقعة]».

240. 'Abd Ibn Ḥumayd narrated to us; Muṣ'ab Ibn al-Miqdām narrated to us; Al-Mubārak Ibn Faḍalah narrated to us that Al-Ḥasan [al-Baṣri] said:

> 'An old woman came to the Prophet (ﷺ) and said: 'O Messenger of Allāh, pray to Allāh that He enters me into Paradise.' He (ﷺ) replied: "O Mother of so-and-so, no old woman will enter Paradise!" She went off weeping, so he said: "Inform her that she will not enter it as an old woman, as Allāh the Most High says:
>
> "We have created them a new creation. And made them virgins, loving, equal in age.'"[244,245]

[243] Aḥmad in his *Musnad*, #12669.

[244] *Al-Waqi'ah* (56): 35-37

[245] This ḥadith is weak but supported by another narration found in Tabarani in *Al-Awsat*, #5545 on the authority of 'A'ishah (*raḍiyAllāhu 'anha*).

CHAPTER THIRTY-SEVEN

بابُ مَا جَاءَ فِي صِفَةِ كَلَامِ رَسُولِ اللهِ ﷺ فِي الشِّعْرِ

What has been narrated concerning the Poetry (*shi'r*) of the Messenger of Allāh (ﷺ)

٢٤١ـ حَدَّثَنَا عَلِيُّ بْنُ حُجْرٍ، قَالَ: حَدَّثَنَا شَرِيكٌ، عَنِ الْمِقْدَامِ بْنِ شُرَيْحٍ، عَنْ أَبِيهِ، عَنْ عَائِشَةَ، قَالَتْ: قِيلَ لَهَا: هَلْ كَانَ النَّبِيُّ ﷺ يَتَمَثَّلُ بِشَيْءٍ مِنَ الشِّعْرِ؟ قَالَتْ: «كَانَ يَتَمَثَّلُ بِشِعْرِ ابْنِ رَوَاحَةَ، وَيَتَمَثَّلُ بِقَوْلِهِ: وَيَأْتِيكَ بِالأَخْبَارِ مَنْ لَمْ تُزَوِّدِ».

241. 'Alī Ibn Ḥujr narrated to us; Sharīk narrated to us; from Al-Miqdām Ibn Shurayḥ; from his father that 'Ā'ishah (*raḍiyAllāhu 'anhā*) said that she was asked:

> 'Did the Prophet (ﷺ) imitate any form of poetry (*shi'r*)?' She said: 'He used imitate the poetry of ['Abdullāh] Ibn Rawāhah and he would cite his couplets:
>
> *"You will be brought the news by one whom you have not supplied with provisions."*'[246]

٢٤٢ـ حَدَّثَنَا مُحَمَّدُ بْنُ بَشَّارٍ، قَالَ: حَدَّثَنَا عَبْدُ الرَّحْمَنِ بْنُ مَهْدِيٍّ، قَالَ: حَدَّثَنَا

[246] Tirmidhī, #2848.

سُفْيَانُ الثَّوْرِيُّ، عَنْ عَبْدِ المَلِكِ بْنِ عُمَيْرٍ، قَالَ: حَدَّثَنَا أَبُو سَلَمَةَ، عَنْ أَبِي هُرَيْرَةَ قَالَ: قَالَ رَسُولُ اللهِ ﷺ: «إِنَّ أَصْدَقَ كَلِمَةٍ قَالَهَا الشَّاعِرُ كَلِمَةُ لَبِيدٍ: أَلَا كُلُّ شَيْءٍ مَا خَلَا اللهَ بَاطِلٌ»، وَكَادَ أُمَيَّةُ بْنُ أَبِي الصَّلْتِ أَنْ يُسْلِمَ.

242. Muḥammad Ibn Bashshār narrated to us; 'Abdu'l-Raḥmān Ibn Mahdi narrated to us; Sufyān al-Thawrī narrated to us; from 'Abdu'l-Mālik Ibn 'Umayr; Abū Salamah narrated to us that Abū Hurayrah (*raḍiyAllāhu 'anhu*) said:

> 'The Messenger of Allāh (ﷺ) said: "The truest words spoken by a poet is the saying of Labid [Ibn Rabī'ah]: 'Indeed everything besides Allāh is futile.' [The poet] Umayyah Ibn Abī Ṣalt was on the verge of embracing Islām."'[247]

٢٤٣ـ حَدَّثَنَا مُحَمَّدُ بْنُ المُثَنَّى، قَالَ: حَدَّثَنَا مُحَمَّدُ بْنُ جَعْفَرٍ، قَالَ: حَدَّثَنَا شُعْبَةُ، عَنِ الأَسْوَدِ بْنِ قَيْسٍ، عَنْ جُنْدُبِ بْنِ سُفْيَانَ البَجَلِيِّ، قَالَ: أَصَابَ حَجَرٌ أُصْبُعَ رَسُولِ اللهِ ﷺ فَدَمِيَتْ، فَقَالَ:

«هَلْ أَنْتِ إِلَّا أُصْبُعٌ دَمِيتِ وَفِي سَبِيلِ اللهِ مَا لَقِيتِ»

243. Muḥammad Ibn al-Muthannāh narrated to us; Muḥammad Ibn Jā'far narrated to us; Shu'bah narrated to us; from Al-Aswad Ibn Qays that Jundub Ibn Sufyān al-Bajalī said:

> 'A stone struck the toe of the Messenger of Allāh (ﷺ) [in battle], causing it to bleed, so he said:
>
> *"You are nothing except a toe that bled*
> *What you endured was on the path of Allāh."*[248]

[247] Bukhārī, #3841, Muslim, #2246, and Tirmidhī, #2849.
[248] Bukhārī, #2802, Muslim, #1796, and Tirmidhī, #3345.

٢٤٤ـ حَدَّثَنَا ابْنُ أَبِي عُمَرَ، قَالَ: حَدَّثَنَا سُفْيَانُ بْنُ عُيَيْنَةَ، عَنِ الأَسْوَدِ ابْنِ قَيْسٍ، عَنْ جُنْدُبِ بْنِ عَبْدِ اللهِ البَجَلِيِّ، نَحْوَهُ.

244. Ibn Abī 'Umar narrated to us; Sufyān Ibn 'Uyaynah narrated to us; from Al-Aswad Ibn Qays that Jundub Ibn 'Abdullāh al-Bajalī said something similar to the above tradition.

٢٤٥ـ حَدَّثَنَا مُحَمَّدُ بْنُ بَشَّارٍ، قَالَ: حَدَّثَنَا يَحْيَى بْنُ سَعِيدٍ، قَالَ: حَدَّثَنَا سُفْيَانُ الثَّوْرِيُّ، قَالَ: أَنْبَأَنَا أَبُو إِسْحَاقَ، عَنِ البَرَاءِ بْنِ عَازِبٍ، قَالَ: قَالَ لَهُ رَجُلٌ: أَفَرَرْتُمْ عَنْ رَسُولِ اللهِ ﷺ يَا أَبَا عُمَارَةَ؟! فَقَالَ: لَا، وَاللهِ مَا وَلَّى رَسُولُ اللهِ ﷺ، وَلَكِنْ وَلَّى سَرَعَانُ النَّاسِ تَلَقَّتْهُمْ هَوَازِنُ بِالنَّبْلِ، وَرَسُولُ اللهِ ﷺ عَلَى بَغْلَتِهِ، وَأَبُو سُفْيَانَ ابْنُ الحَارِثِ بْنِ عَبْدِ المُطَّلِبِ آخِذٌ بِلِجَامِهَا، وَرَسُولُ اللهِ يَقُولُ:

«أَنَـــا النَّبِـــيُّ لا كَـــذِبْ أَنَـا ابْـنُ عبـد المطَّلِـبْ»

245. Muḥammad Ibn Bashshār narrated to us; Yaḥyā Sa'īd narrated to us; Sufyān al-Thawrī narrated to us; Abū Isḥāq informed us that Barā'a Ibn 'Āzib (*raḍiyAllāhu 'anhu*) said:

> 'A man said to him: 'Did you all flee [at the Day of Ḥunayn], leaving the Messnger of Allāh (ﷺ) exposed, O Abū 'Umārah?' He replied: 'No, by Allāh, the Messenger of Allāh (ﷺ) did not retreat. But some who were hasty retreated, and were received by arrows from the Hawāzin. The Messenger of Allāh (ﷺ) was mounted on a mule with Abū Sufyān Ibn al-Ḥārith Ibn 'Abdul-Muṭṭālib (*raḍiyAllāhu 'anhu*) holding onto its rein, and the Messenger of Allāh (ﷺ) was reciting:
>
> *"I am the Prophet, no lie!*

I am the son of 'Abdu'l-Muṭṭālib!"[249]

٢٤٦ـ حَدَّثَنَا إِسْحَاقُ بْنُ مَنْصُورٍ، قَالَ: حَدَّثَنَا عَبْدُ الرَّزَّاقِ، قَالَ: حَدَّثَنَا جَعْفَرُ بْنُ سُلَيْمَانَ، قَالَ: حَدَّثَنَا ثَابِتٌ، عَنْ أَنَسٍ: أَنَّ النَّبِيَّ ﷺ دَخَلَ مَكَّةَ فِي عُمْرَةِ القَضَاءِ، وَابْنُ رَوَاحَةَ يَمْشِي بَيْنَ يَدَيْهِ، وَهُوَ يَقُولُ:

خَلُّوا بَنِي الكُفَّارِ عَنْ سَبِيلِهِ   اليَوْمَ نَضْرِبْكُمْ عَلَى تَنْزِيلِهِ
ضَرْبًا يُزِيلُ الهَامَ عَنْ مَقِيلِهِ   وَيُذْهِلُ الخَلِيلَ عَنْ خَلِيلِهِ

فَقَالَ لَهُ عُمَرُ: يَا ابْنَ رَوَاحَةَ! بَيْنَ يَدَيْ رَسُولِ اللهِ ﷺ، وَفِي حَرَمِ اللهِ تَقُولُ الشِّعْرَ! فَقَالَ ﷺ: «خَلِّ عَنْهُ يَا عُمَرُ! فَلَهِيَ أَسْرَعُ فِيهِمْ مِنْ نَضْحِ النَّبْلِ».

246. Isḥāq Ibn Manṣūr narrated to us; 'Abdu'l-Razzāq narrated to us; Jā'far Ibn Sulaymān narrated to us; Thābit narrated to us that Anas (*raḍiyAllāhu 'anhu*) said:

> 'The Prophet (ﷺ) entered Makkah during his missed 'umrah (*'umrah al-qaḍā'*), and Ibn Rawāhah walked in front of him, chanting:
>
> *'Clear, O children of the disbelievers, from his path,*
> *For today we shall strike you with such force,*
> *A blow that will sever the head from its neck,*
> *And distract a dear friend from his dear friend.'*
>
> 'Umar (*raḍiyAllāhu 'anhu*) said to him: 'O Ibn Rawāhah, in the presence of the Messenger of Allāh (ﷺ) and in Allāh's Sanctuary, you chant poetry?' He (ﷺ) said: "Leave him alone, O 'Umar, for it will strike them down quicker than the firing of arrows."'[250]

[249] Bukhārī, #2824, Muslim, #1796, and Tirmidhī, #1688.
[250] Tirmidhī, #2847 and others

٢٤٧- حَدَّثَنَا عَلِيُّ بْنُ حُجْرٍ، قَالَ: حَدَّثَنَا شَرِيكٌ، عَنْ سِمَاكِ بْنِ حَرْبٍ، عَنْ جَابِرِ بْنِ سَمُرَةَ، قَالَ: «جَالَسْتُ النَّبِيَّ ﷺ أَكْثَرَ مِنْ مِائَةِ مَرَّةٍ، وَكَانَ أَصْحَابُهُ يَتَنَاشَدُونَ الشِّعْرَ، وَيَتَذَاكَرُونَ أَشْيَاءَ مِنْ أَمْرِ الجَاهِلِيَّةِ، وَهُوَ سَاكِتٌ، وَرُبَّمَا تَبَسَّمَ مَعَهُمْ».

247. ʿAlī Ibn Ḥujr narrated to us; Sharīk narrated to us; from Simāk Ibn Ḥarb that Jābir Ibn Samurah (*raḍiyAllāhu ʿanhu*) said:

> "I sat with Prophet (ﷺ) more than a hundred times, and his Companions used to recite poetry to one another. They would reminisce about things from the Jāhilīyyah (pagan era), while he would sit silently, and sometimes even smile with them."[251]

٢٤٨- حَدَّثَنَا عَلِيُّ بْنُ حُجْرٍ، قَالَ: حَدَّثَنَا شَرِيكٌ، عَنْ عَبْدِ المَلِكِ بْنِ عُمَيْرٍ، عَنْ أَبِي سَلَمَةَ، عَنْ أَبِي هُرَيْرَةَ، عَنِ النَّبِيِّ ﷺ، قَالَ: «أَشْعَرُ كَلِمَةٍ تَكَلَّمَتْ بِهَا العَرَبُ كَلِمَةُ لَبِيدٍ: أَلَا كُلُّ شَيْءٍ مَا خَلَا اللهَ بَاطِلٌ».

248. ʿAlī Ibn Ḥujr narrated to us; Sharīk narrated to us; from ʿAbdu'l-Mālik Ibn ʿUmayr; from Abū Salamah that Abū Hurayrah (*raḍiyAllāhu ʿanhu*) said:

> 'The Prophet (ﷺ) said: "The best of poetic saying spoken by the Arabs is the saying of Labeed:
>
> *'Indeed everything besides Allāh is futile.'"*[252]

---

[251] Tirmidhī, #2850, this is a weak tradition but is supported by another narration reported in Nasā'ī, #1359.

[252] Bukhārī, #3841, Muslim, #2246, and Tirmidhī, #2849.

٢٤٩ـ حَدَّثَنَا أَحْمَدُ بْنُ مَنِيعٍ، قَالَ: حَدَّثَنَا مَرْوَانُ بْنُ مُعَاوِيَةَ، عَنْ عَبْدِ اللهِ ابْنِ عَبْدِ الرَّحْمَنِ الطَّائِفِيِّ، عَنْ عَمْرِو بْنِ الشَّرِيدِ، عَنْ أَبِيهِ، قَالَ: كُنْتُ رِدْفَ النَّبِيِّ ﷺ فَأَنْشَدْتُهُ مِائَةَ قَافِيَةٍ مِنْ قَوْلِ أُمَيَّةَ بْنِ أَبِي الصَّلْتِ الثَّقَفِيِّ، كُلَّمَا أَنْشَدْتُهُ بَيْتًا قَالَ لِيَ النَّبِيُّ ﷺ: «هِيهْ»، حَتَّى أَنْشَدْتُهُ مِائَةً ـ يَعْنِي بَيْتًا ـ فَقَالَ النَّبِيُّ ﷺ: «إِنْ كَادَ لَيُسْلِمُ».

249. Aḥmad Ibn Manīʿ narrated to us; Marwān Ibn Muʿāwiyah narrated to us; from ʿAbdullāh Ibn ʿAbdu'l-Raḥmān al-Ṭā'ifī; from ʿAmr Ibn Sharīd that his father (*raḍiyAllāhu ʿanhu*) said:

> 'I rode behind the Prophet (ﷺ), and I recited to him a hundred poetic verses of Umayyah Ibn Abī Ṣalt al-Thaqafī. Whenever I recited a verse to him, the Prophet (ﷺ) said to me: "Recite more to me!" until I eventually recited a hundred verses to him.' The Prophet (ﷺ) then said: "He was on the verge of embracing Islām."'[253]

٢٥٠ـ حَدَّثَنَا إِسْمَاعِيلُ بْنُ مُوسَى الْفَزَارِيُّ، وَعَلِيُّ بْنُ حُجْرٍ، وَالْمَعْنَى وَاحِدٌ، قَالَا: حَدَّثَنَا عَبْدُ الرَّحْمَنِ بْنُ أَبِي الزِّنَادِ، عَنْ هِشَامِ بْنِ عُرْوَةَ، عَنْ أَبِيهِ، عَنْ عَائِشَةَ، قَالَتْ: كَانَ رَسُولُ اللهِ ﷺ يَضَعُ لِحَسَّانَ بْنِ ثَابِتٍ مِنْبَرًا فِي الْمَسْجِدِ يَقُومُ عَلَيْهِ قَائِمًا يُفَاخِرُ عَنْ رَسُولِ اللهِ ﷺ ـ أَوْ قَالَ: يُنَافِحُ ـ عَنْ رَسُولِ اللهِ ﷺ، وَيَقُولُ ﷺ: «إِنَّ اللهَ يُؤَيِّدُ حَسَّانَ بِرُوحِ الْقُدُسِ مَا يُنَافِحُ ـ أَوْ يُفَاخِرُ ـ عَنْ رَسُولِ اللهِ ﷺ».

250. Ismāʿīl Ibn Mūsā al-Fazarī and ʿAlī Ibn Ḥujr—one and the same—narrated to us; ʿAbdu'l-Raḥmān Ibn Abī al-Zinnād narrated to us; from Hishām Ibn ʿUrwah; from his father that ʿĀ'ishah (*raḍiyAllāhu ʿanhā*) said:

[253] Muslim, #2255.

'The Prophet (ﷺ) used to set up a pulpit in the *masjid* for Ḥassān Ibn Thābit. He would stand upon it, praising the Messenger of Allāh (ﷺ)—or he said—defending the Messenger of Allāh (ﷺ). He (ﷺ) would say: "Allāh the Most High supports Ḥassān with the Spirit (*Rūḥ al-Quds*),[254] as long as he praises—or defends—the Messenger of Allāh (ﷺ)."'[255]

٢٥١ـ حَدَّثَنَا إِسْمَاعِيلُ بْنُ مُوسَى، وَعَلِيُّ بْنُ حُجْرٍ، قَالَا: حَدَّثَنَا ابْنُ أَبِي الزِّنَادِ، عَنْ أَبِيهِ، عَنْ عُرْوَةَ، عَنْ عَائِشَةَ، عَنِ النَّبِيِّ ﷺ مِثْلَهُ.

251. Ismā'īl Ibn Mūsā al-Fazarī and 'Alī Ibn Ḥujr—one and the same—narrated to us; 'Abdu'l-Raḥmān Ibn Abī al-Zinnād narrated to us; from Hisham Ibn 'Urwah; from his father; 'Ā'ishah (*raḍiyAllāhu 'anhā*) reported a similar tradition through a different chain.

[254] *Rūḥ al-Quds* refers to the Archangel Jibrā'īl (*'alayhis-salām*).

[255] Abū Dāwūd, #5015 and Tirmidhī, #2846.

CHAPTER THIRTY-EIGHT

بابُ مَا جَاءَ فِي كَلَامِ رَسُولِ اللهِ ﷺ فِي السَّمَرِ

What has been narrated concerning the Conversations at night (*samar*) of the Messenger of Allāh (ﷺ)

٢٥٢ـ حَدَّثَنَا الحَسَنُ بْنُ صَبَّاحٍ البَزَّارُ، قَالَ: حَدَّثَنَا أَبُو النَّضْرِ، قَالَ: حَدَّثَنَا أَبُو عَقِيلٍ الثَّقَفِيُّ عَبْدُ اللهِ بنُ عَقِيلٍ، عَنْ مُجَالِدٍ، عَنِ الشَّعْبِيِّ، عَنْ مَسْرُوقٍ، عَنْ عَائِشَةَ، قَالَتْ: حَدَّثَ رَسُولُ اللهِ ﷺ ذَاتَ لَيْلَةٍ نِسَاءَهُ حَدِيثًا، فَقَالَتِ امْرَأَةٌ مِنْهُنَّ: كَأَنَّ الحَدِيثَ حَدِيثُ خُرَافَةَ، فَقَالَ: «أَتَدْرُونَ مَا خُرَافَةُ؟ إِنَّ خُرَافَةَ كَانَ رَجُلًا مِنْ عُذْرَةَ، أَسَرَتْهُ الجِنُّ فِي الجَاهِلِيَّةِ فَمَكَثَ فِيهِمْ دَهْرًا، ثُمَّ رَدُّوهُ إِلَى الإِنْسِ فَكَانَ يُحَدِّثُ النَّاسَ بِمَا رَأَى فِيهِمْ مِنَ الأَعَاجِيبِ، فَقَالَ النَّاسُ: حَدِيثُ خُرَافَةَ».

252. Al-Ḥasan Ibn Subbāḥ al-Bazzār narrated to us; Abū Naḍr narrated to us; Abū ʿAqīl al-Thaqafī ʿAbdullāh Ibn ʿAqīl narrated to us; from Mujālid; from Al-Shaʿbī; from Masrūq that ʿĀ'ishah (*raḍiyAllāhu ʿanhā*) said:

> 'The Messenger of Allāh (ﷺ) narrated to his wives a story one night, and one of them said: 'It is as if you are relating a story of Khurāfah?' He replied: "Do you know Khurāfah? Khurāfah was a man from [the tribe

of] 'Udhrah. The jinn kidnapped him in *al-jāhiliīyah*, so he stayed with them for a while. When they eventually returned him to the people, he began to narrate to the people about the extraordinary things that he saw among them, so the people said: 'The story of Khurāfah.'"[256]

٢٥٣ـ حَدَّثَنَا عَلِيُّ بْنُ حُجْرٍ، قَالَ: حَدَّثَنَا عِيسَى بْنُ يُونُسَ، عَنْ هِشَامِ ابْنِ عُرْوَةَ، عَنِ أَخِيهِ عَبْدِ اللهِ بْنِ عُرْوَةَ، عَنْ عُرْوَةَ، عَنْ عَائِشَةَ، قَالَتْ: جَلَسَتْ إِحْدَى عَشْرَةَ امْرَأَةً فَتَعَاهَدْنَ وَتَعَاقَدْنَ أَنْ لَا يَكْتُمْنَ مِنْ أَخْبَارِ أَزْوَاجِهِنَّ شَيْئًا:

فَقَالَتِ الأُولَى: زَوْجِي لَحْمُ جَمَلٍ غَثٍّ، عَلَى رَأْسِ جَبَلٍ وَعْرٍ، لَا سَهْلٌ فَيُرْتَقَى، وَلَا سَمِينٌ فَيُنْتَقَلُ.

قَالَتِ الثَّانِيَةُ: زَوْجِي لَا أَبُثُّ خَبَرَهُ، إِنِّي أَخَافُ أَنْ لَا أَذَرَهُ، إِنْ أَذْكُرْهُ أَذْكُرْ عُجَرَهُ وَبُجَرَهُ.

قَالَتِ الثَّالِثَةُ: زَوْجِي العَشَنَّقُ؛ إِنْ أَنْطِقْ أُطَلَّقْ، وَإِنْ أَسْكُتْ أُعَلَّقْ.

قَالَتِ الرَّابِعَةُ: زَوْجِي كَلَيْلِ تِهَامَةَ؛ لَا حَرٌّ وَلَا قُرٌّ، وَلَا مَخَافَةَ وَلَا سَآمَةَ.

قَالَتِ الخَامِسَةُ: زَوْجِي إِنْ دَخَلَ فَهِدَ، وَإِنْ خَرَجَ أَسِدَ، وَلَا يَسْأَلُ عَمَّا عَهِدَ.

قَالَتِ السَّادِسَةُ: زَوْجِي إِنْ أَكَلَ لَفَّ، وَإِنْ شَرِبَ اشْتَفَّ، وَإِنِ اضْطَجَعَ التَفَّ، وَلَا يُولِجُ الكَفَّ لِيَعْلَمَ البَثَّ.

قَالَتِ السَّابِعَةُ: زَوْجِي عَيَايَاءُ ـ أَوْ غَيَايَاءُ ـ طَبَاقَاءُ، كُلُّ دَاءٍ لَهُ دَاءٌ، شَجَّكِ أَوْ فَلَّكِ، أَوْ جَمَعَ كُلًّا لَكِ.

قَالَتِ الثَّامِنَةُ: زَوْجِي المَسُّ مَسُّ أَرْنَبٍ، وَالرِّيحُ رِيحُ زَرْنَبٍ.

---

[256] Aḥmad in his *Musnad*, #25244, this ḥadīth is weak.

قَالَتِ التَّاسِعَةُ: زَوْجِي رَفِيعُ العِمَادِ، طَوِيلُ النِّجَادِ، عَظِيمُ الرَّمَادِ، قَرِيبُ البَيْتِ مِنَ النَّادِ.

قَالَتِ العَاشِرَةُ: زَوْجِي مَالِكٌ وَمَا مَالِكٌ! مَالِكٌ خَيْرٌ مِنْ ذَلِكِ، لَهُ إِبِلٌ كَثِيرَاتُ المَبَارِكِ، قَلِيلاتُ المَسَارِحِ، إِذَا سَمِعْنَ صَوْتَ المِزْهَرِ أَيْقَنَّ أَنَّهُنَّ هَوَالِكُ.

قَالَتِ الحَادِيَةَ عَشْرَةَ: زَوْجِي أَبُو زَرْعٍ وَمَا أَبُو زَرْعٍ؟ أَنَاسَ مِنْ حُلِيٍّ أُذُنَيَّ، وَمَلأَ مِنْ شَحْمٍ عَضُدَيَّ، وَبَجَّحَنِي فَبَجَحَتْ إِلَيَّ نَفْسِي، وَجَدَنِي فِي أَهْلِ غُنَيْمَةٍ بِشِقٍّ، فَجَعَلَنِي فِي أَهْلِ صَهِيلٍ، وَأَطِيطٍ، وَدَائِسٍ، وَمُنَقٍّ، فَعِنْدَهُ أَقُولُ: فَلا أُقَبَّحُ، وَأَرْقُدُ فَأَتَصَبَّحُ، وَأَشْرَبُ فَأَتَقَمَّحُ.

أُمُّ أَبِي زَرْعٍ فَمَا أُمُّ أَبِي زَرْعٍ؟! عُكُومُهَا رَدَاحٌ، وَبَيْتُهَا فَسَاحٌ.

ابْنُ أَبِي زَرْعٍ، فَمَا ابْنُ أَبِي زَرْعٍ؟! مَضْجَعُهُ كَمَسَلِّ شَطْبَةٍ، وَتُشْبِعُهُ ذِرَاعُ الجَفْرَةِ.

بِنْتُ أَبِي زَرْعٍ، فَمَا بِنْتُ أَبِي زَرْعٍ؟! طَوْعُ أَبِيهَا وَطَوْعُ أُمِّهَا، مِلءُ كِسَائِهَا، وَغَيْظُ جَارَتِهَا.

جَارِيَةُ أَبِي زَرْعٍ، فَمَا جَارِيَةُ أَبِي زَرْعٍ؟! لَا تَبُثُّ حَدِيثَنَا تَبْثِيثًا، وَلا تُنَقِّثُ مِيرَتَنَا تَنْقِيثًا، وَلَا تَمْلأُ بَيْتَنَا تَعْشِيشًا.

قَالَتْ: خَرَجَ أَبُو زَرْعٍ وَالأَوْطَابُ تُمْخَضُ، فَلَقِيَ امْرَأَةً مَعَهَا وَلَدَانِ لَهَا كَالفَهْدَيْنِ، يَلعَبَانِ مِنْ تَحْتِ خَصْرِهَا بِرُمَّانَتَيْنِ، فَطَلَّقَنِي وَنَكَحَهَا، فَنَكَحْتُ بَعْدَهُ رَجُلًا سَرِيًّا، رَكِبَ شَرِيًّا، وَأَخَذَ خَطِّيًّا، وَأَرَاحَ عَلَيَّ نَعَمًا ثَرِيًّا، وَأَعْطَانِي مِنْ كُلِّ رَائِحَةٍ زَوْجًا، وَقَالَ: كُلِي أُمَّ زَرْعٍ، وَمِيرِي أَهْلَكِ، فَلَوْ جَمَعْتُ كُلَّ شَيْءٍ أَعْطَانِيهِ، مَا بَلَغَ أَصْغَرَ آنِيَةِ أَبِي زَرْعٍ.

قَالَتْ عَائِشَةُ: فَقَالَ لِي رَسُولُ اللهِ ﷺ: «كُنْتُ لَكِ كَأَبِي زَرْعٍ لأُمِّ زَرْعٍ».

253. 'Alī Ibn Ḥujr narrated to us; 'Isā Ibn Yūnus narrated to us; from Hishām Ibn 'Urwah; from his brother; from 'Urwah that

'Ā'ishah (*raḍiyAllāhu 'anhā*) said:

'Eleven women sat together, pledged and committed themselves that they would not conceal anything about their husbands.

The first said: 'My husband is like the meat of a scrawny camel (*jamal*) which is kept on the top of a mountain which is neither easy to climb, nor is the meat fleshy enough for it to be carried away [by people to eat].'

The second said: 'My husband, I do not reveal information about him, for fear that I may not be able to finish with him; for if I mention him, I shall mention his apparent and hidden defects.'

The third said: 'My husband is extremely tall and bad mannered (*'ashannaq*). If I speak [about his faults], I will be divorced, and if I remain silent, I am left hanging.'

The fourth said: 'My husband is [moderate] like the night of Tihamah which is neither extremely hot nor cold; neither fearful nor boring.'

The fifth said: 'My husband, if he enters [the house], he pounces like a leopard, and if he leaves, he is bold like a lion, and does not ask about whatever happened [to his wealth].'

The sixth said: 'My husband, if he eats, he eats excessively [due to his gluttonousness], and if he drinks, he gulps all of it, and if he lies down to sleeps, he wraps himself up, and he does not feel his palm [inside my clothes] to know my sorrow.'

The seventh said: 'My husband is incompetent (*'ayāyā'*),

misguided (*ghayāyā'*) and impotent (*ṭabāqā'*), [he is] sick with every sickness (*dā'*), [if he beats] he will cause injury to your skull, or break your bones, or do both to you.'

The eighth said: 'My husband's touch is like the [soft] touch of a rabbit (*arnab*), and [his] scent is like the scent of a sweetsmelling perfume (*zarnab*).'

The ninth said: 'My husband has the loftest of houses (*rafi' al-'imād*), is tall of stature (*ṭawīl al-najād*), is abundantly hospitable (*'aẓīm al-ramād*), and has a house close to the people's assembly (*bayt al-nād*).'

The tenth said: 'My husband is Mālik, and what is [that I can say about] Mālik? Mālik is better than that; he has many camels that are kept [ready to be slaughtered for guests] and a few roam the pastures. If they hear the sound of the lute, they know for certain that they are about to be slaughtered.'

The eleventh said: 'My husband is Abū Zar' and what is [that I can say about] Abū Zar'?

'He has made my ears dangle with jewellery, filled my upper arms with fat, and honoured me until I felt proud of myself. He found me among the poor sherherds in dire straits and then placed me among the owners of horses, camels, and cows that trample crops and workers who thresh seeds. In his presence I can speak, for I shall not be scolded [or rebuked], and when I sleep, I sleep till late in the morning, and when I drink, I drink until I satisfy my thirst.'

'The mother of Abū Zar'and what is [that I can say about] the mother of Abū Zar'? Her sacks are heavy [with provision] and her house is spacious.'

'The son of Abū Zarʿ and what is [that I can say about] the son of Abū Zarʿ? His bed is like a palm-stick stripped of its leaves [because he is very slender], and he is satiated by the foreleg of a lamb (*jafrah*).'

'The daughter of Abū Zarʿ and what is [that I can say about] the daughter of Abū Zarʿ? She is obedient to her father and to her mother. She fills her clothes [and is corpulent], and enrages her female neighbours [because of her beauty].'

'The maidservant of Abū Zarʿ and what is [that I can say about] the maidservant of Abū Zarʿ? She does not broadcast what we say in our conversation, nor does she waste our provisions, and nor does she leave the litter scattered in our house.'

She then added: 'One day it so happened that Abū Zarʿ went out at the time when the milkskins were being churned [to extract butter], and he encountered a woman who had with her two children, like two leopards playing under her waist with two pomegranates. [On seeing her] he divorced me and married her. Thereafter I married a nobleman who rode a sturdy horse and held a spear in his hand, and brought home to me ample livestock, and used to say to me: 'Eat Umm Zarʿ, and feed your family [and relatives]!' Yet, were I to gather everything that he gave me, it would not amount to the smallest of vessels of Abū Zarʿ!'

ʿĀ'ishah (*raḍiyAllāhu ʿanhā*) said: 'The Messenger of Allāh (ﷺ) said to me: "I have been to you as Abū Zarʿ was to Umm Zarʿ."'[257]

[257] Bukhārī, #5189, and Muslim, #2448.

CHAPTER THIRTY-NINE

بَابُ مَا جَاءَ فِي نَوْمِ رَسُولِ اللهِ ﷺ

What has been narrated concerning the Description of the Sleep (*nawm*) of the Messenger of Allāh (ﷺ)

٢٥٤ـ حَدَّثَنَا مُحَمَّدُ بْنُ الْمُثَنَّى، قَالَ: حَدَّثَنَا عَبْدُ الرَّحْمَنِ بْنُ مَهْدِيٍّ، قَالَ: حَدَّثَنَا إِسْرَائِيلُ، عَنْ أَبِي إِسْحَاقَ، عَنْ عَبْدِ اللهِ بْنِ يَزِيدَ، عَنِ الْبَرَاءِ بْنِ عَازِبٍ، أَنَّ النَّبِيَّ ﷺ كَانَ إِذَا أَخَذَ مَضْجَعَهُ وَضَعَ كَفَّهُ الْيُمْنَى تَحْتَ خَدِّهِ الأَيْمَنِ، وقَالَ: «رَبِّ قِنِي عَذَابَكَ يَوْمَ تَبْعَثُ عِبَادَكَ».

254. Muḥammad Ibn al-Muthannā narrated to us; Abdu'l-Raḥmān Ibn Mahdī narrated to us; Isrā'īl narrated to us; from Abū Isḥāq; from 'Abdullāh Ibn Yazīd that al-Barā'a Ibn 'Āzib (*raḍiyAllāhu 'anhu*) said:

> 'When the Prophet (ﷺ) lay down to sleep, he placed his right palm under his right cheek, and said: *"Rabbī qiynī 'adhābaka yawma tab'athu 'ibādak."*—"O my Lord, protect me from Your torment on the day when You resurrect Your servants."'[258]

---

[258] Aḥmad in his *Musnad*, #18672.

٢٥٥ـ حَدَّثَنَا مُحَمَّدُ بْنُ الْمُثَنَّى، قَالَ: حَدَّثَنَا عَبْدُ الرَّحْمَنِ، قَالَ: حَدَّثَنَا إِسْرَائِيلُ، عَنْ أَبِي إِسْحَاقَ، عَنْ أَبِي عُبَيْدَةَ، عَنْ عَبْدِ اللهِ مِثْلَهُ، وَقَالَ: «يَوْمَ تَجْمَعُ عِبَادَكَ».

255. Muḥammad Ibn al-Muthannā narrated to us; ʿAbdu'l-Raḥmān narrated to us; Isrā'īl narrated to us; from Abū Isḥāq; from Abū ʿUbadah that ʿAbdullāh [Ibn Masʿūd] said the same but with the exception of:

> *"...yawma tajmaʿ ʿibādak."*—"...on the Day You will gather Your servants."

٢٥٦ـ حَدَّثَنَا مَحْمُودُ بْنُ غَيْلَانَ، قَالَ: حَدَّثَنَا عَبْدُ الرَّزَّاقِ، قَالَ: حَدَّثَنَا سُفْيَانُ، عَنْ عَبْدِ الْمَلِكِ بْنِ عُمَيْرٍ، عَنْ رِبْعِيِّ بْنِ حِرَاشٍ، عَنْ حُذَيْفَةَ، قَالَ: كَانَ النَّبِيُّ ﷺ إِذَا أَوَى إِلَى فِرَاشِهِ، قَالَ: «اللَّهُمَّ بِاسْمِكَ أَمُوتُ وَأَحْيَا»، وَإِذَا اسْتَيْقَظَ قَالَ: «الْحَمْدُ للهِ الَّذِي أَحْيَانَا بَعْدَمَا أَمَاتَنَا، وَإِلَيْهِ النُّشُورُ».

256. Maḥmūd Ibn Ghaylān narrated to us; ʿAbdu'l-Razzāq narrated to us; Sufyān narrated to us; from ʿAbdu'l-Mālik Ibn ʿUmayr; from Rabīʿ Ibn Harāsh that Hudhayfah (*raḍiyAllāhu ʿanhu*) said:

> 'When the Prophet (ﷺ) would retire to his bedding (firāsh), he would say: *"Allāhumma bi'smika amūtu wa aḥyā."*—"O Allāh! By Your Name I shall die and live."
>
> When he woke up, he would say: *"Al-ḥamdu-li'-llāhi 'illahī aḥyānā baʿda mā amātanā wa ilayhil-nushūr."*—"Praise be to Allāh who revived us after He caused us to die, and to Him is [our] final return."'[259]

[259] Bukhārī, #6312, Abū Dāwūd, #5049 and Tirmidhī, #3418.

٢٥٧ـ حَدَّثَنَا قُتَيْبَةُ بْنُ سَعِيدٍ، قَالَ: حَدَّثَنَا الْمُفَضَّلُ بْنُ فَضَالَةَ، عَنْ عُقَيْلٍ، أُرَاهُ عَنِ الزُّهْرِيِّ، عَنْ عُرْوَةَ، عَنْ عَائِشَةَ قَالَتْ: «كَانَ رَسُولُ اللهِ ﷺ إِذَا أَوَى إِلَى فِرَاشِهِ كُلَّ لَيْلَةٍ جَمَعَ كَفَّيْهِ فَنَفَثَ فِيهِمَا، وَقَرَأَ فِيهِمَا ﴿قُلْ هُوَ ٱللَّهُ أَحَدٌ﴾ وَ﴿قُلْ أَعُوذُ بِرَبِّ ٱلْفَلَقِ﴾ وَ﴿قُلْ أَعُوذُ بِرَبِّ ٱلنَّاسِ﴾، ثُمَّ مَسَحَ بِهِمَا مَا اسْتَطَاعَ مِنْ جَسَدِهِ، يَبْدَأُ بِهِمَا رَأْسَهُ وَوَجْهَهُ، وَمَا أَقْبَلَ مِنْ جَسَدِهِ، يَصْنَعُ ذَلِكَ ثَلَاثَ مَرَّاتٍ».

257. Qutaybah Ibn Sa'īd narrated to us; Al-Mufaḍḍal Ibn Fuḍālah narrated to us; from 'Uqayl; from al-Zuhrī; from 'Urwah that 'Ā'ishah (*raḍiyAllāhu 'anha*) said:

> 'When the Messenger of Allāh (ﷺ) would retire to his bedding each night, he would join the palms of his hands, then blow into them and recite into them: *"Qul HuwAllāhu Aḥad..."*—"Say: 'He is Allāh, One...!" [*al-Ikhlāṣ* (112): 1] and: *"Qul a'ūdhu bi-Rabbi'l-falaq..."*—"Say: 'I take refuge with the Lord of the Daybreak..." [*al-Falaq* (113): 1] and: *"Qul a'ūdhu bi-Rabbi'l-nās..."*—"Say: 'I take refuge with the Lord of mankind..." [*al-Nās* (114): 1] He would then wipe with them whatever he could of his body, beginning by wiping his head and his face and the front part of his body, doing that three times."'[260]

٢٥٨ـ حَدَّثَنَا مُحَمَّدُ بْنُ بَشَّارٍ، قَالَ: حَدَّثَنَا عَبْدُ الرَّحْمَنِ بْنُ مَهْدِيٍّ، قَالَ: حَدَّثَنَا سُفْيَانُ، عَنْ سَلَمَةَ بْنِ كُهَيْلٍ، عَنْ كُرَيْبٍ، عَنِ ابْنِ عَبَّاسٍ: «أَنَّ رَسُولَ اللهِ ﷺ نَامَ حَتَّى نَفَخَ، وَكَانَ إِذَا نَامَ نَفَخَ، فَأَتَاهُ بِلَالٌ فَآذَنَهُ بِالصَّلَاةِ، فَقَامَ وَصَلَّى وَلَمْ يَتَوَضَّأْ» وَفِي الْحَدِيثِ قِصَّةٌ.

[260] Bukhārī, #5017, Abū Dāwūd, #6056 and Tirmidhī, #3402.

٢٥٨ـ حَدَّثَنَا مُحَمَّدُ بْنُ بَشَّارٍ، قَالَ: حَدَّثَنَا عَبْدُ الرَّحْمَنِ بْنُ مَهْدِيٍّ، قَالَ: حَدَّثَنَا سُفْيَانُ، عَنْ سَلَمَةَ بْنِ كُهَيْلٍ، عَنْ كُرَيْبٍ، عَنِ ابْنِ عَبَّاسٍ: «أَنَّ رَسُولَ اللهِ ﷺ نَامَ حَتَّى نَفَخَ، وَكَانَ إِذَا نَامَ نَفَخَ، فَأَتَاهُ بِلَالٌ فَآذَنَهُ بِالصَّلَاةِ، فَقَامَ وَصَلَّى وَلَمْ يَتَوَضَّأْ» وَفِي الْحَدِيثِ قِصَّةٌ .

258. Muḥammad Ibn Bashshār narrated to us; Abdu'l-Raḥmān Ibn Mahdī narrated to us; Sufyān narrated to us; from Salamah Ibn Kuhayl; from Kurayb that Ibn ʿAbbās (*raḍiyAllāhu ʿanhumā*) said:

> 'The Messenger of Allāh (ﷺ) slept until he was breathing heavily, and when he would sleep, he breathed heavily, so Bilāl came to him and notified him for ritual prayer, whereupon he got up and performed the ritual prayer without performing riual ablution.'

This tradition has a detailed incident.[261]

٢٥٩ـ حَدَّثَنَا إِسْحَاقُ بْنُ مَنْصُورٍ، قَالَ: حَدَّثَنَا عَفَّانُ، قَالَ: حَدَّثَنَا حَمَّادُ بْنُ سَلَمَةَ، عَنْ ثَابِتٍ، عَنْ أَنَسِ بْنِ مَالِكٍ، أَنَّ رَسُولَ اللهِ ﷺ كَانَ إِذَا أَوَى إِلَى فِرَاشِهِ، قَالَ: «الْحَمْدُ للهِ الَّذِي أَطْعَمَنَا، وَسَقَانَا، وَكَفَانَا، وَآوَانَا، فَكَمْ مِمَّنْ لَا كَافِيَ لَهُ، وَلَا مُؤْوِيَ» .

259. Isḥāq Ibn Manṣūr narrated to us; ʿAffān narrated to us; Ḥammād Ibn Salamah narrated to us; from Thābit that Anas Ibn Mālik (*raḍiyAllāhu ʿanhu*) said:

> 'When the Messenger of Allāh (ﷺ) would retire to his bedding, he would say:
>
> *"Al-ḥamdu-li'-llāhi 'illahee aṭʿamanā wa saqānā wa kafānā wa āwānā, fakam miman lā kāfiyah lahu wa lā mu'wiyī."*

[261] Bukhārī, #138, and Tirmidhī, #232.

> "Praise be to Allāh, who fed us and gave us drink, and sufficed us and sheltered us, for how many there are who have neither anyone to take care of them nor anyone to provide shelter!"[262]

٢٦٠ـ حَدَّثَنَا الْحُسَيْنُ بْنُ مُحَمَّدٍ الْجَرِيْرِيُّ، قَالَ: حَدَّثَنَا سُلَيْمَانُ بْنُ حَرْبٍ، قَالَ: حَدَّثَنَا حَمَّادُ بْنُ سَلَمَةَ، عَنْ حُمَيْدٍ، عَنْ بَكْرِ بْنِ عَبْدِ اللهِ الْمُزَنِيِّ، عَنْ عَبْدِ اللهِ بْنِ رَبَاحٍ، عَنْ أَبِي قَتَادَةَ: «أَنَّ النَّبِيَّ ﷺ كَانَ إِذَا عَرَّسَ بِلَيْلٍ اضْطَجَعَ عَلَى شِقِّهِ الأَيْمَنِ، وَإِذَا عَرَّسَ قُبَيْلَ الصُّبْحِ نَصَبَ ذِرَاعَهُ، وَوَضَعَ رَأْسَهُ عَلَى كَفِّهِ» .

260. Al-Ḥusayn Ibn Muḥammad al-Jarīrī narrated to us; Sulaymān Ibn Ḥarb narrated to us; Ḥammād Ibn Salamah narrated to us; from Ḥumayd; from Bakr Ibn 'Abdulllāh al-Muzanī; from 'Abdullāh Ibn Rabāḥ that Abū Qatādah (*raḍiyAllāhu 'anhu*) said:

> 'When the Prophet (ﷺ) would stop over for rest on a journey at night, he would recline on his right side, and when he would stop over to rest on a journey just before the morning, he would position his forearm upright and place his head on the palm of his hand.'[263]

[262] Muslim, #2715, and Tirmidhī, #3396.

[263] Muslim, #2715.

CHAPTER FORTY

بَابُ مَا جَاءَ فِي عِبَادَةِ رَسُولِ اللهِ ﷺ

What has been narrated concerning the Worship (*ʿibadah*) of the Messenger of Allāh (ﷺ)

٢٦١ـ حَدَّثَنَا قُتَيْبَةُ بْنُ سَعِيدٍ، وَبِشْرُ بْنُ مُعَاذٍ، قَالَا: حَدَّثَنَا أَبُو عَوَانَةَ، عَنْ زِيَادِ بْنِ عِلَاقَةَ، عَنِ الْمُغِيرَةِ بْنِ شُعْبَةَ قَالَ: صَلَّى رَسُولُ اللهِ ﷺ حَتَّى انْتَفَخَتْ قَدَمَاهُ، فَقِيلَ لَهُ: أَتَتَكَلَّفُ هَذَا وَقَدْ غَفَرَ اللهُ لَكَ مَا تَقَدَّمَ مِنْ ذَنْبِكَ وَمَا تَأَخَّرَ؟ قَالَ: «أَفَلَا أَكُونُ عَبْدًا شَكُورًا» .

261. Qutaybah Ibn Saʿīd and Bishr Ibn Muʿādh narrated to us; Abū ʿAwānah narrated to us; from Ziyād Ibn ʿAlāqah that Mughīrah Ibn Shuʿbah (*raḍiyAllāhu ʿanhu*) said:

> 'The Messenger of Allāh (ﷺ) prayed until his feet became swollen, when he was asked: 'Why do endure this when Allāh has forgiven you your former and your latter sins? (*dhanb*).' He (ﷺ) replied: "Should I not be a thankful servant (*ʿabd shakūr*)?"[264]

[264] Bukhārī, #1130, Muslim, #2819, and Tirmidhī, #412.

٢٦٢- حَدَّثَنَا أَبُو عَمَّارٍ الْحُسَيْنُ بْنُ حُرَيْثٍ، قَالَ: حَدَّثَنَا الْفَضْلُ بْنُ مُوسَى، عَنْ مُحَمَّدِ بْنِ عَمْرٍو، عَنْ أَبِي سَلَمَةَ، عَنْ أَبِي هُرَيْرَةَ، قَالَ: كَانَ رَسُولُ اللهِ ﷺ يُصَلِّي حَتَّى تَرِمَ قَدَمَاهُ، قَالَ: فَقِيلَ لَهُ: أَتَفْعَلُ هَذَا وَقَدْ جَاءَكَ أَنَّ اللهَ قَدْ غَفَرَ لَكَ مَا تَقَدَّمَ مِنْ ذَنْبِكَ وَمَا تَأَخَّرَ؟ قَالَ: «أَفَلَا أَكُونُ عَبْدًا شَكُورًا».

262. Abū ʿAmmār al-Ḥusayn Ibn Ḥurayth narrated to us; Al-Faḍl Ibn Mūsā narrated to us; from Muḥammad Ibn ʿAmr; from Abū Salamah that Abū Hurayrah (*raḍiyAllāhu ʿanhu*) said:

> 'The Messenger of Allāh (ﷺ) used to perform the prayer until his feet had swollen, when he was asked: 'Must you do this, when it has come to you that Allāh has already forgiven you your former and your latter sins?' He (ﷺ) replied: "Should I not be a thankful servant (*ʿabd shakūr*)?"[265]

٢٦٣- حَدَّثَنَا عِيسَى بْنُ عُثْمَانَ بْنِ عِيسَى بْنِ عَبْدِ الرَّحْمَنِ الرَّمْلِيُّ، قَالَ: حَدَّثَنَا عَمِّي يَحْيَى بْنُ عِيسَى الرَّمْلِيُّ، عَنِ الْأَعْمَشِ، عَنْ أَبِي صَالِحٍ، عَنْ أَبِي هُرَيْرَةَ، قَالَ: كَانَ رَسُولُ اللهِ ﷺ يَقُومُ يُصَلِّي حَتَّى تَنْتَفِخَ قَدَمَاهُ، فَيُقَالُ لَهُ: يَا رَسُولَ اللهِ! تَفْعَلُ هَذَا وَقَدْ غَفَرَ اللهُ لَكَ مَا تَقَدَّمَ مِنْ ذَنْبِكَ وَمَا تَأَخَّرَ؟ قَالَ: «أَفَلَا أَكُونُ عَبْدًا شَكُورًا» .

263. ʿIsā Ibn ʿUthmān Ibn ʿIsā Ibn ʿAbdu'l-Raḥmān al-Ramlī narrated to us; My paternal uncle Yaḥyā Ibn ʿIsā al-Ramlī narrated to us; from al-Aʿmash; from Abū Ṣāliḥ that Abū Hurayrah (*raḍiyAllāhu ʿanhu*) said:

> 'The Messenger of Allāh (ﷺ) used to perform the prayer until his feet had become swollen, when he was asked:

[265] Ibn Mājah, #1420.

> 'Must you do this, when Allāh has already forgiven you your former and your latter sins?' He (ﷺ) replied: "Should I not be a thankful servant (*'abd shakūr*)?"[266]

٢٦٤ـ حَدَّثَنَا مُحَمَّدُ بْنُ بَشَّارٍ، قَالَ: حَدَّثَنَا مُحَمَّدُ بْنُ جَعْفَرٍ، قَالَ: حَدَّثَنَا شُعْبَةُ، عَنْ أَبِي إِسْحَاقَ، عَنِ الأَسْوَدِ بْنِ يَزِيدَ، قَالَ: سَأَلْتُ عَائِشَةَ، عَنْ صَلاَةِ رَسُولِ الله ﷺ بِاللَّيْلِ؟ فَقَالَتْ: «كَانَ يَنَامُ أَوَّلَ اللَّيْلِ ثُمَّ يَقُومُ، فَإِذَا كَانَ مِنَ السَّحَرِ أَوْتَرَ، ثُمَّ أَتَى فِرَاشَهُ، فَإِذَا كَانَ لَهُ حَاجَةٌ أَلَمَّ بِأَهْلِهِ، فَإِذَا سَمِعَ الأَذَانَ وَثَبَ، فَإِنْ كَانَ جُنُبًا أَفَاضَ عَلَيْهِ مِنَ المَاءِ، وَإِلَّا تَوَضَّأَ وَخَرَجَ إِلَى الصَّلَاةِ».

264. Muḥammad Ibn Bashshār narrated to us; Muḥammad Ibn Jā'far narrated to us; Shu'bah narrated to us; from Abū Isḥāq that Al-Aswad Ibn Yazīd said:

> 'I asked 'Ā'ishah (*raḍiyAllāhu 'anhā*) about the nighttime prayer of the Messenger of Allāh (ﷺ).' She replied: He would sleep the first portion of the night and then he would get up [to perform the prayer]. Then, when it was the latter portion of the night, he would perform the witr [prayer]. Thereafter, he went to his bedding and if he had a need, he had sexual intercourse with his wife [and then slept]. When he heard the call to prayer, he sprang up, and if he was in a state of major impurity (*junub*), he would pour water over his entire body, otherwise he would perform ablution and went out to ritual prayer.'[267]

[266] This ḥadīth and the one previous together strengthen each other, as well as the ḥadīth of Al-Mughīrah which has preceeded, see number 261.
[267] Bukhārī, #1146, and Muslim, #739.

٢٦٥ـ حَدَّثَنَا قُتَيْبَةُ بْنُ سَعِيدٍ، عَنْ مَالِكِ بْنِ أَنَسٍ، (ح) وَحَدَّثَنَا إِسْحَاقُ ابْنُ مُوسَى الأَنْصَارِيُّ، قَالَ: حَدَّثَنَا مَعْنٌ، عَنْ مَالِكٍ، عَنْ مَخْرَمَةَ بْنِ سُلَيْمَانَ، عَنْ كُرَيْبٍ، عَنِ ابْنِ عَبَّاسٍ، «أَنَّهُ أَخْبَرَهُ أَنَّهُ بَاتَ عِنْدَ مَيْمُونَةَ وَهِيَ خَالَتُهُ، قَالَ: فَاضْطَجَعْتُ فِي عَرْضِ الوِسَادَةِ، وَاضْطَجَعَ رَسُولُ اللهِ ﷺ فِي طُولِهَا، فَنَامَ رَسُولُ اللهِ ﷺ حَتَّى إِذَا انْتَصَفَ اللَّيْلُ أَوْ قَبْلَهُ بِقَلِيلٍ أَوْ بَعْدَهُ بِقَلِيلٍ، فَاسْتَيْقَظَ رَسُولُ اللهِ ﷺ فَجَعَلَ يَمْسَحُ النَّوْمَ عَنْ وَجْهِهِ، ثُمَّ قَرَأَ العَشْرَ الآيَاتِ الخَوَاتِيمَ مِنْ سُورَةِ آلِ عِمْرَانَ، ثُمَّ قَامَ إِلَى شَنٍّ مُعَلَّقٍ فَتَوَضَّأَ مِنْهَا، فَأَحْسَنَ الوُضُوءَ، ثُمَّ قَامَ يُصَلِّي، قَالَ عَبْدُ اللهِ بْنُ عَبَّاسٍ: فَقُمْتُ إِلَى جَنْبِهِ فَوَضَعَ رَسُولُ اللهِ ﷺ يَدَهُ اليُمْنَى عَلَى رَأْسِي، ثُمَّ أَخَذَ بِأُذُنِي اليُمْنَى فَفَتَلَهَا، فَصَلَّى رَكْعَتَيْنِ، ثُمَّ رَكْعَتَيْنِ، ثُمَّ رَكْعَتَيْنِ، ثُمَّ رَكْعَتَيْنِ، ثُمَّ رَكْعَتَيْنِ، ثُمَّ رَكْعَتَيْنِ ـ قَالَ مَعْنٌ: سِتَّ مَرَّاتٍ ـ ثُمَّ أَوْتَرَ، ثُمَّ اضْطَجَعَ».

265. Qutaybah Ibn Sa'īd narrated to us; from Mālik Ibn Anas and Isḥāq Ibn Mūsā al-Anṣārī narrated to us; Ma'an narrated to us; from Mālik; from Makhramah Ibn Sulaymān; from Kurayb that Ibn 'Abbās (*raḍiyAllāhu 'anhumā*) informed him that he spent the night in the home of his maternal aunt Maymūnah, and said:

> 'I lay on the width of the pillow, while the Messenger of Allāh (ﷺ) lay on it lengthwise. The Messenger of Allāh (ﷺ) slept until the middle of the night, or just a little before or after it. The Messenger of Allāh (ﷺ) then wiped the [traces of] sleep from his face, and then recited the final ten verses of *Surah Āl-'Imrān*. He then approached a suspended waterskin, performed ablution [from the water in it] and did so excellently, after which he performed the prayer.

> 'Abdullāh Ibn 'Abbās (*raḍiyAllāhu 'anhumā*) said: 'Then, I stood next to him, whereupon the Messenger of Allāh (ﷺ) placed his right hand on my head, and took me by

my right ear and twisted it. He then prayed two cycles [of prayer], followed by another two, and then another two, and then another two, and then another two, and then two.'

Ma'an said: '...six times-after which he performed the witr prayer, after which he laid down."[268]

٢٦٦ـ حَدَّثَنَا أَبُو كُرَيْبٍ مُحَمَّدُ بْنُ العَلَاءِ، قَالَ: حَدَّثَنَا وَكِيعٌ، عَنْ شُعْبَةَ، عَنْ أَبِي جَمْرَةَ، عَنِ ابْنِ عَبَّاسٍ، قَالَ: «كَانَ النَّبِيُّ ﷺ يُصَلِّي مِنَ اللَّيْلِ ثَلَاثَ عَشْرَةَ رَكْعَةً».

266. Abū Kurayb Muḥammad Ibn al-A'lā narrated to us; Wakī' narrated to us; from Shu'bah; from Abū Jamrah that Ibn 'Abbās (*raḍiyAllāhu 'anhuma*) said:

> 'The Prophet (ﷺ) used to perform thirteen cycles (*rak'ah*) during the night.'[269]

٢٦٧ـ حَدَّثَنَا قُتَيْبَةُ بْنُ سَعِيدٍ، قَالَ: حَدَّثَنَا أَبُو عَوَانَةَ، عَنْ قَتَادَةَ، عَنْ زُرَارَةَ ابْنِ أَوْفَى، عَنْ سَعْدِ بْنِ هِشَامٍ، عَنْ عَائِشَةَ: أَنَّ النَّبِيَّ ﷺ كَانَ إِذَا لَمْ يُصَلِّ بِاللَّيْلِ مَنَعَهُ مِنْ ذَلِكَ النَّوْمُ، أَوْ غَلَبَتْهُ عَيْنَاهُ، صَلَّى مِنَ النَّهَارِ ثِنْتَيْ عَشْرَةَ رَكْعَةً

267. Qutabah Ibn Sa'īd narrated to us; Abū 'Awānah narrated to us; from Qatādah; from Zurarah Ibn Awfā; from Sa'd Ibn Hishām that 'Ā'ishah (*raḍiyAllāhu 'anhā*) said:

> 'If the Prophet (ﷺ) did not perform the prayer at night due to being prevented by sleep or being overcome by intense drowsiness, he would perform twelve cycles dur-

[268] Bukhārī, #138, and Tirmidhī, #232.

[269] Bukhārī, #1138, Muslim, #764, and Tirmidhī, #442.

ing the day.'[270]

٢٦٨ـ حَدَّثَنَا مُحَمَّدُ بْنُ الْعَلَاءِ، قَالَ: حَدَّثَنَا أَبُو أُسَامَةَ، عَنْ هِشَامٍ ـ يَعْنِي ابْنَ حَسَّانَ ـ، عَنْ مُحَمَّدِ بْنِ سِيرِينَ، عَنْ أَبِي هُرَيْرَةَ، عَنِ النَّبِيِّ ﷺ قَالَ: «إِذَا قَامَ أَحَدُكُمْ مِنَ اللَّيْلِ فَلْيَفْتَتِحْ صَلَاتَهُ بِرَكْعَتَيْنِ خَفِيفَتَيْنِ».

268. Muḥammad Ibn al-A'lā' narrated to us; Abū Usamah narrated to us; from Hishām Ibn Ḥassan; from Muḥammad Ibn Sirin that Abū Hurayrah (*raḍiyAllāhu 'anhu*) said that the Prophet (ﷺ) said:

> "When one of you gets up at night, let him begin his prayer with two short cycles."[271]

٢٦٩ـ حَدَّثَنَا قُتَيْبَةُ بْنُ سَعِيدٍ، عَنْ مَالِكِ بْنِ أَنَسٍ، (ح) وَحَدَّثَنَا إِسْحَاقُ ابْنُ مُوسَى، قَالَ: حَدَّثَنَا مَعْنٌ قَالَ: حَدَّثَنَا مَالِكٌ، عَنْ عَبْدِ اللهِ بْنِ أَبِي بَكْرٍ، عَنْ أَبِيهِ، أَنَّ عَبْدَ اللهِ بْنَ قَيْسِ بْنِ مَخْرَمَةَ، أَخْبَرَهُ عَنْ زَيْدِ بْنِ خَالِدٍ الْجُهَنِيِّ، أَنَّهُ قَالَ: «لَأَرْمُقَنَّ صَلَاةَ النَّبِيِّ ﷺ، فَتَوَسَّدْتُ عَتَبَتَهُ، أَوْ فُسْطَاطَهُ فَصَلَّى رَسُولُ اللهِ ﷺ رَكْعَتَيْنِ خَفِيفَتَيْنِ، ثُمَّ صَلَّى رَكْعَتَيْنِ طَوِيلَتَيْنِ، طَوِيلَتَيْنِ، طَوِيلَتَيْنِ، ثُمَّ صَلَّى رَكْعَتَيْنِ وَهُمَا دُونَ اللَّتَيْنِ قَبْلَهُمَا، ثُمَّ صَلَّى رَكْعَتَيْنِ وَهُمَا دُونَ اللَّتَيْنِ قَبْلَهُمَا، ثُمَّ صَلَّى رَكْعَتَيْنِ وَهُمَا دُونَ اللَّتَيْنِ قَبْلَهُمَا، ثُمَّ صَلَّى رَكْعَتَيْنِ وَهُمَا دُونَ اللَّتَيْنِ قَبْلَهُمَا، ثُمَّ أَوْتَرَ فَذَلِكَ ثَلَاثَ عَشْرَةَ رَكْعَةً».

Isḥāq Ibn Mūsā narrated to us; Ma'an narrated to us; from 'Abdullāh Ibn Abū Bakr; from his father that 'Abdullāh Ibn Qays Ibn Makh-

[270] Muslim, #746, and Tirmidhī, #445.
[271] Muslim, #768.

ramah informed us that Zayd Ibn Khalid al-Jahuhanī said:

> 'I was observing the prayer of the Prophet (ﷺ) closely, so I laid my head on his doorstep or his tent. The Messenger of Allāh (ﷺ) performed two brisk cycles of prayer. After this he performed two lengthy, two lengthy, two lengthy cycles. Then he performed two cycles which were shorter than those before them. Then he performed two cycles which were shorter than those before them. Then he performed two cycles which were shorter than those before them. Then he performed two cycles which were shorter than those before them. Then finally he performed a single cycle of *witr*, so that added to a total of thirteen cycles [altogether].'[272]

٢٧٠ـ حَدَّثَنَا إِسْحَاقُ بْنُ مُوسَى، قَالَ: حَدَّثَنَا مَعْنٌ، قَالَ: حَدَّثَنَا مَالِكٌ، عَنْ سَعِيدِ بْنِ أَبِي سَعِيدٍ الْمَقْبُرِيِّ، عَنْ أَبِي سَلَمَةَ بْنِ عَبْدِ الرَّحْمَنِ، أَنَّهُ أَخْبَرَهُ أَنَّهُ سَأَلَ عَائِشَةَ، كَيْفَ كَانَتْ صَلَاةُ رَسُولِ اللهِ ﷺ فِي رَمَضَانَ؟ فَقَالَتْ: مَا كَانَ رَسُولُ اللهِ ﷺ لِيَزِيدَ فِي رَمَضَانَ، وَلَا فِي غَيْرِهِ عَلَى إِحْدَى عَشْرَةَ رَكْعَةً، يُصَلِّي أَرْبَعًا لَا تَسْأَلْ عَنْ حُسْنِهِنَّ وَطُولِهِنَّ، ثُمَّ يُصَلِّي أَرْبَعًا لَا تَسْأَلْ عَنْ حُسْنِهِنَّ وَطُولِهِنَّ، ثُمَّ يُصَلِّي ثَلَاثًا، قَالَتْ عَائِشَةُ: قُلْتُ: يَا رَسُولَ اللهِ! أَتَنَامُ قَبْلَ أَنْ تُوتِرَ؟ فَقَالَ: يَا عَائِشَةُ! «إِنَّ عَيْنَيَّ تَنَامَانِ وَلَا يَنَامُ قَلْبِي».

narrated to us; from Sa'īd Ibn Abī Sa'īd al-Maqbūrī; from Abū Salamah Ibn 'Abdu'l-Raḥmān that he informed him that he asked 'Ā'ishah (*raḍiyAllāhu 'anhā*):

'How was the prayer of the Messenger of Allāh (ﷺ)

[272] Muslim, #765.

during Ramaḍān?' So she said: 'The Messenger of Allāh (ﷺ) would pray no more than eleven cycles in or outside Ramaḍān; do not ask about their excellence and their length. Then he would pray another four cycles; do not ask about their excellence and their length. Then he would perform three cycles.'

'Ā'ishah (*raḍiyAllāhu 'anha*) said: 'I said: 'O Messenger of Allāh, do you sleep before you perform witr?' He said: "O 'Ā'ishah, my eyes sleep, but my heart does not sleep."''[273]

٢٧١- حَدَّثَنَا إِسْحَاقُ بْنُ مُوسَى، قَالَ: حَدَّثَنَا مَعْنٌ، قَالَ: حَدَّثَنَا مَالِكٌ، عَنِ ابْنِ شِهَابٍ، عَنْ عُرْوَةَ، عَنْ عَائِشَةَ: «أَنَّ رَسُولَ اللهِ ﷺ كَانَ يُصَلِّي مِنَ اللَّيْلِ إِحْدَى عَشْرَةَ رَكْعَةً يُوتِرُ مِنْهَا بِوَاحِدَةٍ، فَإِذَا فَرَغَ مِنْهَا اضْطَجَعَ عَلَى شِقِّهِ الأَيْمَنِ».

271. Isḥāq Ibn Mūsā narrated to us; Ma'an narrated to us; Mālik narrated to us; from Ibn Shihab; from 'Urwah that 'Ā'ishah (*raḍiyAllāhu 'anhā*) said:

'The Messenger of Allāh (ﷺ) performed eleven cycles of prayer during the night, of which one cycle was of witr, and when had finished, he reclined on his right side.'[274]

٢٧٢- حَدَّثَنَا ابْنُ أَبِي عُمَرَ، قَالَ: حَدَّثَنَا مَعْنٌ، عَنْ مَالِكٍ، عَنِ ابْنِ شِهَابٍ، نَحْوَهُ (ح)، وَحَدَّثَنَا قُتَيْبَةُ، عَنْ مَالِكٍ، عَنِ ابْنِ شِهَابٍ، نَحْوَهُ.

272. Ibn Abī 'Umar narrated to us; Ma'an narrated to us; from Mālik; from Ibn Shihāb and likewise from Qutabah; from Mālik;

[273] Bukhārī, #1147, Muslim, #738, and Tirmidhī, #439.
[274] Bukhārī, #994, Muslim, #736, and Tirmidhī, #440.

from Ibn Shihāb similar to the previous one.

٢٧٣ـ حَدَّثَنَا هَنَّادٌ، قَالَ: حَدَّثَنَا أَبُو الأَحْوَصِ، عَنِ الأَعْمَشِ، عَنْ إِبْرَاهِيمَ، عَنِ الأَسْوَدِ، عَنْ عَائِشَةَ، قَالَتْ: «كَانَ رَسُولُ اللهِ ﷺ يُصَلِّي مِنَ اللَّيْلِ تِسْعَ رَكَعَاتٍ» .

273. Hannād narrated to us; Abū'l-Aḥwaṣ narrated to us; from al-'Amash; from Ibrāhīm; from al-Aswad that 'Ā'ishah (*raḍiyAllāhu 'anhā*) said:

> 'The Messenger of Allāh (ﷺ) used to perform nine cycles of prayer during the night.'[275]

٢٧٤ـ حَدَّثَنَا مَحْمُودُ بْنُ غَيْلَانَ، قَالَ: حَدَّثَنَا يَحْيَى بْنُ آدَمَ، قَالَ: حَدَّثَنَا سُفْيَانُ الثَّوْرِيُّ، عَنِ الأَعْمَشِ، نَحْوَهُ.

274. Maḥmūd Ibn Ghaylān narrated to us; Yaḥyā Ibn Ādam narrated to us; Sufyān al-Thawrī narrated to us; from al-A'mash. This ḥadīth is similar to the previous but with a slightly different chain of narration.

٢٧٥ـ حَدَّثَنَا مُحَمَّدُ بْنُ الْمُثَنَّى، قَالَ: حَدَّثَنَا مُحَمَّدُ بْنُ جَعْفَرٍ، قَالَ: حَدَّثَنَا شُعْبَةُ، عَنْ عَمْرِو بْنِ مُرَّةَ، عَنْ أَبِي حَمْزَةَ، رَجُلٍ مِنَ الأَنْصَارِ، عَنْ رَجُلٍ مِنْ بَنِي عَبْسٍ، عَنْ حُذَيْفَةَ بْنِ الْيَمَانِ، «أَنَّهُ صَلَّى مَعَ النَّبِيِّ ﷺ مِنَ اللَّيْلِ، قَالَ: فَلَمَّا دَخَلَ فِي الصَّلَاةِ، قَالَ: اللهُ أَكْبَرُ ذُو الْمَلَكُوتِ وَالْجَبَرُوتِ وَالْكِبْرِيَاءِ وَالْعَظَمَةِ، قَالَ: ثُمَّ قَرَأَ الْبَقَرَةَ، ثُمَّ رَكَعَ رُكُوعَهُ نَحْوًا مِنْ قِيَامِهِ، وَكَانَ يَقُولُ: سُبْحَانَ رَبِّيَ الْعَظِيمِ، سُبْحَانَ رَبِّيَ الْعَظِيمِ ثُمَّ

[275] Tirmidhī, #443, and Ibn Mājah, #1360.

رَفَعَ رَأْسَهُ فَكَانَ قِيَامُهُ نَحْوًا مِنْ رُكُوعِهِ، وَكَانَ يَقُولُ: لِرَبِّيَ الحَمْدُ، لِرَبِّيَ الحَمْدُ ثُمَّ سَجَدَ فَكَانَ سُجُودُهُ نَحْوًا مِنْ قِيَامِهِ، وَكَانَ يَقُولُ: سُبْحَانَ رَبِّيَ الأَعْلَى، سُبْحَانَ رَبِّيَ الأَعْلَى ثُمَّ رَفَعَ رَأْسَهُ، فَكَانَ مَا بَيْنَ السَّجْدَتَيْنِ نَحْوًا مِنَ السُّجُودِ، وَكَانَ يَقُولُ: رَبِّ اغْفِرْ لِي، رَبِّ اغْفِرْ لِي، حَتَّى قَرَأَ البَقَرَةَ وَآلَ عِمْرَانَ وَالنِّسَاءَ وَالمَائِدَةَ أَوِ الأَنْعَامَ»، شُعْبَةُ الَّذِي شَكَّ فِي المَائِدَةِ وَالأَنْعَامِ .

275. Muḥammad Ibn al-Muthannā narrated to us; Muḥammad Ibn Jā'far narrated to us; Shu'bah narrated to us; from 'Amr Ibn Murrah; from Abū Ḥamzah, a man from the al-Anṣār; from a man from Banu 'Abas; that Hudhayfah Ibn al-Yamān (*raḍiyAllāhu 'anhu*) performed the prayer with the Prophet (ﷺ) during one night, and he said: 'After commencing the prayer he recited

> *"Allāh akbar dhu'l-malakūt wa'l-jabarūt wa'l-kibriya wa'l-'aẓamah."*—"Allāh is Supreme! Lord of sovereignty, power, magnificence and sublimity."
>
> Then he recited *al-Baqarah*, and then bowed down, and his bowing was similar to his standing in duration. He then read in his bowing: *"Subḥāna rabbi al-'aẓīm, Subḥāna rabbi al-'aẓīm"*—"Glory be to my Lord the Great! Glory be to my Lord the Great!
>
> Then, he raised his head, and his standing was similar to his bowing in duration, saying: *"li-rabbi al-ḥamd, li-rabbi al-ḥamd"*—"To my Lord belongs all praise! To my Lord belongs all praise!" Then he prostrated, and his prostration was similar to his standing in duration, saying: *"Subḥāna rabbi al-A'lā, Subḥāna rabbi al-A'lā"*—"Glory be to my Lord, the Most High! Glory be to my Lord, the Most High!" Then he raised his head, and the pause between two prostrations was similar to his prostration in duration. During

> his pause, saying: *"Rabbi ighfirlī, Rabbi ighfirlī"*—"My Lord, forgive me! My Lord, forgive me!" [He continued] until he had read *al-Baqarah*, *Āl-'Imrān*, *al-Nisā'*, *al-Mā'idah* or *al-An'ām*.'

Abū 'Isā said: 'The narrator Shu'bah is in doubt regarding as to whether he read *al-Mā'idah* or *al-An'ām*.'[276]

٢٧٦ـ حَدَّثَنَا أَبُو بَكْرٍ مُحَمَّدُ بْنُ نَافِعٍ البَصْرِيُّ، قَالَ: حَدَّثَنَا عَبْدُ الصَّمَدِ ابْنُ عَبْدِ الوَارِثِ، عَنْ إِسْمَاعِيلَ بْنِ مُسْلِمٍ العَبْدِيِّ، عَنْ أَبِي المُتَوَكِّلِ، عَنْ عَائِشَةَ، قَالَتْ: «قَامَ رَسُولُ اللهِ ﷺ بِآيَةٍ مِنَ القُرْآنِ لَيْلَةً».

276. Abū Bakr Muḥammad Ibn Nāfi' al-Baṣrī narrated to us; 'Abdu'l-Ṣamad Ibn 'Abdu'l-Wārith narrated to us; from Ismā'īl Ibn Muslim al-'Abdī; from Abū'l-Mutawakkil that 'Ā'ishah (*raḍiyAllāhu 'anhā*) said:

> 'The Messenger of Allāh (ﷺ) stood [praying] the night reciting a single verse from the Qur'ān.'[277]

٢٧٧ـ حَدَّثَنَا مَحْمُودُ بْنُ غَيْلَانَ، قَالَ: حَدَّثَنَا سُلَيْمَانُ بْنُ حَرْبٍ، قَالَ: حَدَّثَنَا شُعْبَةُ، عَنِ الأَعْمَشِ، عَنْ أَبِي وَائِلٍ، عَنْ عَبْدِ اللهِ بْنِ مَسْعُودٍ، قَالَ: «صَلَّيْتُ لَيْلَةً مَعَ رَسُولِ اللهِ ﷺ فَلَمْ يَزَلْ قَائِمًا حَتَّى هَمَمْتُ بِأَمْرِ سُوءٍ، قِيلَ لَهُ: وَمَا هَمَمْتَ بِهِ؟ قَالَ: هَمَمْتُ أَنْ أَقْعُدَ وَأَدَعَ النَّبِيَّ ﷺ».

277. Maḥmūd Ibn Ghaylān narrated to us; Sulaymān Ibn Harb narrated to us; Shu'bah narrated to us; from al-A'mash; from Abū

[276] Abu Dawud, #874 and is authentic.
[277] Tirmidhī, #448.

Waa'il that 'Abdullāh Ibn Mas'ūd (*raḍiyAllāhu 'anhu*) said:

> 'One night I prayed alongside the Messenger of Allāh (ﷺ) and he remained standing for so long, that I was on the verge of doing something evil (*sū'*).' He was asked: 'What were you on the verge of doing?' He replied: 'I was about to sit down and leave the Prophet (ﷺ)!'[278]

٢٧٨ـ حَدَّثَنَا سُفْيَانُ بْنُ وَكِيعٍ، قَالَ: حَدَّثَنَا جَرِيرٌ، عَنِ الأَعْمَشِ، نَحْوَهُ.

278. Sufyān Ibn Wakī' narrated to us; Jarīr narrated to us likewise, on the authority of al-A'mash.

٢٧٩ـ حَدَّثَنَا إِسْحَاقُ بْنُ مُوسَى الأَنْصَارِيُّ، قَالَ: حَدَّثَنَا مَعْنٌ، قَالَ: حَدَّثَنَا مَالِكٌ، عَنْ أَبِي النَّضْرِ، عَنْ أَبِي سَلَمَةَ، عَنْ عَائِشَةَ: «أَنَّ النَّبِيَّ ﷺ كَانَ يُصَلِّي جَالِسًا فَيَقْرَأُ وَهُوَ جَالِسٌ، فَإِذَا بَقِيَ مِنْ قِرَاءَتِهِ قَدْرُ مَا يَكُونُ ثَلَاثِينَ أَوْ أَرْبَعِينَ آيَةً، قَامَ فَقَرَأَ وَهُوَ قَائِمٌ، ثُمَّ رَكَعَ وَسَجَدَ، ثُمَّ صَنَعَ فِي الرَّكْعَةِ الثَّانِيَةِ مِثْلَ ذَلِكَ».

279. Isḥāq Ibn Mūsā al-Anṣārī narrated to us; Ma'an narrated to us; Mālik narrated to us; from Abū Naḍr; from Abū Salamah that 'Ā'ishah (*raḍiyAllāhu 'anhā*) said:

> "The Prophet (ﷺ) used to pray sitting, and he would recite sitting. When the amount of what is between thirty or forty verses remained of his recitation, he would stand up and recite standing. Then he would bow and prostrate. Then, he would do likewise in the second cycle [*rak'ah*]."[279]

[278] Bukhārī, #1135 and Muslim, #773.

[279] Bukhārī, #1119, Muslim, #731 and Tirmidhī, #374.

٢٨٠ـ حَدَّثَنَا أَحْمَدُ بْنُ مَنِيعٍ، قَالَ: حَدَّثَنَا هُشَيْمٌ، قَالَ: حَدَّثَنَا خَالِدٌ الحَذَّاءُ، عَنْ عَبْدِ اللهِ بْنِ شَقِيقٍ، قَالَ: سَأَلْتُ عَائِشَةَ عَنْ صَلَاةِ رَسُولِ اللهِ ﷺ عَنْ تَطَوُّعِهِ، فَقَالَتْ: «كَانَ يُصَلِّي لَيْلاً طَوِيلًا قَائِمًا، وَلَيْلًا طَوِيلًا قَاعِدًا، فَإِذَا قَرَأَ وَهُوَ قَائِمٌ رَكَعَ وَسَجَدَ وَهُوَ قَائِمٌ، وَإِذَا قَرَأَ وَهُوَ جَالِسٌ رَكَعَ وَسَجَدَ وَهُوَ جَالِسٌ».

280. Aḥmad Ibn Manīʿ narrated to us; Ḥusayn narrated to us; Khālid al-Ḥadhadhā' narrated to us; from 'Abdullāh Ibn Shaqīq said:

> 'I asked 'Ā'ishah (*raḍiyAllāhu 'anhā*) regarding the voluntary prayers of the Messenger of Allāh (ﷺ) and she replied: "He would pray a substantial part of the night while standing (*qā'im*), and a substantial part of the night while sitting (*qā'id*), so if he recited while standing, he would bow and prostrate from a standing position, and if recited while sitting (*jālis*), he would bow and prostrate from the sitting position."'[280]

٢٨١ـ حَدَّثَنَا إِسْحَاقُ بْنُ مُوسَى الأَنْصَارِيُّ، قَالَ: حَدَّثَنَا مَعْنٌ، قَالَ: حَدَّثَنَا مَالِكٌ، عَنِ ابْنِ شِهَابٍ، عَنِ السَّائِبِ بنِ يَزِيدَ، عَنِ المُطَّلِبِ بن أَبِي وَدَاعَةَ السَّهْمِيِّ، عَنْ حَفْصَةَ، زَوْجِ النَّبِيِّ ﷺ قَالَتْ: «كَانَ رَسُولُ اللهِ ﷺ يُصَلِّي فِي سُبْحَتِهِ قَاعِدًا وَيَقْرَأُ بِالسُّورَةِ وَيُرَتِّلُهَا حَتَّى تَكُونَ أَطْوَلَ مِنْ أَطْوَلَ مِنْهَا».

281. Isḥāq Ibn Mūsā al-Anṣārī narrated to us; Maʿan narrated to us; Mālik narrated to us; from Ibn Shihāb; from al-Sā'ib Ibn Yazīd; from al-Muṭṭalib Ibn Abī Wadāʿa that Ḥafsah (*raḍiyAllāhu 'anhā*), the wife of the Prophet (ﷺ), said

[280] Muslim, #730 and Tirmidhī, #375.

"The Messenger of Allāh (ﷺ) used to perform his voluntary prayer (*subḥah*) while sitting down (*qā'id*), and he would recite a *surah* and recite it slowly (*tartil*), so that it would seem to be longer than [a *surah*] longer than it."[281]

٢٨٢ـ حَدَّثَنَا الحَسَنُ بْنُ مُحَمَّدٍ الزَّعْفَرَانِيُّ، قَالَ: حَدَّثَنَا الحَجَّاجُ بْنُ مُحَمَّدٍ، عَنِ ابْنِ جُرَيْجٍ، قَالَ: أَخْبَرَنِي عُثْمَانُ بْنُ أَبِي سُلَيْمَانَ، أَنَّ أَبَا سَلَمَةَ بْنَ عَبْدِ الرَّحْمَنِ، أَخْبَرَهُ أَنَّ عَائِشَةَ، أَخْبَرَتْهُ «أَنَّ النَّبِيَّ ﷺ لَمْ يَمُتْ حَتَّى كَانَ أَكْثَرُ صَلَاتِهِ وَهُوَ جَالِسٌ».

282. Al-Ḥasan Ibn Muḥammad al-Za'farānī narrated to us; Al-Ḥajjāj Ibn Muḥammad narrated to us that Ibn Jurayj said: "Uthman Ibn Abī Sulaymān informed us that Abū Salamah Ibn 'Abdu'l-Raḥmān informed him that 'Ā'ishah (*raḍiyAllāhu 'anhā*) said:

"The Prophet (ﷺ) did not pass away until most of his voluntary prayers were perfomed sitting (*jālis*)."[282]

٢٨٣ـ حَدَّثَنَا أَحْمَدُ بْنُ مَنِيعٍ، قَالَ: حَدَّثَنَا إِسْمَاعِيلُ بْنُ إِبْرَاهِيمَ، قَالَ: حَدَّثَنَا أَيُّوبُ، عَنْ نَافِعٍ، عَنِ ابْنِ عُمَرَ، قَالَ: «صَلَّيْتُ مَعَ النَّبِيِّ ﷺ رَكْعَتَيْنِ قَبْلَ الظُّهْرِ، وَرَكْعَتَيْنِ بَعْدَهَا، وَرَكْعَتَيْنِ بَعْدَ المَغْرِبِ فِي بَيْتِهِ، وَرَكْعَتَيْنِ بَعْدَ العِشَاءِ فِي بَيْتِهِ».

283. Aḥmad Ibn Mani' narrated to us; Ismā'īl Ibn Ibrāhīm narrated to us; Ayyūb narrated to us; from Nāfi' that Ibn 'Umar (*raḍiyAllāhu 'anhumā*) said:

'I performed two cycles [of ritual prayer] with the Messenger of Allāh (ﷺ) before the *ẓuhr* prayer, and two cycles after it, and two cycles after the *maghrib* prayer in his house,

[281] Muslim, #733 and Tirmidhī, #373.

[282] *Musannaf* of 'Abdu'l-Razzāq, #3959

and two cycles after the *'ishā'* prayer in his house."[283]

٢٨٤ـ حَدَّثَنَا أَحْمَدُ بْنُ مَنِيعٍ، قَالَ: حَدَّثَنَا إِسْمَاعِيلُ بْنُ إِبْرَاهِيمَ، قَالَ: حَدَّثَنَا أَيُّوبُ، عَنْ نَافِعٍ، عَنِ ابْنِ عُمَرَ، قَالَ: حَدَّثَتْنِي حَفْصَةُ: «أَنَّ رَسُولَ اللهِ ﷺ كَانَ يُصَلِّي رَكْعَتَيْنِ حِينَ يَطْلُعُ الفَجْرُ وَيُنَادِي المُنَادِي».

قَالَ أَيُّوبُ: وَأُرَاهُ قَالَ: خَفِيفَتَيْنِ.

284. Aḥmad Ibn Manīʿ narrated to us; Ismāʿīl Ibn Ibrāhīm narrated to us; Ayyūb narrated to us; from Nāfiʿ that Ibn 'Umar said: 'Ḥafsah (*raḍiyAllāhu 'anhum*) said:

> "The Messenger of Allah (ﷺ) would perform two cycles of prayer at the time of dawn break."[284]

And Ayyūb (one of the narrators) said: 'I think he described them as short and light cycles.'

٢٨٥ـ حَدَّثَنَا قُتَيْبَةُ بْنُ سَعِيدٍ، قَالَ: حَدَّثَنَا مَرْوَانُ بْنُ مُعَاوِيَةَ الفَزَارِيُّ، عَنْ جَعْفَرِ بْنِ بُرْقَانَ، عَنْ مَيْمُونِ بْنِ مِهْرَانَ، عَنِ ابْنِ عُمَرَ، قَالَ: «حَفِظْتُ مِنْ رَسُولِ اللهِ ﷺ ثَمَانِيَ رَكَعَاتٍ: رَكْعَتَيْنِ قَبْلَ الظُّهْرِ، وَرَكْعَتَيْنِ بَعْدَهَا، وَرَكْعَتَيْنِ بَعْدَ المَغْرِبِ، وَرَكْعَتَيْنِ بَعْدَ العِشَاءِ، قَالَ ابْنُ عُمَرَ: وَحَدَّثَتْنِي حَفْصَةُ بِرَكْعَتَي الغَدَاةِ، وَلَمْ أَكُنْ أَرَاهُمَا مِنَ النَّبِيِّ ﷺ».

285. Qutaybah Ibn Saʿīd narrated to us; Marwān Ibn Muʿāwwiyah al-Fazārī narrated to us; from Jāʿfar Ibn Burqān; from Maymūn Ibn

[283] Bukhārī, #937, Muslim, #729 and Tirmidhī, #425.
[284] Bukhārī, #937 and Muslim, #729

Mihran that Ibn 'Umar (*raḍiyAllāhu 'anhumā*) said:

> 'I recall eight cycles performed by the Messenger of Allāh (ﷺ): two cycles before the *ẓuhr* prayer and two cycles after it, two cycles after the *magrib* prayer, and two cycles after the *'ishā'* prayer.'

Ibn 'Umar (*raḍiyAllāhu 'anhumā*) said: 'Ḥafsah also narrated to me about the two cycles of the *fajr* prayer, but I did not see them performed by the Prophet (ﷺ).'[285]

٢٨٦ـ حَدَّثَنَا أَبُو سَلَمَةَ يَحْيَى بْنُ خَلَفٍ، قَالَ: حَدَّثَنَا بِشْرُ بْنُ الْمُفَضَّلِ، عَنْ خَالِدٍ الْحَذَّاءِ، عَنْ عَبْدِ اللهِ بنِ شَقِيقٍ، قَالَ: سَأَلْتُ عَائِشَةَ عَنْ صَلَاةِ النَّبِيِّ ﷺ قَالَتْ: «كَانَ يُصَلِّي قَبْلَ الظُّهْرِ رَكْعَتَيْنِ وَبَعْدَهَا رَكْعَتَيْنِ، وَبَعْدَ الْمَغْرِبِ رَكْعَتَيْنِ، وَبَعْدَ الْعِشَاءِ رَكْعَتَيْنِ، وَقَبْلَ الْفَجْرِ ثِنْتَيْنِ».

286. Abū Salamah Yaḥyā Ibn Khalaf narrated to us; Bishr Ibn Ibn al-Mufaḍḍal narrated to us; from Khālid al-Ḥadhdhā' that 'Abdullāh Ibn Shaqīq (*raḍiyAllāhu 'anhu*) said:

> 'I asked 'Ā'ishah (*raḍiyAllāhu 'anhā*) about voluntary prayers of the Prophet (ﷺ), and she said: 'He used to perform two cycles before the *ẓuhr* prayer and two cycles after it, two cycles after the *maghrib* prayer, two cycles after the *'ishā'* prayer, and two before the *fajr* prayer.'[286]

٢٨٧ـ حَدَّثَنَا مُحَمَّدُ بْنُ الْمُثَنَّى، قَالَ: حَدَّثَنَا مُحَمَّدُ بْنُ جَعْفَرٍ، قَالَ: حَدَّثَنَا

---

285 Bukhārī, #937, Muslim, #729 and Tirmidhī, #425.

286 Muslim, #730 and Tirmidhī, #375.

شُعْبَةُ، عَنْ أَبِي إِسْحَاقَ، قَالَ: سَمِعْتُ عَاصِمَ بْنَ ضَمْرَةَ، يَقُولُ: سَأَلْنَا عَلِيًّا عَنْ صَلَاةِ رَسُولِ اللهِ ﷺ مِنَ النَّهَارِ، فَقَالَ: «إِنَّكُمْ لَا تُطِيقُونَ ذَلِكَ، قَالَ: فَقُلْنَا: مَنْ أَطَاقَ ذَلِكَ مِنَّا صَلَّى، فَقَالَ: كَانَ إِذَا كَانَتِ الشَّمْسُ مِنْ هَهُنَا كَهَيْئَتِهَا مِنْ هَهُنَا عِنْدَ العَصْرِ صَلَّى رَكْعَتَيْنِ، وَإِذَا كَانَتِ الشَّمْسُ مِنْ هَهُنَا كَهَيْئَتِهَا مِنْ هَهُنَا عِنْدَ الظُّهْرِ صَلَّى أَرْبَعًا، وَيُصَلِّي قَبْلَ الظُّهْرِ أَرْبَعًا، وَبَعْدَهَا رَكْعَتَيْنِ، وَقَبْلَ العَصْرِ أَرْبَعًا، يَفْصِلُ بَيْنَ كُلِّ رَكْعَتَيْنِ بِالتَّسْلِيمِ عَلَى المَلَائِكَةِ المُقَرَّبِينَ وَالنَّبِيِّينَ، وَمَنْ تَبِعَهُمْ مِنَ المُؤْمِنِينَ وَالمُسْلِمِينَ».

287. Muḥammad Ibn al-Muthannā narrated to us; Muḥammad Ibn Jā'far narrated to us; Shu'bah narrated to us that Abū Isḥāq said: 'I heard 'Āṣim Ibn Ḍamrah say

> 'We asked 'Alī (*radiyAllāhu 'anhu*) about the voluntary prayers of the Messenger of Allāh (ﷺ) during the daytime, and he said: 'You are unable to endure that,' so we said: 'Whoever of us is able to endure that will pray.' He therefore said: 'When the sun would appear from over here [pointing east], like its appearance from here [pointing west], at the time of late noon, he would perform two cycles of prayer, and when the sun was from over here [pointing east], like its appearance from here [pointing before the *zuhr* prayer and two after it, and four before the *'asr* prayer, separating each of the two cycles with a greeting of peace upon the angels drawn near, and upon the Prophets and the believers and Muslims who follow them."[287]

[287] Tirmidhī, #599.

CHAPTER FORTY-ONE

بَابُ صَلَاةِ الضُّحَى

What has been narrated concerning the Mid-morning Prayer (*ṣalat al-ḍuḥā*) [of the Messenger of Allāh (ﷺ)]

٢٨٨ـ حَدَّثَنَا مَحْمُودُ بْنُ غَيْلَانَ، قَالَ: حَدَّثَنَا أَبُو دَاوُدَ الطَّيَالِسِيُّ، قَالَ: حَدَّثَنَا شُعْبَةُ، عَنْ يَزِيدَ الرِّشْكِ، قَالَ: سَمِعْتُ مُعَاذَةَ، قَالَتْ: «قُلْتُ لِعَائِشَةَ: أَكَانَ النَّبِيُّ ﷺ يُصَلِّي الضُّحَى؟ قَالَتْ: نَعَمْ، أَرْبَعَ رَكَعَاتٍ وَيَزِيدُ مَا شَاءَ اللهُ ﷻ».

288. Maḥmūd Ibn Ghaylān narrated to us; Abū Dāwūd al-Ṭayālisī narrated to us; Shu'bah narrated to us that Yazīd al-Rishk said:

> 'I heard Mu'adha say: 'I asked 'Ā'ishah (*raḍiyAllāhu 'anhā*): 'Did the Prophet (ﷺ) used to perform the mid-morning (*ḍuḥā*) prayer?' She said: 'Yes, four cycles, and he would add whatever Allāh, Almighty and the Majestic, wills."[288]

٢٨٩ـ حَدَّثَنَا مُحَمَّدُ بْنُ الْمُثَنَّى، قَالَ: حَدَّثَنِي حَكِيمُ بْنُ مُعَاوِيَةَ الزِّيَادِيُّ، قَالَ:

---

[288] Muslim, #819.

حَدَّثَنَا زِيَادُ بْنُ عُبَيْدِ اللهِ بْنِ الرَّبِيعِ الزِّيَادِيُّ، عَنْ حُمَيْدٍ الطَّوِيلِ، عَنْ أَنَسِ بْنِ مَالِكٍ: «أَنَّ النَّبِيَّ ﷺ كَانَ يُصَلِّي الضُّحَى سِتَّ رَكَعَاتٍ».

289. Muḥammad Ibn al-Muthannā narrated to us; Ḥakīm Ibn Muʿāwiyah al-Zayādī narrated to us; Ziyād Ibn ʿUbaydullāh Ibn al-Rabīʿ al-Zayādī narrated to us; from Ḥumayd al-Ṭawīl that Anas Ibn Mālik (*raḍiyAllāhu ʿanhu*) said:

> "The Prophet (ﷺ) used to perform the mid-morning (*ḍuḥā*) prayer as six cycles."[289]

٢٩٠ـ حَدَّثَنَا مُحَمَّدُ بْنُ الْمُثَنَّى، قَالَ: حَدَّثَنَا مُحَمَّدُ بْنُ جَعْفَرٍ، قَالَ: حَدَّثَنَا شُعْبَةُ، عَنْ عَمْرِو بْنِ مُرَّةَ، عَنْ عَبْدِ الرَّحْمَنِ بْنِ أَبِي لَيْلَى، قَالَ: مَا أَخْبَرَنِي أَحَدٌ أَنَّهُ رَأَى النَّبِيَّ ﷺ يُصَلِّي الضُّحَى إِلَّا أُمُّ هَانِئٍ، فَإِنَّهَا حَدَّثَتْ «أَنَّ رَسُولَ اللهِ ﷺ دَخَلَ بَيْتَهَا يَوْمَ فَتْحِ مَكَّةَ فَاغْتَسَلَ فَسَبَّحَ ثَمَانِيَ رَكَعَاتٍ، مَا رَأَيْتُهُ ﷺ صَلَّى صَلَاةً قَطُّ أَخَفَّ مِنْهَا، غَيْرَ أَنَّهُ كَانَ يُتِمُّ الرُّكُوعَ وَالسُّجُودَ».

290. Muḥammad Ibn al-Muthannā narrated to us; Muḥammad Ibn Jāʿfar narrated to us; Shuʿbah narrated to us; from ʿAmr Ibn Murrah that ʿAbdu'l-Raḥmān Ibn Abī Laylā said:

> 'I have never heard anyone mention seeing the Prophet (ﷺ) performing the mid-morning (*ḍuḥā*) prayer other than Umm Hānī' (*raḍiyAllāhu ʿanhā*).'
>
> She related that the Messenger of Allāh (ﷺ) entered her house on the Day of the Conquest of Makkah, and then he performed a bath (*ghusl*) and glorified Allāh in eight cycles. I never saw him (ﷺ) perform a prayer shorter in

[289] Ṭabarānī in *Al-Awsaṭ*, #1276.

form than that, even though he completed the bowing (*rukū'*) and the prostration (*sujūd*)."[290]

٢٩١ـ حَدَّثَنَا ابْنُ أَبِي عُمَرَ، قَالَ: حَدَّثَنَا وَكِيعٌ، قَالَ: حَدَّثَنَا كَهْمَسُ بْنُ الْحَسَنِ، عَنْ عَبْدِ اللهِ بْنِ شَقِيقٍ، قَالَ: قُلْتُ لِعَائِشَةَ: «أَكَانَ النَّبِيُّ ﷺ يُصَلِّي الضُّحَى؟ قَالَتْ: لَا، إِلَّا أَنْ يَجِيءَ مِنْ مَغِيبِهِ».

291. Ibn Abī 'Umar narrated to us; Wakī' narrated to us; Kahmas Ibn al-Ḥasan narrated to us that 'Abdullāh Ibn Shaqīq (*raḍiyAllāhu 'anhu*) related:

> 'I asked 'Ā'ishah (*raḍiyAllāhu 'anhā*): 'Would the Prophet (ﷺ) perform the mid-morning (*ḍuḥā*) prayer?' She said: 'No, unless he returned after being away."[291]

٢٩٢ـ حَدَّثَنَا زِيَادُ بْنُ أَيُّوبَ الْبَغْدَادِيُّ، قَالَ: حَدَّثَنَا مُحَمَّدُ بْنُ رَبِيعَةَ، عَنْ فُضَيْلِ بْنِ مَرْزُوقٍ، عَنْ عَطِيَّةَ، عَنْ أَبِي سَعِيدٍ الْخُدْرِيِّ قَالَ: «كَانَ النَّبِيُّ ﷺ يُصَلِّي الضُّحَى حَتَّى نَقُولَ: لَا يَدَعُهَا، وَيَدَعُهَا حَتَّى نَقُولَ: لَا يُصَلِّيهَا».

292. Ziyād Ibn Ayyūb al-Baghdadī narrated to us; Muḥammad Ibn Rabī'ah narrated to us; from Fuḍayl Ibn Mazruq; from 'Aṭṭiyah that Abū Sa'īd al-Khudrī (*raḍiyAllāhu 'anhu*) said:

> 'The Prophet (ﷺ) would perform the mid-morning (*ḍuḥā*) prayer [so frequently], so much so that we would say: 'He does not fail to pray it.' Then he would leave it [so frequently], so much so that we would say: 'He does not pray it."[292]

---

[290] Bukhārī, #1103, Muslim, #336, and Tirmidhī, #474.

[291] Muslim, #336.

[292] Tirmidhī, #477. This hadīth has a weak chain.

٢٩٣ـ حَدَّثَنَا أَحْمَدُ بْنُ مَنِيعٍ، عَنْ هُشَيْمٍ، قَالَ: حَدَّثَنَا عُبَيْدَةُ، عَنْ إِبْرَاهِيمَ، عَنْ سَهْمِ بْنِ مِنْجَابٍ، عَنْ قَرْثَعٍ الضَّبِّيِّ، أَوْ عَنْ قَزَعَةَ، عَنْ قَرْثَعٍ، عَنْ أَبِي أَيُّوبَ الأَنْصَارِيِّ، «أَنَّ النَّبِيَّ ﷺ كَانَ يُدْمِنُ أَرْبَعَ رَكَعَاتٍ عِنْدَ زَوَالِ الشَّمْسِ، فَقُلْتُ: يَا رَسُولَ اللهِ! إِنَّكَ تُدْمِنُ هَذِهِ الأَرْبَعَ رَكَعَاتٍ عِنْدَ زَوَالِ الشَّمْسِ، فَقَالَ: إِنَّ أَبْوَابَ السَّمَاءِ تُفْتَحُ عِنْدَ زَوَالِ الشَّمْسِ فَلَا تُرْتَجُ حَتَّى تُصَلَّى الظُّهْرُ، فَأُحِبُّ أَنْ يَصْعَدَ لِي فِي تِلْكَ السَّاعَةِ خَيْرٌ، قُلْتُ: أَفِي كُلِّهِنَّ قِرَاءَةٌ؟ قَالَ: نَعَمْ، قُلْتُ: هَلْ فِيهِنَّ تَسْلِيمٌ فَاصِلٌ؟ قَالَ: لَا».

293. Aḥmad Ibn Manīʿ narrated to us; Hushaym narrated to us; ʿUbaydah narrated to us; from Ibrāhīm; Sahm Ibn Minjab; from Qarthaʿ al-Ḍabbī or Qazaʿah; from Qarthaʿ that Abū Ayyūb al-Anṣārī (*raḍiyAllāhu ʿanhu*) said:

> 'The Prophet (ﷺ) would consistently perform four cycles of prayer at high noon (*zawāl al-shāms*), so I said: 'O Messenger, you consistently pray these four cycles at hign noon.' He explained: "The gates of heavens are open at hign noon, and then they are unlocked until the *ẓuhr* prayer is performed; I therefore love to have a good deed of mine to ascend at that time." I asked: 'Is there recitation in each of them [the four cycles]?' He said: "Yes." So I asked: 'Do they contain a separating salutation of peace (*taslīm*)?' He said: "No."[293]

٢٩٤ـ أَخْبَرَنِي أَحْمَدُ بْنُ مَنِيعٍ، قَالَ: حَدَّثَنَا أَبُو مُعَاوِيَةَ، قَالَ: حَدَّثَنَا عُبَيْدَةُ، عَنْ إِبْرَاهِيمَ، عَنْ سَهْمِ بْنِ مِنْجَابٍ، عَنْ قَزَعَةَ، عَنْ قَرْثَعٍ، عَنْ أَبِي أَيُّوبَ الأَنْصَارِيِّ، عَنِ النَّبِيِّ ﷺ نَحْوَهُ.

---

[293] Aḥmad in his *Musnad*, 23/532, this hadīth is weak but is supported by the next hadīth.

294. Aḥmad Ibn Manī' narrated to us; Abū Mu'āwiyyah narrated to us; 'Ubaydah narrated to us; from Ibrahim; Sahm Ibn Minjāb; from Qaza'ah; from Qartha'; from Abū Ayyūb al-Anṣārī (*raḍiyAllāhu 'anhu*) who said that the Prophet (ﷺ) said likewise [to the previous hadith with a different chain].

٢٩٥ـ حَدَّثَنَا مُحَمَّدُ بْنُ الْمُثَنَّى، قَالَ: حَدَّثَنَا أَبُو دَاوُدَ، قَالَ: حَدَّثَنَا مُحَمَّدُ بْنُ مُسْلِمِ ابْنِ أَبِي الْوَضَّاحِ، عَنْ عَبْدِ الْكَرِيمِ الْجَزَرِيِّ، عَنْ مُجَاهِدٍ، عَنْ عَبْدِ اللهِ بْنِ السَّائِبِ، «أَنَّ رَسُولَ اللهِ ﷺ كَانَ يُصَلِّي أَرْبَعًا بَعْدَ أَنْ تَزُولَ الشَّمْسُ قَبْلَ الظُّهْرِ، وَقَالَ: إِنَّهَا سَاعَةٌ تُفْتَحُ فِيهَا أَبْوَابُ السَّمَاءِ، فَأُحِبُّ أَنْ يَصْعَدَ لِي فِيهَا عَمَلٌ صَالِحٌ».

295. Muḥammad Ibn al-Muthannā narrated to us; Abū Dāwūd narrated to us; Muḥammad Ibn Muslim Ibn Abū'l-Waḍḍāh; from 'Abdu'l-Karīm al-Jazārī; from Mujāhid that 'Abdullāh Ibn Sā'ib (*raḍiyAllāhu 'anhu*) reported:

> 'The Messenger of Allāh (ﷺ) used to perform four cycles after the sun has passed its zenith before the *ẓuhr* prayer, and he said: "It is a time in which the gates of heavens are open, I therefore love to have a righteous deed ascend for me [in it]."'[294]

٢٩٦ـ حَدَّثَنَا أَبُو سَلَمَةَ يَحْيَى بْنُ خَلَفٍ، قَالَ: حَدَّثَنَا عُمَرُ بْنُ عَلِيٍّ الْمُقَدَّمِيُّ، عَنْ مِسْعَرِ بْنِ كِدَامٍ، عَنْ أَبِي إِسْحَاقَ، عَنْ عَاصِمِ بْنِ ضَمْرَةَ، عَنْ عَلِيٍّ، «أَنَّهُ كَانَ يُصَلِّي قَبْلَ الظُّهْرِ أَرْبَعًا، وَذَكَرَ أَنَّ رَسُولَ اللهِ ﷺ كَانَ يُصَلِّيهَا عِنْدَ الزَّوَالِ وَيَمُدُّ فِيهَا».

296. Abū Salamah Yaḥyā Ibn Khalaf narrated to us; 'Umar Ibn 'Alī al-Muqaddamī narrated to us; from Mis'ar Ibn Kidām; from

[294] Tirmidhī, #478.

Abū Isḥāq; from 'Āṣim Ibn Ḍamrah that 'Alī (*raḍiyAllāhu 'anhu*) said:

> 'He used to perform four cycles before the *ẓuhr* prayer, and he mentioned he used to perform them at the time of sun's zenith (*zawāl*), and he used to prolong them.'[295]

[295] Tirmidhī, #424

CHAPTER FORTY-TWO

بَابُ صَلَاةِ التَّطَوُّعِ فِي الْبَيْتِ

What has been narrated concerning the Voluntary Prayer (*salāt al-taṭawwu'*) [of the Messenger of Allāh (ﷺ)] in the Home

٢٩٧ـ حَدَّثَنَا عَبَّاسٌ الْعَنْبَرِيُّ، قَالَ: حَدَّثَنَا عَبْدُ الرَّحْمَنِ بْنُ مَهْدِيٍّ، عَنْ مُعَاوِيَةَ بْنِ صَالِحٍ، عَنِ الْعَلَاءِ بْنِ الْحَارِثِ، عَنْ حَرَامِ بْنِ مُعَاوِيَةَ، عَنْ عَمِّهِ عَبْدِ اللهِ ابْنِ سَعْدٍ قَالَ: سَأَلْتُ رَسُولَ اللهِ ﷺ عَنِ الصَّلَاةِ فِي بَيْتِي وَالصَّلَاةِ فِي الْمَسْجِدِ قَالَ: «قَدْ تَرَى مَا أَقْرَبَ بَيْتِي مِنَ الْمَسْجِدِ، فَلَأَنْ أُصَلِّيَ فِي بَيْتِي أَحَبُّ إِلَيَّ مِنْ أَنْ أُصَلِّيَ فِي الْمَسْجِدِ إِلَّا أَنْ تَكُونَ صَلَاةً مَكْتُوبَةً».

297. 'Abbās al-'Anbarī narrated to us; 'Abdu'l-Raḥmān Ibn Mahdī narrated to us; from Mu'āwiyah Ibn Ṣāliḥ; from al-A'lā' Ibn al-Ḥārith; from Ḥaram Ibn Mu'āwiyah; from his paternal uncle that 'Abdullāh Ibn Sa'd (*raḍiyAllāhu 'anhu*) said:

> 'I asked the Messenger of Allāh (ﷺ) about performing [voluntary] prayer in my home, and performing it in *masjid.*

He (ﷺ) said: "Do you observe how near my home is to the *masjid*? I prefer to perform the prayer in my home over praying in the *masjid*, except for the prescribed prayers.'"[296]

[296] Tirmidhī, #133, Abū Dāwūd, #311 and Ibn Mājah, #651. This chain is weak but it has supporting evidence from Bukhārī, #731.

CHAPTER FORTY-THREE

بَابُ مَا جَاءَ فِي صَوْمِ رَسُولِ اللهِ ﷺ

What has been narrated concerning the Description of the Fasting (*ṣawm*) of the Messenger of Allāh (ﷺ)

٢٩٨ـ حَدَّثَنَا قُتَيْبَةُ بْنُ سَعِيدٍ، قَالَ: حَدَّثَنَا حَمَّادُ بْنُ زَيْدٍ، عَنْ أَيُّوبَ، عَنْ عَبْدِ اللهِ ابْنِ شَقِيقٍ، قَالَ: سَأَلْتُ عَائِشَةَ، عَنْ صِيَامِ رَسُولِ اللهِ ﷺ، قَالَتْ: «كَانَ يَصُومُ حَتَّى نَقُولَ قَدْ صَامَ، وَيُفْطِرُ حَتَّى نَقُولَ قَدْ أَفْطَرَ. قَالَتْ: وَمَا صَامَ رَسُولُ اللهِ ﷺ شَهْرًا كَامِلًا مُنْذُ قَدِمَ الْمَدِينَةَ إِلَّا رَمَضَانَ».

298. Qutaybah Ibn Sa'īd narrated to us; Ḥammād Ibn Zayd narrated to us; from Ayyūb that 'Abdullāh Ibn Shaqīq (*raḍiyAllāhu 'anhu*) said:

> 'I asked 'Ā'ishah (*raḍiyAllāhu 'anhā*) about the [voluntary] fasting of the Messenger of Allāh (ﷺ). She said: 'He would fast, so much so that we would say: 'He [always] fasts.' Then he would also not observe the fast, so much so that we would say: 'He does not observe the fast.' She also said: 'The Messenger of Allāh (ﷺ) did not fast for a

whole month after arriving in Medinah, with the exception of Ramaḍān.'"[297]

٢٩٩ـ حَدَّثَنَا عَلِيُّ بْنُ حُجْرٍ، قَالَ: حَدَّثَنَا إِسْمَاعِيلُ بْنُ جَعْفَرٍ، عَنْ حُمَيْدٍ، عَنْ أَنَسِ بْنِ مَالِكٍ، أَنَّهُ سُئِلَ عَنْ صَوْمِ النَّبِيِّ ﷺ، فَقَالَ: «كَانَ يَصُومُ مِنَ الشَّهْرِ حَتَّى نَرَى أَنْ لَا يُرِيدَ أَنْ يُفْطِرَ مِنْهُ، وَيُفْطِرُ مِنْهُ حَتَّى نَرَى أَنْ لَا يُرِيدَ أَنْ يَصُومَ مِنْهُ شَيْئًا، وَكُنْتَ لَا تَشَاءُ أَنْ تَرَاهُ مِنَ اللَّيْلِ مُصَلِّيًا إِلَّا رَأَيْتَهُ مُصَلِّيًا، وَلَا نَائِمًا إِلَّا رَأَيْتَهُ نَائِمًا».

299. 'Alī Ibn Ḥujr narrated to us; Ismā'īl Ibn Jā'far narrated to us; from Ḥumayd that Anas Ibn Mālik (*raḍiyAllāhu 'anhu*) was asked about the fasting of the Prophet (ﷺ), so he said:

> 'He used to fast [continuously] during the month, so much so that we would assume that he did not intend to leave it. Then he would not observe the fast, so much so that we would assume that he does not intend to fast at all. [In fact], never would you wish to see him praying during the night except you saw him praying, nor sleeping except you saw him sleeping.'[298]

٣٠٠ـ حَدَّثَنَا مَحْمُودُ بْنُ غَيْلَانَ، قَالَ: حَدَّثَنَا أَبُو دَاوُدَ قَالَ: حَدَّثَنَا شُعْبَةُ، عَنْ أَبِي بِشْرٍ، قَالَ: سَمِعْتُ سَعِيدَ بْنَ جُبَيْرٍ، عَنِ ابْنِ عَبَّاسٍ قَالَ: «كَانَ النَّبِيُّ ﷺ يَصُومُ حَتَّى نَقُولَ مَا يُرِيدُ أَنْ يُفْطِرَ مِنْهُ، وَيُفْطِرُ حَتَّى نَقُولَ مَا يُرِيدُ أَنْ يَصُومَ، وَمَا صَامَ شَهْرًا كَامِلًا مُنْذُ قَدِمَ الْمَدِينَةَ إِلَّا رَمَضَانَ».

300. Maḥmūd Ibn Ghaylān narrated to us; Abū Dāwūd narrated

[297] Muslim, #1156, and Tirmidhī, #768.
[298] Bukhārī, #1141, and Tirmidhī, #768.

to us; Shuʿbah narrated to us that Abū Bishr said: 'I heard Saʿīd Ibn Jubayr say that Ibn ʿAbbās (*raḍiyAllāhu ʿanhumā*) said:

> 'The Prophet (ﷺ) used to fast, so much so that we would say that he did not intend to leave it. Then he would not observe the fast, so much so that we would say that he does not intend to fast at all. He did not fast for a whole month after arriving in Medīnah, with the exception of Ramaḍān.'[299]

٣٠١ـ حَدَّثَنَا مُحَمَّدُ بْنُ بَشَّارٍ، قَالَ: حَدَّثَنَا عَبْدُ الرَّحْمَنِ بْنُ مَهْدِيٍّ، عَنْ سُفْيَانَ، عَنْ مَنْصُورٍ، عَنْ سَالِمِ بْنِ أَبِي الجَعْدِ، عَنْ أَبِي سَلَمَةَ، عَنْ أُمِّ سَلَمَةَ، قَالَتْ: مَا رَأَيْتُ النَّبِيَّ ﷺ يَصُومُ شَهْرَيْنِ مُتَتَابِعَيْنِ إِلَّا شَعْبَانَ وَرَمَضَانَ.

301. Muḥammad Ibn Bashshār narrated to us; ʿAbdu'l-Raḥmān Ibn Mahdī narrated to us; from Sufyān; from Manṣūr; Sālim Ibn Abū'l-Jaʿd; from Abū Salamah that Umm Salamah (*raḍiyAllāhu ʿanhumā*) said:

> 'I did not see the Prophet fast (ﷺ) for two consecutive months, other than [the months of] Shaʿbān and Ramaḍān.'[300]

٣٠٢ـ حَدَّثَنَا هَنَّادٌ، قَالَ: حَدَّثَنَا عَبْدَةُ، عَنْ مُحَمَّدِ بْنِ عَمْرٍو، قَالَ: حَدَّثَنَا أَبُو سَلَمَةَ، عَنْ عَائِشَةَ، قَالَتْ: «لَمْ أَرَ رَسُولَ اللهِ ﷺ يَصُومُ فِي شَهْرٍ أَكْثَرَ مِنْ صِيَامِهِ للهِ فِي شَعْبَانَ، كَانَ يَصُومُ شَعْبَانَ إِلَّا قَلِيلًا، بَلْ كَانَ يَصُومُهُ كُلَّهُ».

302. Hannād narrated to us; ʿAbdah narrated to us; from

[299] Bukhārī, #1971, and Muslim, #1157.
[300] Tirmidhī, #736, Abū Dāwūd, #2336, and Ibn Mājah, #1648.

Muḥammad Ibn ʿAmr; from Abū Salamah narrated to us that ʿĀ'ishah (*raḍiyAllāhu ʿanhā*) said:

> 'I did not see the Messenger of Allāh (ﷺ) fast during any month more than his fasting for Allāh's sake during [the month of] Shaʿbān. He used to fast during all but a little of Shaʿbān; no indeed, he would fast through all of it.'[301]

٣٠٣ـ حَدَّثَنَا القَاسِمُ بْنُ دِينَارٍ الكُوفِيُّ، قَالَ: حَدَّثَنَا عُبَيْدُ اللهِ بْنُ مُوسَى، وَطَلْقُ ابْنُ غَنَّامٍ، عَنْ شَيْبَانَ، عَنْ عَاصِمٍ، عَنْ زِرِّ بْنِ حُبَيْشٍ، عَنْ عَبْدِ اللهِ قَالَ: «كَانَ رَسُولُ اللهِ ﷺ يَصُومُ مِنْ غُرَّةِ كُلِّ شَهْرٍ ثَلاثَةَ أَيَّامٍ، وَقَلَّمَا كَانَ يُفْطِرُ يَوْمَ الجُمُعَةِ».

303. al-Qāsim Ibn Dinār al-Kūfī narrated to us; ʿUbadullāh Ibn Mūsā and Ṭalq Ibn Ghannām narrated to us; from Shaybān; from ʿĀṣim; from Zirr Ibn Khubaysh that ʿAbdullāh [Ibn Masʿūd] (*raḍiyAllāhu ʿanhu*) said:

> 'The Messenger of Allāh (ﷺ) used to fast three days in the beginning of every [new] month, and it was rare for him to fast on a Friday.'[302]

٣٠٤ـ حَدَّثَنَا أَبُو حَفْصٍ عَمْرُو بْنُ عَلِيٍّ، قَالَ: حَدَّثَنَا عَبْدُ اللهِ بْنُ دَاوُدَ، عَنْ ثَوْرِ بْنِ يَزِيدَ، عَنْ خَالِدِ بْنِ مَعْدَانَ، عَنْ رَبِيعَةَ الجُرَشِيِّ، عَنْ عَائِشَةَ، قَالَتْ: «كَانَ النَّبِيُّ ﷺ يَتَحَرَّى صَوْمَ الاثْنَيْنِ وَالخَمِيسِ».

304. Abū Ḥafs ʿAmr Ibn ʿAlī narrated to us; ʿAbdullāh Ibn Dāwūd narrated to us; from Thawr Ibn Yazīd; from Khālid Ibn Maʿdān; from

[301] Bukhārī, #1969, Muslim, #1156, and Tirmidhī, #737.

[302] Abū Dāwūd, #2450, Ibn Mājah, #1725.

Rabīʿah al-Jurashī that ʿĀ'ishah (*raḍiyAllāhu ʿanhā*) said

> 'The Prophet (ﷺ) was eagerly committed to fasting every Monday and Thursday.'[303]

٣٠٥- حَدَّثَنَا مُحَمَّدُ بْنُ يَحْيَى، قَالَ: حَدَّثَنَا أَبُو عَاصِمٍ، عَنْ مُحَمَّدِ بْنِ رِفَاعَةَ، عَنْ سُهَيْلِ بْنِ أَبِي صَالِحٍ، عَنْ أَبِيهِ، عَنْ أَبِي هُرَيْرَةَ، أَنَّ النَّبِيَّ ﷺ قَالَ: «تُعْرَضُ الأَعْمَالُ يَوْمَ الاثْنَيْنِ وَالخَمِيسِ، فَأُحِبُّ أَنْ يُعْرَضَ عَمَلِي وَأَنَا صَائِمٌ».

305. Muḥammad Ibn Yaḥyā narrated to us; Abū ʿĀṣim narrated to us; from Muḥammad Ibn Rifāʿah; from Suhayl Ibn Abū Ṣāliḥ; from his father that Abū Hurayrah (*raḍiyAllāhu ʿanhu*) said:

> 'The Prophet (ﷺ) said: "Deeds are presented [before Allāh, the Most High] on Mondays and Thursdays. I therefore love for my deeds to presented while I am fasting."'[304]

٣٠٦- حَدَّثَنَا مَحْمُودُ بْنُ غَيْلَانَ، قَالَ: حَدَّثَنَا أَبُو أَحْمَدَ، وَمُعَاوِيَةُ بْنُ هِشَامٍ، قَالَا: حَدَّثَنَا سُفْيَانُ، عَنْ مَنْصُورٍ، عَنْ خَيْثَمَةَ، عَنْ عَائِشَةَ، قَالَتْ: «كَانَ النَّبِيُّ ﷺ يَصُومُ مِنَ الشَّهْرِ السَّبْتَ وَالأَحَدَ وَالاثْنَيْنِ، وَمِنَ الشَّهْرِ الآخَرِ الثُّلَاثَاءَ وَالأَرْبِعَاءَ وَالخَمِيسَ».

306. Maḥmūd Ibn Ghaylān narrated to us; Abū Aḥmad and Muʿawwiyah narrated to us; Abū Sufyān narrated to us; from Manṣūr; from Khathamah that ʿĀ'ishah (*raḍiyAllāhu ʿanhā*) said:

---

303 Tirmidhī, #745, and Ibn Mājah, #1649.
304 Tirmidhī, #747, the chain has a weakness but is supported by other evidence see *Irwā' Galīl*, #948, #948.

> 'The Prophet (ﷺ) used fast during one month on the Saturday, and on the Sunday, and on the Monday, and during another month on the Tuesday, and on the Wednesday and on the Thursday.'[305]

307. Abū Muṣʿab al-Madanī narrated to us; from Mālik Ibn Anas; from Abū'l-Naḍr; from Abū Salamah Ibn ʿAbdu'l-Raḥmān that ʿĀ'ishah (*raḍiyAllāhu ʿanhā*) said:

> 'The Messenger of Allāh (ﷺ) would not fast in any month more than he did in [the month of] Shaʿbān.'[306]

٣٠٨ـ حَدَّثَنَا مَحْمُودُ بْنُ غَيْلَانَ، قَالَ: حَدَّثَنَا أَبُو دَاوُدَ، قَالَ: حَدَّثَنَا شُعْبَةُ، عَنْ يَزِيدَ الرِّشْكِ، قَالَ: سَمِعْتُ مُعَاذَةَ، قَالَتْ: قُلْتُ لِعَائِشَةَ: «أَكَانَ رَسُولُ اللهِ ﷺ يَصُومُ ثَلَاثَةَ أَيَّامٍ مِنْ كُلِّ شَهْرٍ؟ قَالَتْ: نَعَمْ، قُلْتُ: مِنْ أَيِّهِ كَانَ يَصُومُ؟ قَالَتْ: كَانَ لَا يُبَالِي مِنْ أَيِّهِ صَامَ».

308. Maḥmūd Ibn Ghaylān narrated to us; Abū Dāwūd narrated to us; Shuʿbah narrated to us; from Yazīd al-Rishk, who said: I heard from Muʿādhah say:

> 'I asked ʿĀ'ishah (*raḍiyAllāhu ʿanhā*): 'Did the the Messenger of Allāh (ﷺ) used to fast three days of every month?' She replied:'Yes,' I then asked: 'During which days would he fast?' She replied: 'He would not mind about which days he fasted.''[307]

---

[305] Tirmidhī, #746.

[306] Bukhārī, #1969, Muslim, #1156, and Tirmidhī, #737.

[307] Muslim, #1160, and Tirmidhī, #763.

قَالَ أَبُو عِيسَى: يَزِيدُ الرِّشْكُ هُوَ يَزِيدُ الضُّبَعِيُّ البَصْرِيُّ، وَهُوَ ثِقَةٌ، رَوَى عَنْهُ شُعْبَةُ، وَعَبْدُ الوَارِثِ بْنُ سَعِيدٍ، وَحَمَّادُ بْنُ زَيْدٍ، وَإِسْمَاعِيلُ بْنُ إِبْرَاهِيمَ، وَغَيْرُ وَاحِدٍ مِنَ الأَئِمَّةِ، وَهُوَ يَزِيدُ القَاسِمُ، وَيُقَالُ: القَسَّامُ، وَالرِّشْكُ بِلُغَةِ أَهْلِ البَصْرَةِ هُوَ القَسَّامُ.

Abū ʿIsā said: 'Yazīd al-Rishk is Yazīd al-Ḍabʿī al-Baṣrī, he is reliable and transmitted by way of Shuʿbah. ʿAbdu'l-Wārith Ibn Saʿīd, Ḥammād Ibn Zayd, Ismāʿīl Ibn Ibrāhīm, and more than of the Imāms. He is also known as Yazīd al-Qāsim and Yazīd al-Qassām.'

٣٠٩ـ حَدَّثَنَا هَارُونُ بْنُ إِسْحَاقَ الهَمْدَانِيُّ، قَالَ: حَدَّثَنَا عَبْدَةُ بْنُ سُلَيْمَانَ، عَنْ هِشَامِ بْنِ عُرْوَةَ، عَنْ أَبِيهِ، عَنْ عَائِشَةَ، قَالَتْ: «كَانَ عَاشُورَاءُ يَوْمًا تَصُومُهُ قُرَيْشٌ فِي الجَاهِلِيَّةِ، وَكَانَ رَسُولُ اللهِ ﷺ يَصُومُهُ، فَلَمَّا قَدِمَ المَدِينَةَ صَامَهُ وَأَمَرَ بِصِيَامِهِ، فَلَمَّا افْتُرِضَ رَمَضَانُ كَانَ رَمَضَانُ هُوَ الفَرِيضَةُ وَتُرِكَ عَاشُورَاءُ، فَمَنْ شَاءَ صَامَهُ وَمَنْ شَاءَ تَرَكَهُ».

309. Hārun Ibn Isḥāq al-Hamdānī narrated to us; ʿAbdah Ibn Sulaymān narrated to us; from Hishām Ibn ʿUrwah; from his father that ʿĀ'ishah (*raḍiyAllāhu ʿanhā*) said:

> '*ʿĀshūrā'* was a day on which the Quraysh used to fast in the days of *al-jāhilīyyah* (pagan era), and the Messenger of Allāh (ﷺ) used to fast it as well. Then, when he arrived in Medīnah, he fasted during it and ordered its fast. Thereafter, when Ramaḍān was made obligatory, Ramaḍān was obligatory fast and *'Āshūrā'* was left. So whoever wants

may fast during it; and whoever wants may leave it.'[308]

٣١٠- حَدَّثَنَا مُحَمَّدُ بْنُ بَشَّارٍ، قَالَ: حَدَّثَنَا عَبْدُ الرَّحْمَنِ بْنُ مَهْدِيٍّ، قَالَ: حَدَّثَنَا سُفْيَانُ، عَنْ مَنْصُورٍ، عَنِ إِبْرَاهِيمَ، عَنْ عَلْقَمَةَ، قَالَ: سَأَلْتُ عَائِشَةَ، «أَكَانَ رَسُولُ اللهِ ﷺ يَخُصُّ مِنَ الأَيَّامِ شَيْئًا؟ قَالَتْ: كَانَ عَمَلُهُ دِيمَةً، وَأَيُّكُمْ يُطِيقُ مَا كَانَ رَسُولُ اللهِ ﷺ يُطِيقُ».

310. Muḥammad Ibn Bashshār narrated to us; 'Abdu'l-Raḥmān Ibn Mahdī narrated to us; Sufyān narrated to us; from Manṣūr; from Ibrāhīm that 'Alqamah (*raḍiyAllāhu 'anhu*) said:

> 'I asked 'Ā'ishah (*raḍiyAllāhu 'anhā*): 'Did the Messenger of Allāh (ﷺ) single out any of the days?' She replied: 'His deeds were consistent. Indeed, who among you is able to endure what the Messenger of Allāh (ﷺ) was able to endure?"[309]

٣١١- حَدَّثَنَا هَارُونُ بْنُ إِسْحَاقَ، قَالَ: حَدَّثَنَا عَبْدَةُ، عَنْ هِشَامِ بْنِ عُرْوَةَ، عَنْ أَبِيهِ، عَنْ عَائِشَةَ، قَالَتْ: دَخَلَ عَلَيَّ رَسُولُ اللهِ ﷺ وَعِنْدِي امْرَأَةٌ، فَقَالَ: «مَنْ هَذِهِ؟» قُلْتُ: فُلَانَةُ لَا تَنَامُ اللَّيْلَ، فَقَالَ رَسُولُ اللهِ ﷺ: «عَلَيْكُمْ مِنَ الأَعْمَالِ مَا تُطِيقُونَ، فَوَاللهِ لَا يَمَلُّ اللهُ حَتَّى تَمَلُّوا»، وَكَانَ أَحَبَّ ذَلِكَ إِلَى رَسُولِ اللهِ ﷺ الَّذِي يَدُومُ عَلَيْهِ صَاحِبُهُ.

311. Hārun Ibn Isḥāq al-Hamdānī narrated to us; 'Abdah [Ibn Sulaymān] narrated to us; from Hishām Ibn 'Urwah; from his father

[308] Bukhārī, #1952, Muslim, #1125, and Tirmidhī, #753.
[309] Bukhārī, #1987, and Muslim, #783.

that 'Ā'ishah (*raḍiyAllāhu 'anhā*) said:

> 'The Messenger of Allāh (ﷺ) [once] entered upon me while there was a woman with me, so he said: "Who is this woman?" I replied: 'So-and-so. She does not sleep at night.' The Messenger of Allāh (ﷺ) then said: "Adhere to actions which you are able to cope with; for by Allāh, Allāh will not become weary until you become weary!" In fact, the actions most beloved to the Messenger of Allāh (ﷺ) were those which a person could perform consistently.'[310]

٣١٢ـ حَدَّثَنَا أَبُو هِشَامٍ مُحَمَّدُ بْنُ يَزِيدَ الرِّفَاعِيُّ، قَالَ: حَدَّثَنَا ابْنُ فُضَيْلٍ، عَنِ الأَعْمَشِ، عَنْ أَبِي صَالِحٍ، قَالَ: سَأَلْتُ عَائِشَةَ، وَأُمَّ سَلَمَةَ، «أَيُّ العَمَلِ كَانَ أَحَبَّ إِلَى رَسُولِ اللهِ ﷺ؟ قَالَتَا: مَا دِيمَ عَلَيْهِ وَإِنْ قَلَّ».

312. Abū Hishām Muḥammad Ibn al-Rifā'ī narrated to us; Ibn Fuḍayl narrated to us; from al-A'mash that Abū Ṣāliḥ said:

> 'I asked 'Ā'ishah and Umm Salamah (*raḍiyAllāhu 'anhumā*), 'Which deed was most beloved by the Messenger of Allāh (ﷺ)?' They replied: 'That which is performed consistently, even if it was small.'[311]

٣١٣ـ حَدَّثَنَا مُحَمَّدُ بْنُ إِسْمَاعِيلَ، قَالَ: حَدَّثَنَا عَبْدُ اللهِ بْنُ صَالِحٍ، قَالَ: حَدَّثَنِي مُعَاوِيَةُ بْنُ صَالِحٍ، عَنْ عَمْرِو بْنِ قَيْسٍ، أَنَّهُ سَمِعَ عَاصِمَ بْنَ حُمَيْدٍ، قَالَ: سَمِعْتُ عَوْفَ بْنَ مَالِكٍ يَقُولُ: «كُنْتُ مَعَ رَسُولِ اللهِ ﷺ لَيْلَةً فَاسْتَاكَ ثُمَّ تَوَضَّأَ ثُمَّ قَامَ يُصَلِّي،

[310] Bukhārī, #43, and Muslim, #785.
[311] Tirmidhī, #2856.

فَقُمْتُ مَعَهُ، فَبَدَأَ فَاسْتَفْتَحَ البَقَرَةَ فَلَا يَمُرُّ بِآيَةِ رَحْمَةٍ إِلَّا وَقَفَ فَسَأَلَ، وَلَا يَمُرُّ بِآيَةِ عَذَابٍ إِلَّا وَقَفَ فَتَعَوَّذَ، ثُمَّ رَكَعَ فَمَكَثَ رَاكِعًا بِقَدْرِ قِيَامِهِ، وَيَقُولُ فِي رُكُوعِهِ: سُبْحَانَ ذِي الجَبَرُوتِ وَالمَلَكُوتِ وَالكِبْرِيَاءِ وَالعَظَمَةِ، ثُمَّ سَجَدَ بِقَدْرِ رُكُوعِهِ، وَيَقُولُ فِي سُجُودِهِ: سُبْحَانَ ذِي الجَبَرُوتِ وَالمَلَكُوتِ وَالكِبْرِيَاءِ وَالعَظَمَةِ، ثُمَّ قَرَأَ آلَ عِمْرَانَ ثُمَّ سُورَةً سُورَةً يَفْعَلُ مِثْلَ ذَلِكَ».

313. Muḥammad Ibn Ismāʿīl narrated to us; ʿAbdullāh Ibn Ṣāliḥ narrated to us; Muʿāwiyyah Ibn Ṣāliḥ narrated to me; from ʿAmr Ibn Qays that he heard ʿĀṣim Ibn Ḥumayd say: 'I heard ʿUrf Ibn Mālik say:

> 'I was with the Messenger of Allāh (ﷺ) one night when he brushed his teeth with the tooth-stick, after which he performed ablution and then stood praying, so I stood up with him, whereupon he commenced with [*surah*] *al-Baqarah*, and he would not pass by a verse referring to mercy (*raḥmah*) except he paused and asked [for that mercy], nor would he pass by a verse of torment (*ʿadhāb*) except he paused and sought refuge [from the torment].
>
> Then he bowed down and remained bowing (*rukūʿ*) for the duration of his standing (*qiyām*), saying:
>
> *"Subḥān dhi-al-jabrūti wa'l-malakūti wa'l-kibriyā'i wa'l-ʿaẓamati."*—"Glory be to the Lord of power (*jabrūt*), sovereignty (*malakūt*), grandeur (*kibriyāʾ*) and exaltedness (*ʿaẓama*)!"
>
> Then he prostrated (*sujūd*) for the duration of his bowing (*rukūʿ*), saying:
>
> *"Subḥān dhi-al-jabrūti wa'l-malakūti wa'l-kibriyā'i wa'l-*

'azamati."—"Glory be to the Lord of power (*jabrūt*), sovereignty (*malakūt*), grandeur (*kibriyā'*) and exaltedness (*'azama*)!"

Then he recited the [*Surah*] *Āl-'Imrān*, followed by another *Surah*, and he did this in every cycle [of prayer].'[312]

[312] Abū Dāwūd, #783.

CHAPTER FORTY-FOUR

بَابُ مَا جَاءَ فِي قِرَاءَةِ رَسُولِ اللهِ ﷺ

What has been narrated concerning the Recitation (*qirā'a*) of the Messenger of Allāh (ﷺ)

٣١٤ـ حَدَّثَنَا قُتَيْبَةُ بْنُ سَعِيدٍ، قَالَ: حَدَّثَنَا اللَّيْثُ، عَنِ ابْنِ أَبِي مُلَيْكَةَ، عَنْ يَعْلَى بْنِ مَمْلَكٍ «أَنَّهُ سَأَلَ أُمَّ سَلَمَةَ، عَنْ قِرَاءَةِ رَسُولِ اللهِ ﷺ فَإِذَا هِيَ تَنْعَتُ قِرَاءَةً مُفَسَّرَةً حَرْفًا حَرْفًا».

314. Qutaybah Ibn Sa'īd narrated to us; Al-Layth narrated to us; from Ibn Abī Mulaykah that Ya'lā Ibn Mamlak said:

> 'He asked Umm Salamah (*raḍiyAllāhu 'anhā*) about the recitation (*qirā'a*) of the Messenger of Allāh (ﷺ), whereupon she began to describe it as recitation in which each letter (*harf*) would be clearly distinguished from the other.'[313]

٣١٥ـ حَدَّثَنَا مُحَمَّدُ بْنُ بَشَّارٍ، قَالَ: حَدَّثَنَا وَهْبُ بْنُ جَرِيرِ بْنِ حَازِمٍ، قَالَ:

[313] Tirmidhī, #2923, and Abū Dāwūd, #1466, the chain is weak but the meaning is supported by other narrations which will follow.

حَدَّثَنَا أَبِي، عَنْ قَتَادَةَ، قَالَ: قُلْتُ لأَنَسِ بْنِ مَالِكٍ: «كَيْفَ كَانَتْ قِرَاءَةُ رَسُولِ اللهِ ﷺ؟ فَقَالَ: مَدًّا».

315. Muḥammad Ibn Bashshār narrated to us; Wahb Ibn Jarīr Ibn Ḥāzim narrated to us; My father narrated to us that Qatādah said:

> 'I asked Anas Ibn Mālik (*raḍiyAllāhu 'anhu*): 'How was the recitation (*qirā'a*) of the Messenger of Allāh (ﷺ)?' He said: "Elongated (*madd*)."'[314]

٣١٦ـ حَدَّثَنَا عَلِيُّ بْنُ حُجْرٍ، قَالَ: حَدَّثَنَا يَحْيَى بْنُ سَعِيدٍ الأُمَوِيُّ، عَنِ ابْنِ جُرَيْجٍ، عَنِ ابْنِ أَبِي مُلَيْكَةَ، عَنْ أُمِّ سَلَمَةَ، قَالَتْ: «كَانَ النَّبِيُّ ﷺ يُقَطِّعُ قِرَاءَتَهُ يَقُولُ: ﴿ٱلْحَمْدُ لِلَّهِ رَبِّ ٱلْعَٰلَمِينَ ۝﴾ ثُمَّ يَقِفُ، ثُمَّ يَقُولُ: ﴿ٱلرَّحْمَٰنِ ٱلرَّحِيمِ ۝﴾ ثُمَّ يَقِفُ، وَكَانَ يَقْرَأُ ﴿مَٰلِكِ يَوْمِ ٱلدِّينِ ۝﴾».

316. 'Alī Ibn Ḥujr narrated to us; Yaḥyā Ibn Sa'īd al- Umawī narrated to us; from Ibn Jurayj; from Ibn Abī Mulaykah that Umm Salamah said:

> 'The Prophet (ﷺ) used to divide his recitation (*qirā'a*) [into parts]. He would say: *"al-hamdu li'llaahi Rabbi'l-'alamin"*—"Praise be to Allāh, the Lord of all the worlds", then he would pause, then he would say: *"al-Raḥmān al-Raheem"*—"The All-Merciful, the All-Compassionate", then he would pause, then he would say: *"Māliki yawmi'd-din"*—"Master of the Day of Reckoning."'[315]

[314] Bukhārī, #5045.
[315] Tirmidhī, #2927.

٣١٧ـ حَدَّثَنَا قُتَيْبَةُ، قَالَ: حَدَّثَنَا اللَّيْثُ، عَنْ مُعَاوِيَةَ بْنِ صَالِحٍ، عَنْ عَبْدِ اللهِ ابْنِ أَبِي قَيْسٍ قَالَ: سَأَلْتُ عَائِشَةَ، عَنْ قِرَاءَةِ النَّبِيِّ ﷺ أَكَانَ يُسِرُّ بِالْقِرَاءَةِ أَمْ يَجْهَرُ؟ قَالَتْ: «كُلُّ ذَلِكَ قَدْ كَانَ يَفْعَلُ، قَدْ كَانَ رُبَّمَا أَسَرَّ وَرُبَّمَا جَهَرَ، فَقُلْتُ: الْحَمْدُ لله الَّذِي جَعَلَ فِي الأَمْرِ سَعَةً».

317. Qutaybah Ibn Saʿīd narrated to us; Al-Layth narrated to us; from Muʿāwiyyah Ibn Ṣāliḥ that ʿAbdullāh Ibn Abī Qays said:

> 'I asked ʿĀ'ishah (*raḍiyAllāhu ʿanhā*) about the recitation (*qirā'a*) of the Prophet (ﷺ): 'Would he recite softly or audibly?' She replied: 'He used to do both: sometimes he used to recite softly while other times he used to recite audibly.' So I said: 'Praise be to Allāh, who has ordained ease in the matter."[316]

٣١٨ـ حَدَّثَنَا مَحْمُودُ بْنُ غَيْلَانَ، قَالَ: حَدَّثَنَا وَكِيعٌ، قَالَ: حَدَّثَنَا مِسْعَرٌ، عَنْ أَبِي الْعَلَاءِ الْعَبْدِيِّ، عَنْ يَحْيَى بْنِ جَعْدَةَ، عَنْ أُمِّ هَانِئٍ، قَالَتْ: «كُنْتُ أَسْمَعُ قِرَاءَةَ النَّبِيِّ ﷺ بِاللَّيْلِ وَأَنَا عَلَى عَرِيشِي».

318. Maḥmūd Ibn Ghaylān narrated to us; Wakīʿ narrated to us; Misʿar narrated to us; from Abū'l-ʿAlā' al-ʿAbdī; from Yaḥyā Ibn Jaʿdah that Umm Hānī (*raḍiyAllāhu ʿanhā*) said:

> 'I would hear the recitation (*qirā'a*) of the Prophet (ﷺ) during the night, while I would be in my bed [sleeping].'[317]

---

[316] Abū Dāwūd, #226 and Tirmidhī, #449.
[317] Ibn Mājah, #1349.

٣١٩ـ حَدَّثَنَا مَحْمُودُ بْنُ غَيْلَانَ، قَالَ: حَدَّثَنَا أَبُو دَاوُدَ، قَالَ: حَدَّثَنَا شُعْبَةُ، عَنْ مُعَاوِيَةَ بْنِ قُرَّةَ، قَالَ: سَمِعْتُ عَبْدَ اللهِ بْنَ مُغَفَّلٍ، يَقُولُ: «رَأَيْتُ النَّبِيَّ ﷺ عَلَى نَاقَتِهِ يَوْمَ الْفَتْحِ وَهُوَ يَقْرَأُ: ﴿إِنَّا فَتَحْنَا لَكَ فَتْحًا مُّبِينًا ۝١ لِّيَغْفِرَ لَكَ اللَّهُ مَا تَقَدَّمَ مِن ذَنبِكَ وَمَا تَأَخَّرَ﴾ [الفتح: ٢]، قَالَ: فَقَرَأَ وَرَجَّعَ».

قَالَ: وَقَالَ مُعَاوِيَةُ بْنُ قُرَّةَ: لَوْلَا أَنْ يَجْتَمِعَ النَّاسُ عَلَيَّ لَأَخَذْتُ لَكُمْ فِي ذَلِكَ الصَّوْتِ أَوْ قَالَ: اللَّحْنِ .

319. Maḥmūd Ibn Ghaylān narrated to us; Abū Dāwūd narrated to us; Shu'bah narrated to us; that Mu'āwiyyah Ibn Qurrah said: 'I heard 'Abdullāh Ibn Mughaffal (*raḍiyAllāhu 'anhu*) said:

> 'I saw the Prophet (ﷺ) on his she-camel on the Day of Victory, and he was reciting:
>
> *"innaa fatahnaa la-ka fathan mubeena: li-yaghfira la-ka Allaahu maa taqaddama min dhanbi-ka wa maa ta'akhkhara"*—
>
> "Verily, We have granted you a manifest victory that Allāh may forgive you your sin of the past and those to follow, and complete His favour upon you." [*al-Fatḥ* (48): 1-2]
>
> He recited it and recited it beautifully.'
>
> Mu'āwiyyah Ibn Qurrah also said: 'Were it not that the people would gather around me, I would have recited it to you in that voice (*sawt*) or that tone (*laḥn*).'[318]

[318] Bukhārī, #4581, and Muslim, #794.

٣٢٠ـ حَدَّثَنَا قُتَيْبَةُ بْنُ سَعِيدٍ، قَالَ: حَدَّثَنَا نُوحُ بْنُ قَيْسٍ الْحُدَّانِيُّ، عَنْ حُسَامِ ابْنِ مِصَكٍّ، عَنْ قَتَادَةَ قَالَ: «مَا بَعَثَ اللهُ نَبِيًّا إِلَّا حَسَنَ الْوَجْهِ، حَسَنَ الصَّوْتِ، وَكَانَ نَبِيُّكُمْ ﷺ حَسَنَ الْوَجْهِ، حَسَنَ الصَّوْتِ، وَكَانَ لَا يُرَجِّعُ».

320. Qutaybah Ibn Saʿīd narrated to us; Nuḥ Ibn Qays al-Ḥuddānī narrated to us; from Ḥusām Ibn Misakk that Qatādah (*raḍiyAllāhu ʿanhu*) said:

> 'Allāh did not send a Prophet except one who had a handsome face (*ḥasan al-wajh*) and a beautiful voice (*ḥasan al-sawt*), and your Prophet had a handsome face and a beautiful voice, and he did not recite repeatedly in a singing manner.'[319]

٣٢١ـ حَدَّثَنَا عَبْدُ اللهِ بْنُ عَبْدِ الرَّحْمَنِ، قَالَ: حَدَّثَنَا يَحْيَى بْنُ حَسَّانَ، قَالَ: حَدَّثَنَا عَبْدُ الرَّحْمَنِ بْنُ أَبِي الزِّنَادِ، عَنْ عَمْرِو بْنِ أَبِي عَمْرٍو، عَنْ عِكْرِمَةَ، عَنِ ابْنِ عَبَّاسٍ قَالَ: «كَانَتْ قِرَاءَةُ النَّبِيِّ ﷺ رُبَّمَا يَسْمَعُهَا مَنْ فِي الْحُجْرَةِ وَهُوَ فِي الْبَيْتِ».

321. ʿAbdullāh Ibn ʿAbdu'l-Raḥmān narrated to us; Yaḥyā Ibn Ḥassān narrated to us; ʿAbdu'l-Raḥmān Ibn Abī Zinād narrated to us; from ʿAmr Ibn Abī ʿAmr; from ʿIkrīmah that Ibn ʿAbbās (*raḍiyAllāhu ʿanhumā*) said:

> 'The recitation (*qirā'a*) of the Prophet (ﷺ) was sometimes heard by those in the courtyard, while he was in his house.'[320]

[319] *Ṭabaqāt Ibn Saʿd*, #879, this hadīth has a weak chain.
[320] Abū Dāwūd, #1327.

CHAPTER FORTY-FIVE

بَابُ مَا جَاءَ فِي بُكَاءِ رَسُولِ اللهِ

What has been narrated concerning the Weeping (*bukā'*) of the Messenger of Allāh (ﷺ)

٣٢٢- حَدَّثَنَا سُوَيْدُ بْنُ نَصْرٍ، قَالَ: حَدَّثَنَا عَبْدُ اللهِ بْنُ الْمُبَارَكِ، عَنْ حَمَّادِ ابْنِ سَلَمَةَ، عَنْ ثَابِتٍ، عَنْ مُطَرِّفٍ وَهُوَ ابْنُ عَبْدِ اللهِ بْنِ الشِّخِّيرِ، عَنْ أَبِيهِ، قَالَ: أَتَيْتُ رَسُولَ اللهِ ﷺ وَهُوَ يُصَلِّي وَلِجَوْفِهِ أَزِيزٌ كَأَزِيزِ الْمِرْجَلِ مِنَ الْبُكَاءِ.

322. Suwayd Ibn Naṣr narrated to us; 'Abdullāh Ibn al-Mubārak narrated to us; from Ḥammād Ibn Salamah; from Thābit; from Muṭarrif 'Abdullāh Ibn al-Shikhkhīr (*raḍiyAllāhu 'anhu*) that his father said:

> 'I came to the Messenger of Allāh (ﷺ) as he was praying, and a sound, like the hissing of cooking pot, was emanating from his inner body due to his weeping (*bukā'*).'[321]

٣٢٣- حَدَّثَنَا مَحْمُودُ بْنُ غَيْلَانَ، قَالَ: حَدَّثَنَا مُعَاوِيَةُ بْنُ هِشَامٍ، قَالَ: حَدَّثَنَا

[321] Abū Dāwūd, #904.

سُفْيَانُ، عَنِ الأَعْمَشِ، عَنْ إِبْرَاهِيمَ، عَنْ عَبِيدَةَ، عَنْ عَبْدِ اللهِ بْنِ مَسْعُودٍ، قَالَ: قَالَ لِي رَسُولُ اللهِ ﷺ: اقْرَأْ عَلَيَّ، فَقُلْتُ: يَا رَسُولَ اللهِ! أَقْرَأُ عَلَيْكَ وَعَلَيْكَ أُنْزِلَ؟ قَالَ: إِنِّي أُحِبُّ أَنْ أَسْمَعَهُ مِنْ غَيْرِي، فَقَرَأْتُ سُورَةَ النِّسَاءِ، حَتَّى بَلَغْتُ ﴿وَجِئْنَا بِكَ عَلَىٰ هَٰؤُلَاءِ شَهِيدًا ﴿٤١﴾﴾ [النساء] قَالَ: فَرَأَيْتُ عَيْنَيْ رَسُولِ اللهِ تَهْمِلَانِ.

323. Maḥmūd Ibn Ghaylān narrated to us; Muʿāwiyyah Ibn Hishām narrated to us; Sufyān narrated to us; from al-Aʿmash; from Ibrāhīm; from ʿUbaydah that ʿAbdullāh Ibn Masʿūd (*raḍiyAllāhu ʿanhu*) said:

> 'The Messenger of Allāh (ﷺ) said to me: "Recite the Qur'ān to me." So I said: 'O Messenger of Allāh, shall I recite to you when to you it was revealed?' He said: "I love to hear it from someone else." So I recited from *Surah al-Nisā'* until I reached the [the words]: *"wa ji'nābika ʿalā hā'ulā'i shahīdā"*—"And We brought you as a witness against these." [*al-Nisā'* (4): 41], whereupon I saw tears flowing from the eyes of the Messenger of Allāh (ﷺ).'[322]

٣٢٤ـ حَدَّثَنَا قُتَيْبَةُ، قَالَ: حَدَّثَنَا جَرِيرٌ، عَنْ عَطَاءِ بْنِ السَّائِبِ، عَنْ أَبِيهِ، عَنْ عَبْدِ اللهِ بْنِ عَمْرٍو، قَالَ: «انْكَسَفَتِ الشَّمْسُ يَوْمًا عَلَى عَهْدِ رَسُولِ اللهِ ﷺ فَقَامَ رَسُولُ اللهِ ﷺ يُصَلِّي، حَتَّى لَمْ يَكَدْ يَرْكَعُ ثُمَّ رَكَعَ، فَلَمْ يَكَدْ يَرْفَعُ رَأْسَهُ، ثُمَّ رَفَعَ رَأْسَهُ، فَلَمْ يَكَدْ أَنْ يَسْجُدَ، ثُمَّ سَجَدَ، فَلَمْ يَكَدْ أَنْ يَرْفَعَ رَأْسَهُ، ثُمَّ رَفَعَ رَأْسَهُ، فَلَمْ يَكَدْ أَنْ يَسْجُدَ، ثُمَّ سَجَدَ، فَلَمْ يَكَدْ أَنْ يَرْفَعَ رَأْسَهُ، فَجَعَلَ يَنْفُخُ وَيَبْكِي، وَيَقُولُ: رَبِّ أَلَمْ تَعِدْنِي أَنْ لَا تُعَذِّبَهُمْ وَأَنَا فِيهِمْ؟ رَبِّ أَلَمْ تَعِدْنِي أَنْ لَا تُعَذِّبَهُمْ وَهُمْ يَسْتَغْفِرُونَ؟ وَنَحْنُ نَسْتَغْفِرُكَ، فَلَمَّا

[322] Bukhārī, #4582, Muslim, #800, and Tirmidhī, #3025.

صَلَّى رَكْعَتَيْنِ انْجَلَتِ الشَّمْسُ، فَقَامَ فَحَمِدَ اللهَ تَعَالَى وَأَثْنَى عَلَيْهِ، ثُمَّ قَالَ: إِنَّ الشَّمْسَ وَالقَمَرَ آيَتَانِ مِنْ آيَاتِ اللهِ لَا يَنْكَسِفَانِ لِمَوْتِ أَحَدٍ وَلَا لِحَيَاتِهِ، فَإِذَا انْكَسَفَا فَافْزَعُوا إِلَى ذِكْرِ اللهِ تَعَالَى».

324. Qutaybah narrated to us; Jarīr narrated to us; from 'Aṭā' Ibn al-Sā'ib; from his father that 'Abdullāh Ibn 'Amr (*raḍiyAllāhu 'anhumā*) said:

> 'One day during the lifetime of the Messenger of Allāh (ﷺ) the sun eclipsed, so the Messenger of Allāh (ﷺ) stood praying until he could hardly bow down, then he bowed down and could hardly raise his head, then he raised his head and could hardly prostrate himself, then he prostrated himself and could hardly raise his head. Then he began to breathe heavily and weep, while saying: "My Lord, did You not promise me that You will not punish them as long as I am amongst them? My Lord, did You not promise me that You will not punish them as long as they seek forgiveness, and we are seeking Your forgiveness?" when he had prayed the two cycles, the sun became visible, so he stood up praised Allāh, the Most High and extolled Him. Then he said: "The sun and the moon are two of Allāh's signs. They are not eclipsed due to the death or birth of any person. If they are eclipsed, then hasten to the remembrance of Allāh, the Most High."'[323]

٣٢٥ـ حَدَّثَنَا مَحْمُودُ بْنُ غَيْلَانَ، قَالَ: حَدَّثَنَا أَبُو أَحْمَدَ، قَالَ: حَدَّثَنَا سُفْيَانُ، عَنْ عَطَاءِ بْنِ السَّائِبِ، عَنْ عِكْرِمَةَ، عَنِ ابْنِ عَبَّاسٍ، قَالَ: أَخَذَ رَسُولُ اللهِ ﷺ ابْنَةً لَهُ تَقْضِي فَاحْتَضَنَهَا فَوَضَعَهَا بَيْنَ يَدَيْهِ فَمَاتَتْ وَهِيَ بَيْنَ يَدَيْهِ، وَصَاحَتْ أُمُّ أَيْمَنَ فَقَالَ

[323] Aḥmad, #6483.

ـ يَعْنِي ﷺ ـ: «أَتَبْكِينَ عِنْدَ رَسُولِ اللهِ؟» فَقَالَتْ: أَلَسْتُ أَرَاكَ تَبْكِي؟ قَالَ: «إِنِّي لَسْتُ أَبْكِي، إِنَّمَا هِيَ رَحْمَةٌ، إِنَّ الْمُؤْمِنَ بِكُلِّ خَيْرٍ عَلَى كُلِّ حَالٍ، إِنَّ نَفْسَهُ تُنْزَعُ مِنْ بَيْنِ جَنْبَيْهِ، وَهُوَ يَحْمَدُ اللهَ ﷻ».

325. Maḥmūd Ibn Ghaylān narrated to us; Abū Aḥmad narrated to us; Sufyān narrated to us; from 'Aṭā' Ibn Sā'ib; from 'Ikrimah that Ibn 'Abbās (*raḍiyAllāhu 'anhumā*) said:

> 'The Messenger of Allāh (ﷺ) took hold of a daughter of his who was dying, then embraced her and she died in his arms. Then, when Umm Ayman screamed, he said: "Are you weeping in the presence of the Messenger of Allāh?" She replied: 'Do I not see you crying?' He (ﷺ) replied: "I am not crying. They are merely [due to] mercy. A believer's condition is always good. His soul is removed from between his sides yet he praises Allāh, the Most High."'[324]

٣٢٦ـ حَدَّثَنَا مُحَمَّدُ بْنُ بَشَّارٍ، قَالَ: حَدَّثَنَا عَبْدُ الرَّحْمَنِ بْنُ مَهْدِيٍّ قَالَ: حَدَّثَنَا سُفْيَانُ، عَنْ عَاصِمِ بْنِ عُبَيْدِ اللهِ، عَنِ الْقَاسِمِ بْنِ مُحَمَّدٍ، عَنْ عَائِشَةَ: «أَنَّ رَسُولَ اللهِ ﷺ قَبَّلَ عُثْمَانَ بْنَ مَظْعُونٍ وَهُوَ مَيِّتٌ، وَهُوَ يَبْكِي، أَوْ قَالَ: عَيْنَاهُ تُهْرَاقَانِ».

326. Muḥammad Ibn Bashshār narrated to us; 'Abdu'l-Raḥmān Ibn Mahdī narrated to us; Sufyān narrated to us; from 'Āṣim Ibn 'Ubaydullāh; from al-Qāsim Ibn Muḥammad that 'Ā'ishah (*raḍiyAllāhu 'anhā*) said:

> 'The Messenger of Allāh (ﷺ) kissed [the forehead of] 'Uthman Ibn Maz'ūn as he lay dead, while weeping or [the

[324] Aḥmad, #2412 and Nasā'ī, #1843.

narrator] said: 'His eyes were shedding tears.'"[325]

٣٢٧ـ حَدَّثَنَا إِسْحَاقُ بْنُ مَنْصُورٍ، قَالَ: أَخْبَرَنَا أَبُو عَامِرٍ، قَالَ: حَدَّثَنَا فُلَيْحٌ وَهُوَ ابْنُ سُلَيْمَانَ، عَنْ هِلَالِ بْنِ عَلِيٍّ، عَنْ أَنَسِ بْنِ مَالِكٍ، قَالَ: «شَهِدْنَا ابْنَةً لِرَسُولِ اللهِ ﷺ وَرَسُولُ اللهِ جَالِسٌ عَلَى القَبْرِ، فَرَأَيْتُ عَيْنَيْهِ تَدْمَعَانِ، فَقَالَ: أَفِيكُمْ رَجُلٌ لَمْ يُقَارِفِ اللَّيْلَةَ؟ قَالَ أَبُو طَلْحَةَ: أَنَا قَالَ: انْزِلْ فَنَزَلَ فِي قَبْرِهَا».

327. Isḥāq Ibn Manṣūr narrated to us; Abū 'Āmir informed us; Fulayḥ Ibn Sulaymān narrated to us; from Ḥilāl Ibn 'Alī that Anas Ibn Mālik (*raḍiyAllāhu 'anhu*) said:

> 'We saw the Messenger of Allāh (ﷺ), sitting on the grave of a daughter of his, and I saw his eyes shedding tears. He then said: "Is there a man amongst you who did not engage in intercourse last night?" Abū Ṭalḥah replied: 'I' He told him: "Descend! And so he descended into her grave.'[326]

[325] Abū Dāwūd, #3163, Tirmidhī, #989, and Ibn Mājah, #1456, this chain has a weakness.
[326] Bukhārī, #1285.

CHAPTER FORTY-SIX

بَابُ مَا جَاءَ فِي فِرَاشِ رَسُولِ اللهِ ﷺ

What has been narrated concerning the Mattress (*firāsh*) of the Messenger of Allāh (ﷺ)

٣٢٨ـ حَدَّثَنَا عَلِيُّ بْنُ حُجْرٍ، قَالَ: حَدَّثَنَا عَلِيُّ بْنُ مُسْهِرٍ، عَنْ هِشَامِ بْنِ عُرْوَةَ، عَنْ أَبِيهِ، عَنْ عَائِشَةَ، قَالَتْ: «إِنَّمَا كَانَ فِرَاشُ رَسُولِ اللهِ ﷺ الَّذِي يَنَامُ عَلَيْهِ مِنْ أَدَمٍ حَشْوُهُ لِيفٌ».

328. 'Alī Ibn Ḥujr narrated to us; 'Alī Ibn Mus'hir narrated to us; from Hishām Ibn 'Urwah; from his father that 'Ā'ishah (*raḍiyAllāhu 'anhā*) said:

> 'The mattress (*firāsh*) on which the Messenger of Allāh (ﷺ) used to sleep was made of tanned leather whose filling consisted of palm fibre.'[327]

٣٢٩ـ حَدَّثَنَا أَبُو الخَطَّابِ زِيَادُ بْنُ يَحْيَى البَصْرِيُّ، قَالَ: حَدَّثَنَا عَبْدُ اللهِ ابْنُ مَيْمُونٍ، قَالَ: حَدَّثَنَا جَعْفَرُ بْنُ مُحَمَّدٍ، عَنْ أَبِيهِ قَالَ: سُئِلَتْ عَائِشَةُ، مَا كَانَ فِرَاشُ

[327] Bukhārī, #6456, Muslim, #2082, and Tirmidhī, #1761.

رَسُولِ اللهِ ﷺ فِي بَيْتِكِ؟ قَالَتْ: مِنْ أَدَمٍ حَشْوُهُ مِنْ لِيفٍ.

وَسُئِلَتْ حَفْصَةُ: مَا كَانَ فِرَاشُ رَسُولِ اللهِ ﷺ فِي بَيْتِكِ؟ قَالَتْ: مِسْحًا نَثْنِيهِ ثِنْيَتَيْنِ فَيَنَامُ عَلَيْهِ، فَلَمَّا كَانَ ذَاتَ لَيْلَةٍ قُلْتُ: لَوْ ثَنَيْتُهُ أَرْبَعَ ثِنْيَاتٍ لَكَانَ أَوْطَأَ لَهُ فَثَنَيْنَاهُ لَهُ بِأَرْبَعِ ثِنْيَاتٍ، فَلَمَّا أَصْبَحَ، قَالَ: مَا فَرَشْتُمْ لِي اللَّيْلَةَ؟ قَالَتْ: قُلْنَا: هُوَ فِرَاشُكَ إِلَّا أَنَّا ثَنَيْنَاهُ بِأَرْبَعِ ثِنْيَاتٍ، قُلْنَا: هُوَ أَوْطَأُ لَكَ، قَالَ: رُدُّوهُ لِحَالَتِهِ الأُولَى، فَإِنَّهُ مَنَعَتْنِي وَطَاءَتُهُ صَلَاتِيَ اللَّيْلَةَ.

329. Abū'l-Khaṭṭāb Ziyād Ibn Yaḥyā al-Baṣrī narrated to us; 'Abdullāh Ibn Maymūn narrated to us; Jā'far Ibn Muḥammad narrated to us that his father [Muḥammad al-Bāqir (*raḍiyAllāhu 'anhu*)] said: 'Ā'ishah (*raḍiyAllāhu 'anhā*) was asked:

> 'How was the mattress (*firāsh*) of the Messenger of Allāh (ﷺ) in your home?' She said: '[It was made] of tanned leather whose filling consisted of palm fibre.'
>
> Hafsah (*raḍiyAllāhu 'anhā*) was [also] asked: 'How was the mattress (*firāsh*) of the Messenger of Allāh (ﷺ) in your house? She said: 'A coarse woollen sheet which we would fold into two layers, upon which he would sleep.' Then one night I said: 'If only I was to fold it into four layers, it would be more comfortable for him.' So I folded it into four layers for him. When morning came, he asked: What did you spread out as a mattress for me to sleep last night?"' She said: 'We said: 'It is your [normal] mattress, except that we folded it four times. We said [to ourselves] it would be softer for you.' He said: "Restore it to its original condition, for its softness hindered me from praying at night."'[328]

[328] *Akhlāq al-Nabī*, #456, this hadīth is very weak; however the first part is authentic see hadīth #328

CHAPTER FORTY-SEVEN

بَابُ مَا جَاءَ فِي تَوَاضُعِ رَسُولِ اللهِ ﷺ

What has been narrated concerning the Humility (*tawāḍu'*) of the Messenger of Allāh (ﷺ)

٣٣٠ـ حَدَّثَنَا أَحْمَدُ بْنُ مَنِيعٍ، وَسَعِيدُ بْنُ عَبْدِ الرَّحْمَنِ الْمَخْزُومِيُّ، وَغَيْرُ وَاحِدٍ قَالُوا: حَدَّثَنَا سُفْيَانُ بْنُ عُيَيْنَةَ، عَنِ الزُّهْرِيِّ، عَنْ عُبَيْدِ اللهِ، عَنِ ابْنِ عَبَّاسٍ، عَنْ عُمَرَ ابْنِ الْخَطَّابِ قَالَ: قَالَ رَسُولُ اللهِ ﷺ: «لَا تُطْرُونِي كَمَا أَطْرَتِ النَّصَارَى ابْنَ مَرْيَمَ، إِنَّمَا أَنَا عَبْدٌ فَقُولُوا: عَبْدُ اللهِ وَرَسُولُهُ».

330. Aḥmad Ibn Manī' narrated to us; Sa'īd Ibn 'Abdu'l-Raḥmān al-Makhzūmī narrated to us; Sufyān Ibn 'Uyaynah narrated to us; from al-Zuhrī; from 'Ubaydullāh; from Ibn 'Abbās (*raḍiyAllāhu 'anhumā*) that 'Umar Ibn al-Khaṭṭāb (*raḍiyAllāhu 'anhu*) said:

> 'The Messenger of Allāh (ﷺ) said: "Do not exceed the limits in praising me as did the Christians with the son of Maryam. I am merely a servant, so say: "[He is] the servant of Allāh and His Messenger."'[329]

---

[329] Bukhārī, #2462, Muslim, #1691, and Tirmidhī, #1432.

٣٣١- حَدَّثَنَا عَلِيُّ بْنُ حُجْرٍ، قَالَ: حَدَّثَنَا سُوَيْدُ بْنُ عَبْدِ الْعَزِيزِ، عَنْ حُمَيْدٍ، عَنْ أَنَسِ بْنِ مَالِكٍ، أَنَّ امْرَأَةً جَاءَتْ إِلَى النَّبِيِّ ﷺ، فَقَالَتْ لَهُ: إِنَّ لِي إِلَيْكَ حَاجَةً. فَقَالَ: «اجْلِسِي فِي أَيِّ طَرِيقِ الْمَدِينَةِ شِئْتِ أَجْلِسْ إِلَيْكِ».

331. 'Alī Ibn Ḥujr narrated to us; Suwayd Ibn 'Abdu'l-'Azīz narrated to us; from Ḥumayd that Anas Ibn Mālik (*raḍiyAllāhu 'anhu*) said:

> 'A woman came to the Prophet and said to him: 'I have a need to ask of you.' So he said: "Sit in whichever road of the city (*al-Medīnah*) you wish and I will sit with you."'[330]

٣٣٢- حَدَّثَنَا عَلِيُّ بْنُ حُجْرٍ، قَالَ: حَدَّثَنَا عَلِيُّ بْنُ مُسْهِرٍ، عَنْ مُسْلِمٍ الأَعْوَرِ، عَنْ أَنَسِ بْنِ مَالِكٍ، قَالَ: «كَانَ رَسُولُ اللهِ ﷺ يَعُودُ الْمَرِيضَ، وَيَشْهَدُ الْجَنَائِزَ، وَيَرْكَبُ الْحِمَارَ، وَيُجِيبُ دَعْوَةَ الْعَبْدِ، وَكَانَ يَوْمَ بَنِي قُرَيْظَةَ عَلَى حِمَارٍ مَخْطُومٍ بِحَبْلٍ مِنْ لِيفٍ، وَعَلَيْهِ إِكَافٌ مِنْ لِيفٍ».

332. 'Alī Ibn Ḥujr narrated to us; 'Alī Ibn Mus'hir narrated to us; from Muslim al-A'war that Anas Ibn Mālik (*raḍiyAllāhu 'anhu*) said:

> 'The Messenger of Allāh (ﷺ) used to visit the sick (*marīḍ*), attend funerals (*janā'iz*), ride donkeys (*himār*) and accept the invitation of a slave (*'abd*). On the Day of Banu Quraydah, he was [sitting] on a donkey bridled with a rope made of palm fibres, and on it was a saddle that was also made of palm fibres.'[331]

[330] Abū Dāwūd, #4818, this hadīth is weak but is supported by a narration in Muslim, #2326.
[331] Tirmidhī, #1017, and Ibn Mājah, #2296, this hadīth is weak but the meaning is supported in other narrations.

٣٣٣ـ حَدَّثَنَا وَاصِلُ بْنُ عَبْدِ الأَعْلَى الكُوفِيُّ، قَالَ: حَدَّثَنَا مُحَمَّدُ بْنُ فُضَيْلٍ، عَنِ الأَعْمَشِ، عَنْ أَنَسِ بْنِ مَالِكٍ، قَالَ: كَانَ النَّبِيُّ ﷺ يُدْعَى إِلَى خُبْزِ الشَّعِيرِ وَالإِهَالَةِ السَّنِخَةِ فَيُجِيبُ، وَلَقَدْ كَانَ لَهُ دِرْعٌ عِنْدَ يَهُودِيٍّ، فَمَا وَجَدَ مَا يَفُكُّهَا حَتَّى مَاتَ .

333. Wāsil Ibn 'Abdu'l-A'lā al-Kūfī narrated to us; Muḥammad Ibn Fuḍayl narrated to us; from al-A'mash that Anas Ibn Mālik (*raḍiyAllāhu 'anhu*) said:

> 'When the Prophet (ﷺ) would be invited to to a meal of barley bread and rancid oil he would readily accept. He had armour (*dir'*) that was [put up as collateral] with a Jew, and he died before he could repay the debt to retrieve it.'[332]

٣٣٤ـ حَدَّثَنَا مَحْمُودُ بْنُ غَيْلَانَ، قَالَ: حَدَّثَنَا أَبُو دَاوُدَ الحَفَرِيُّ، عَنْ سُفْيَانَ، عَنِ الرَّبِيعِ بْنِ صَبِيحٍ، عَنْ يَزِيدَ بْنِ أَبَانَ، عَنْ أَنَسِ بْنِ مَالِكٍ، قَالَ: «حَجَّ رَسُولُ اللهِ ﷺ عَلَى رَحْلٍ رَثٍّ، وَعَلَيْهِ قَطِيفَةٌ لَا تُسَاوِي أَرْبَعَةَ دَرَاهِمَ، فَقَالَ: اللَّهُمَّ اجْعَلْهُ حَجًّا لَا رِيَاءَ فِيهِ وَلَا سُمْعَةَ» .

334. Maḥmūd Ibn Ghaylān narrated to us; Abū Dāwūd al-Ḥafarī narrated to us; Sufyān narrated to us; from al-Rabī' Ibn Sabīḥ; from Yazīd Ibn Abān that Anas Ibn Mālik (*raḍiyAllāhu 'anhu*) said:

> 'The Messenger of Allāh (ﷺ) performed Pilgrimage (*ḥajj*) on a worn-out saddle upon which there was a fringed wrap-around worth no more than four dirhams. He said: *"Allāhumma ij'alhu ḥajjā lā riyā' fīhi wa sum'ah."*—"O Allāh, make it a Pilgrimage devoid of ostentation (*riyā'*) or desire for fame (*sum'ah*)."'[333]

---

[332] Aḥmad, 11/993, this chain is weak but supported by a narration in Bukhārī, #2069.
[333] Ibn Mājah, #2890, the chain is weak, but is supported by another narration in *Al-Awsaṭ*, #1378.

٣٣٥ـ حَدَّثَنَا عَبْدُ اللهِ بْنُ عَبْدِ الرَّحْمَنِ، قَالَ: حَدَّثَنَا عَفَّانُ، قَالَ: حَدَّثَنَا حَمَّادُ ابْنُ سَلَمَةَ، عَنْ حُمَيْدٍ، عَنْ أَنَسِ بْنِ مَالِكٍ، قَالَ: «لَمْ يَكُنْ شَخْصٌ أَحَبَّ إِلَيْهِمْ مِنْ رَسُولِ اللهِ ﷺ قَالَ: وَكَانُوا إِذَا رَأَوْهُ لَمْ يَقُومُوا، لِمَا يَعْلَمُونَ مِنْ كَرَاهِيَتِهِ لِذَلِكَ».

335. ʻAbdullāh Ibn ʻAbdu'l-Raḥmān narrated to us; ʻAffān narrated to us; Ḥammād Ibn Salamah narrated to us; from Ḥumayd that Anas Ibn Mālik (*raḍiyAllāhu ʻanhu*) said:

> 'There was no person more beloved to them [the Companions] than the Messenger of Allāh (ﷺ). Yet, they would not stand up [for him] when they would see him [coming] because they knew that he disliked that.'[334]

٣٣٦ـ حَدَّثَنَا سُفْيَانُ بْنُ وَكِيعٍ، قَالَ: حَدَّثَنَا جُمَيْعُ بْنُ عُمَيْرِ بْنِ عَبْدِ الرَّحْمَنِ العِجْلِيُّ، قَالَ: أَنْبَأَنَا رَجُلٌ مِنْ بَنِي تَمِيمٍ مِنْ وَلَدِ أَبِي هَالَةَ زَوْجِ خَدِيجَةَ يُكْنَى أَبَا عَبْدِ اللهِ، عَنِ ابْنِ أَبِي هَالَةَ، عَنِ الحَسَنِ بْنِ عَلِيٍّ، قَالَ: سَأَلْتُ خَالِي هِنْدَ بْنَ أَبِي هَالَةَ، ـ وَكَانَ وَصَّافًا ـ عَنْ حِلْيَةِ رَسُولِ اللهِ ﷺ، وَأَنَا أَشْتَهِي أَنْ يَصِفَ لِي مِنْهَا شَيْئًا، فَقَالَ: كَانَ رَسُولُ اللهِ ﷺ فَخْمًا مُفَخَّمًا، يَتَلأْلأُ وَجْهُهُ تَلأْلُؤَ القَمَرِ لَيْلَةَ البَدْرِ، فَذَكَرَ الحَدِيثَ بِطُولِهِ، قَالَ الحَسَنُ: فَكَتَمْتُهَا الحُسَيْنَ زَمَانًا، ثُمَّ حَدَّثْتُهُ فَوَجَدْتُهُ قَدْ سَبَقَنِي إِلَيْهِ، فَسَأَلَهُ عَمَّا سَأَلْتُهُ عَنْهُ، وَوَجَدْتُهُ قَدْ سَأَلَ أَبَاهُ عَنْ مَدْخَلِهِ وَمَخْرَجِهِ وَشَكْلِهِ فَلَمْ يَدَعْ مِنْهُ شَيْئًا.

قَالَ الحُسَيْنُ: فَسَأَلْتُ أَبِي، عَنْ دُخُولِ رَسُولِ اللهِ ﷺ، فَقَالَ: كَانَ إِذَا أَوَى إِلَى مَنْزِلِهِ جَزَّأَ دُخُولَهُ ثَلَاثَةَ أَجْزَاءٍ، جُزْءًا للهِ، وَجُزْءًا لِأَهْلِهِ، وَجُزْءًا لِنَفْسِهِ، ثُمَّ جَزَّأَ جُزْأَهُ بَيْنَهُ وَبَيْنَ

[334] Tirmidhī, #2754.

النَّاسِ، فَيَرُدُّ ذَلِكَ بِالخَاصَّةِ عَلَى العَامَّةِ، وَلَا يَدَّخِرُ عَنْهُمْ شَيْئًا، وَكَانَ مِنْ سِيرَتِهِ فِي جُزْءِ الأُمَّةِ إِيثَارُ أَهْلِ الفَضْلِ بِإِذْنِهِ، وَقَسْمُهُ عَلَى قَدْرِ فَضْلِهِمْ فِي الدِّينِ؛ فَمِنْهُمْ ذُو الحَاجَةِ، وَمِنْهُمْ ذُو الحَاجَتَيْنِ، وَمِنْهُمْ ذُو الحَوَائِجِ، فَيَتَشَاغَلُ بِهِمْ وَيَشْغَلُهُمْ فِيمَا يُصْلِحُهُمْ وَالأُمَّةَ مِنْ مُسَاءَلَتِهِمْ عَنْهُ، وَإِخْبَارِهِمْ بِالَّذِي يَنْبَغِي لَهُمْ، وَيَقُولُ: لِيُبَلِّغِ الشَّاهِدُ مِنْكُمُ الغَائِبَ، وَأَبْلِغُونِي حَاجَةَ مَنْ لَا يَسْتَطِيعُ إِبْلَاغَهَا؛ فَإِنَّهُ مَنْ أَبْلَغَ سُلطَانًا حَاجَةَ مَنْ لَا يَسْتَطِيعُ إِبْلَاغَهَا ثَبَّتَ اللهُ قَدَمَيْهِ يَوْمَ القِيَامَةِ، لَا يُذْكَرُ عِنْدَهُ إِلَّا ذَلِكَ، وَلَا يَقْبَلُ مِنْ أَحَدٍ غَيْرَهُ، يَدْخُلُونَ رُوَّادًا وَلَا يَفْتَرِقُونَ إِلَّا عَنْ ذَوَاقٍ، وَيَخْرُجُونَ أَدِلَّةً يَعْنِي عَلَى الخَيْرِ.

قَالَ: فَسَأَلْتُهُ عَنْ مَخْرَجِهِ كَيْفَ كَانَ يَصْنَعُ فِيهِ؟ قَالَ: كَانَ رَسُولُ اللهِ ﷺ يَخْزُنُ لِسَانَهُ إِلَّا فِيمَا يَعْنِيهِ، وَيُؤَلِّفُهُمْ وَلَا يُنَفِّرُهُمْ، وَيُكْرِمُ كَرِيمَ كُلِّ قَوْمٍ وَيُوَلِّيهِ عَلَيْهِمْ، وَيَحْذَرُ النَّاسَ وَيَحْتَرِسُ مِنْهُمْ مِنْ غَيْرِ أَنْ يَطْوِيَ عَنْ أَحَدٍ مِنْهُمْ بِشْرَهُ وَخُلُقَهُ، وَيَتَفَقَّدُ أَصْحَابَهُ، وَيَسْأَلُ النَّاسَ عَمَّا فِي النَّاسِ، وَيُحَسِّنُ الحَسَنَ وَيُقَوِّيهِ، وَيُقَبِّحُ القَبِيحَ وَيُوَهِّيهِ، مُعْتَدِلَ الأَمْرِ غَيْرَ مُخْتَلِفٍ، لَا يَغْفُلُ مَخَافَةَ أَنْ يَغْفُلُوا أَوْ يَمِيلُوا، لِكُلِّ حَالٍ عِنْدَهُ عَتَادٌ، لَا يُقَصِّرُ عَنِ الحَقِّ وَلَا يُجَاوِزُهُ، الَّذِينَ يَلُونَهُ مِنَ النَّاسِ خِيَارُهُمْ، أَفْضَلُهُمْ عِنْدَهُ أَعَمُّهُمْ نَصِيحَةً، وَأَعْظَمُهُمْ عِنْدَهُ مَنْزِلَةً أَحْسَنُهُمْ مُوَاسَاةً وَمُؤَازَرَةً.

قَالَ: فَسَأَلْتُهُ عَنْ مَجْلِسِهِ، فَقَالَ: كَانَ رَسُولُ اللهِ ﷺ لَا يَقُومُ وَلَا يَجْلِسُ إِلَّا عَلَى ذِكْرٍ، وَإِذَا انْتَهَى إِلَى قَوْمٍ جَلَسَ حَيْثُ يَنْتَهِي بِهِ المَجْلِسُ، وَيَأْمُرُ بِذَلِكَ، يُعْطِي كُلَّ جُلَسَائِهِ بِنَصِيبِهِ، لَا يَحْسَبُ جَلِيسُهُ أَنَّ أَحَدًا أَكْرَمُ عَلَيْهِ مِنْهُ، مَنْ جَالَسَهُ أَوْ فَاوَضَهُ فِي حَاجَةٍ صَابَرَهُ حَتَّى يَكُونَ هُوَ المُنْصَرِفَ عَنْهُ، وَمَنْ سَأَلَهُ حَاجَةً لَمْ يَرُدَّهُ إِلَّا بِهَا، أَوْ بِمَيْسُورٍ مِنَ القَوْلِ، قَدْ وَسِعَ النَّاسَ بَسْطُهُ وَخُلُقُهُ، فَصَارَ لَهُمْ أَبًا وَصَارُوا عِنْدَهُ فِي الحَقِّ سَوَاءً، مَجْلِسُهُ مَجْلِسُ عِلْمٍ

وَحِلمٍ وَحَيَاءٍ وَأَمَانَةٍ وَصَبْرٍ، لَا تُرْفَعُ فِيهِ الأَصْوَاتُ، وَلَا تُؤْبَنُ فِيهِ الْحُرَمُ، وَلَا تُثْنَى فَلَتَاتُهُ
مُتَعَادِلِينَ، بَلْ كَانُوا يَتَفَاضَلُونَ فِيهِ بِالتَّقْوَى، مُتَوَاضِعِينَ يُوَقِّرُونَ فِيهِ الكَبِيرَ، وَيَرْحَمُونَ فِيهِ
الصَّغِيرَ، وَيُؤْثِرُونَ ذَا الحَاجَةِ، وَيَحْفَظُونَ الغَرِيبَ .

336. Sufyān Ibn Wakīʿ narrated to us; Jumayʿ Ibn ʿUmayr Ibn ʿAbdu'l-Raḥmān al-ʿIjlī narrated to us: I was informed by a man from the Banu Tamīm, one of the children of Abū Hālah, the husband Khadijah, called Abū ʿAbdullāh; from Abū Hālah that al-Ḥasan Ibn ʿAlī (*raḍiyAllāhu ʿanhumā*) said:

> 'I inquired from my maternal uncle Hind Ibn Abī Hālah (*raḍiyAllāhu ʿanhā*) about the noble features of the Messenger of Allāh (ﷺ). He had often described the noble features of the Messenger of Allāh (ﷺ) in detail. I felt that I should hear from him personally, some of the noble appearance (*ḥilyah*) of the Messenger of Allāh (ﷺ), so that I could make his description a proof and testimony for myself and also memorise them, and, if possible, try to emulate and adopt them, so he said: "The Messenger of Allāh (ﷺ) was majestic and esteemed. His face would shine with the radiance of the moon on the moonlit night.' Then he related the tradition in its full length.[335]
>
> Ḥasan [Ibn 'Ali] (*raḍiyAllāhu ʿanhumā*) said: 'I concealed it from al-Ḥusayn for some time, but then I related it to him only to find that he had beaten me to him. He therefore asked him about what he had asked him about, and he found that he had asked his father about his entrance and his exit and his outward appearance, so he did not leave anything out of it.'

[335] See ḥadīth #8 for the full tradition p.70.

Ḥusayn [Ibn 'Alī] (*raḍiyAllāhu 'anhumā*) said: 'I asked my father about the entry in which the Messenger of Allāh (ﷺ) would enter his home.' He replied: 'When the Messenger of Allāh (ﷺ) entered his home he divided his time into three portions; a portion for Allāh; a portion for his wives; and a portion for himself. Then he divided his portion [further] between himself and the people, and he was assigning that in particular to the common folk, and he was not keeping anything from them. As regards the portion assigned for the nation, it was his practice to give preference to people of excellence and virtue, with his permission, and its allotment according to the value of their religious merit. Some of them would have a single need, some two, and some multiple. He would therefore preoccupy himself with them, and preoccupy them with what would benefit them and the nation [in general], including questioning them about it and informing them of what would be appropriate for them. He would say: "Let those amongst you who are present convey to those absent, and convey to me the need of whoever is unable to relay it [in person], for whoever conveys to a ruler (*sulṭān*) the need of someone who is unable to convey it himself, Allāh shall make his feet firm on the Day of Resurrection." Nothing but that will be mentioned in his presence, and it will not be accepted from anyone other than him. They would enter as seekers (*ruwwād*), and only part after having tasted something, and emerge as guides—meaning—to goodness.'

He said: 'Then I asked him about how he was when he left his home: 'What would he do in this regard?' He replied: 'The Messenger of Allāh (ﷺ) would withhold his tongue from what did not concern him, and he would bring people together and not alienate them. He would honour the noble of each tribe and appoint him over them as leader. He would caution people and be wary of them, without concealing his good humour and fine character. He would enquire about his Companions, and ask the people about their affairs. He would approve of whatever is good and support it, and he would disapprove of the vile and weaken it. He was equitable, and not argumentative. He remained vigilant lest others be negligent or deviate from the right path, and he had a means of dealing with every situation. He would neither fall short of the truth, nor overstep it [limits]. Those who followed him were the best of people, and were the most virtuous. The best of them were in his eyes those who offered the most sincere advice (*naṣiḥah*) and those holding the greatest rank were the most generous and helpful.'

He [further] said: 'Then I asked him about his assemblies, so he said: 'The Messener of Allāh (ﷺ) would neither stand up nor sit down without observing the remembrance of Allāh. When he would join an assembly of people, he would take whatever seat was available, and he instructed others to the same. He would give each and every person who sat with him his share [of time and attention]; no one sitting with him would think that anyone else was dearer to him than him. Whoever sat with him or to consult or discuss with him about a need, he would bear with him patiently. Whoever asked him of a need, he would not turn him away without what he had requested, or offering a word of comfort. His cheery contenance and good character extended to all people such that he became a father to them and they became equal to him. His assembly was an assembly of knowledge (*'ilm*), forbearance (*ḥilm*), modesty (*ḥayā'*), trust (*amānah*) and patience (*ṣabr*). Voices would not be raised therein, nor would anyone's honour be tarnished, nor were any mistakes broadcast. They would treat each other equally, contending with each other only in piety (*taqwā*), while showing humility. They would

> honour the elderly and show compassion for the young. They would give the needy preference over themselves, and take good care of the strangers.'"[336]

٣٣٧ـ حَدَّثَنَا مُحَمَّدُ بْنُ عَبْدِ اللهِ بْنِ بَزِيعٍ، قَالَ: حَدَّثَنَا بِشْرُ بْنُ الْمُفَضَّلِ، قَالَ: حَدَّثَنَا سَعِيدٌ، عَنْ قَتَادَةَ، عَنْ أَنَسِ بْنِ مَالِكٍ، قَالَ: قَالَ رَسُولُ اللهِ ﷺ: «لَوْ أُهْدِيَ إِلَيَّ كُرَاعٌ لَقَبِلْتُ، وَلَوْ دُعِيتُ عَلَيْهِ لأَجَبْتُ».

337. Muḥammad Ibn 'Abdulllāh Ibn Bazī' narrated to us; Bishr Ibn al-Mufaḍḍal narrated to us; Sa'id narrated to us; from Qatādah that Anas Ibn Mālik (*raḍiyAllāhu 'anhu*) said:

> 'The Messenger of Allāh (ﷺ) said: "If a hoof was sent to me as a gift, I would accept, and if I was invited to partake of it, I would accept the invitation."'[337]

٣٣٨ـ حَدَّثَنَا مُحَمَّدُ بْنُ بَشَّارٍ، قَالَ: حَدَّثَنَا عَبْدُ الرَّحْمَنِ، قَالَ: حَدَّثَنَا سُفْيَانُ، عَنْ مُحَمَّدِ بْنِ الْمُنْكَدِرِ، عَنْ جَابِرٍ، قَالَ: «جَاءَنِي رَسُولُ اللهِ ﷺ لَيْسَ بِرَاكِبِ بَغْلٍ، وَلَا بِرْذَوْنٍ».

338. Muḥammad Ibn Bashshār narrated to us; 'Abdu'l-Raḥmān Ibn Mahdī narrated to us; Sufyān narrated to us; from Muḥammad Ibn al-Munkadir that Jabir (*raḍiyAllāhu 'anhu*) said:

> 'The Messenger of Allāh (ﷺ) came to visit me [while I was ill], yet he was neither riding a mule nor a non-Arabian horse.'[338]

[336] Refer to ḥadīth number 8 of this book.
[337] Tirmidhī, #1337.
[338] Bukhārī, #194, Muslim, #1616, and Tirmidhī, #3851.

٣٣٩ـ حَدَّثَنَا عَبْدُ اللهِ بْنُ عَبْدِ الرَّحْمَنِ، قَالَ: حَدَّثَنَا أَبُو نُعَيْمٍ، قَالَ: أَنْبَأَنَا يَحْيَى ابْنُ أَبِي الْهَيْثَمِ الْعَطَّارُ، قَالَ: سَمِعْتُ يُوسُفَ بْنَ عَبْدِ اللهِ بْنِ سَلَامٍ، قَالَ: «سَمَّانِي رَسُولُ اللهِ ﷺ يُوسُفَ، وَأَقْعَدَنِي فِي حِجْرِهِ، وَمَسَحَ عَلَى رَأْسِي».

339. ʿAbdullāh Ibn ʿAbdu'l-Raḥmān narrated to us; Abū Nuʿaym narrated to us; Yaḥyā Ibn Abū'l-Haytham al-ʿAṭṭār informed us saying:

> 'I heard Yūsuf Ibn ʿAbdullāh Ibn Salām (*raḍiyAllāhu ʿanhu*) say: 'The Messenger of Allāh (ﷺ) named me Yūsuf, and he sat me on his lap and wiped my head.'[339]

٣٤٠ـ حَدَّثَنَا إِسْحَاقُ بْنُ مَنْصُورٍ، قَالَ: حَدَّثَنَا أَبُو دَاوُدَ الطَّيَالِسِيُّ، قَالَ: حَدَّثَنَا الرَّبِيعُ وَهُوَ ابْنُ صَبِيحٍ، قَالَ: حَدَّثَنَا يَزِيدُ الرَّقَاشِيُّ، عَنْ أَنَسِ بْنِ مَالِكٍ، «أَنَّ رَسُولَ اللهِ ﷺ حَجَّ عَلَى رَحْلٍ رَثٍّ وَقَطِيفَةٍ، كُنَّا نَرَى ثَمَنَهَا أَرْبَعَةَ دَرَاهِمَ، فَلَمَّا اسْتَوَتْ بِهِ رَاحِلَتُهُ قَالَ: لَبَّيْكَ بِحَجَّةٍ لَا سُمْعَةَ فِيهَا وَلَا رِيَاءَ».

340. Isḥāq Ibn Manṣūr narrated to us; Abū Dāwūd al-Ṭayālisī narrated to us; al-Rabīʿ—Ibn Sabīḥ—narrated to us; Yazīd al-Raqāshī narrated to us that Anas Ibn Mālik (*raḍiyAllāhu ʿanhu*) said:

> 'The Messenger of Allāh (ﷺ) performed Pilgrimage (*hajj*) on a worn-out saddle upon which there was a fringed wrap-around worth no more than four dirhams. He said: "*Labbayk bi- ḥajjatin lā sumʿah fīhi wa lā riyāʾ.*"—"At Your service, with a Pilgrimage in which there is no desire for fame (*sumʿah*) and no ostentation (*riyāʾ*)."'[340]

[339] Aḥmad, 16/404.
[340] Refer to the hadith number 334 of this book.

٣٤١- حَدَّثَنَا إِسْحَاقُ بْنُ مَنْصُورٍ، قَالَ: حَدَّثَنَا عَبْدُ الرَّزَّاقِ، قَالَ: حَدَّثَنَا مَعْمَرٌ، عَنْ ثَابِتٍ الْبُنَانِيِّ، وَعَاصِمٍ الأَحْوَلِ، عَنْ أَنَسِ بْنِ مَالِكٍ، «أَنَّ رَجُلًا خَيَّاطًا دَعَا رَسُولَ اللهِ ﷺ فَقَرَّبَ مِنْهُ ثَرِيدًا عَلَيْهِ دُبَّاءٌ، قَالَ: فَكَانَ رَسُولُ اللهِ ﷺ يَأْخُذُ الدُّبَّاءَ، وَكَانَ يُحِبُّ الدُّبَّاءَ».

قَالَ ثَابِتٌ: فَسَمِعْتُ أَنَسًا يَقُولُ: فَمَا صُنِعَ لِي طَعَامٌ أَقْدِرُ عَلَى أَنْ يُصْنَعَ فِيهِ دُبَّاءٌ إِلَّا صُنِعَ.

341. Isḥāq Ibn Manṣūr narrated to us; ʿAbdu'l-Razzāq narrated to us; Miʿmar narrated to us; from Thābit al-Bānī and ʿĀṣim al-Aḥwal that Anas Ibn Mālik (*raḍiyAllāhu ʿanhu*) said:

> 'A tailor invited the Messenger of Allāh (ﷺ) and served him a dish sopped bread, meat and broth (*tharīd*), with some pumpkin (*dubbā'*) on it. The Messenger of Allāh (ﷺ) used to love pumpkin.'
>
> Thābit said: 'I heard Anas say: 'After that no dish was prepared for me, wherein if pumpkin could be added, was added.''[341]

٣٤٢- حَدَّثَنَا مُحَمَّدُ بْنُ إِسْمَاعِيلَ، قَالَ: حَدَّثَنَا عَبْدُ اللهِ بْنُ صَالِحٍ، قَالَ: حَدَّثَنَا مُعَاوِيَةُ بْنُ صَالِحٍ، عَنْ يَحْيَى بْنِ سَعِيدٍ، عَنْ عَمْرَةَ، قَالَتْ: قِيلَ لِعَائِشَةَ: مَاذَا كَانَ يَعْمَلُ رَسُولُ اللهِ ﷺ فِي بَيْتِهِ؟ قَالَتْ: «كَانَ بَشَرًا مِنَ الْبَشَرِ، يَفْلِي ثَوْبَهُ، وَيَحْلُبُ شَاتَهُ، وَيَخْدُمُ نَفْسَهُ».

342. Muḥammad Ibn Ismāʿīl narrated to us; ʿAbdullāh Ibn Ṣāliḥ narrated to us; Muʿāwiyah Ibn Ṣāliḥ narrated to us; from Yaḥyā Ibn

[341] Muslim, #2041.

Sa'īd that 'Amrah [bint 'Abdu'l-Raḥmān] said:

> "Ā'ishah (*raḍiyAllāhu 'anhā*) was asked: 'What was the usual practice of the Messenger of Allāh (ﷺ) at home?' She replied: 'He was a man from amongst men. He used to examine [and amend] his clothes, milk his sheep, and serve himself."[342]

[342] Bukhārī in *Adab al-Mufrid*, #541.

CHAPTER FORTY-EIGHT

بَابُ مَا جَاءَ فِي خُلُقِ رَسُولِ اللهِ ﷺ

What has been narrated concerning the Character (*khuluq*) of the Messenger of Allāh (ﷺ)

٣٤٣ـ حَدَّثَنَا عَبَّاسُ بْنُ مُحَمَّدٍ الدُّورِيُّ، قَالَ: حَدَّثَنَا عَبْدُ اللهِ بْنُ يَزِيدَ الْمُقْرِئُ، قَالَ: حَدَّثَنَا لَيْثُ بْنُ سَعْدٍ، قَالَ: حَدَّثَنِي أَبُو عُثْمَانَ الْوَلِيدُ بْنُ أَبِي الْوَلِيدِ، عَنْ سُلَيْمَانَ ابْنِ خَارِجَةَ، عَنْ خَارِجَةَ بْنِ زَيْدِ بْنِ ثَابِتٍ، قَالَ: دَخَلَ نَفَرٌ عَلَى زَيْدِ بْنِ ثَابِتٍ، فَقَالُوا لَهُ: حَدِّثْنَا أَحَادِيثَ رَسُولِ اللهِ ﷺ، قَالَ: «مَاذَا أُحَدِّثُكُمْ؟ كُنْتُ جَارَهُ فَكَانَ إِذَا نَزَلَ عَلَيْهِ الْوَحْيُ بَعَثَ إِلَيَّ فَكَتَبْتُهُ لَهُ، فَكُنَّا إِذَا ذَكَرْنَا الدُّنْيَا ذَكَرَهَا مَعَنَا، وَإِذَا ذَكَرْنَا الآخِرَةَ ذَكَرَهَا مَعَنَا، وَإِذَا ذَكَرْنَا الطَّعَامَ ذَكَرَهُ مَعَنَا، فَكُلُّ هَذَا أُحَدِّثُكُمْ عَنْ رَسُولِ اللهِ ﷺ».

343. ʿAbbās Ibn Muḥammad al-Dūrī narrated to us; ʿAbdullāh Ibn Yazīd al-Muqrī narrated to us; Layth Ibn Saʿd narrated to us; Abū ʿUthmān al-Walīd Ibn Abū'l-Walīd narrated to me; from Sulaymān Ibn Khārijah that Khārijah Ibn Zayd Ibn Thābit (*raḍiyAllāhu ʿanhu*) said:

ʿA group of people (*nafar*) came to visit Zayd Ibn Thābit

> [his father] and said to him: 'Relate to us the traditions of the Messenger of Allāh (ﷺ).' He replied: 'What shall I relate to you? As I was his neighbour, whenever he received revelation he would summon me and I would write it down for him. Whenever we would mention this world, he would mention them along with us, and whenever we would mention the Hereafter, he would mention it along with us, and whenever we would mention food, he would mention it along with us. So I shall relate to you what the Messenger of Allāh (ﷺ) had to say regarding all of this."[343]

٣٤٤ـ حَدَّثَنَا إِسْحَاقُ بْنُ مُوسَى، قَالَ: حَدَّثَنَا يُونُسُ بْنُ بُكَيْرٍ، عَنْ مُحَمَّدِ ابْنِ إِسْحَاقَ، عَنْ زِيَادِ بْنِ أَبِي زِيَادٍ، عَنْ مُحَمَّدِ بْنِ كَعْبٍ الْقُرَظِيِّ، عَنْ عَمْرِو بْنِ الْعَاصِ، قَالَ: «كَانَ رَسُولُ اللهِ ﷺ يُقْبِلُ بِوَجْهِهِ وَحَدِيثِهِ عَلَى أَشَرِّ الْقَوْمِ يَتَأَلَّفُهُمْ بِذَلِكَ، فَكَانَ يُقْبِلُ بِوَجْهِهِ وَحَدِيثِهِ عَلَيَّ حَتَّى ظَنَنْتُ أَنِّي خَيْرُ الْقَوْمِ، فَقُلْتُ: يَا رَسُولَ اللهِ! أَنَا خَيْرٌ أَوْ أَبُو بَكْرٍ؟ قَالَ: أَبُو بَكْرٍ، فَقُلْتُ: يَا رَسُولَ اللهِ! أَنَا خَيْرٌ أَوْ عُمَرُ؟ فَقَالَ: عُمَرُ، فَقُلْتُ: يَا رَسُولَ اللهِ! أَنَا خَيْرٌ أَوْ عُثْمَانُ؟ قَالَ: عُثْمَانُ، فَلَمَّا سَأَلْتُ رَسُولَ اللهِ ﷺ فَصَدَقَنِي، فَلَوَدِدْتُ أَنِّي لَمْ أَكُنْ سَأَلْتُهُ».

344. Isḥāq Ibn Mūsā narrated to us; Yūnus Ibn Bukayr narrated to us; from Muḥammad Ibn Isḥāq; from Ziyād Ibn Abī Ziyād; from Muḥammad Ibn Ka'b al-Quraẓī that 'Amr Ibn al-'Āṣ (*raḍiyAllāhu 'anhumā*) said:

> 'The Messenger of Allāh (ﷺ) used to speak directly with the worst of people, thereby winning their hearts. He used to do the same with me until I thought I was the best of the people, so I asked: 'O Messenger of Allāh, am I better,

[343] *Sunan al-Kubrah*, #12345, this chain is weak.

> or Abū Bakr?' He said: "Abū Bakr." I then asked: 'O Messenger of Allāh, am I better, or 'Umar [Ibn al-Khaṭṭāb]?' He said: "'Umar." I then asked: 'O Messenger of Allāh, am I better, or 'Uthmān [Ibn 'Affān]?' He said: "'Uthmān." When ever I asked the the Messenger of Allāh, he told me the truth, so I wished I had not asked him."[344]

٣٤٥ـ حَدَّثَنَا قُتَيْبَةُ بْنُ سَعِيدٍ، قَالَ: حَدَّثَنَا جَعْفَرُ بْنُ سُلَيْمَانَ الضُّبَعِيُّ، عَنْ ثَابِتٍ، عَنْ أَنَسِ بْنِ مَالِكٍ، قَالَ: «خَدَمْتُ رَسُولَ اللهِ ﷺ عَشْرَ سِنِينَ، فَمَا قَالَ لِي أُفٍّ قَطُّ، وَمَا قَالَ لِشَيْءٍ صَنَعْتُهُ لِمَ صَنَعْتَهُ، وَلَا لِشَيْءٍ تَرَكْتُهُ لِمَ تَرَكْتَهُ، وَكَانَ رَسُولُ اللهِ ﷺ مِنْ أَحْسَنِ النَّاسِ خُلُقًا، وَلَا مَسَسْتُ خَزًّا، وَلَا حَرِيرًا، وَلَا شَيْئًا كَانَ أَلْيَنَ مِنْ كَفِّ رَسُولِ اللهِ ﷺ، وَلَا شَمَمْتُ مِسْكًا قَطُّ، وَلَا عِطْرًا كَانَ أَطْيَبَ مِنْ عَرَقِ النَّبِيِّ ﷺ».

345. Qutaybah Ibn Sa'īd narrated to us; Jāf'ar Ibn Sulaymān al-Ḍuba'ī narrated to us; from Thābit that Anas Ibn Mālik (*raḍiyAllāhu 'anhu*) said:

> 'I served the Messenger of Allāh (ﷺ) for ten years, and he never said "*Uff!*" to me. He never asked me about something I had done, saying: "Why did you do?" nor about something I had left undone, saying: Why did you leave it undone?" The Messenger of Allāh (ﷺ) was the best of people in character (*khuluq*). I never felt any silk, or anything at all, that was softer than the palm (*kaff*) of the Messenger of Allāh (ﷺ). I never smelled any musk, nor any pefume, more fragrant than the perspiration (*'arq*) the Messenger of Allāh (ﷺ).'[345]

[344] *Tahdhīb al-Kamāl*, #939, this hadīth is weak.

[345] Bukhārī, #6041, Muslim, #2330, Abū Dāwūd, #4773 and Tirmidhī, #2015.

٣٤٦ـ حَدَّثَنَا قُتَيْبَةُ بْنُ سَعِيدٍ، وَأَحْمَدُ بْنُ عَبْدَةَ هُوَ الضَّبِّيُّ، وَالْمَعْنَى وَاحِدٌ، قَالَا: حَدَّثَنَا حَمَّادُ بْنُ زَيْدٍ، عَنْ سَلْمٍ الْعَلَوِيِّ، عَنْ أَنَسِ بْنِ مَالِكٍ، «عَنْ رَسُولِ اللهِ ﷺ أَنَّهُ كَانَ عِنْدَهُ رَجُلٌ بِهِ أَثَرُ صُفْرَةٍ، قَالَ: وَكَانَ رَسُولُ اللهِ ﷺ لَا يَكَادُ يُوَاجِهُ أَحَدًا بِشَيْءٍ يَكْرَهُهُ، فَلَمَّا قَامَ قَالَ لِلْقَوْمِ: لَوْ قُلْتُمْ لَهُ يَدَعُ هَذِهِ الصُّفْرَةَ».

346. Qutaybah Ibn Saʿīd and Aḥmad Ibn ʿAbdah al Ḍabbī narrated to us; Ḥammād Ibn Yazīd narrated to us; from Salm al-ʿAlawī that Anas Ibn Mālik (*raḍiyAllāhu ʿanhu*) said:

> 'According to the Messenger of Allāh (ﷺ), there was a man with the Messenger of Allāh (ﷺ) who had a trace of saffron upon him [or his garment]; and since the Messenger of Allāh (ﷺ) could barely confront someone with something on him that he found disgusting, so when he got up and left, he (ﷺ) said to the people: "If only you would tell him to get rid of this saffron!"'[346]

٣٤٧ـ حَدَّثَنَا مُحَمَّدُ بْنُ بَشَّارٍ، قَالَ: حَدَّثَنَا مُحَمَّدُ بْنُ جَعْفَرٍ، قَالَ: حَدَّثَنَا شُعْبَةُ، عَنْ أَبِي إِسْحَاقَ، عَنْ أَبِي عَبْدِ اللهِ الْجَدَلِيِّ ـ وَاسْمُهُ عَبْدُ بْنُ عَبْدٍ ـ عَنْ عَائِشَةَ، أَنَّهَا قَالَتْ: «لَمْ يَكُنْ رَسُولُ اللهِ ﷺ فَاحِشًا وَلَا مُتَفَحِّشًا، وَلَا صَخَّابًا فِي الْأَسْوَاقِ، وَلَا يَجْزِي بِالسَّيِّئَةِ السَّيِّئَةَ، وَلَكِنْ يَعْفُو وَيَصْفَحُ».

347. Muḥammad Ibn Bashshār narrated to us; Muḥammad Ibn Jāʿfar narrated to us; Shuʿbah narrated to us; from Abū Ishāq; Abū ʿAbdullāh al-Jadalī that ʿĀ'ishah (*raḍiyAllāhu ʿanhā*) said:

---

[346] Abū Dāwūd, #4182, this chain is weak. Saffron is a colour that is specific to the disbelievers or their religion and therefore why the Messenger of Allāh (ﷺ) disliked it.

> 'The Messenger of Allāh (ﷺ) was neither obscene (*fāhish*), nor immoral (*mutafahish*), nor boisterous (*ṣakhāb*) in the markets, and he would not repay a wrong (*sayyi'ah*) with a wrong (*sayyi'ah*), but rather he would pardon and overlook.'[347]

٣٤٨ـ حَدَّثَنَا هَارُونُ بْنُ إِسْحَاقَ الهَمْدَانِيُّ، قَالَ: حَدَّثَنَا عَبْدَةُ، عَنْ هِشَامِ ابْنِ عُرْوَةَ، عَنْ أَبِيهِ، عَنْ عَائِشَةَ، قَالَتْ: «مَا ضَرَبَ رَسُولُ اللهِ ﷺ بِيَدِهِ شَيْئًا قَطُّ إِلَّا أَنْ يُجَاهِدَ فِي سَبِيلِ اللهِ! وَلَا ضَرَبَ خَادِمًا، وَلَا امْرَأَةً».

348. Hārun Ibn Ishāq al-Hamdānī narrated to us; 'Abdah narrated to us; from Hishām Ibn 'Urwah; from his father that 'Ā'ishah (*raḍiyAllāhu 'anhā*) said:

> 'The Messenger of Allāh (ﷺ) never struck anything with his hand unless he happened to be fighting in the way of Allāh, nor did he ever srike a servant or a woman.'[348]

٣٤٩ـ حَدَّثَنَا أَحْمَدُ بْنُ عَبْدَةَ الضَّبِّيُّ، قَالَ: حَدَّثَنَا فُضَيْلُ بْنُ عِيَاضٍ، عَنْ مَنْصُورٍ، عَنِ الزُّهْرِيِّ، عَنْ عُرْوَةَ، عَنْ عَائِشَةَ، قَالَتْ: «مَا رَأَيْتُ رَسُولَ اللهِ ﷺ مُنْتَصِرًا مِنْ مَظْلَمَةٍ ظُلِمَهَا قَطُّ مَا لَمْ يُنْتَهَكْ مِنْ مَحَارِمِ اللهِ تَعَالَى شَيْءٌ، فَإِذَا انْتُهِكَ مِنْ مَحَارِمِ اللهِ شَيْءٌ كَانَ مِنْ أَشَدِّهِمْ فِي ذَلِكَ غَضَبًا، وَمَا خُيِّرَ بَيْنَ أَمْرَيْنِ إِلَّا اخْتَارَ أَيْسَرَهُمَا مَا لَمْ يَكُنْ مَأْثَمًا».

349. Aḥmad Ibn 'Abdah al-Ḍabbī narrated to us; Fuḍayl Ibn 'Iyāḍ narrated to us; from Manṣūr; from al-Zuhrī; from 'Urwah that

[347] Tirmidhī, #2016 and Aḥmad, 6/174

[348] Muslim, #2328, Abū Dāwūd, #4786 and Ibn Mājah, #1984

'Ā'ishah (*raḍiyAllāhu 'anhā*) said:

> 'I never saw the Messenger of Allāh (ﷺ) take revenge for a wrong committed against him as long as Allāh's prohibitions were not violated. If any of Allāh's prohibitions (*maḥārim*) were violated, he would be enraged. Whenever he was given the choice between two matters, he would choose the easier of the two so long as it was not a sin.'[349]

٣٥٠ـ حَدَّثَنَا ابْنُ أَبِي عُمَرَ، قَالَ: حَدَّثَنَا سُفْيَانُ، عَنْ مُحَمَّدِ بْنِ الْمُنْكَدِرِ، عَنْ عُرْوَةَ، عَنْ عَائِشَةَ، قَالَتْ: «اسْتَأْذَنَ رَجُلٌ عَلَى رَسُولِ اللهِ ﷺ وَأَنَا عِنْدَهُ، فَقَالَ: بِئْسَ ابْنُ الْعَشِيرَةِ أَوْ أَخُو الْعَشِيرَةِ، ثُمَّ أَذِنَ لَهُ، فَأَلَانَ لَهُ الْقَوْلَ، فَلَمَّا خَرَجَ قُلْتُ: يَا رَسُولَ اللهِ! قُلْتَ مَا قُلْتَ ثُمَّ أَلَنْتَ لَهُ الْقَوْلَ؟ فَقَالَ: يَا عَائِشَةُ! إِنَّ مِنْ شَرِّ النَّاسِ مَنْ تَرَكَهُ النَّاسُ، أَوْ وَدَعَهُ النَّاسُ اتِّقَاءَ فُحْشِهِ».

350. Ibn Abī 'Umar narrated to us; Sufyān narrated to us; from Muḥammad Ibn al-Munkadir; from 'Urwah that 'Ā'ishah (*raḍiyAllāhu 'anhā*) said:

> 'A man sought permission to come in to see the Messenger of Allāh (ﷺ) while I was with him, so he said: "What a vile man he is!" then he gave him permission to enter, and when he entered, he spoke to him gently. After he had left, I said: 'O Messenger of Allāh, you said what you said, and then spoke to him gently!' He said: "O 'Ā'ishah, one of the worst of people is one whom the people avoid to protect themselves from his ill-manners"'[350]

---

[349] Bukhārī, #3560, Muslim, #2327 and Abū Dāwūd, #4785.
[350] Bukhārī, #6032, Muslim, #2591, and Tirmidhī, #1996.

٣٥١ـ حَدَّثَنَا سُفْيَانُ بْنُ وَكِيعٍ، قَالَ: حَدَّثَنَا جُمَيْعُ بْنُ عُمَيْرِ بْنِ عَبْدِ الرَّحْمَنِ الْعِجْلِيُّ، قَالَ: أَنْبَأَنَا رَجُلٌ مِنْ بَنِي تَمِيمٍ مِنْ وَلَدِ أَبِي هَالَةَ زَوْجِ خَدِيجَةَ وَيُكْنَى أَبَا عَبْدِ اللهِ، عَنِ ابْنٍ لِأَبِي هَالَةَ، عَنِ الْحَسَنِ بْنِ عَلِيٍّ، قَالَ: قَالَ الْحُسَيْنُ: سَأَلْتُ أَبِي عَنْ سِيرَةِ النَّبِيِّ ﷺ فِي جُلَسَائِهِ، فَقَالَ: كَانَ رَسُولُ اللهِ ﷺ دَائِمَ الْبِشْرِ، سَهْلَ الْخُلُقِ، لَيِّنَ الْجَانِبِ، لَيْسَ بِفَظٍّ وَلَا غَلِيظٍ، وَلَا صَخَّابٍ وَلَا فَحَّاشٍ، وَلَا عَيَّابٍ وَلَا مُشَاحٍّ، يَتَغَافَلُ عَمَّا لَا يَشْتَهِي، وَلَا يُؤْيِسُ مِنْهُ رَاجِيهِ وَلَا يُخَيَّبُ فِيهِ، قَدْ تَرَكَ نَفْسَهُ مِنْ ثَلَاثٍ: الْمِرَاءِ وَالْإِكْثَارِ وَمَا لَا يَعْنِيهِ.

وَتَرَكَ النَّاسَ مِنْ ثَلَاثٍ: كَانَ لَا يَذُمُّ أَحَدًا وَلَا يَعِيبُهُ، وَلَا يَطْلُبُ عَوْرَتَهُ، وَلَا يَتَكَلَّمُ إِلَّا فِيمَا رَجَا ثَوَابَهُ، وَإِذَا تَكَلَّمَ أَطْرَقَ جُلَسَاؤُهُ كَأَنَّمَا عَلَى رُؤُوسِهِمُ الطَّيْرُ، فَإِذَا سَكَتَ تَكَلَّمُوا لَا يَتَنَازَعُونَ عِنْدَهُ الْحَدِيثَ، وَمَنْ تَكَلَّمَ عِنْدَهُ أَنْصَتُوا لَهُ حَتَّى يَفْرُغَ، حَدِيثُهُمْ عِنْدَهُ حَدِيثُ أَوَّلِهِمْ، يَضْحَكُ مِمَّا يَضْحَكُونَ مِنْهُ، وَيَتَعَجَّبُ مِمَّا يَتَعَجَّبُونَ مِنْهُ، وَيَصْبِرُ لِلْغَرِيبِ عَلَى الْجَفْوَةِ فِي مَنْطِقِهِ وَمَسْأَلَتِهِ، حَتَّى إِنْ كَانَ أَصْحَابُهُ لَيَسْتَجْلِبُونَهُمْ وَيَقُولُ: إِذَا رَأَيْتُمْ طَالِبَ حَاجَةٍ يَطْلُبُهَا فَأَرْفِدُوهُ، وَلَا يَقْبَلُ الثَّنَاءَ إِلَّا مِنْ مُكَافِئٍ، وَلَا يَقْطَعُ عَلَى أَحَدٍ حَدِيثَهُ حَتَّى يَجُوزَ فَيَقْطَعُهُ بِنَهْيٍ أَوْ قِيَامٍ».

351. Sufyān Ibn Wakī' narrated to us; Jumay' Ibn 'Umayr Ibn 'Abdu'l-Raḥmān al-'Ijlī narrated to us: I was informed by a man from the Banu Tamīm, one of the children of Abū Ḥālah, the husband Khadijah, called Abū 'Abdullāh; from Abū Ḥālah that al-Ḥasan Ibn 'Alī (*raḍiyAllāhu 'anhumā*) said:

> 'Al-Ḥusayn said: 'I asked my father about the conduct of the Messenger of Allāh (ﷺ) amongst those who would sit with him.' So he said: 'The Messenger of Allāh (ﷺ) was always cheerful (*dā'im al-bishr*), easy-going (*sahl al-khuluq)* and mild mannered (*layyin al-jānib*). He was neither harsh

(*fazz*), nor hard-hearted (*ghalīz*), nor boisterous (*ṣakhāb*), nor obscene (*fahhāsh*), nor fault-finding (*'ayāb*), nor avaricious (*mushāh*). He would take no interest in what he did not desire, he would not leave anyone who pleaded with him hopeless and disappointed. There were three things he avoided: hypocrisy (*mirā'*), excess (*ikthār*) and leaving what did not concern him. Similarly, he would not rebuke anyone, nor criticise him, nor pry into his personal affairs. He would only say that in which he hoped for reward.

When he spoke, those sitting with him would lower their heads in such a manner, as if there were birds sitting on their heads, and only when he fell silent they would speak. They would not argue with each other in his presence, they would remain silent for him [to speak] until he finished [speaking]. The first of them would be the first to speak before him. He would laugh at whatever made them laugh, and express surprise at whatever surprised them.

He used to exercise patience with a stranger's rough manner of speaking or questioning, so much that his Companions would bring them. He used to say: "If you see someone in need, then assist him." He would only accept praise in moderation, and he would not interrupt someone who was speaking unless he overstepped a limit, in which case he would interrupt him with a prohibition or by standing up [and leaving]."[351]

٣٥٢ـ حَدَّثَنَا مُحَمَّدُ بْنُ بَشَّارٍ، قَالَ: حَدَّثَنَا عَبْدُ الرَّحْمَنِ بْنُ مَهْدِيٍّ، قَالَ: حَدَّثَنَا سُفْيَانُ، عَنْ مُحَمَّدِ بْنِ الْمُنْكَدِرِ، قَالَ: سَمِعْتُ جَابِرَ بْنَ عَبْدِ اللهِ، يَقُولُ: «مَا سُئِلَ رَسُولُ اللهِ ﷺ شَيْئًا قَطُّ فَقَالَ: لَا».

[351] Refer to hadīth number 8 of this book p.70

352. Muḥammad Ibn Bashshār narrated to us; 'Abdu'l-Raḥmān Ibn Mahdī narrated to us; Sufyān narrated to us; from Muḥammad Ibn al-Munkadir said:

> 'I heard that Jābir Ibn 'Abdullāh (*radiyAllāhu 'anhu*) say: 'Never did the Messenger of Allāh (ﷺ) say "No." to anyone who asked for something of him."[352]

٣٥٣ـ حَدَّثَنَا عَبْدُ اللهِ بْنُ عِمْرَانَ أَبُو القَاسِمِ القُرَشِيُّ المَكِّيُّ، قَالَ: حَدَّثَنَا إِبْرَاهِيمُ ابْنُ سَعْدٍ، عَنِ ابْنِ شِهَابٍ، عَنْ عُبَيْدِ اللهِ، عَنِ ابْنِ عَبَّاسٍ، قَالَ: «كَانَ رَسُولُ اللهِ ﷺ أَجْوَدَ النَّاسِ بِالخَيْرِ، وَكَانَ أَجْوَدَ مَا يَكُونُ فِي شَهْرِ رَمَضَانَ، حَتَّى يَنْسَلِخَ فَيَأْتِيهِ جِبْرِيلُ فَيَعْرِضُ عَلَيْهِ القُرْآنَ، فَإِذَا لَقِيَهُ جِبْرِيلُ كَانَ رَسُولُ اللهِ ﷺ أَجْوَدَ بِالخَيْرِ مِنَ الرِّيحِ المُرْسَلَةِ».

353. 'Abdullāh Ibn 'Imrān Abū'l-Qāsim al-Qurashī al-Makkī narrated to us; Ibrāhīm Ibn Sa'd narrated to us; from Ibn Shihāb; from 'Ubaydullāh that Ibn 'Abbās (*raḍiyAllāhu 'anhumā*) said:

> 'The Messenger of Allāh (ﷺ) was the most generous of people in charity, and he was most charitable in the month of Ramaḍān, until it came to an end. Jibrīl would come to him and he would recite to him the Qur'ān. When Jibrīl would meet him, the Messenger of Allāh (ﷺ) would be most generous in charity than the winds sent with showering rain."[353]

٣٥٤ـ حَدَّثَنَا قُتَيْبَةُ بْنُ سَعِيدٍ، قَالَ: أَخْبَرَنَا جَعْفَرُ بْنُ سُلَيْمَانَ، عَنْ ثَابِتٍ، عَنْ أَنَسِ بْنِ مَالِكٍ قَالَ: «كَانَ النَّبِيُّ ﷺ لَا يَدَّخِرُ شَيْئًا لِغَدٍ».

[352] Bukhārī, #6034, and Muslim, #2311.
[353] Bukhārī, #1902, and Muslim, #2308.

354. Qutaybah Ibn Sa'īd narrated to us; Jā'far Ibn Sulaymān informed us; from Thābit that Anas Ibn Mālik (*raḍiyAllāhu 'anhu*) said:

> 'The Prophet (ﷺ) never stored anything for the morrow.'[354]

٣٥٥- حَدَّثَنَا هَارُونُ بْنُ مُوسَى بْنِ أَبِي عَلْقَمَةَ الْمَدِينِيُّ، قَالَ: حَدَّثَنِي أَبِي، عَنْ هِشَامِ بْنِ سَعْدٍ، عَنْ زَيْدِ بْنِ أَسْلَمَ، عَنْ أَبِيهِ، عَنْ عُمَرَ بْنِ الْخَطَّابِ، أَنَّ رَجُلًا جَاءَ إِلَى النَّبِيِّ ﷺ فَسَأَلَهُ أَنْ يُعْطِيَهُ، فَقَالَ النَّبِيُّ ﷺ: مَا عِنْدِي شَيْءٌ وَلَكِنِ ابْتَعْ عَلَيَّ، فَإِذَا جَاءَنِي شَيْءٌ قَضَيْتُهُ، فَقَالَ عُمَرُ: يَا رَسُولَ اللهِ! قَدْ أَعْطَيْتَهُ فَمَا كَلَّفَكَ اللهُ مَا لَا تَقْدِرُ عَلَيْهِ، فَكَرِهَ النَّبِيُّ ﷺ قَوْلَ عُمَرَ، فَقَالَ رَجُلٌ مِنَ الْأَنْصَارِ: يَا رَسُولَ اللهِ! أَنْفِقْ وَلَا تَخَفْ مِنْ ذِي الْعَرْشِ إِقْلَالًا، فَتَبَسَّمَ رَسُولُ اللهِ ﷺ وَعُرِفَ فِي وَجْهِهِ الْبِشْرُ لِقَوْلِ الْأَنْصَارِيِّ، ثُمَّ قَالَ: بِهَذَا أُمِرْتُ».

355. Hārun Ibn Musā Ibn Abī 'Alqamah al-Madyanī narrated to us; my father narrated to us; from Hishām Ibn Sa'd; Zayd Ibn Aslam; from his father that 'Umar Ibn al-Khaṭṭāb (*raḍiyAllāhu 'anhu*) said:

> 'A man came to the Prophet (ﷺ) and asked him to give him a gift, so the Prophet (ﷺ) said: "I do not have anything with me, but purchase at my expense, and when something comes my way, I will settle the debt." 'Umar said: 'O Messenger of Allāh, you have already given him, Allāh has not burdened you with what is beyond your means!' The Prophet (ﷺ) disliked what 'Umar said, whereupon a man from the Anṣār said: 'O Messenger of Allāh, spend and fear not poverty from the Lord of the Throne!' Whereupon the Messenger of Allāh (ﷺ) smiled, and it was clear

[354] Tirmidhī, #2362.

from the look on his face that he was pleased with the words of the Anṣārī. Then he said: "This is what I have been commanded to do.'"[355]

٣٥٦ـ حَدَّثَنَا عَلِيُّ بْنُ حُجْرٍ، قَالَ: أَخْبَرَنَا شَرِيكٌ، عَنْ عَبْدِ اللهِ بْنِ مُحَمَّدِ ابْنِ عَقِيلٍ، عَنِ الرُّبَيِّعِ بِنْتِ مُعَوِّذِ بْنِ عَفْرَاءَ، قَالَتْ: «أَتَيْتُ النَّبِيَّ ﷺ بِقِنَاعٍ مِنْ رُطَبٍ وَأَجْرٍ زُغْبٍ فَأَعْطَانِي مِلْءَ كَفِّهِ حُلِيًّا وَذَهَبًا».

356. 'Alī Ibn Ḥujr narrated to us; Sharīk narrated to us; from 'Abdullāh Ibn Muḥammad Ibn 'Aqīl that Al-Rabī' bint Mu'awwidh Ibn 'Afrā' (*raḍiyAllāhu 'anhā*) said:

> 'I came to the Prophet (ﷺ) with a tray of fresh ripe dates and pieces of cucumber. He gave me a handful of jewellery or she said gold.'[356]

٣٥٧ـ حَدَّثَنَا عَلِيُّ بْنُ خَشْرَمٍ، وَغَيْرُ وَاحِدٍ، قَالُوا: حَدَّثَنَا عِيسَى بْنُ يُونُسَ، عَنْ هِشَامِ بْنِ عُرْوَةَ، عَنْ أَبِيهِ، عَنْ عَائِشَةَ: «أَنَّ النَّبِيَّ ﷺ كَانَ يَقْبَلُ الْهَدِيَّةَ وَيُثِيبُ عَلَيْهَا».

357. 'Alī Ibn Khashram narrated to us; 'Isā Ibn Yūnus narrated to us; from Hishām Ibn 'Urwah; from his father that 'Ā'ishah (*raḍiyAllāhu 'anhā*) said:

> 'The Prophet (ﷺ) used to accept gifts, and reciprocate them.'[357]

[355] Bazzār, #3662, this hadīth is weak.
[356] Aḥmad in his *Musnad*, #27020.
[357] Bukhārī, #2585, and Tirmidhī, #1953.

CHAPTER FORTY-NINE

بَابُ مَا جَاءَ فِي حَيَاءِ رَسُولِ اللهِ ﷺ

What has been narrated concerning the Modesty (*ḥaya'*) of the Messenger of Allāh (ﷺ)

٣٥٨ـ حَدَّثَنَا مَحْمُودُ بْنُ غَيْلَانَ، قَالَ: حَدَّثَنَا أَبُو دَاوُدَ، قَالَ: حَدَّثَنَا شُعْبَةُ، عَنْ قَتَادَةَ، قَالَ: سَمِعْتُ عَبْدَ اللهِ بْنَ أَبِي عُتْبَةَ، يُحَدِّثُ عَنْ أَبِي سَعِيدٍ الْخُدْرِيِّ، قَالَ: «كَانَ النَّبِيُّ ﷺ أَشَدَّ حَيَاءً مِنَ الْعَذْرَاءِ فِي خِدْرِهَا، وَكَانَ إِذَا كَرِهَ شَيْئًا عَرَفْنَاهُ فِي وَجْهِهِ».

358. Maḥmūd Ibn Ghaylān narrated to us; Abū Dāwūd narrated to us; Shu'bah narrated to us that Qatādah said: 'I heard 'Abdullāh Ibn Abī 'Utbah that Abū Sa'īd Khudrī (*raḍiyAllāhu 'anhu*) said:

> 'The Prophet (ﷺ) was more bashful (*ḥayā'*) than a virgin girl in her chambers, when he disapproved of something, we knew it from the expression on his face."[358]

٣٥٩ـ حَدَّثَنَا مَحْمُودُ بْنُ غَيْلَانَ، قَالَ: حَدَّثَنَا وَكِيعٌ، قَالَ: حَدَّثَنَا سُفْيَانُ، عَنْ مَنْصُورٍ، عَنْ مُوسَى بْنِ عَبْدِ اللهِ بْنِ يَزِيدَ الْخَطْمِيِّ، عَنْ مَوْلًى لِعَائِشَةَ، قَالَ: قَالَتْ عَائِشَةُ:

---

[358] Bukhārī, #3562, and Muslim, #2320.

«مَا نَظَرْتُ إِلَى فَرْجِ رَسُولِ اللهِ ﷺ»، أَوْ قَالَتْ: «مَا رَأَيْتُ فَرْجَ رَسُولِ اللهِ ﷺ قَطُّ».

359. Maḥmūd Ibn Ghaylān narrated to us; Wakīʿ narrated to us; Sufyān narrated to us; from Manṣūr; from Mūsā Ibn ʿAbdullāh Ibn Yazīd al-Khamī that a freed slave of ʿĀ'ishah (*raḍiyAllāhu ʿanhā*) said:

> 'I never looked at the private parts of the Messenger of Allāh (ﷺ).' Or she said: 'I never saw the private parts of the Messenger of Allāh (ﷺ).''[359]

[359] Ibn Mājah, #662 and Aḥmad, 6/63.

CHAPTER FIFTY

بَابُ مَا جَاءَ فِي حِجَامَةِ رَسُولِ اللهِ ﷺ

What has been narrated concerning the Cupping (*ḥijāma*) of the Messenger of Allāh (ﷺ)

٣٦٠- حَدَّثَنَا عَلِيُّ بْنُ حُجْرٍ، قَالَ: حَدَّثَنَا إِسْمَاعِيلُ بْنُ جَعْفَرٍ، عَنْ حُمَيْدٍ، قَالَ: سُئِلَ أَنَسُ بْنُ مَالِكٍ عَنْ كَسْبِ الْحَجَّامِ، فَقَالَ: «احْتَجَمَ رَسُولُ اللهِ ﷺ، حَجَمَهُ أَبُو طَيْبَةَ، فَأَمَرَ لَهُ بِصَاعَيْنِ مِنْ طَعَامٍ، وَكَلَّمَ أَهْلَهُ فَوَضَعُوا عَنْهُ مِنْ خَرَاجِهِ، وَقَالَ: إِنَّ أَفْضَلَ مَا تَدَاوَيْتُمْ بِهِ الْحِجَامَةُ، أَوْ إِنَّ مِنْ أَمْثَلِ دَوَائِكُمُ الْحِجَامَةَ» .

360. ʿAlī Ibn Ḥujr narrated to us; Ismāʿīl Ibn Jāʿfar narrated to us that Ḥumayd said: ʿAnas Ibn Mālik (*raḍiyAllāhu ʿanhu*) was asked about earnings of the cupper (*ḥajjām*).' So he said:

> 'The Messenger of Allāh (ﷺ) underwent cupping (*ḥijāmah*) by Abū Ṭayybah and ordered that he be paid two (*ṣāʿ*) measures of food, so he spoke to his people, so they deducted some of his tax (*kharāj*) and said: "Cupping is the most excellent means by which you can provide medical treatment." Or he said: "Cupping is one of the most effective treatments for you."'[360]

[360] Bukhārī, #2102, and Muslim, #1577, and Tirmidhī, #1278.

٣٦١- حَدَّثَنَا عَمْرُو بْنُ عَلِيٍّ، قَالَ: حَدَّثَنَا أَبُو دَاوُدَ، قَالَ: حَدَّثَنَا وَرْقَاءُ ابْنُ عُمَرَ، عَنْ عَبْدِ الأَعْلَى، عَنْ أَبِي جَمِيلَةَ، عَنْ عَلِيٍّ: «أَنَّ النَّبِيَّ ﷺ احْتَجَمَ وَأَمَرَنِي فَأَعْطَيْتُ الحَجَّامَ أَجْرَهُ».

361. ʿAmr Ibn ʿAlī narrated to us; Abū Dāwūd narrated to us; Warqā' narrated to us; from ʿAbdu'l-Aʿlā; from Abū Jamīlah that ʿAlī (*raḍiyAllāhu ʿanhu*) said:

> 'The Prophet (ﷺ) had cupping performed upon him, and instructed me to give the cupper (*ḥajjām*) his fee.'[361]

٣٦٢- حَدَّثَنَا هَارُونُ بْنُ إِسْحَاقَ الهَمْدَانِيُّ، قَالَ: حَدَّثَنَا عَبْدَةُ، عَنْ سُفْيَانَ الثَّوْرِيِّ، عَنْ جَابِرٍ، عَنِ الشَّعْبِيِّ، عَنِ ابْنِ عَبَّاسٍ، قَالَ: «إِنَّ النَّبِيَّ ﷺ احْتَجَمَ فِي الأَخْدَعَيْنِ وَبَيْنَ الكَتِفَيْنِ، وَأَعْطَى الحَجَّامَ أَجْرَهُ، وَلَوْ كَانَ حَرَامًا لَمْ يُعْطِهِ».

362. Hārun Ibn Isḥāq al-Hamdānī narrated to us; ʿAbdah narrated to us; from Sufyān al-Thawrī; from Jābir; from al-Shaʿbī that Ibn ʿAbbās (*raḍiyAllāhu ʿanhumā*) said:

> 'The Prophet (ﷺ) had cupping performed between the two veins of the neck and between the shoulders. He also gave the cupper (*ḥajjām*) his fee, which he would not have done if cupping (*ḥijāmah*) had been unlawful (*ḥarām*).'[362]

٣٦٣- حَدَّثَنَا هَارُونُ بْنُ إِسْحَاقَ، قَالَ: حَدَّثَنَا عَبْدَةُ، عَنِ ابْنِ أَبِي لَيْلَى، عَنْ

---

[361] Ibn Mājah, #2163, this chain has a weakness but is supported by the narrations before and after it.

[362] This ḥadīth is weak but is supported by narrations in Bukhārī, #2103 and Muslim, #1202.

[363] Ṭabarānī in his *al-Muʿjam al-Kabir*, #12427.

نَافِعٍ، عَنِ ابْنِ عُمَرَ، «أَنَّ النَّبِيَّ ﷺ دَعَا حَجَّامًا فَحَجَمَهُ، وَسَأَلَهُ: كَمْ خَرَاجُكَ؟ فَقَالَ: ثَلَاثَةُ آصُعٍ، فَوَضَعَ عَنْهُ صَاعًا وَأَعْطَاهُ أَجْرَهُ».

363. Harun Ibn Ishāq narrated to us; 'Abdah narrated to us; from Ibn Abī laylā; from Nāfi' that Ibn 'Umar (*raḍiyAllāhu 'anhumā*) said:

> 'The Prophet (ﷺ) summoned a cupper (*ḥajjām*), so he cupped him. Then he asked him: "How much is your tax (*kharāj*)." He said: 'Three measures.' So he reduced his tax by one measure (*sā'*) and gave him his fee."[363]

٣٦٤ـ حَدَّثَنَا عَبْدُ الْقُدُّوسِ بْنُ مُحَمَّدٍ الْعَطَّارُ الْبَصْرِيُّ، قَالَ: حَدَّثَنَا عَمْرُو ابْنُ عَاصِمٍ، قَالَ: حَدَّثَنَا هَمَّامٌ، وَجَرِيرُ بْنُ حَازِمٍ، قَالَا: حَدَّثَنَا قَتَادَةُ، عَنْ أَنَسِ بْنِ مَالِكٍ قَالَ: «كَانَ رَسُولُ اللهِ ﷺ يَحْتَجِمُ فِي الْأَخْدَعَيْنِ وَالْكَاهِلِ، وَكَانَ يَحْتَجِمُ لِسَبْعَ عَشْرَةَ وَتِسْعَ عَشْرَةَ وَإِحْدَى وَعِشْرِينَ».

364. 'Abdu'l-Quddūs Ibn Muḥammad al-'Aṭṭār al-Baṣrī narrated to us; 'Amr Ibn 'Āṣim narrated to us; Hammām and Jarīr Ibn Ḥāzim narrated to us; Qatādah narrated to us that Anas Ibn Mālik (*raḍiyAllāhu 'anhu*) said:

> 'The Messenger of Allāh (ﷺ) used to undergo cupping between the two veins of the neck and in the upper portion of the back, and he would undergo cupping on the seventeenth, nineteenth or the twenty-first days of the [lunar] month.'[364]

[364] Tirmidhī, #2051, Abū Dāwūd, #3860, and Ibn Mājah, #3483.

٣٦٥ـ حَدَّثَنَا إِسْحَاقُ بْنُ مَنْصُورٍ، قَالَ: أَنْبَأَنَا عَبْدُ الرَّزَّاقِ، عَنْ مَعْمَرٍ، عَنْ قَتَادَةَ، عَنْ أَنَسِ بْنِ مَالِكٍ: «أَنَّ رَسُولَ اللهِ ﷺ احْتَجَمَ وَهُوَ مُحْرِمٌ بِمَلَلٍ عَلَى ظَهْرِ الْقَدَمِ» .

365. Isḥāq Ibn Manṣūr narrated to us; ʿAbdu'l-Razzāq in formed us; from Maʿmar; from Qatādah that Anas Ibn Mālik (*raḍiyAllāhu ʿanhu*) said:

> 'The Messenger of Allāh (ﷺ) underwent cupping on the top of his foot, while he was in the state of Ihrām (*muḥrim*) in Malal [a place between Makkah and Madīnah].'[365]

[365] Abū Dāwūd, #1837.

CHAPTER FIFTY-ONE

بَابُ مَا جَاءَ فِي أَسْمَاءِ رَسُولِ اللهِ ﷺ

What has been narrated concerning Names (*asmā'*) of the Messenger of Allāh (ﷺ)

٣٦٦- حَدَّثَنَا سَعِيدُ بْنُ عَبْدِ الرَّحْمَنِ الْمَخْزُومِيُّ، وَغَيْرُ وَاحِدٍ، قَالُوا: حَدَّثَنَا سُفْيَانُ، عَنِ الزُّهْرِيِّ، عَنْ مُحَمَّدِ بْنِ جُبَيْرِ بْنِ مُطْعِمٍ، عَنْ أَبِيهِ، قَالَ: قَالَ رَسُولُ اللهِ ﷺ: «إِنَّ لِي أَسْمَاءً أَنَا مُحَمَّدٌ، وَأَنَا أَحْمَدُ، وَأَنَا الْمَاحِي الَّذِي يَمْحُو اللهُ بِيَ الْكُفْرَ، وَأَنَا الْحَاشِرُ الَّذِي يُحْشَرُ النَّاسُ عَلَى قَدَمِي، وَأَنَا الْعَاقِبُ»، وَالْعَاقِبُ: الَّذِي لَيْسَ بَعْدَهُ نَبِيٌّ.

366. Sa'īd Ibn 'Abdu'l-Raḥmān al-Makhzūmī narrated to us; Sufyān narrated to us; from al-Zuhrī; from Muḥammad Ibn Jubayr Ibn Muṭ'im that his father (*raḍiyAllāhu 'anhu*) said:

> 'The Messenger of Allāh (ﷺ) said: "I have several names: I am Muḥammad, I am Aḥmad, and I am al-Māhī (the Obliterator), through whom Allāh will obliterate disbelief (*kufr*). I am al-Ḥāshir (the Gatherer), at whose feet mankind shall gather, and I am al-'Āqib (the Last in Succession), after whom there shall be no other Prophet."'[366]

[366] Bukhārī, #3532, and Muslim, #2354, and Tirmidhī, #2840.

٣٦٧ـ حَدَّثَنَا مُحَمَّدُ بْنُ طَرِيفٍ الكُوفِيُّ، قَالَ: حَدَّثَنَا أَبُو بَكْرِ بْنُ عَيَّاشٍ، عَنْ عَاصِمٍ، عَنْ أَبِي وَائِلٍ، عَنْ حُذَيْفَةَ، قَالَ: لَقِيتُ النَّبِيَّ ﷺ فِي بَعْضِ طُرُقِ المَدِينَةِ فَقَالَ: «أَنَا مُحَمَّدٌ، وَأَنَا أَحْمَدُ، وَأَنَا نَبِيُّ الرَّحْمَةِ، وَنَبِيُّ التَّوْبَةِ، وَأَنَا المُقَفَّى، وَأَنَا الحَاشِرُ، وَنَبِيُّ المَلَاحِمِ».

367. Muḥammad Ibn Ṭarīf al-Kūfī narrated to us; Abū Bakr Ibn 'Ayyāsh narrated to us; from 'Āṣim; from Abū Wā'il that Hudhayfah (*raḍiyAllāhu 'anhu*) said:

> 'I encounted the Prophet (ﷺ) in one of the streets of Medīnah, and he said: "I am Muḥammad; and I am Aḥmad; and I am the Prophet of Mercy (*nabī al-raḥmah*); and I am the Prophet of Repentance (*nabī al-taubah*); and I am the Follower [of the earlier Prophets] (*al-Muqaffā*); and I am the Gatherer (*al-Ḥāshir*), and the Prophet of Wars (*nabī al-malāḥim*)."'[367]

٣٦٨ـ حَدَّثَنَا إِسْحَاقُ بْنُ مَنْصُورٍ قَالَ: حَدَّثَنَا النَّضْرُ بْنُ شُمَيْلٍ، قَالَ: أَنْبَأَنَا حَمَّادُ ابْنُ سَلَمَةَ، عَنْ عَاصِمٍ، عَنْ زِرٍّ، عَنْ حُذَيْفَةَ، عَنِ النَّبِيِّ ﷺ نَحْوَهُ بِمَعْنَاهُ.

هَكَذَا قَالَ حَمَّادُ بْنُ سَلَمَةَ، عَنْ عَاصِمٍ، عَنْ زِرٍّ، عَنْ حُذَيْفَةَ.

368. Isḥāq Ibn Manṣūr narrated to us; Al-Naḍr Ibn Shumayl narrated to us; Ḥammād Ibn Salamah informed us; from 'Āṣim; from Zirr; from Hudayfah (*raḍiyAllāhu 'anhu*) that the Prophet (ﷺ) transmitted similar meaning in a similar form. Likewise, Ḥammād Ibn Salamah said by way of 'Āṣim; from Zirr; from Hudayfah (*raḍiyAllāhu 'anhu*).

[367] Aḥmad, 23/445, see Apendix one for additional names p.328

CHAPTER FIFTY-TWO

بَابُ مَا جَاءَ فِي عَيْشِ النَّبِيِّ ﷺ

What has been narrated concerning the Subsistence (*ʿaish*) of the Messenger of Allāh (ﷺ)

٣٦٩ـ حَدَّثَنَا قُتَيْبَةُ بْنُ سَعِيدٍ، قَالَ: حَدَّثَنَا أَبُو الأَحْوَصِ، عَنْ سِمَاكِ بْنِ حَرْبٍ قَالَ: سَمِعْتُ النُّعْمَانَ بْنَ بَشِيرٍ يَقُولُ: «أَلَسْتُمْ فِي طَعَامٍ وَشَرَابٍ مَا شِئْتُمْ؟ لَقَدْ رَأَيْتُ نَبِيَّكُمْ ﷺ وَمَا يَجِدُ مِنَ الدَّقَلِ مَا يَمْلأُ بَطْنَهُ».

369. Qutaybah narrated to us; Abū'l-Aḥwaṣ narrated to us that Simāk Ibn Ḥarb said:

> 'I heard al-Nuʿmān Ibn Bashīr (*raḍiyAllāhu ʿanhu*) say: 'Do you not indulge in whatever food and drink you wish?' I saw that your Prophet (ﷺ) was unable to find poor-quality dates (*daqal*) with which to fill his stomach.'"[368]

[368] Muslim, #2977 and Tirmidhī, #2372. *Daqal* are dried out poor-dates. See *Tuḥfat Al-Aḥwadhī*.

٣٧٠ـ حَدَّثَنَا هَارُونُ بْنُ إِسْحَاقَ، قَالَ: حَدَّثَنَا عَبْدَةُ، عَنْ هِشَامِ بْنِ عُرْوَةَ، عَنْ أَبِيهِ، عَنْ عَائِشَةَ، قَالَتْ: «إِنْ كُنَّا آلَ مُحَمَّدٍ نَمكُثُ شَهْرًا مَا نَسْتَوْقِدُ بِنَارٍ، إِنْ هُوَ إِلَّا التَّمْرُ وَالمَاءُ».

370. Hārun Ibn Isḥāq narrated to us; ʿAbdah narrated to us; from Hishām Ibn ʿUrwah ; from his father that ʿĀ'ishah (*raḍiyAllāhu ʿanhā*) said:

> 'We the family of Muḥammad (ﷺ), would go an entire month without cooking anything over a fire, and with nothing to eat and drink but dates and water.'[369]

٣٧١ـ حَدَّثَنَا عَبْدُ اللهِ بْنُ أَبِي زِيَادٍ، قَالَ: حَدَّثَنَا سَيَّارٌ، قَالَ: حَدَّثَنَا سَهْلُ ابْنُ أَسْلَمَ، عَنْ يَزِيدَ بْنِ أَبِي مَنْصُورٍ، عَنْ أَنَسٍ، عَنْ أَبِي طَلْحَةَ، قَالَ: شَكَوْنَا إِلَى رَسُولِ اللهِ ﷺ الجُوعَ وَرَفَعْنَا عَنْ بُطُونِنَا عَنْ حَجَرٍ حَجَرٍ، فَرَفَعَ رَسُولُ اللهِ ﷺ عَنْ بَطْنِهِ عَنْ حَجَرَيْنِ.

قَالَ أَبُو عِيسَى: هَذَا حَدِيثٌ غَرِيبٌ مِنْ حَدِيثِ أَبِي طَلْحَةَ، لَا نَعْرِفُهُ إِلَّا مِنْ هَذَا الوَجْهِ، وَمَعْنَى قَوْلِهِ: «وَرَفَعْنَا عَنْ بُطُونِنَا عَنْ حَجَرٍ حَجَرٍ»، كَانَ أَحَدُهُمْ يَشُدُّ فِي بَطْنِهِ الحَجَرَ مِنَ الجُهْدِ وَالضَّعْفِ الَّذِي بِهِ مِنَ الجُوعِ.

371. ʿAbdullāh Ibn Abī Ziyād narrated to us; Siyyār narrated to us; Sahl Ibn Aslam narrated to us; from Yazīd Ibn Manṣūr; from Anas that Abū Talhah (*raḍiyAllāhu ʿanhu*) said:

> 'We complained to the Messenger of Allāh (ﷺ) of severe hunger, and we exposed our stomachs, each revealing a stone [fastened to it], so the Messenger of Allāh (ﷺ) exposed his stomach, revealing two stones [fastened to

[369] Bukhārī, #6458, Muslim, #2971, and Tirmidhī, #2471.

it].'[370]

Abū ʿIsā said: 'This tradition is strange from the tradition of Abū Ṭalḥah (*raḍiyAllāhu ʿanhu*). We do not know of it except from this route.' He said: 'Each of them would strap a stone to his stomach, so thin was he and exhausted with severe hunger.'

٣٧٢ـ حَدَّثَنَا مُحَمَّدُ بْنُ إِسْمَاعِيلَ، قَالَ: حَدَّثَنَا آدَمُ بْنُ أَبِي إِيَاسٍ، قَالَ: حَدَّثَنَا شَيْبَانُ أَبُو مُعَاوِيَةَ، قَالَ: حَدَّثَنَا عَبْدُ الْمَلِكِ بْنُ عُمَيْرٍ، عَنْ أَبِي سَلَمَةَ بْنِ عَبْدِ الرَّحْمَنِ، عَنْ أَبِي هُرَيْرَةَ، قَالَ: خَرَجَ رَسُولُ اللهِ ﷺ فِي سَاعَةٍ لَا يَخْرُجُ فِيهَا، وَلَا يَلْقَاهُ فِيهَا أَحَدٌ، فَأَتَاهُ أَبُو بَكْرٍ، فَقَالَ: «مَا جَاءَ بِكَ يَا أَبَا بَكْرٍ؟» قَالَ: خَرَجْتُ أَلْقَى رَسُولَ اللهِ ﷺ وَأَنْظُرُ فِي وَجْهِهِ، وَالتَّسْلِيمَ عَلَيْهِ، فَلَمْ يَلْبَثْ أَنْ جَاءَ عُمَرُ، فَقَالَ: «مَا جَاءَ بِكَ يَا عُمَرُ؟» قَالَ: الْجُوعُ يَا رَسُولَ اللهِ! قَالَ ﷺ: «وَأَنَا قَدْ وَجَدْتُ بَعْضَ ذَلِكَ»، فَانْطَلَقُوا إِلَى مَنْزِلِ أَبِي الْهَيْثَمِ بْنِ التَّيِّهَانِ الْأَنْصَارِيِّ، وَكَانَ رَجُلًا كَثِيرَ النَّخْلِ وَالشَّاءِ، وَلَمْ يَكُنْ لَهُ خَدَمٌ، فَلَمْ يَجِدُوهُ، فَقَالُوا لِامْرَأَتِهِ: أَيْنَ صَاحِبُكِ؟ فَقَالَتِ: انْطَلَقَ يَسْتَعْذِبُ لَنَا الْمَاءَ، فَلَمْ يَلْبَثُوا أَنْ جَاءَ أَبُو الْهَيْثَمِ بِقِرْبَةٍ يَزْعَبُهَا، فَوَضَعَهَا ثُمَّ جَاءَ يَلْتَزِمُ النَّبِيَّ ﷺ وَيُفَدِّيهِ بِأَبِيهِ وَأُمِّهِ، ثُمَّ انْطَلَقَ بِهِمْ إِلَى حَدِيقَتِهِ فَبَسَطَ لَهُمْ بِسَاطًا، ثُمَّ انْطَلَقَ إِلَى نَخْلَةٍ فَجَاءَ بِقِنْوٍ فَوَضَعَهُ، فَقَالَ النَّبِيُّ ﷺ: «أَفَلَا تَنَقَّيْتَ لَنَا مِنْ رُطَبِهِ؟» فَقَالَ: يَا رَسُولَ اللهِ! إِنِّي أَرَدْتُ أَنْ تَخْتَارُوا، أَوْ تَخَيَّرُوا مِنْ رُطَبِهِ وَبُسْرِهِ، فَأَكَلُوا وَشَرِبُوا مِنْ ذَلِكَ الْمَاءِ، فَقَالَ ﷺ: «هَذَا وَالَّذِي نَفْسِي بِيَدِهِ مِنَ النَّعِيمِ الَّذِي تُسْأَلُونَ عَنْهُ يَوْمَ الْقِيَامَةِ ظِلٌّ بَارِدٌ، وَرُطَبٌ طَيِّبٌ، وَمَاءٌ بَارِدٌ»، فَانْطَلَقَ أَبُو الْهَيْثَمِ لِيَصْنَعَ لَهُمْ طَعَامًا، فَقَالَ النَّبِيُّ ﷺ: «لَا تَذْبَحَنَّ ذَاتَ دَرٍّ»، فَذَبَحَ لَهُمْ عَنَاقًا أَوْ جَدْيًا، فَأَتَاهُمْ بِهَا فَأَكَلُوا، فَقَالَ ﷺ: «هَلْ لَكَ خَادِمٌ؟» قَالَ: لَا، قَالَ: «فَإِذَا أَتَانَا سَبْيٌ فَأْتِنَا»، فَأُتِيَ النَّبِيُّ ﷺ

[370] Tirmidhī, #2371, this hadīth is weak but supported in meaning by another narration in Bukhārī, #4101. Likewise, it is supported by Ṭabarānī in his *al-Awsaṭ*, 1/445 on the authority of Sahl Ibn Aslam.

بِرَأْسَيْنِ لَيْسَ مَعَهُمَا ثَالِثٌ، فَأَتَاهُ أَبُو الهَيْثَمِ، فَقَالَ النَّبِيُّ ﷺ: «اخْتَرْ مِنْهُمَا»، فَقَالَ: يَا رَسُولَ اللهِ! اخْتَرْ لِي، فَقَالَ النَّبِيُّ ﷺ: «إِنَّ المُسْتَشَارَ مُؤْتَمَنٌ، خُذْ هَذَا فَإِنِّي رَأَيْتُهُ يُصَلِّي، وَاسْتَوْصِ بِهِ مَعْرُوفًا»، فَانْطَلَقَ أَبُو الهَيْثَمِ إِلَى امْرَأَتِهِ، فَأَخْبَرَهَا بِقَوْلِ رَسُولِ اللهِ ﷺ، فَقَالَتِ امْرَأَتُهُ: مَا أَنْتَ بِبَالِغٍ حَقَّ مَا قَالَ فِيهِ النَّبِيُّ ﷺ إِلَّا بِأَنْ تَعْتِقَهُ، قَالَ: فَهُوَ عَتِيقٌ، فَقَالَ ﷺ: «إِنَّ اللهَ لَمْ يَبْعَثْ نَبِيًّا وَلَا خَلِيفَةً إِلَّا وَلَهُ بِطَانَتَانِ: بِطَانَةٌ تَأْمُرُهُ بِالمَعْرُوفِ وَتَنْهَاهُ عَنِ المُنْكَرِ، وَبِطَانَةٌ لَا تَأْلُوهُ خَبَالًا، وَمَنْ يُوقَ بِطَانَةَ السُّوءِ فَقَدْ وُقِيَ».

372. Muḥammad Ibn Ismā'īl narrated to us; Adam Ibn Abī Iyās narrated to us; Shaybān narrated to us; 'Abdu'l-Mālik Ibn 'Umayr narrated to us; from Abū Salamah Ibn 'Abdu'l-Raḥmān that Abū Hurayrah (*raḍiyAllāhu 'anhu*) said:

> 'The Messenger of Allāh (ﷺ) went out during an hour in which he did not usually go out and in which no one used to meet him, but Abū Bakr came to him, so he said: "What brings you here, O Abū Bakr?" He replied: 'I came out to meet the Messenger of Allāh (ﷺ) and gaze upon his face and greet him with salutation of peace.'It was not long before 'Umar turned up. He said: "What brings you here, O 'Umar?" He replied: 'Hunger, O Messenger of Allāh!' He said: "I have also experienced some of that."
>
> Then they went to the home of Abū'l-Haytham al-Tayyihan Al-Ansari He was a man with many datepalms and sheep, but he had no servants so they did not find him there. They said to his wife: "Where is your companion?"She said: 'He has gone to fetch us some fresh water.' It was not long before Abū'l-Haytham came along hauling a large water-skin which he put down. Then he came and embraced the Prophet (ﷺ) and exclaiming that his father and mother be ransomed for him. Then he took them to his [date palm]

garden, and spread a carpet for them. Then they went to a grove of his and he spread out a mat for them. Then he went to a date-palm and returned with a cluster of dates and set it down. The Prophet (ﷺ) said: "Why not selct for us from its ripe dates?" He replied: 'O Messenger of Allāh! I wanted you to select from both its ripe dates and the unripened dates.' So they ate and they drank from that water. The Messenger of Allāh (ﷺ) said: "By the One in Whose Hand is my soul! This is among the favours which you shall be asked about on the Day of Resurrection: cool shade, wholesome ripe dates, and cold water!"

Abū'l-Haytham left to prepare some food for them. The Prophet said: "Do not slaughter for us a milch goat." So he slaughtered a young she-goat or a young male goat, and brought it to them so they could eat it. The Prophet (ﷺ) said: "Do you have a servant?" He said: 'No' so he then said: "If we get some captives we shall bring them for you." Then he (ﷺ) was brought two captives, without a third. Abū'l-Haytham then came to him, and the Prophet (ﷺ) said: "Chose from the pair of them." So he said: 'O Messenger of Allāh, chose for me!'

The Prophet (ﷺ) said: "Indeed the one consulted is entrusted. Take this one for I have seen him pray, and treat him well." So Abū'l-Haytham went to his wife and informed her of what the Messenger of Allāh (ﷺ) said. So his wife said: 'You will not be able to fulfil the right stated by the Prophet (ﷺ) about him unless you free.' So he said: 'He is free, then!' So the Prophet (ﷺ) said: "Indeed Allāh has not sent any Prophet, nor a Caliph, without his having two consultees (*biṭānatān*): one who commands him to do what is right and fair, and forbids him to do what is wrong and unfair, and one who will spare no effort to corrupt him. Whoever is guarded against an evil companion is truly guarded."[371]

٣٧٣- حَدَّثَنَا عُمَرُ بْنُ إِسْمَاعِيلَ بْنِ مُجَالِدِ بْنِ سَعِيدٍ، قَالَ: حَدَّثَنِي أَبِي، عَنْ بَيَانِ بْنِ بِشْرٍ، عَنْ قَيْسِ بْنِ أَبِي حَازِمٍ، قَالَ: سَمِعْتُ سَعْدَ بْنَ أَبِي وَقَّاصٍ، يَقُولُ: إِنِّي لَأَوَّلُ رَجُلٍ أَهْرَاقَ دَمًا فِي سَبِيلِ اللهِ ﷻ، وَإِنِّي لَأَوَّلُ رَجُلٍ رَمَى بِسَهْمٍ فِي سَبِيلِ اللهِ، لَقَدْ رَأَيْتُنِي أَغْزُو فِي العِصَابَةِ مِنْ أَصْحَابِ مُحَمَّدٍ - عَلَيْهِ الصَّلَاةُ وَالسَّلَامُ - مَا نَأْكُلُ إِلَّا وَرَقَ الشَّجَرِ وَالْحُبْلَةِ حَتَّى تَقَرَّحَتْ أَشْدَاقُنَا، وَإِنَّ أَحَدَنَا لَيَضَعُ كَمَا تَضَعُ الشَّاةُ وَالبَعِيرُ، وَأَصْبَحَتْ بَنُو أَسَدٍ يُعَزِّرُونِي فِي الدِّينِ، لَقَدْ خِبْتُ وَخَسِرْتُ إِذًا وَضَلَّ عَمَلِي .

373. 'Umar Ibn Ismā'īl Ibn Mujālid Ibn Sa'īd narrated to us; my father narrated to me; from Bayān Ibn Bashīr that Qays Ibn Abī Hāzim said:

> 'I am the first man who shed blood in the cause of Allāh, and I am the first man who shot an arrow in the cause of Allāh. I found myself in a military expedition among the Companion of Muḥammad (ﷺ). We ate nothing but the leaves of trees and pods of the acacia tortilis fruit (*ḥublah*), until the insides of our mouths were covered with ulcers and blisters. One of us would excrete as do sheep and camel. Yet, Banū Asad began to censure me about the religion. I would have been deprived of any good and ruined in that case, and my deeds would have been wasted.'[372]

[371] Tirmidhī, #2369, Abū Dāwūd, #5128 and Ibn Mājah, #2745.
[372] Bukhārī, #3728, Muslim, #2966, and Tirmidhī, #2365.

٣٧٤ـ حَدَّثَنَا مُحَمَّدُ بْنُ بَشَّارٍ، قَالَ: حَدَّثَنَا صَفْوَانُ بْنُ عِيسَى، قَالَ: حَدَّثَنَا عَمْرُو ابْنُ عِيسَى أَبُو نَعَامَةَ العَدَوِيُّ، قَالَ: سَمِعْتُ خَالِدَ بْنَ عُمَيْرٍ، وَشُوَيْسًا أَبَا الرُّقَادِ، قَالَا: بَعَثَ عُمَرُ بْنُ الخَطَّابِ عُتْبَةَ بْنَ غَزْوَانَ، وَقَالَ: انطَلِقْ أَنْتَ وَمَنْ مَعَكَ، حَتَّى إِذَا كُنْتُمْ فِي أَقْصَى بِلَادِ العَرَبِ وَأَدْنَى بِلَادِ العَجَمِ، فَأَقْبَلُوا حَتَّى إِذَا كَانُوا بِالمِرْبَدِ وَجَدُوا هَذَا الكَذَّانَ، فَقَالُوا: مَا هَذِهِ؟ قَالُوا: هَذِهِ البَصْرَةُ فَسَارُوا حَتَّى إِذَا بَلَغُوا حِيَالَ الجِسْرِ الصَّغِيرِ، فَقَالُوا: هَهُنَا أُمِرْتُمْ، فَنَزَلُوا ـ فَذَكَرُوا الحَدِيثَ بِطُولِهِ ـ.

قَالَ: فَقَالَ عُتْبَةُ بْنُ غَزْوَانَ: لَقَدْ رَأَيْتُنِي وَإِنِّي لَسَابِعُ سَبْعَةٍ مَعَ رَسُولِ اللهِ ﷺ مَا لَنَا طَعَامٌ إِلَّا وَرَقُ الشَّجَرِ، حَتَّى تَقَرَّحَتْ أَشْدَاقُنَا، فَالتَقَطْتُ بُرْدَةً قَسَمْتُهَا بَيْنِي وَبَيْنَ سَعْدٍ، فَمَا مِنَّا مِنْ أُولَئِكَ السَّبْعَةِ أَحَدٌ إِلَّا وَهُوَ أَمِيرُ مِصْرٍ مِنَ الأَمْصَارِ وَسَتُجَرِّبُونَ الأُمَرَاءَ بَعْدَنَا».

374. Muḥammad Ibn Bashshār narrated to us; Sufyān Ibn 'Isā narrated to us; 'Amr Ibn 'Isā Abū Nu'āmah al-'Adawī said:

> 'I heard Khālid Ibn 'Umayr and Shuwaysa Abū'l-Ruqād say: 'Umar Ibn al-Khaṭṭāb (*raḍiyAllāhu 'anhu*) dispatched 'Utbah Ibn Ghazwān, and he said: 'Go, you and whoever is with you, until you are in the furthest Arab land and the nearest non-Arab land.' So they proceeded, until when they reached the Mirbad, they found these soft white stones, so they said [to one another]: 'What is this?' They were told: 'It is Basrah.' They continued the journey until, when they reached the vicinity of the small bridge. They said: 'Here is our appointed destination,' so they alighted and then mentioned the entire tradition.
>
> 'Utbah Ibn Ghazwān said: 'I found myself the seventh of seven with the Messenger of Allāh (ﷺ). We ate nothing but

> tree leaves until the corners of our mouths were covered with ulcers and blisters. I happened to find a mantle which I divided between me and Sa'd, for there is not a single one of us seven except he is a governor of a city, and you will put the governors to the test after us."[373]

٣٧٥ـ حَدَّثَنَا عَبْدُ اللهِ بْنُ عَبْدِ الرَّحْمَنِ، قَالَ: حَدَّثَنَا رَوْحُ بْنُ أَسْلَمَ أَبُو حَاتِمٍ البَصْرِيُّ، قَالَ: حَدَّثَنَا حَمَّادُ بْنُ سَلَمَةَ، قَالَ: حَدَّثَنَا ثَابِتٌ، عَنْ أَنَسٍ، قَالَ: قَالَ رَسُولُ اللهِ ﷺ: «لَقَدْ أُخِفْتُ فِي اللهِ وَمَا يُخَافُ أَحَدٌ، وَلَقَدْ أُوذِيتُ فِي اللهِ وَمَا يُؤْذَى أَحَدٌ، وَلَقَدْ أَتَتْ عَلَيَّ ثَلَاثُونَ مِنْ بَيْنِ لَيْلَةٍ وَيَوْمٍ وَمَا لِي وَلِبِلَالٍ طَعَامٌ يَأْكُلُهُ ذُو كَبِدٍ إِلَّا شَيْءٌ يُوَارِيهِ إِبْطُ بِلَالٍ».

375. 'Abdullāh Ibn 'Abdu'l-Raḥmān narrated to us; Rūḥ Ibn Aslam Abū Hātim al-Baṣrī narrated to us; Ḥammād Ibn Salamah narrated to us; Thābit narrated to us that Anas (*raḍiyAllāhu 'anhu*) said:

> 'The Messenger of Allāh (ﷺ) said: "I have been frightened [through threats] for Allāh's sake, while no one else was frightened, and I have been hurt for Allāh's sake, while no one else was hurt. Thirty days and nights passed by me and Bilāl without any food fit for a human or an animal to eat except something [so meagre] tucked under Bilāl's armpit."'[374]

٣٧٦ـ حَدَّثَنَا عَبْدُ اللهِ بْنُ عَبْدِ الرَّحْمَنِ، قَالَ: حَدَّثَنَا عَفَّانُ بْنُ مُسْلِمٍ، قَالَ:

---

[373] Muslim, #2967, Ibn Mājah, #4156 and Ṭabarānī in his *al-Awsaṭ*, 4/243.
[374] Tirmidhī, #2372, Ibn Mājah, #151, the chain is weak but supported by a narration in *Musnad* of Aḥmad, 14/055.

حَدَّثَنَا أَبَانُ بْنُ يَزِيدَ الْعَطَّارُ، قَالَ: حَدَّثَنَا قَتَادَةُ، عَنْ أَنَسِ بْنِ مَالِكٍ: أَنَّ النَّبِيَّ ﷺ لَمْ يَجْتَمِعْ عِنْدَهُ غَدَاءٌ وَلَا عَشَاءٌ مِنْ خُبْزٍ وَلَحْمٍ إِلَّا عَلَى ضَفَفٍ.

قَالَ عَبْدُ اللهِ: قَالَ بَعْضُهُمْ: هُوَ كَثْرَةُ الْأَيْدِي.

376. ʿAbdullāh Ibn ʿAbdu'l-Raḥmān narrated to us; ʿAffān Ibn Muslim narrated to us; Abān Ibn Yazīd al-ʿAṭṭār narrated to us; Qatādah narrated to us that Anas Ibn Mālik (*raḍiyAllāhu ʿanhu*) said:

> 'Neither a morning nor evening meal of bread and meat was assembled in the presence of the Prophet (ﷺ) [in one day], except if he was invited as a guest.'[375]

٣٧٧ـ حَدَّثَنَا عَبْدُ بْنُ حُمَيْدٍ، قَالَ: حَدَّثَنَا مُحَمَّدُ بْنُ إِسْمَاعِيلَ بْنِ أَبِي فُدَيْكٍ، قَالَ: حَدَّثَنَا ابْنُ أَبِي ذِئْبٍ، عَنْ مُسْلِمِ بْنِ جُنْدُبٍ، عَنْ نَوْفَلِ بْنِ إِيَاسٍ الْهُذَلِيِّ، قَالَ: كَانَ عَبْدُ الرَّحْمَنِ بْنُ عَوْفٍ لَنَا جَلِيسًا، وَكَانَ نِعْمَ الْجَلِيسُ، وَإِنَّهُ انْقَلَبَ بِنَا ذَاتَ يَوْمٍ حَتَّى إِذَا دَخَلْنَا بَيْتَهُ دَخَلَ فَاغْتَسَلَ، ثُمَّ خَرَجَ وَأُتِينَا بِصَحْفَةٍ فِيهَا خُبْزٌ وَلَحْمٌ، فَلَمَّا وُضِعَتْ بَكَى عَبْدُ الرَّحْمَنِ فَقُلْتُ: يَا أَبَا مُحَمَّدٍ! مَا يُبْكِيكَ؟ فَقَالَ: هَلَكَ رَسُولُ اللهِ ﷺ وَلَمْ يَشْبَعْ هُوَ وَأَهْلُ بَيْتِهِ مِنْ خُبْزِ الشَّعِيرِ، فَلَا أُرَانَا أُخِّرْنَا لِمَا هُوَ خَيْرٌ لَنَا».

377. ʿAbd Ibn Ḥumayd narrated to us; Muḥammad Ibn Ismāʿīl Ibn Abī Fudayk narrated to us; Ibn Abī Dhi'b narrated to us; from Muslim Ibn Jundub that Nawfal Ibn Iyās al-Hudhalī said:

> ʿAbdu'l-Raḥmān Ibn ʿAwf (*raḍiyAllāhu ʿanhu*) would host gatherings for us, and an excellent host was he! After he had returned from a journey with us one day, we entered his house. When we entered his house, he entered and

[375] Aḥmad, 13/859.

had a bath. He then came out and brought us a platter of bread and meat, and when it was served, 'Abdu'l-Raḥmān wept, so I said: 'O Abū Muḥammad, what makes you weep?' He replied: 'The Messenger of Allāh (ﷺ) passed away while neither he nor his family ever had their fill of barley bread. But I do not think our circumstances are any better for us.'"[376]

[376] *Musnad 'Abd Ibn Ḥāmid*, #161, this tradition is weak however; there is a supporting narration in Bukhārī, #1274.

CHAPTER FIFTY-THREE

بَابُ مَا جَاءَ فِي سِنِّ رَسُولِ اللهِ ﷺ

What has been narrated concerning the Age (*sinn*) of the Messenger of Allāh (ﷺ)

٣٧٨ـ حَدَّثَنَا أَحْمَدُ بْنُ مَنِيعٍ، قَالَ: حَدَّثَنَا رَوْحُ بْنُ عُبَادَةَ، قَالَ: حَدَّثَنَا زَكَرِيَّا ابْنُ إِسْحَاقَ، قَالَ: حَدَّثَنَا عَمْرُو بْنُ دِينَارٍ، عَنِ ابْنِ عَبَّاسٍ قَالَ: «مَكَثَ النَّبِيُّ ﷺ بِمَكَّةَ ثَلَاثَ عَشْرَةَ سَنَةً يُوحَى إِلَيْهِ، وَبِالْمَدِينَةِ عَشْرًا، وَتُوُفِّيَ وَهُوَ ابْنُ ثَلَاثٍ وَسِتِّينَ».

378. Aḥmad Ibn Manīʿ narrated to us; Rūḥ Ibn ʿUbādah narrated to us; Zakariyāh Ibn Isḥāq narrated to us; ʿAmr Ibn Dinār narrated to us that Ibn ʿAbbās (*raḍiyAllāhu ʿanhumā*) said:

> 'The Prophet (ﷺ) stayed in Makkah for thirteen years, in which he received revelation, and in Medīnah for ten years, and passed away when he was sixty-three years of age.'[377]

[377] Bukhārī, #3903, Muslim, #2351, and Tirmidhī, #3652.

٣٧٩ـ حَدَّثَنَا مُحَمَّدُ بْنُ بَشَّارٍ، قَالَ: حَدَّثَنَا مُحَمَّدُ بْنُ جَعْفَرٍ، عَنْ شُعْبَةَ، عَنْ أَبِي إِسْحَاقَ، عَنْ عَامِرِ بْنِ سَعْدٍ، عَنْ جَرِيرٍ، عَنْ مُعَاوِيَةَ، أَنَّهُ سَمِعَهُ يَخْطُبُ، قَالَ: «مَاتَ رَسُولُ اللهِ ﷺ وَهُوَ ابْنُ ثَلَاثٍ وَسِتِّينَ وَأَبُو بَكْرٍ وَعُمَرُ، وَأَنَا ابْنُ ثَلَاثٍ وَسِتِّينَ».

379. Muḥammad Ibn Bashshār narrated to us; Muḥammad Ibn Jāʿfar narrated to us; Shuʿbah narrated to us; from Abū Isḥāq; from ʿĀmir Ibn Saʿd; from Jarīr that Muʿāwiyah (*raḍiyAllāhu ʿanhu*) said in a sermon:

> 'The Prophet (ﷺ) passed away when he was sixty-three years of age, as did Abū Bakr and ʿUmar, and I am now sixty-three years of age. [378]

٣٨٠ـ حَدَّثَنَا حُسَيْنُ بْنُ مَهْدِيٍّ الْبَصْرِيُّ، قَالَ: حَدَّثَنَا عَبْدُ الرَّزَّاقِ، عَنِ ابْنِ جُرَيْجٍ، عَنِ الزُّهْرِيِّ، عَنْ عُرْوَةَ، عَنْ عَائِشَةَ: «أَنَّ النَّبِيَّ ﷺ مَاتَ وَهُوَ ابْنُ ثَلَاثٍ وَسِتِّينَ سَنَةً».

380. Ḥusayn Ibn Mahdī al-Baṣrī narrated to us; ʿAbdu'l-Razzāq narrated to us; from Ibn Jurayj; from al-Zuhrī; from ʿUrwah that ʿĀ'ishah (*raḍiyAllāhu ʿanhā*) said:

> 'The Prophet (ﷺ) passed away when he was sixty-three years of age.'[379]

٣٨١ـ حَدَّثَنَا أَحْمَدُ بْنُ مَنِيعٍ، وَيَعْقُوبُ بْنُ إِبْرَاهِيمَ الدَّوْرَقِيُّ، قَالَا: حَدَّثَنَا إِسْمَاعِيلُ بْنُ عُلَيَّةَ، عَنْ خَالِدٍ الْحَذَّاءِ، قَالَ: أَنْبَأَنَا عَمَّارٌ مَوْلَى بَنِي هَاشِمٍ قَالَ: سَمِعْتُ

[378] Muslim, #2352, and Tirmidhī, #3653.
[379] Bukhārī, #3536, Muslim, #2349, and Tirmidhī, #3654.

ابْنَ عَبَّاسٍ يَقُولُ: تُوُفِّيَ رَسُولُ اللهِ ﷺ وَهُوَ ابْنُ خَمْسٍ وَسِتِّينَ.

381. Aḥmad Ibn Manīʿ and Yaʿqūb Ibn Ibrāhīm al-Dawaqrī narrated to us; Ismāʿīl Ibn ʿUlayyah narrated to us; from Khālid al-Ḥadhdhā'; ʿAmmār, the Mawla of Banu Hāshim informed us:

> 'I heard Ibn ʿAbbas (*raḍiyAllāhu ʿanhumā*) say: 'The Messenger of Allāh (ﷺ) passed away when he was sixty-five years of age.''[380]

٣٨٢ـ حَدَّثَنَا مُحَمَّدُ بْنُ بَشَّارٍ، وَمُحَمَّدُ بْنُ أَبَانَ، قَالَا: حَدَّثَنَا مُعَاذُ بْنُ هِشَامٍ، قَالَ: حَدَّثَنِي أَبِي، عَنْ قَتَادَةَ، عَنِ الْحَسَنِ، عَنْ دَغْفَلِ بْنِ حَنْظَلَةَ: «أَنَّ النَّبِيَّ ﷺ قُبِضَ وَهُوَ ابْنُ خَمْسٍ وَسِتِّينَ».

قَالَ أَبُو عِيسَى: «وَدَغْفَلُ لَا نَعْرِفُ لَهُ سَمَاعًا مِنَ النَّبِيِّ ﷺ، وَكَانَ فِي زَمَنِ النَّبِيِّ ﷺ رَجُلًا».

382. Muḥammad Ibn Bashshār and Muḥammad Ibn Abān narrated to us; Muʿādh Ibn Hishām narrated to us; my father narrated to me; from Qatādah; from Ḥasan that Daghfal Ibn Ḥanzalah (*raḍiyAllāhu ʿanhu*) said:

> 'The Prophet (ﷺ) passed away when he was sixty-three years of age.'[381]

Abū ʿIsā said: 'As for Daghfal, we do not know of him having heard anything from the Prophet (ﷺ), though he was in the time of the Prophet (ﷺ).

[380] Muslim, #2353, and Tirmidhī, #3650.
[381] See hadīth 380 p.300

٣٨٣ـ حَدَّثَنَا إِسْحَاقُ بْنُ مُوسَى الأَنْصَارِيُّ، قَالَ: حَدَّثَنَا مَعْنٌ، حَدَّثَنَا مَالِكُ ابْنُ أَنَسٍ، عَنْ رَبِيعَةَ بْنِ أَبِي عَبْدِ الرَّحْمَنِ، عَنْ أَنَسِ بْنِ مَالِكٍ، أَنَّهُ سَمِعَهُ يَقُولُ: «كَانَ رَسُولُ اللهِ ﷺ لَيْسَ بِالطَّوِيلِ البَائِنِ، وَلَا بِالقَصِيرِ، وَلَا بِالأَبْيَضِ الأَمْهَقِ، وَلَا بِالآدَمِ، وَلَا بِالجَعْدِ القَطَطِ، وَلَا بِالسَّبِطِ، بَعَثَهُ اللهُ تَعَالَى عَلَى رَأْسِ أَرْبَعِينَ سَنَةً، فَأَقَامَ بِمَكَّةَ عَشْرَ سِنِينَ، وَبِالمَدِينَةِ عَشْرَ سِنِينَ، وَتَوَفَّاهُ اللهُ عَلَى رَأْسِ سِتِّينَ سَنَةً وَلَيْسَ فِي رَأْسِهِ وَلِحْيَتِهِ عِشْرُونَ شَعْرَةً بَيْضَاءَ».

383. Abū Rajā', Qutaybah Ibn Sa'īd informed us; from Mālik Ibn Anas; from Rabī'ah Ibn Abū 'Abdu'l-Raḥmān; that he heard Anas Ibn Mālik (*raḍiyAllāhu 'anhu*) saying:

> 'The Messenger of Allāh (ﷺ) was neither [excessively] tall, nor short. In complexion, he was neither pale white, nor very dark; neither was his hair tightly curled nor completely straight [but slightly wavy]. When he reached the age of forty, Allāh the Exalted granted him Prophethood. He stayed for ten years in Makkah and in Madīnah for ten years. Allāh took his soul upon the completion of sixty years, at that time there were no more than twenty white hairs on his head and beard."[382]

٣٨٤ـ حَدَّثَنَا قُتَيْبَةُ بْنُ سَعِيدٍ، عَنْ مَالِكِ بْنِ أَنَسٍ، عَنْ رَبِيعَةَ بْنِ أَبِي عَبْدِ الرَّحْمَنِ، عَنْ أَنَسِ بْنِ مَالِكٍ، نَحْوَهُ.

384. Qutaybah Ibn Sa'īd informed us; from Mālik Ibn Anas; from Rabī'ah Ibn Abū 'Abdu'l-Raḥmān; that he heard Anas Ibn Mālik (*raḍiyAllāhu 'anhu*) said likewise.

[382] Bukhārī, #5899, Muslim, #2347 and Tirmidhī, #362.

CHAPTER FIFTY-FOUR

بَابُ مَا جَاءَ فِي وَفَاةِ رَسُولِ اللهِ ﷺ

What has been narrated concerning the Demise (*wafāt*) of the Messenger of Allāh (ﷺ)

٣٨٥ـ حَدَّثَنَا أَبُو عَمَّارٍ الْحُسَيْنُ بْنُ حُرَيْثٍ، وَقُتَيْبَةُ بْنُ سَعِيدٍ، وَغَيْرُ وَاحِدٍ، قَالُوا: حَدَّثَنَا سُفْيَانُ بْنُ عُيَيْنَةَ، عَنِ الزُّهْرِيِّ، عَنْ أَنَسِ بْنِ مَالِكٍ قَالَ: «آخِرُ نَظْرَةٍ نَظَرْتُهَا إِلَى رَسُولِ اللهِ ﷺ كَشْفُ السِّتَارَةِ يَوْمَ الاِثْنَيْنِ، فَنَظَرْتُ إِلَى وَجْهِهِ كَأَنَّهُ وَرَقَةُ مُصْحَفٍ وَالنَّاسُ خَلْفَ أَبِي بَكْرٍ، فَأَشَارَ إِلَى النَّاسِ أَنِ اثْبُتُوا، وَأَبُو بَكْرٍ يَؤُمُّهُمْ وَأَلْقَى السِّجْفَ، وَتُوُفِّيَ رَسُولُ اللهِ ﷺ مِنْ آخِرِ ذَلِكَ الْيَوْمِ».

385. Abū ʿAmmār al-Ḥusayn Ibn Ḥurayth and Qutaybah Ibn Saʿīd, and others narrated to us; Sufyān Ibn ʿUyaynah narrated to us; from al-Zuhrī that Anas Ibn Mālik (*raḍiyAllāhu ʿanhu*) said

> 'The very last time I gazed at the Messenger of Allāh (ﷺ) was when he drew back the curtain on Monday as people stood behind Abū Bakr. I looked at his face as if it were a page of the Qur'ān (*muṣḥaf*) [in beauty and radiance], as the people were performing the prayer behind Abū Bakr.

> So when the people were getting restless, he signalled to them to stay in their places, as Abū Bakr led them in prayer, and he drew the curtain. The Messenger of Allāh (ﷺ) passed away at the end of that day.'[383]

٣٨٦- حَدَّثَنَا حُمَيْدُ بْنُ مَسْعَدَةَ الْبَصْرِيُّ، قَالَ: حَدَّثَنَا سُلَيْمُ بْنُ أَخْضَرَ، عَنِ ابْنِ عَوْنٍ، عَنْ إِبْرَاهِيمَ، عَنِ الأَسْوَدِ، عَنْ عَائِشَةَ، قَالَتْ: «كُنْتُ مُسْنِدَةَ النَّبِيِّ ﷺ إِلَى صَدْرِي - أَوْ قَالَتْ: إِلَى حِجْرِي - فَدَعَا بِطَسْتٍ لِيَبُولَ فِيهِ، ثُمَّ بَالَ، فَمَاتَ».

386. Ḥumayd Ibn Mas'adah al-Baṣrī narrated to us; Sulaym Ibn Akhḍar narrated to us; from Ibn 'Awn; from Ibrāhīm; from al-Aswad that 'Ā'ishah (*raḍiyAllāhu 'anhā*) said:

> 'I had the Prophet (ﷺ) resting against my chest—or she said: 'my lap'—when he asked for a vessel to urinate in. Then he urinated and passed away soon after.'[384]

٣٨٧- حَدَّثَنَا قُتَيْبَةُ، قَالَ: حَدَّثَنَا اللَّيْثُ، عَنِ ابْنِ الْهَادِ، عَنْ مُوسَى ابْنِ سَرْجِسَ، عَنِ الْقَاسِمِ بْنِ مُحَمَّدٍ، عَنْ عَائِشَةَ، أَنَّهَا قَالَتْ: رَأَيْتُ رَسُولَ اللهِ ﷺ وَهُوَ بِالْمَوْتِ وَعِنْدَهُ قَدَحٌ فِيهِ مَاءٌ، وَهُوَ يُدْخِلُ يَدَهُ فِي الْقَدَحِ ثُمَّ يَمْسَحُ وَجْهَهُ بِالْمَاءِ، ثُمَّ يَقُولُ: «اللَّهُمَّ أَعِنِّي عَلَى مُنْكَرَاتِ - أَوْ قَالَ: عَلَى سَكَرَاتِ - الْمَوْتِ».

387. Qutaybah narrated to us; al-Layth narrated to us; from Ibn al-Hād; from Mūsā Ibn Sarjis; from al-Qāsim Ibn Muḥammad that 'Ā'ishah (*raḍiyAllāhu 'anhā*) said:

> 'I saw the Messenger of Allāh (ﷺ) as he was on the verge

[383] Bukhārī, #680, and Muslim, #419.

[384] Bukhārī, #741, and Muslim, #1636.

of dying, and besides him there was vessel containing water. He inserted his hand into the vessel, then wiped his face with the water, saying: *"Allāhumma a'ini 'alā munkarāt..."*—"O Allāh, help me against the atrocities..." Or he (ﷺ) said: *"...sakarāt al-mawt"* —"...the agonies of death."[385]

٣٨٨ـ حَدَّثَنَا الحَسَنُ بْنُ الصَّبَّاحِ البَزَّارُ، قَالَ: حَدَّثَنَا مُبَشِّرُ بْنُ إِسْمَاعِيلَ، عَنْ عَبْدِ الرَّحْمَنِ بْنِ العَلَاءِ، عَنْ أَبِيهِ، عَنِ ابْنِ عُمَرَ، عَنْ عَائِشَةَ، قَالَتْ: «لَا أَغْبِطُ أَحَدًا بِهَوْنِ مَوْتٍ بَعْدَ الَّذِي رَأَيْتُ مِنْ شِدَّةِ مَوْتِ رَسُولِ اللهِ ﷺ».

388. al-Ḥasan Ibn al-Ṣabbāḥ al-Bazzāz narrated to us; al-Mubashshir Ibn Ismā'īl narrated to us; from 'Abdu'l-Raḥmān Ibn al-'Alā'; from his father; from Ibn 'Umar (*raḍiyAllāhu 'anhumā*) that 'Ā'ishah (*raḍiyAllāhu 'anhā*) said:

> 'I will never envy anyone for an easy death now that I have witnessed the difficulty (*shidda*) in the Messenger of Allāh (ﷺ) in his passing.'[386]

٣٨٩ـ حَدَّثَنَا أَبُو كُرَيْبٍ مُحَمَّدُ بْنُ العَلَاءِ، قَالَ: حَدَّثَنَا أَبُو مُعَاوِيَةَ، عَنْ عَبْدِ الرَّحْمَنِ ابْنِ أَبِي بَكْرٍ وَهُوَ ابْنُ الْمُلَيْكِيِّ، عَنِ ابْنِ أَبِي مُلَيْكَةَ، عَنْ عَائِشَةَ، قَالَتْ: «لَـمَّا قُبِضَ رَسُولُ اللهِ ﷺ اخْتَلَفُوا فِي دَفْنِهِ، فَقَالَ أَبُو بَكْرٍ: سَمِعْتُ مِنْ رَسُولِ اللهِ ﷺ شَيْئًا مَا نَسِيتُهُ قَالَ: «مَا قَبَضَ اللهُ نَبِيًّا إِلَّا فِي الْمَوْضِعِ الَّذِي يُحِبُّ أَنْ يُدْفَنَ فِيهِ»، ادْفِنُوهُ فِي مَوْضِعِ فِرَاشِهِ».

389. Abū Kurayb Muḥammad Ibn al-'Alā' narrated to us; Abū Mu'āwiyah narrated to us; from 'Abdu'l-Raḥmān Ibn Abī Bakr—Ibn

[385] Tirmidhī, #978, this is a weak hadīth but supported by a narration in Bukhārī, #6510.
[386] Tirmidhī, #979, this is a weak hadīth but supported by a narration in Bukhārī, #4446.

al-Mālikī; from Ibn Abī Mulaykah that ʿĀ'ishah (*raḍiyAllāhu ʿanhā*) said:

> 'When the Messenger of Allāh (ﷺ) passed away, they [the Companions] disagreed over where to bury him. Abū Bakr (*raḍiyAllāhu ʿanhu*) said: 'I heard the Messenger of Allāh (ﷺ) say something which I did not forget. He said: "Allāh will never take a Prophet except in the place in which he loved to be buried." So bury him in the spot where his bed is!"[387]

٣٩٠ـ حَدَّثَنَا مُحَمَّدُ بْنُ بَشَّارٍ، وَعَبَّاسٌ العَنْبَرِيُّ، وَسَوَّارُ بْنُ عَبْدِ الله، وَغَيْرُ وَاحِدٍ قَالُوا: حَدَّثَنَا يَحْيَى بْنُ سَعِيدٍ، عَنْ سُفْيَانَ الثَّوْرِيِّ، عَنْ مُوسَى بْنِ أَبِي عَائِشَةَ، عَنْ عُبَيْدِ الله ابْنِ عَبْدِ الله، عَنِ ابْنِ عَبَّاسٍ، وَعَائِشَةَ، أَنَّ أَبَا بَكْرٍ قَبَّلَ النَّبِيَّ ﷺ بَعْدَ مَا مَاتَ .

390. Muḥammad Ibn Bashshār narrated to us; by ʿIyāsh Ibn al-ʿAnbarī and Siwār Ibn ʿAbdullāh and others; Yaḥyā Ibn Saʿīd informed us; from Sufyān al-Thawrī; from Mūsā Ibn Abī ʿĀ'ishah; from ʿUbaydullāh Ibn ʿAbdullāh that Ibn ʿAbbās (*raḍiyAllāhu ʿanhumā*) and ʿĀ'ishah (*raḍiyAllāhu ʿanhā*) said:

> 'Abū Bakr kissed [the forehead of] the Prophet (ﷺ) after he passed away.'[388]

٣٩١ـ حَدَّثَنَا نَصْرُ بْنُ عَلِيٍّ الجَهْضَمِيُّ، قَالَ: حَدَّثَنَا مَرْحُومُ بْنُ عَبْدِ العَزِيزِ العَطَّارُ، عَنِ أَبِي عِمْرَانَ الجَوْنِيِّ، عَنْ يَزِيدَ بْنِ بَابَنُوسَ، عَنْ عَائِشَةَ، أَنَّ أَبَا بَكْرٍ، دَخَلَ

[387] Tirmidhī, #1018, this hadīth is weak but the meaning is correct due to other supporting narrations.

[388] Bukhārī, #4451.

عَلَى النَّبِيِّ ﷺ بَعْدَ وَفَاتِهِ فَوَضَعَ فَمَهُ بَيْنَ عَيْنَيْهِ، وَوَضَعَ يَدَيْهِ عَلَى سَاعِدَيْهِ، وَقَالَ: وَانَبِيَّاهُ! وَاصَفِيَّاهُ! وَاخَلِيلَاهُ!».

391. Naṣr Ibn ʿAlī al-Jahdamī narrated to us; Marhūm Ibn ʿAbdu'l-ʿAzīz al-ʿAṭṭār narrated to us; from ʿImrān al-Jawzī; from Yazīd Ibn Bābanūs that ʿĀ'ishah (*raḍiyAllāhu ʿanhā*) said:

> 'Abū Bakr entered to see the Prophet (ﷺ) after his demise, and he placed his mouth between his eyes [and kissed him], and his forearms and said: 'O Prophet! O true friend! O intimate friend!''[389]

٣٩٢- حَدَّثَنَا بِشْرُ بْنُ هِلَالٍ الصَّوَّافُ الْبَصْرِيُّ، قَالَ: حَدَّثَنَا جَعْفَرُ بْنُ سُلَيْمَانَ، عَنْ ثَابِتٍ، عَنْ أَنَسٍ قَالَ: «لَمَّا كَانَ الْيَوْمُ الَّذِي دَخَلَ فِيهِ رَسُولُ اللهِ ﷺ الْمَدِينَةَ أَضَاءَ مِنْهَا كُلُّ شَيْءٍ، فَلَمَّا كَانَ الْيَوْمُ الَّذِي مَاتَ فِيهِ أَظْلَمَ مِنْهَا كُلُّ شَيْءٍ، وَمَا نَفَضْنَا أَيْدِينَا مِنَ التُّرَابِ، وَإِنَّا لَفِي دَفْنِهِ ﷺ حَتَّى أَنْكَرْنَا قُلُوبَنَا».

392. Bishr Ibn Hilāl al-Ṣawwāf al-Baṣrī narrated to us; Jāʿfar Ibn Sulaymān narrated to us; from Thābit that Anas (*raḍiyAllāhu ʿanhu*) said:

> 'On the day when the Messenger of Allāh (ﷺ) entered Medīnah, everything was illuminated and bright, and on the day when he died, everything turned dark and gloomy. We had barely cleared the dust off our hands [after his burial] until we no longer recognised our own hearts [due to his loss].'[390]

[389] Abū Dāwūd, #2137.
[390] Tirmidhī, #3618, and Ibn Mājah, #1631.

٣٩٣- حَدَّثَنَا مُحَمَّدُ بْنُ حَاتِمٍ، قَالَ: حَدَّثَنَا عَامِرُ بْنُ صَالِحٍ، عَنْ هِشَامِ بْنِ عُرْوَةَ، عَنْ أَبِيهِ، عَنْ عَائِشَةَ، قَالَتْ: «تُوُفِّيَ رَسُولُ اللهِ ﷺ يَوْمَ الاثْنَيْنِ».

393. Muḥammad Ibn Ḥātim narrated to us; ʿĀmir Ibn Ṣāliḥ narrated to us; from Hisham Ibn ʿUrwah; from his father that ʿĀ'ishah (*raḍiyAllāhu ʿanhā*) said:

> 'The Messenger of Allāh (ﷺ) passed away on a Monday.'[391]

٣٩٤- حَدَّثَنَا مُحَمَّدُ بْنُ أَبِي عُمَرَ، قَالَ: حَدَّثَنَا سُفْيَانُ بْنُ عُيَيْنَةَ، عَنْ جَعْفَرِ ابْنِ مُحَمَّدٍ، عَنْ أَبِيهِ قَالَ: قُبِضَ رَسُولُ اللهِ ﷺ يَوْمَ الاثْنَيْنِ، فَمَكَثَ ذَلِكَ الْيَوْمَ وَلَيْلَةَ الثُّلاثَاءِ، وَدُفِنَ مِنَ اللَّيْلِ.

وَقَالَ سُفْيَانُ: وَقَالَ غَيْرُهُ: يُسْمَعُ صَوْتُ الْمَسَاحِي مِنْ آخِرِ اللَّيْلِ.

394. Muḥammad Ibn Abī ʿUmar narrated to us; Sufyān Ibn ʿUyaynah narrated to us; from Jāʿfar Ibn Muḥammad that his father [Muḥammad al-Bāqir] (*raḍiyAllāhu ʿanhum*) said:

> 'The Messenger of Allāh (ﷺ) passed away on Monday, after which he remained that day and Tuesaday night and he was buried during the night.'[392]

According to Sufyān and others: 'The sound of shovels could be heard during the latter part of the night.'

٣٩٥- حَدَّثَنَا قُتَيْبَةُ بْنُ سَعِيدٍ، قَالَ: حَدَّثَنَا عَبْدُ الْعَزِيزِ بْنُ مُحَمَّدٍ، عَنْ شَرِيكِ ابْنِ

[391] Tirmidhī, #996, and this hadīth is weak.

[392] Sunan al-Bayhaqī, #6216, and *Musannaf* ʿAbdu'l-Razzāq, #6209, this tradition is Mursal (weak).

عَبْدِ اللهِ بْنِ أَبِي نَمِرٍ، عَنْ أَبِي سَلَمَةَ بْنِ عَبْدِ الرَّحْمَنِ بْنِ عَوْفٍ، قَالَ: «تُوُفِّيَ رَسُولُ اللهِ ﷺ يَوْمَ الاثْنَيْنِ، وَدُفِنَ يَوْمَ الثُّلَاثَاءِ».

قَالَ أَبُو عِيسَى: هَذَا حَدِيثٌ غَرِيبٌ.

395. Qutaybah Ibn Sa'īd narrated to us; 'Abdu'l-'Azīz Ibn Muḥammad narrated to us; from Sharīk Ibn 'Abdullāh Ibn Abī Namir that Abū Salamah Ibn 'Abdu'l-Raḥmān Ibn 'Awf (*raḍiyAllāhu 'anhu*) said:

> 'The Messenger of Allāh (ﷺ) passed away on a Monday, and was buried on a Tuesday.'[393]

Abū 'Isā said: 'This is a strange tradition.'

٣٩٦- حَدَّثَنَا نَصْرُ بْنُ عَلِيٍّ الْجَهْضَمِيُّ، قَالَ: حَدَّثَنَا عَبْدُ اللهِ بْنُ دَاوُدَ، قَالَ: حَدَّثَنَا سَلَمَةُ بْنُ نُبَيْطٍ، عَنْ نُعَيْمِ بْنِ أَبِي هِنْدَ، عَنْ نُبَيْطِ بْنِ شَرِيطٍ، عَنْ سَالِمِ بْنِ عُبَيْدٍ، وَكَانَتْ لَهُ صُحْبَةٌ، قَالَ: أُغْمِيَ عَلَى رَسُولِ اللهِ ﷺ فِي مَرَضِهِ فَأَفَاقَ، فَقَالَ: حَضَرَتِ الصَّلَاةُ؟ فَقَالُوا: نَعَمْ، فَقَالَ: مُرُوا بِلَالًا فَلْيُؤَذِّنْ، وَمُرُوا أَبَا بَكْرٍ أَنْ يُصَلِّيَ لِلنَّاسِ - أَوْ قَالَ: بِالنَّاسِ - قَالَ: ثُمَّ أُغْمِيَ عَلَيْهِ، فَأَفَاقَ، فَقَالَ: حَضَرَتِ الصَّلَاةُ؟ فَقَالُوا: نَعَمْ، فَقَالَ: مُرُوا بِلَالًا فَلْيُؤَذِّنْ، وَمُرُوا أَبَا بَكْرٍ فَلْيُصَلِّ بِالنَّاسِ، فَقَالَتْ عَائِشَةُ: إِنَّ أَبِي رَجُلٌ أَسِيفٌ، إِذَا قَامَ ذَلِكَ الْمَقَامَ بَكَى فَلَا يَسْتَطِيعُ، فَلَوْ أَمَرْتَ غَيْرَهُ، قَالَ: ثُمَّ أُغْمِيَ عَلَيْهِ فَأَفَاقَ، فَقَالَ: مُرُوا بِلَالًا فَلْيُؤَذِّنْ، وَمُرُوا أَبَا بَكْرٍ فَلْيُصَلِّ بِالنَّاسِ، فَإِنَّكُنَّ صَوَاحِبُ أَوْ صَوَاحِبَاتُ يُوسُفَ، قَالَ: فَأُمِرَ بِلَالٌ فَأَذَّنَ، وَأُمِرَ أَبُو بَكْرٍ فَصَلَّى بِالنَّاسِ، ثُمَّ إِنَّ رَسُولَ اللهِ ﷺ وَجَدَ خِفَّةً، فَقَالَ: انْظُرُوا لِي مَنْ أَتَّكِئُ عَلَيْهِ، فَجَاءَتْ بَرِيرَةُ وَرَجُلٌ آخَرُ، فَاتَّكَأَ عَلَيْهِمَا فَلَمَّا رَآهُ أَبُو بَكْرٍ ذَهَبَ لِيَنْكِصَ،

[393] Muwaṭṭā' of Imām Mālik , #539

فَأَوْمَأَ إِلَيْهِ أَنْ يَثْبُتَ مَكَانَهُ، حَتَّى قَضَى أَبُو بَكْرٍ صَلَاتَهُ، ثُمَّ إِنَّ رَسُولَ اللهِ ﷺ قُبِضَ، فَقَالَ عُمَرُ: وَاللهِ لَا أَسْمَعُ أَحَدًا يَذْكُرُ أَنَّ رَسُولَ اللهِ ﷺ قُبِضَ إِلَّا ضَرَبْتُهُ بِسَيْفِي هَذَا قَالَ: وَكَانَ النَّاسُ أُمِّيِّينَ لَمْ يَكُنْ فِيهِمْ نَبِيٌّ قَبْلَهُ، فَأَمْسَكَ النَّاسُ، فَقَالُوا: يَا سَالِمُ! انْطَلِقْ إِلَى صَاحِبِ رَسُولِ اللهِ ﷺ فَادْعُهُ، فَأَتَيْتُ أَبَا بَكْرٍ وَهُوَ فِي الْمَسْجِدِ فَأَتَيْتُهُ أَبْكِي دَهِشًا، فَلَمَّا رَآنِي قَالَ: أَقُبِضَ رَسُولُ اللهِ ﷺ؟ قُلْتُ: إِنَّ عُمَرَ يَقُولُ: لَا أَسْمَعُ أَحَدًا يَذْكُرُ أَنَّ رَسُولَ اللهِ ﷺ قُبِضَ إِلَّا ضَرَبْتُهُ بِسَيْفِي هَذَا، فَقَالَ لِي: انْطَلِقْ، فَانْطَلَقْتُ مَعَهُ، فَجَاءَ هُوَ وَالنَّاسُ قَدْ دَخَلُوا عَلَى رَسُولِ اللهِ ﷺ فَقَالَ: يَا أَيُّهَا النَّاسُ! أَفْرِجُوا لِي، فَأَفْرَجُوا لَهُ فَجَاءَ حَتَّى أَكَبَّ عَلَيْهِ وَمَسَّهُ، فَقَالَ: ﴿إِنَّكَ مَيِّتٌ وَإِنَّهُم مَّيِّتُونَ ۝٣٠﴾ [سورة الزمر]، ثُمَّ قَالُوا: يَا صَاحِبَ رَسُولِ اللهِ ﷺ! أَقُبِضَ رَسُولُ اللهِ ﷺ؟ قَالَ: نَعَمْ، فَعَلِمُوا أَنْ قَدْ صَدَقَ، قَالُوا: يَا صَاحِبَ رَسُولِ اللهِ ﷺ! أَيُصَلَّى عَلَى رَسُولِ اللهِ؟ قَالَ: نَعَمْ، قَالُوا: وَكَيْفَ؟ قَالَ: يَدْخُلُ قَوْمٌ فَيُكَبِّرُونَ وَيُصَلُّونَ وَيَدْعُونَ، ثُمَّ يَخْرُجُونَ، ثُمَّ يَدْخُلُ قَوْمٌ فَيُكَبِّرُونَ وَيُصَلُّونَ وَيَدْعُونَ، ثُمَّ يَخْرُجُونَ، حَتَّى يَدْخُلَ النَّاسُ، قَالُوا: يَا صَاحِبَ رَسُولِ اللهِ! أَيُدْفَنُ رَسُولُ اللهِ ﷺ؟ قَالَ: نَعَمْ، قَالُوا: أَيْنَ؟ قَالَ: فِي الْمَكَانِ الَّذِي قَبَضَ اللهُ فِيهِ رُوحَهُ، فَإِنَّ اللهَ لَمْ يَقْبِضْ رُوحَهُ إِلَّا فِي مَكَانٍ طَيِّبٍ، فَعَلِمُوا أَنْ قَدْ صَدَقَ، ثُمَّ أَمَرَهُمْ أَنْ يُغَسِّلَهُ بَنُو أَبِيهِ، وَاجْتَمَعَ الْمُهَاجِرُونَ يَتَشَاوَرُونَ، فَقَالُوا: انْطَلِقْ بِنَا إِلَى إِخْوَانِنَا مِنَ الْأَنْصَارِ نُدْخِلْهُمْ مَعَنَا فِي هَذَا الْأَمْرِ، فَقَالَتِ الْأَنْصَارُ: مِنَّا أَمِيرٌ وَمِنْكُمْ أَمِيرٌ، فَقَالَ عُمَرُ ابْنُ الْخَطَّابِ: مَنْ لَهُ مِثْلُ هَذِهِ الثَّلَاثِ: ﴿ثَانِيَ ٱثْنَيْنِ إِذْ هُمَا فِى ٱلْغَارِ إِذْ يَقُولُ لِصَـٰحِبِهِۦ لَا تَحْزَنْ إِنَّ ٱللَّهَ مَعَنَا﴾ [سورة التوبة: ٤٠] مَنْ هُمَا؟ قَالَ: ثُمَّ بَسَطَ يَدَهُ فَبَايَعَهُ وَبَايَعَهُ النَّاسُ بَيْعَةً حَسَنَةً جَمِيلَةً.

396. Naṣr Ibn ʿAlī al-Jahdamī narrated to us; ʿAbdullāh Ibn Dāwūd

narrated to us; Salamah Ibn Nubayṭ narrated to us; from Nu'aym Ibn Abī Hind; from Nubayṭ Ibn Sharīk that Sālim Ibn 'Ubayd, who had companionship with him, said:

> 'The Messenger of Allāh (ﷺ) lost consciousness in his illness, then he regained consciousness and said: "Is it time for prayer?" They replied: 'Yes.' He said: "Order Bilāl to give the call to prayer (*adhān*) and order Abū Bakr to lead the people in prayer." Then he lost consciousness, and when he regained his consciousness, he asked: "Is it time for prayer?" They replied: 'Yes.' He said: "Order Bilāl to give the call to prayer (*adhān*) and order Abū Bakr to lead the people in prayer." 'Ā'ishah (*raḍiyAllāhu 'anhā*) said: 'My father is a man who is easily grief-stricken and brought to tears if he is given that responsibility, he will weep [profusely] and will be unable [to lead the people in prayer], so if only you would appoint someone else!' Then he lost consciousness, and when he regained his consciousness, he said: "Order Bilāl to give the call to prayer (*adhān*) and order Abū Bakr to lead the people in prayer, for you are the female companions of Yūsuf!"
>
> Bilāl was therefore ordered, so he gave the call to prayer (*adhān*), and Abū Bakr was ordered, so he led the people in prayer. Then when the Messenger of Allāh (ﷺ) found some relief, and he said: "Find me someone I can lean on!" Barīrah and another man came and so he leaned on them. When Abū Bakr saw him, he began to step back, but he signalled for him to stay in his place until Abū Bakr completed his prayer.
>
> Thereafter, the Messenger of Allāh (ﷺ) passed away. 'Umar (*raḍiyAllāhu 'anhu*) said: 'By Allāh, I will not hear anyone mention that the Messenger of Allāh (ﷺ) has passed away, otherwise I will strike him with this sword of mine!'

He [Sālim] said: The people were unlettered among whom there had never come a Prophet before, so they withheld and said: 'O Sālim, go the Companion of the Messenger of Allāh (ﷺ) and call him. So I went to Abū Bakr, who was in the *masjid.* I came up to him weeping and perplexed, so when he saw me, he said: 'Has the Messenger of Allāh (ﷺ) passed away?' I replied: "Umar is saying: 'I will not hear anyone mention that the Messenger of Allāh (ﷺ) has passed away, otherwise I will strike him with this sword of mine!' he then said to me: 'Go outside!' so I went outside with him. He came and found the people in the presence of the Messenger of Allāh (ﷺ). He therefore said: 'O people, make room for me.' They made room for him, and then he leaned over him and touched him, saying:

"You will surely die, and they will surely die." [*al-Zumar* (39): 30]

Then they asked: 'O Companion of the Messenger of Allāh, has the Messenger of Allāh passed away?' He replied: 'Yes' when they realised that he was telling the truth, they asked:

'O Companion of the Messenger of Allāh, should the funeral prayer be performed for the Messenger of Allāh?' He replied: 'Yes' They asked: 'And how?' He replied: 'A group will, proclaim the Greatness of Allāh, perform the prayer and offer supplication. Then they will leave so that other people may enter.' Then they asked: 'O Companion of the Messenger of Allāh, should the Messenger of Allāh (ﷺ) be buried?' He replied: 'Yes' They asked: 'Where?' He replied: 'In the place in which Allāh took his soul (*rūḥ*), for Allāh does not take his soul but at a pure place (*makān ṭayyib*).' They realised that he was telling the truth.

Then he instructed the family of Messenger of Allāh (ﷺ) to bathe [and carry out the preparation of his shrouding].

The Emigrants (*al-Muhajirūn*) assembled, consulting one another. They said: 'Let us go to our brothers from among the Helpers (*al-Anṣār*) and include them in this matter. The Helpers said: 'There should be a leader from among us and a leader among you.' So 'Umar Ibn Khaṭṭāb (*raḍiyAllāhu 'anhu*) said: 'Who has the like of these three [excellent merits of Abū Bakr]?

"The second of the two; when the two of them were in cave, when he said to his companion: 'Do not grieve. Allāh is with us." [*al-Taubah* (9): 40]

Who are the two of them?' Then he extended his hand, so they pledged allegiance (*bay'ah*) to him [Abū Bakr], and the people [too] pledged allegiance to him in an excellent and beautiful manner."[394]

٣٩٧ـ حَدَّثَنَا نَصْرُ بْنُ عَلِيٍّ، قَالَ: حَدَّثَنَا عَبْدُ اللهِ بْنُ الزُّبَيْرِ، شَيْخٌ بَاهِلِيٌّ قَدِيمٌ بَصْرِيٌّ، قَالَ: حَدَّثَنَا ثَابِتٌ الْبُنَانِيُّ، عَنْ أَنَسِ بْنِ مَالِكٍ قَالَ: «لَـمَّا وَجَدَ رَسُولُ اللهِ ﷺ مِنْ كُرَبِ الْمَوْتِ مَا وَجَدَ، قَالَتْ فَاطِمَةُ: وَاكَرْبَاهُ! فَقَالَ النَّبِيُّ ﷺ: «لَا كَرْبَ عَلَى أَبِيكِ بَعْدَ الْيَوْمِ، إِنَّهُ قَدْ حَضَرَ مِنْ أَبِيكِ مَا لَيْسَ بِتَارِكٍ مِنْهُ أَحَدًا الْمُوَافَاةُ يَوْمَ الْقِيَامَةِ».

397. Naṣr Ibn 'Alī narrated to us; 'Abdullāh Ibn al-Zubayr—Shaikh Bāhilī Qadim Baṣrī—narrated to us; from Thābit al-Bunānī that Anas Ibn Mālik (*raḍiyAllāhu 'anhu*) said:

[394] Ibn Mājah, #1234. The three excellent merits for Abū Bakr (*raḍiyAllāhu 'anhu*) mentioned in this verse are that he was the second of the two in the cave, and his companionship and Allāh being with him (*ma'iyyah*).

> 'When the Messenger of Allāh (ﷺ) was enduring the agony of death, Fāṭimah exclaimed: 'Alas, what agony!' to which the Prophet (ﷺ) replied: "Your father shall not suffer any agony after today. Your father has met the fate from which no one can escape. [Our] reunion is on Resurrection Day."'[395]

٣٩٨ـ حَدَّثَنَا أَبُو الخَطَّابِ زِيَادُ بْنُ يَحْيَى البَصْرِيُّ، وَنَصْرُ بْنُ عَلِيٍّ، قَالَا: حَدَّثَنَا عَبْدُ رَبِّهِ بْنُ بَارِقٍ الحَنَفِيُّ قَالَ: سَمِعْتُ جَدِّي أَبَا أُمِّي سِمَاكَ بْنَ الوَلِيدِ، يُحَدِّثُ أَنَّهُ سَمِعَ ابْنَ عَبَّاسٍ، يُحَدِّثُ أَنَّهُ سَمِعَ رَسُولَ اللهِ ﷺ يَقُولُ: «مَنْ كَانَ لَهُ فَرَطَانِ مِنْ أُمَّتِي أَدْخَلَهُ اللهُ تَعَالَى بِهِمَا الجَنَّةَ»، فَقَالَتْ عَائِشَةُ: فَمَنْ كَانَ لَهُ فَرَطٌ مِنْ أُمَّتِكَ؟ قَالَ: «وَمَنْ كَانَ لَهُ فَرَطٌ يَا مُوَفَّقَةُ!» قَالَتْ: فَمَنْ لَمْ يَكُنْ لَهُ فَرَطٌ مِنْ أُمَّتِكَ؟ قَالَ: «فَأَنَا فَرَطٌ لِأُمَّتِي، لَنْ يُصَابُوا بِمِثْلِي».

398. Abū'l-Khaṭṭāb Ziyād Ibn Yaḥyā al-Baṣrī and Naṣr Ibn 'Alī narrated to us; 'Abd Rabbih Ibn Bāriq al-Ḥanafī narrated to us: 'I heard my maternal grandfather, Simāk Ibn al-Walīd relate that he heard Ibn 'Abbās (*raḍiyAllāhu 'anhumā*) say:

> 'The Messenger of Allāh (ﷺ) said: "Whoever from my nation has two children who died [in infancy], Allāh will cause him to enter the Garden of Paradise on their account." So 'Ā'ishah (*raḍiyAllāhu 'anhā*) asked: "What about someone who only had one child from your nation who has died?' He said: "Also whoever has only one child who has died, O successful lady." She then asked: 'What about someone from your nation who has no child who died [in infancy]?' He replied: "Then I will be an intercessor for my nation, for never will they be afflicted by the loss of the likes of me!"'[396]

[395] Ibn Mājah, #1629.

[396] Tirmidhī, #1062, this ḥadīth is weak.

CHAPTER FIFTY-FIVE

بَابُ مَا جَاءَ فِي مِيرَاثِ رَسُولِ اللهِ ﷺ

What has been narrated concerning the Legacy (*mirāth*) of the Messenger of Allāh (ﷺ)

٣٩٩ـ حَدَّثَنَا أَحْمَدُ بْنُ مَنِيعٍ، قَالَ: حَدَّثَنَا حُسَيْنُ بْنُ مُحَمَّدٍ، قَالَ: حَدَّثَنَا إِسْرَائِيلُ، عَنْ أَبِي إِسْحَاقَ، عَنْ عَمْرِو بْنِ الحَارِثِ، أَخِي جُوَيْرِيَةَ ـ لَهُ صُحْبَةٌ ـ قَالَ: «مَا تَرَكَ رَسُولُ اللهِ ﷺ إِلَّا سِلَاحَهُ، وَبَغْلَتَهُ، وَأَرْضًا جَعَلَهَا صَدَقَةً».

399. Aḥmad Ibn Manīʿ narrated to us; Ḥusayn Ibn Muḥammad narrated to us; Isrāʾīl narrated to us; from Abū Isḥāq that ʿAmr Ibn al-Ḥārith, the brother of [the Mother of the Believers] Juwayriyyah (*raḍiyAllāhu ʿanhumā*) said:

> 'The Messenger of Allāh (ﷺ) did not leave behind anything other than his weapons, his mule and a plot of land which he designated as charity (*ṣadaqah*).'[397]

٤٠٠ـ حَدَّثَنَا مُحَمَّدُ بْنُ الْمُثَنَّى، قَالَ: حَدَّثَنَا أَبُو الوَلِيدِ، قَالَ: حَدَّثَنَا حَمَّادُ بْنُ سَلَمَةَ،

---

[397] Bukhārī, #2739.

عَنْ مُحَمَّدِ بْنِ عَمْرٍو، عَنْ أَبِي سَلَمَةَ، عَنْ أَبِي هُرَيْرَةَ، قَالَ: جَاءَتْ فَاطِمَةُ إِلَى أَبِي بَكْرٍ، فَقَالَتْ: مَنْ يَرِثُكَ؟ فَقَالَ: أَهْلِي وَوَلَدِي، فَقَالَتْ: مَا لِي لَا أَرِثُ أَبِي؟ فَقَالَ أَبُو بَكْرٍ: سَمِعْتُ رَسُولَ اللهِ ﷺ يَقُولُ: «لَا نُورَثُ»، وَلَكِنِّي أَعُولُ مَنْ كَانَ رَسُولُ اللهِ ﷺ يَعُولُهُ، وَأُنْفِقُ عَلَى مَنْ كَانَ رَسُولُ اللهِ ﷺ يُنْفِقُ عَلَيْهِ.

400. Muḥammad Ibn al-Muthannāh narrated to us; Abū'l-Walīd narrated to us; Hammād Ibn Salamah narrated to us; from Muḥammad Ibn 'Amr; from Abū Salamah that Abū Hurayrah (*raḍiyAllāhu 'anhu*) said:

> 'Fatimah came to Abū Bakr and asked: 'Who will inherit from you?' He replied: 'My wife and children.' She said: 'Why is it then that I cannot inherit from my father?' Abū Bakr replied: 'I heard the Messenger of Allāh (ﷺ) said: "No one inherits from us." But, I shall support those whom the Messenger of Allāh (ﷺ) used to support and spend for those for whom the Messenger of Allāh (ﷺ) used to spend on."[398]

٤٠١- حَدَّثَنَا مُحَمَّدُ بْنُ الْمُثَنَّى، قَالَ: حَدَّثَنَا يَحْيَى بْنُ كَثِيرٍ الْعَنْبَرِيُّ أَبُو غَسَّانَ، قَالَ: حَدَّثَنَا شُعْبَةُ، عَنْ عَمْرِو بْنِ مُرَّةَ، عَنْ أَبِي الْبَخْتَرِيِّ، أَنَّ الْعَبَّاسَ، وَعَلِيًّا، جَاءَا إِلَى عُمَرَ يَخْتَصِمَانِ يَقُولُ كُلُّ وَاحِدٍ مِنْهُمَا لِصَاحِبِهِ: أَنْتَ كَذَا، أَنْتَ كَذَا، فَقَالَ عُمَرُ، لِطَلْحَةَ، وَالزُّبَيْرِ، وَعَبْدِ الرَّحْمَنِ بْنِ عَوْفٍ، وَسَعْدٍ: أَنْشُدُكُمْ بِاللهِ أَسَمِعْتُمْ رَسُولَ اللهِ ﷺ يَقُولُ: «كُلُّ مَالِ نَبِيٍّ صَدَقَةٌ، إِلَّا مَا أَطْعَمَهُ، إِنَّا لَا نُورَثُ؟»، وَفِي الْحَدِيثِ قِصَّةٌ.

401. Muḥammad Ibn al-Muthannāh narrated to us; Yaḥyā Ibn

---

[398] Tirmidhī, #1608.

Kathīr al-ʿAnbarī Abū Ghassān narrated to us; Shuʿbah narrated to us; from Muḥammad Ibn ʿAmr; from Abū'l-Bakhtarī that al-ʿAbbās and ʿAlī came quarrelling, each saying to the other: 'You are such-and-such, you are such-and such!' So ʿUmar said to Ṭalḥah, al-Zubayr, ʿAbdu'l-Raḥmān Ibn ʿAwf and Saʿd (*raḍiyAllāhu ʿanhum*):

> 'I implore you by Allāh, have you heard the Messenger of Allāh (ﷺ) say: "Each possession of a Prophet is charity (*ṣadaqah*), except what provides him with food. No one shall inherit from us [the Prophets]!"'

This tradition is part of a longer story.[399]

٤٠٢ـ حَدَّثَنَا مُحَمَّدُ بْنُ الْمُثَنَّى، قَالَ: حَدَّثَنَا صَفْوَانُ بْنُ عِيسَى، عَنْ أُسَامَةَ ابْنِ زَيْدٍ، عَنِ الزُّهْرِيِّ، عَنْ عُرْوَةَ، عَنْ عَائِشَةَ، أَنَّ رَسُولَ اللهِ ﷺ قَالَ: «لَا نُورَثُ مَا تَرَكْنَا فَهُوَ صَدَقَةٌ».

402. Muḥammad Ibn al-Muthannāh narrated to us; Ṣafwān Ibn ʿIsā narrated to us; from Usāmah Ibn Zayd; from al-Zuhrī; from ʿUrwah that ʿĀ'ishah (*raḍiyAllāhu ʿanhā*) said:

> 'The Messsenger of Allāh (ﷺ) said: "We [the Prophets] are not inherited from. Whatever we leave behind is charity (*ṣadaqah*)."'[400]

٤٠٣ـ حَدَّثَنَا مُحَمَّدُ بْنُ بَشَّارٍ، قَالَ: حَدَّثَنَا عَبْدُ الرَّحْمَنِ بْنُ مَهْدِيٍّ، قَالَ: حَدَّثَنَا سُفْيَانُ، عَنْ أَبِي الزِّنَادِ، عَنِ الأَعْرَجِ، عَنْ أَبِي هُرَيْرَةَ، عَنِ النَّبِيِّ ﷺ قَالَ: «لَا يَقْتَسِمُ وَرَثَتِي دِينَارًا وَلَا دِرْهَمًا، مَا تَرَكْتُ بَعْدَ نَفَقَةِ نِسَائِي، وَمُؤْنَةِ عَامِلِي فَهُوَ صَدَقَةٌ».

[399] Abū Dāwūd, #2963, this is a weak tradition but supported by the following narrations.
[400] Bukhārī, #4035, and Muslim, #1758.

403. Muḥammad Ibn Bashshār narrated to us; 'Abdu'l-Raḥmān Ibn Mahdī narrated to us; Sufyān narrated to us; from Abū'l-Zinād; from al-'Araj that Abū Hurayrah (*raḍiyAllāhu 'anhu*) said:

> 'The Messenger of Allāh (ﷺ) said: "My heirs must not distribute a single *dinar* or a *dirham*. Whatever I leave beyond support for my wives and the provisions for my workman will be charity (*ṣadaqah*)."'[401]

٤٠٤ـ حَدَّثَنَا الحَسَنُ بْنُ عَلِيٍّ الخَلاَّلُ، قَالَ: حَدَّثَنَا بِشْرُ بْنُ عُمَرَ، قَالَ: سَمِعْتُ مَالِكَ بْنَ أَنَسٍ، عَنِ الزُّهْرِيِّ، عَنْ مَالِكِ بْنِ أَوْسِ بْنِ الحَدَثَانِ، قَالَ: دَخَلتُ عَلَى عُمَرَ فَدَخَلَ عَلَيْهِ عَبْدُ الرَّحْمَنِ بْنُ عَوْفٍ، وَطَلحَةُ، وَسَعْدٌ، وَجَاءَ عَلِيٌّ، وَالعَبَّاسُ، يَخْتَصِمَانِ، فَقَالَ لَهُمْ عُمَرُ: أَنْشُدُكُمْ بِالَّذِي بِإِذْنِهِ تَقُومُ السَّمَاءُ وَالأَرْضُ، أَتَعْلَمُونَ أَنَّ رَسُولَ اللهِ ﷺ قَالَ: «لَا نُورَثُ، مَا تَرَكْنَاهُ صَدَقَةٌ»؟ فَقَالُوا: اللَّهُمَّ نَعَمْ، وَفِي الحَدِيثِ قِصَّةٌ طَوِيلَةٌ .

404. al-Ḥusayn Ibn 'Alī al-Khallāl narrated to us; Bishr Ibn 'Umar narrated to us; I heard from Mālik Ibn Anas say from al-Zuhrī that Mālik Ibn al-Ḥadathān said:

> 'I came to visit 'Umar at his house, and soon after 'Abdu'l-Raḥmān Ibn 'Awf, Ṭalḥah and Sa'd also came to visit him. Then 'Alī and al-'Abbas came quarrelling, so 'Umar said to them: 'I implore you by the One with whose permission the heaven and the earth exist, do you know that the Messenger of Allāh (ﷺ) said: "We [the Prophets] are not inherited from. Whatever we leave behind is charity (*ṣadaqah*)." They all said: 'O Allāh, certainly [we attest]."

[401] Bukhārī, #2776, and Muslim, #1760.

This tradition is part of a longer story.[402]

٤٠٥- حَدَّثَنَا مُحَمَّدُ بْنُ بَشَّارٍ، قَالَ: حَدَّثَنَا عَبْدُ الرَّحْمَنِ بْنُ مَهْدِيٍّ، قَالَ: حَدَّثَنَا سُفْيَانُ، عَنْ عَاصِمِ ابْنِ بَهْدَلَةَ، عَنْ زِرِّ بْنِ حُبَيْشٍ، عَنْ عَائِشَةَ، قَالَتْ: مَا تَرَكَ رَسُولُ اللهِ ﷺ دِينَارًا، وَلَا دِرْهَمًا، وَلَا شَاةً، وَلَا بَعِيرًا ، قَالَ: وَأَشُكُّ فِي الْعَبْدِ وَالأَمَةِ.

405. Muḥammad Ibn Bashshār narrated to us; 'Abdu'l-Raḥmān Ibn Mahdī narrated to us; Sufyān narrated to us; from 'Āzib Ibn Bahdalah; from Zirr Ibn Ḥubaysh that 'Ā'ishah (*raḍiyAllāhu 'anha*) said:

> 'The Messenger of Allāh (ﷺ) did not leave behind dinars, nor dirhams, nor a sheep, nor a camel.' [The narrator of this tradition] said: 'I am in doubt if she said: 'nor a male or female slave'[403]

[402] Bukhārī, #3094, Muslim, #1757, and Tirmidhī, #1610.
[403] Aḥmad, 25/053

CHAPTER FIFTY-SIX

بَابُ مَا جَاءَ فِي رُؤْيَةِ رَسُولِ اللهِ ﷺ فِي الـمَنَامِ

What has been narrated concerning the Vision (*ru'yah*) of the Messenger of Allāh (ﷺ) in a Dream

٤٠٦ـ حَدَّثَنَا مُحَمَّدُ بْنُ بَشَّارٍ، قَالَ: حَدَّثَنَا عَبْدُ الرَّحْمَنِ بْنُ مَهْدِيٍّ، قَالَ: حَدَّثَنَا سُفْيَانُ، عَنْ أَبِي إِسْحَاقَ، عَنْ أَبِي الأَحْوَصِ، عَنْ عَبْدِ اللهِ بْنِ مَسْعُودٍ، عَنِ النَّبِيِّ ﷺ قَالَ: «مَنْ رَآنِي فِي الْمَنَامِ فَقَدْ رَآنِي؛ فَإِنَّ الشَّيْطَانَ لَا يَتَمَثَّلُ بِي».

406. Muḥammad Ibn Bashshār narrated to us; 'Abdu'l-Raḥmān Ibn Mahdī narrated to us; Sufyān narrated to us; from Abū Isḥāq; from Abū'l-Aḥwaṣ; on the authority of 'Abdullāh Ibn Mas'ūd (*raḍiyAllāhu 'anhu*) that the Prophet (ﷺ) said:

> "Whoever sees me in his dream (*manām*), he has indeed seen me, for Satan cannot imitate me (*lā yatamathalu bī*)."[404]

٤٠٧ـ حَدَّثَنَا مُحَمَّدُ بْنُ بَشَّارٍ، وَمُحَمَّدُ بْنُ الْمُثَنَّى، قَالَا: حَدَّثَنَا مُحَمَّدُ بْنُ جَعْفَرٍ، قَالَ:

[404] Tirmidhī, #2276, and Ibn Mājah, #3900.
[405] Bukhārī, #110, and Muslim, #6056.

حَدَّثَنَا شُعْبَةُ، عَنْ أَبِي حَصِينٍ، عَنْ أَبِي صَالِحٍ، عَنْ أَبِي هُرَيْرَةَ، قَالَ: قَالَ رَسُولُ اللهِ ﷺ: «مَنْ رَآنِي فِي الْمَنَامِ فَقَدْ رَآنِي، فَإِنَّ الشَّيْطَانَ لَا يَتَصَوَّرُ، أَوْ قَالَ: لَا يَتَشَبَّهُ بِي».

407. Muḥammad Ibn Bashshār narrated to us; Muḥammad Ibn al-Muthannāh narrated to us; Muḥammad Ibn Jāʿfar narrated to us; Shuʿbah narrated to us; from Abū Ḥusayn; from Abū Ṣāliḥ that Abū Hurayrah (*raḍiyAllāhu ʿanhu*) said:

> 'The Messenger of Allāh (ﷺ) said: "Whosoever sees me (*ra'ānī*) in a dream, he has indeed seen me (*faqad ra'ānī*), as Satan cannot take on my appearance (*lā yataṣuwaru*)." Or he (ﷺ) said: cannot resemble me (*lā yatashabbhu bī*).'"[405]

٤٠٨ـ حَدَّثَنَا قُتَيْبَةُ، قَالَ: حَدَّثَنَا خَلَفُ بْنُ خَلِيفَةَ، عَنْ أَبِي مَالِكٍ الأَشْجَعِيِّ، عَنْ أَبِيهِ قَالَ: قَالَ رَسُولُ اللهِ ﷺ: «مَنْ رَآنِي فِي الْمَنَامِ فَقَدْ رَآنِي».

قَالَ أَبُو عِيسَى: وَأَبُو مَالِكٍ هَذَا هُوَ: سَعْدُ بْنُ طَارِقِ بْنِ أَشْيَمَ، وَطَارِقُ بْنُ أَشْيَمَ هُوَ مِنْ أَصْحَابِ النَّبِيِّ ﷺ، وَقَدْ رَوَى عَنِ النَّبِيِّ ﷺ أَحَادِيثَ.

سَمِعْتُ عَلِيَّ بْنَ حُجْرٍ، يَقُولُ: قَالَ خَلَفُ بْنُ خَلِيفَةَ: رَأَيْتُ عَمْرَو بْنَ حُرَيْثٍ صَاحِبَ النَّبِيِّ ﷺ وَأَنَا غُلَامٌ صَغِيرٌ.

408. Qutaybah Ibn Saʿīd narrated to us; Khalaf Ibn Khalīfah narrated to us; from Abū Mālik al-Ashjaʿī that his father said:

> 'The Messenger of Allāh (ﷺ) said: "Whosoever sees me in his dream, he has indeed seen me (*faqad ra'ānī*)!"'[406]

Abū ʿIsā said: 'This Abū Mālik is Saʿd Ibn Ṭāriq Ibn Ashyam,

---

[406] Aḥmad, #15880.

and Ṭāriq Ibn Ashyam (*raḍiyAllāhu ʿanhu*) is one of the Companions of the Prophet (ﷺ), and he related traditions from the Prophet (ﷺ).

Similarly, Abū ʿIsā said: I heard ʿAlī Ibn Ḥujr say: 'Khalaf Ibn Khalīfah said: 'I saw ʿAmr Ibn Ḥurayth (*raḍiyAllāhu ʿanhu*), the Companions of the Prophet (ﷺ), when I was a young boy."

٤٠٩ـ حَدَّثَنَا قُتَيبَةُ بْنُ سَعِيدٍ، قَالَ: حَدَّثَنَا عَبْدُ الوَاحِدِ بْنُ زِيَادٍ، عَنْ عَاصِمِ ابْنِ كُلَيْبٍ، قَالَ: حَدَّثَنِي أَبِي، أَنَّهُ سَمِعَ أَبَا هُرَيْرَةَ، يَقُولُ: قَالَ رَسُولُ الله ﷺ: «مَنْ رَآنِي فِي المَنَامِ فَقَدْ رَآنِي؛ فَإِنَّ الشَّيْطَانَ لَا يَتَمَثَّلُنِي»، قَالَ أَبِي: فَحَدَّثْتُ بِهِ ابْنَ عَبَّاسٍ، فَقُلْتُ: قَدْ رَأَيْتُهُ، فَذَكَرْتُ الحَسَنَ بْنَ عَلِيٍّ، فَقُلْتُ: شَبَّهْتُهُ بِهِ، فَقَالَ ابْنُ عَبَّاسٍ: إِنَّهُ كَانَ يُشْبِهُهُ .

409. Qutaybah Ibn Saʿīd narrated to us; ʿAbdu'l-Wāḥid Ibn Ziyād narrated to us; from ʿĀṣim Ibn Kulayb; my father narrated to me that he heard Abū Hurayrah (*raḍiyAllāhu ʿanhu*) say:

> 'The Messsenger of Allāh (ﷺ) said: "Whosoever sees me in a dream, he has indeed seen me (*faqad ra'ānī*), for Satan cannot resemble me (*lā yatamathaluni*)." The father then related this to Ibn ʿAbbās mentioning that he has seen the Prophet (ﷺ). He also mentioned that al-Ḥasan Ibn ʿAlī resembled the Prophet (ﷺ). Upon hearing this Ibn ʿAbbās replied: 'Indeed, he resembles him."[407]

٤١٠ـ حَدَّثَنَا مُحَمَّدُ بْنُ بَشَّارٍ، قَالَ: حَدَّثَنَا ابْنُ أَبِي عَدِيٍّ، وَمُحَمَّدُ بْنُ جَعْفَرٍ، قَالَا: حَدَّثَنَا عَوْفُ بْنُ أَبِي جَمِيلَةَ، عَنْ يَزِيدَ الفَارِسِيِّ ـ وَكَانَ يَكْتُبُ المَصَاحِفَ ـ قَالَ: رَأَيْتُ النَّبِيَّ ﷺ فِي المَنَامِ زَمَنَ ابْنِ عَبَّاسٍ، قَالَ: فَقُلْتُ لابْنِ عَبَّاسٍ: إِنِّي رَأَيْتُ رَسُولَ الله ﷺ فِي

[407] Aḥmad, #7168.

النَّوْمِ، فَقَالَ ابْنُ عَبَّاسٍ: إِنَّ رَسُولَ الله كَانَ يَقُولُ: «إِنَّ الشَّيْطَانَ لَا يَسْتَطِيعُ أَنْ يَتَشَبَّهَ بِي، فَمَنْ رَآنِي فِي النَّوْمِ فَقَدْ رَآنِي»، هَل تَسْتَطِيعُ أَنْ تَنْعَتَ هَذَا الرَّجُلَ الَّذِي رَأَيْتَهُ فِي النَّوْمِ؟ قَالَ: نَعَمْ، أَنْعَتُ لَكَ رَجُلًا بَيْنَ الرَّجُلَيْنِ، جِسْمُهُ ولحمُهُ أَسْمَرُ إِلَى البَيَاضِ، أَكْحَلُ العَيْنَيْنِ، حَسَنُ الضَّحِكِ، جَمِيلُ دَوَائِرِ الوَجْهِ، مَلأَتْ لِحْيَتُهُ مَا بَيْنَ هَذِهِ إِلَى هَذِهِ، قَدْ مَلأَتْ نَحْرَهُ - قَالَ عَوْفٌ: وَلَا أَدْرِي مَا كَانَ مَعَ هَذَا النَّعْتِ - فَقَالَ ابْنُ عَبَّاسٍ: لَوْ رَأَيْتَهُ فِي اليَقَظَةِ مَا اسْتَطَعْتَ أَنْ تَنْعَتَهُ فَوْقَ هَذَا .

قَالَ أَبُو عِيسَى: وَيَزِيدُ الفَارِسِيُّ هُوَ: يَزِيدُ بْنُ هُرْمُزَ، وَهُوَ أَقْدَمُ مِنْ يَزِيدَ الرَّقَاشِيِّ، وَرَوَى يَزِيدُ الفَارِسِيُّ، عَنِ ابْنِ عَبَّاسٍ أَحَادِيثَ، وَيَزِيدُ الرَّقَاشِيُّ لَمْ يُدْرِكِ ابْنَ عَبَّاسٍ، وَهُوَ يَزِيدُ بْنُ أَبَانَ الرَّقَاشِيُّ، وَهُوَ يَرْوِي عَنْ أَنَسِ بْنِ مَالِكٍ. وَيَزِيدُ الفَارِسِيُّ، وَيَزِيدُ الرَّقَاشِيُّ كِلَاهُمَا مِنْ أَهْلِ البَصْرَةِ، وَعَوْفُ بْنُ أَبِي جَمِيلَةَ هُوَ: عَوْفٌ الأَعْرَابِيُّ.

410. Muḥammad Ibn Bashshār narrated to us; Ibn Abī ʿAdī narrated to us; Muḥammad Ibn Jāʿfar narrated to us; ʿAwf Ibn Abī Jamīlah narrated to us; from Yazīd al-Farsī—who used to transcribe copies of the Qur'ān (*muṣāḥif*)—said:

> 'I saw the Messenger of Allāh (ﷺ) in my dream in during the time of Ibn ʿAbbās, so I said to Ibn ʿAbbās: 'I saw the Messenger of Allāh (ﷺ) in my sleep."
>
> Ibn ʿAbbās (*raḍiyAllāhu ʿanhumā*) said: 'The Messenger of Allāh (ﷺ) said: "Satan is unable to resemble me (*lā yastaṭiʿ an yatashabaha bi*). So whosoever sees me in dream, he has indeed seen me." Can you describe this person whom you saw in your dream? He replied: 'Yes, I describe to you a man whose body (*jism*) and flesh (*lahm*) were moderate [in stature], he was fair skinned (*bayāḍ*), having a reddish tinge (*asmar*), his eyes naturally jet black as if lined with kohl, with a pleasant smile (*ḥasan al-ḍaḥik*) and handsome

facial features (*jamīl dawā'ir al-wajh*); his beard went from here to here, and it came down over the top of his chest.'

'Awf said: 'I do not know what could be added to this description.'—so Ibn 'Abbās (*raḍiyAllāhu 'anhumā*) said: 'If you were to see him in wakefulness, you would not be able to describe him more than this.'[408]

٤١١ـ حَدَّثَنَا أَبُو دَاوُدَ سُلَيْمَانُ بْنُ سَلمٍ الْبَلْخِيُّ، قَالَ: حَدَّثَنَا النَّضْرُ بْنُ شُمَيْلٍ قَالَ: قَالَ عَوْفٌ الأَعْرَابِيُّ: أَنَا أَكْبَرُ مِنْ قَتَادَةَ.

411. Abū Dāwūd Sulaymān Ibn Salim al-Balkhī narrated to us; Al-Naḍr Ibn Shumayl said that 'Awf said: 'I am older than Qatādah.'

٤١٢ ـ حَدَّثَنَا عَبْدُ اللهِ بْنُ أَبِي زِيَادٍ، قَالَ: حَدَّثَنَا يَعْقُوبُ بْنُ إِبْرَاهِيمَ بْنِ سَعْدٍ، قَالَ: حَدَّثَنَا ابْنُ أَخِي ابْنِ شِهَابٍ الزُّهْرِيُّ، عَنْ عَمِّهِ قَالَ: قَالَ أَبُو سَلَمَةَ: قَالَ أَبُو قَتَادَةَ: قَالَ رَسُولُ اللهِ ﷺ: «مَنْ رَآنِي ـ يَعْنِي فِي النَّوْمِ ـ فَقَدْ رَأَى الْحَقَّ».

412. 'Abdullāh Ibn Abi Ziyād narrated to us; Ya'qūb Ibn Ibrāhīm Ibn Sa'd narrated to us; the son of the brother of Ibn Shihāb al-Zuhrī narrated to us; from his uncle Abū Salamah that Abū Qatādah (*raḍiyAllāhu 'anhu*) said:

> 'The Messenger of Allāh (ﷺ) said: "Whosoever sees (*man ra'ānī*) me—meaning in his sleep (*nawm*)—he has seen [me] truly (*faqad ra'ā al-ḥaqq*)."'[409]

٤١٣ـ حَدَّثَنَا عَبْدُ اللهِ بْنُ عَبْدِ الرَّحْمَنِ الدَّارِمِيُّ، قَالَ: حَدَّثَنَا مُعَلَّى بْنُ أَسَدٍ،

[408] Aḥmad, #2410.
[409] Bukhārī, #6994, and Muslim, #2267.

قَالَ: حَدَّثَنَا عَبْدُ العَزِيزِ بْنُ الْمُخْتَارِ، قَالَ: حَدَّثَنَا ثَابِتٌ، عَنْ أَنَسٍ: أَنَّ رَسُولَ الله ﷺ قَالَ: «مَنْ رَآنِي فِي الْمَنَامِ فَقَدْ رَآنِي؛ فَإِنَّ الشَّيْطَانَ لَا يَتَخَيَّلُ بِي»، وَقَالَ: «وَرُؤْيَا الْمُؤْمِنِ جُزْءٌ مِنْ سِتَّةٍ وَأَرْبَعِينَ جُزْءًا مِنَ النُّبُوَّةِ».

413. ʿAbdullāh Ibn ʿAbdu'l-Raḥmān al-Dārimī narrated to us; Muʿallā Ibn Asad narrated to us; ʿAbdu'l-ʿAzīz Ibn al-Mukhtār narrated to us; from Thābit that Anas (*raḍiyAllāhu ʿanhu*) said:

> 'The Messenger of Allāh (ﷺ) said: "Whosoever sees me in a dream has indeed seen me, as Satan cannot take on my appearance (*lā yatakhiyyalu bī*).' He (ﷺ) also said: "The dream of a believer is one portion (*juz'*) out of forty-six portions of Prophethood (*nubuwwah*)."'[410]

٤١٤ـ حَدَّثَنَا مُحَمَّدُ بْنُ عَلِيٍّ، قَالَ: سَمِعْتُ أَبِي يَقُولُ: قَالَ عَبْدُ الله بْنُ الْمُبَارَكِ: «إِذَا ابْتُلِيتَ بِالقَضَاءِ فَعَلَيْكَ بِالأَثَرِ».

414. Muḥammad Ibn ʿAlī narrated to us; I heard my father say that ʿAbdullāh Ibn Mubārak said:

> 'If you are afflicted with being appointed as a judge, then adhere to the traditions (*al-athar*).'[411]

٤١٥ـ حَدَّثَنَا مُحَمَّدُ بْنُ عَلِيٍّ، قَالَ: حَدَّثَنَا النَّضْرُ بْنُ شُمَيْلٍ، قَالَ: أَنْبَأَنَا ابْنُ عَوْفٍ، عَنِ ابْنِ سِيرِينَ، قَالَ: «هَذَا الحَدِيثُ دِينٌ؛ فَانْظُرُوا عَمَّنْ تَأْخُذُونَ دِينَكُمْ».

415. Muḥammad Ibn ʿAlī narrated to us; Al-Naḍr Ibn Shumayl

---

[410] Bukhārī, #6994. Muslim, #2264 and Abū Dāwūd, 5018

[411] Meaning refer back to the transmitted judgements of the Prophet (ﷺ) or his Companions (*raḍiyAllāhu ʿanhum*).

narrated to us; Ibn ʿAwn informed us that Ibn Sirīn said:

> 'These traditions (*ḥadīth*) are your religion; then be mindful of whom you learn your religion (*dīn*) from.'[412]

[412] Muslim in his introduction page 26.

APPENDIX ONE

Imām al-Nawawī's Abridged Biography of the Prophet (ﷺ)

The Imām Abū Zakariyyah Yaḥyā Ibn Sharaf al-Nawawī al-Dimashqī, may Allāh have mercy upon him, said:[1]

His (ﷺ) Lineage

He (ﷺ) is: Muḥammad, the Messenger of Allāh (ﷺ), Ibn ʿAbdullāh Ibn ʿAbdu'l-Muṭṭalib Ibn Hāshim Ibn ʿAbd-Manāf Ibn Quṣayy Ibn Kilāb Ibn Murrah Ibn Kaʿb Ibn Lu'ayy Ibn Ghālib Ibn Fihr Ibn Mālik Ibn al-Naḍr Ibn Kinānah Ibn Khuzaymah Ibn Mudrikah Ibn Ilyās Ibn Muḍar Ibn Nizār Ibn Maʿadd Ibn ʿAdnān.[2]

The nation is agreed as to his lineage to this point, after this however they differed greatly concerning his lineage to Ādam (*ʿalayhi as-salām*). The scholars have mentioned that there is nothing authentic

[1] [T] This treatise has been extracted from al-Nawawī's introduction to his *Tahdhīb al-Asmā' wa-l-Lughāt.* Many valuable notes have been added to it by Shaykh Khālid Ibn ʿAbdu'l-Raḥmān al-Shāyiʿ. These have been included in this translation, sometimes translated verbatim and sometimes summarised.

[2] This is the amount that al-Bukhārī sufficed with in mentioning in his ṣaḥīḥ.
Refer to: *al-Fatḥ*, 7/162 and *Zād al-Maʿād*, 1/71. Ibn Ḥajr has discussed this issue in *Fatḥ*, 6/538-539.

concerning this portion of the lineage that can be depended upon.

His (ﷺ) Names and Agnomens

The famous agnomen (*kunyā*) of the Prophet (ﷺ) was Abū al-Qāsim[3] and Jibrīl (*'ālayhi as-salām*) gave him the agnomen, Abū Ibrāhīm.[4]

The Messenger of Allāh (ﷺ) has many names.[5] The Imām and Ḥāfiẓ, Abū al-Qāsim 'Alī Ibn al-Ḥasan Ibn Hibatu-Allāh Ibn 'Abdullāh al-Shāfi'ī al-Dimashqī, famously known as Ibn 'Asākir—may Allāh have mercy upon him, devoted a specific chapter to them in his *Tārīkh Dimashk*.[6] In this chapter he mentioned many names, some of which are mentioned in the Two Ṣaḥīḥs and the remainder in other [books of ḥadīth].

From amongst these names are: Muḥammad, Aḥmad, *al-Ḥāshir* (the Gatherer), *al-'Āqib* (the Ultimate), *al-Muqaffī* (the Tracker), *al-Māḥī* (the Effacer), *Khātimu-n-Nabiyyīn* (the Seal of the Prophets), *Nabiyu-r-Raḥmah* (the Prophet of Mercy), *Nabiyu-l-Malḥamah* (the Prophet of Slaughter)—in one report: *Nabiyu-l-Malāḥim* (the Prophet of Massacres), *Nabiyu-t-Tawbah* (the Prophet of Mercy), *al-Fātiḥ* (the Conqueror), *Ṭahā*, *Yāsīn* and *'Abdullāh* (the Servant of Allāh).[7]

---

[3] Al-Dhahabī, *Tārīkh al-Islām* [p. 33] said, 'it is reported by multiple and consecutive (*mutawātir*) narration that his agnomen was Abū al-Qāsim.'

[4] Refer to: Ibn 'Asākir, *Tahdhīb Tārīkh Dimashq* [1/278]. He said therein, 'this is reported by ad-Dārimī and al-Bayhaqī from Anas (*raḍiyAllāhu 'anhu*).' However its isnād contains Ibn Lahī'ah about whom al-Dhahabī, *Tārīkh al-Islām* [p. 34] said, '*ḍa'īf*'.

I say: It is also reported by al-Ḥākim [2/604] and his isnād also contains Ibn Lahī'ah.

[5] Al-Qasṭalānī, *Mawāhib al-Laduniyyah* [2/11], said, 'a thing having many names is indicative of its nobility and excellence.'

[6] Refer to *Tahdhīb Tārīkh Dimashq* [1/274].

[7] Some of the aforementioned are names and others are titles or descriptions. All of them are proven by authentic narrations except for *al-Fātiḥ*, *Ṭahā* and *Yā sīn*. It is not established that these are included amongst the names of the Prophet (ﷺ).

=

The Imām and Ḥāfiẓ, Abū Bakr Aḥmad Ibn al-Ḥusayn Ibn 'Alī al-Bayhaqī, may Allāh have mercy upon him, said, 'some scholars added to this by saying: in the Qur'ān, He, Mighty and Magnificent, called him *Rasūl* (Messenger), *Nabī* (Prophet), *Ummī* (Unlettered), *Shāhid* (Witness), *Mubashshir* (Bearer of glad-tidings), *Nadhīr* (Warner), a caller to Allāh with His permission and a *Sirāj Munīr* (illuminating torch [of light]), *Ra'ūf* (Kind), *Raḥīm* (Merciful) and *Mudhakkir* (Admonisher). He also appointed him as a mercy, blessing and a guide—(ﷺ).'[8]

Ibn 'Abbās (*raḍiyAllāhu 'anhumā*) reports that the Messenger of Allāh (ﷺ) said,

إِسْـــمِي فِي الْقُرْآنِ مُحَمَّدٌ ، وَفِي الإِنْجِيلِ أَحْمَدُ ، وَفِي التَّوراةِ أُحِيدٌ ، وَ إِنَّما سُمِّيتُ أُحِيدٌ لأَنِّي أُحِيدُ عَنْ أُمَّتِي نارَ جَهَنَّمَ.

> My name in the Qur'ān is Muḥammad, in the Injīl it is Aḥmad and in the Torah it is Uḥīd. I was called Uḥīd because I direct my nation away from the Fire of Hell.[9]

I say: some of these aforementioned names are actually attributes

=

With regards *al-Fātiḥ*, al-Dhahabī said in the section on *Sīrah* in his *Tārīkh Islām* [p. 33] that it is reported via a weak isnād from Abū at-Ṭufail.

With regards *Ṭahā*, it is reported from Ibn 'Abbās via the route of al-Kalbī who is matrūk. It is established from Ibn 'Abbās that the meaning of *Ṭahā* is the call, 'O person!' in the language of the Nabateans [ancient Aran kingdom in SW Asia, now in West Jordan]. This is the opinion that was preferred by the Imām of the Qur'ānic commentators, Ibn Jarīr Ṭabarī, may Allāh have mercy upon him, as per his *Tafsīr* [16/136].

With regards *Yā sīn* (and likewise *Ṭa Hā*), it is not authentically reported that they are included amongst his (ﷺ) names, rather they are names of two chapters of the Qur'ān and in this respect are like [the chapters] Ṣād and Nūn.

[8] Refer to al-Bayhaqī, *Dalā'il an-Nubuwwah* [1/160].

[9] Reported by Ibn 'Adī as mentioned in *Tahdhīb Tārīkh Dimashq* [1/275]. Its isnād contains Isḥāq Ibn Bishr and he is a *khadhdhāb* and *matrūk*. Refer to al-Dhahabī, *Mīzān al-I'tidāl* [1/184].

Therefore this ḥadīth cannot be used to affirm the name Uḥīd. As for the other two, Muḥammad and Aḥmad, they are well established by the Qur'ān itself.

or descriptions [of the Prophet (ﷺ)] and metaphorically referred to as his names.

The Imām and Ḥāfiẓ, Qāḍī Abū Bakr Ibn al-ʿArabī al-Mālikī said in his book, *al-Aḥwadhī fī Sharḥ at-Tirmidhī*,[10] 'some of the Ṣufīs said: Allāh, the Mighty and Magnificent, has one thousand names and the Prophet (ﷺ) has one thousand names.'[11]

Ibn al-ʿArabī continued by saying, 'as for the Names of Allāh, Mighty and Magnificent, then this number is insignificant [as compared to what they really are]. As for the names of the Prophet (ﷺ) then I have counted only those names that are clearly mentioned in the form of obvious names and I have so far collected a total of sixty four names.' Then he mentioned them in detail, commenting upon their meanings comprehensively and in an excellent fashion. Then he said, 'and he has additional names, other than these.'

His (ﷺ) Mother

His mother was Āminah bint Wahb Ibn ʿAbd-Manāf Ibn Zuhrah Ibn Kilāb Ibn Murrah Ibn Kaʿb Ibn Lu'ayy Ibn Ghālib.

[10] 10/280-287.

[11] With regards their confining the names of Allāh, Mighty and Magnificent, to one thousand then this contradicts the authentic ḥadīth, 'I ask you by every name You have named Yourself with, or revealed in Your Book, or taught to one of Your creation, or kept to Yourself in the knowledge of the unseen which is with You...'.

Reported by Aḥmad [1/391, 452], Ibn Ḥibbān [no. 2372] and al-Ḥākim [1/509].

This ḥadīth proves that Allāh has Names that he has kept to Himself in His, Glorious is He, Knowledge.

With regards their saying that the Prophet (ﷺ) has one thousand names then the response to this is that he (ﷺ) has every beautiful name and noble characteristic, however what the Ṣufīs mention has no evidence to support it and actually emanates from their conjectures, their going to extremes with regards the Prophet (ﷺ) and their raising him above his station. The Prophet (ﷺ) severely warned us against this.

His (ﷺ) Birth

The Messenger of Allāh (ﷺ) was born in the Year of the Elephant. It is also postulated that he was born thirty years after it. Al-Ḥākim, Abū Aḥmad said, 'it is postulated that he was born forty years after it or ten years after it,' as reported by al-Ḥāfiẓ Abū al-Qāsim Ibn 'Asākir in *Tārīkh Dimashk*.

The correct and famous opinion is that he was born in the Year of the Elephant. Ibrāhīm Ibn al-Mundhir al-Ḥizāmī—the Shaykh of Bukhārī, Khalīfah Ibn Khayyāṭ and others quoted a consensus concerning this.

They have agreed that he was born on a Monday in the month of Rabī' al-Awwal.[12]

They differed as whether the date was the 2nd, the 8th, the 10th or the 12th of that month. These dates quoted reflect the four famous opinions.[13]

His (ﷺ) Demise

He (ﷺ) passed away during the forenoon of Monday,[14] after twelve

[12] Muslim [2/820] reports that the Messenger of Allāh (ﷺ) was asked about fasting on Mondays to which he replied, 'that was the day in which I was born and that was the day that revelation [first] came to me.'

[13] There is a great deal of difference concerning this. It is not possible to determine the correctness of any one opinion with certainty as they all have their proponents from amongst the scholars.

[14] Some of the scholars were of the opinion that he (ﷺ) died after the sun had begun to decline on that day, taking to the literal sense of the ḥadīth of Anas Ibn Mālik, reported by Bukhārī [no. 4448]. It is mentioned in this ḥadīth that 'he passed away towards the end of that day.' Others said that he died during the forenoon.

Al-Ḥāfiẓ Ibn Ḥajr, *Fath* [8/143] reconciled the two opinions by saying, 'he passed away at the point when the sun had begun to decline, this is time when the forenoon is at its hottest and is also the beginning of the end of the day i.e. the second half of the day has commenced.'

nights had passed of Rabī' al-Awwal, in the year 11 after the Hijrah.[15] The [Islāmic] calendar commences from the date of the Hijrah as has been previously mentioned.[16]

His (ﷺ) Burial Age

He was buried on Tuesday, when the sun had begun to decline. It is also postulated that he was buried on the night of Wednesday.[17]

When he (ﷺ) passed away, he was sixty-three years old. It is also postulated that he was sixty-five or sixty. However the first opinion is most correct and all three opinions have been mentioned in the Ṣaḥīḥ.[18]

---

[15] The scholars are agreed that the Prophet (ﷺ) passed away in 11H, they have agreed that he passed away in the month of Rabī' al-Awwal and that it was on a Monday, this agreement almost reaching the point of consensus. However the scholars have differed as to the date that he passed away, giving the following dates, the 1st, 2nd, 8th, 12th, 13th and others. The most convincing opinions that I have come across are three:

1. The 2nd. This is the opinion of al-Ḥāfiẓ Ibn Ḥajr and others.
2. The 12th. This is the opinion of the majority.
3. The 13th. This was the opinion of some of the scholars and indicated to by more than one person of knowledge.

Refer to: *Fatḥu-l-Bārī* [/129-130]; *al-Bidāyah wa-n-Nihāyah* [5/275-277]; al-Dhahabī, *as-Sīrah* [p. 568]; *Ṭabaqat Ibn Sa'd* [2/272-274]; *Tārīkh at-Ṭabarī* [3/232]; *Laṭā'if al-Ma'ārif* [p. 113].

[16] i.e in *Tahdhīb al-Asmā' wa-Lughāt*, the source of this book.

Al-Ḥāfiẓ Ibn Ḥajr, *Fatḥ* [7/267-269] said, 'some said that it was possible to commence the calendar from four points: 1) His birth. 2) The date of his being commission as a Prophet. 3) The date of his Hijrah. 4). The date of his passing away.

Commencing it from the date of the Hijrah is what they came to determine as being the strongest course. This is because there is a difference as to what year he was born and what year he was commissioned. As for the date of his death, they preferred not to use it due to the feeling of distress that comes about through mentioning his passing away. They commenced the calendar at Muḥarram instead of Rabī' al-Awwal because the resolution to perform the Hijrah occurred in Muḥarram. This is because the pledge of allegiance had taken place during Dhu-l-Ḥijjah which was the starting point of the Hijrah, and the new moon that was born after that was the moon of Muḥarram, hence it was befitting that this be made the beginning of the calendar. This is the strongest reasoning that I have found with regards to commencing the calendar from Muḥarram.

=

The scholars have reconciled these ages by saying: those who mentioned sixty did not include additional number, those who mentioned sixty-five included the year of his birth and death, those who mentioned sixty-three did not.

The correct opinion is sixty-three years and this is also the correct opinion concerning the age of Abū Bakr,[19] 'Umar,[20] 'Alī[21] and 'Ā'ishah[22] (*raḍiyAllāhu 'anhum*), when they passed away.

Al-Ḥākim, Abū Aḥmad—the Shaykh of al-Ḥākim, Abū 'Abdullāh, said, 'it is said that the Prophet (ﷺ) was born on Monday, he was commissioned as a Prophet on Monday, he migrated from Makkah on Monday, he entered Madīnah on Monday and he passed away on Monday.'[23]

It is reported that he (ﷺ) was born circumcised, with the umbilical cord already cut.[24]

=

It is well known that the person to initiate the calendar in this way was 'Umar Ibn al-Khaṭṭab (*raḍiyAllāhu 'anhu*). It is also said that it was Ya'lā Ibn Umayyah in Yemen.'

[17] Al-Ḥāfiẓ Ibn Kathīr, *al-Bidāyah wa-n-Nihāyah* [5/291] said, 'the correct opinion is that he remained unburied the whole of Monday, Tuesday and was buried on the night of Wednesday.... His burial occurred on the night of Wednesday, and this is the opinion that has been textually reported from more than one Imām, both the earlier and later.'

It was this opinion that Khalīfah Khayyāṭ, *Tārīkh* [p. 94] declared with certainty.

[18] Bukhārī [no.'s 3536, 4466] and Muslim [no.'s 2347-2349].

[19] Muslim [no. 2348].

[20] ibid.

[21] Refer to: al-Dhahabī, *Tārīkh al-Islām* [p. 652].

[22] Refer to: al-Dhahabī, *Siyar* [2/193].

[23] This is reported from Ibn 'Abbās as in Aḥmad [1/277] and *Dalā'il an-Nubuwwah* [7/233].

[24] This is reported in a ḥadīth that is not authentic and included by Ibn al-Jawzī in *al-Mawḍū'āt*. [Even if it were true] then this is not considered to be from those matter unique to him because historically many people have been born circumcised as mentioned by Imām Ibn al-Qayyim. He also mentioned a second opinion on this stating that he (ﷺ) was circumcised on the day that the Angels split open his breast while he was being breastfed by Ḥalīmah. He then mentioned a third opinion stating that his grandfather, 'Abdu-l-Muṭṭalib, circumcised

=

The Messenger of Allāh (ﷺ) was shrouded, being wrapped in three white sheets, none of them being a shirt or turban as is established in the Two Ṣaḥīḥs.[25]

Al-Ḥākim, Abū Aḥmad said, 'when the Messenger of Allāh (ﷺ) was wrapped in his burial sheets, he was placed on his bed at the edge of his grave. Then the people entered, group after group, praying [the funeral prayer upon him] with none of them leading.[26] The first to pray upon him was al-'Abbās, then Banū Hāshim, then the *Muhājirūn*, then the *Anṣār*, then everybody else. When the men had finished, the children entered and after them, the women. Then he (ﷺ) was buried and al-'Abbās, 'Alī, al-Faḍl and Qutham—the two sons of al-'Abbās, and Shuqrān lowered him in his grave. It is also said that Usāmah Ibn Zayd and Aws Ibn *Khawlā*[27] were amongst them.'

He was buried in the *laḥd*[28] and therein sun-dried bricks were constructed on top of him (ﷺ). It is said that nine such bricks were employed, then soil was thrown on top and his grave was flattened[29]

=

him on his seventh day, prepared a feast on this occasion and named him Muḥammad. This third opinion has been reported from Ibn 'Abbās and al-Dhahabī inclined towards it in *as-Sīrah an-Nabawiyyah* [p. 28].

Refer to: *atṬabaqāt al-Kubrā* [1/103]; Ibn Kathīr, *as-Sīrah* [1/210]; Ibn al-Qayyim, *Zād al-Ma'ād* [1/81] and *Tuḥafatu-l-Mawdūd* [pp. 121-125].

[25] Bukhārī [no.'s 1264, 1271-1273, 1387] and Muslim [no. 941].

[26] Al-Ḥāfiẓ Ibn Kathīr, *al-Bidāyah wa-n-Nihāyah* [5/286], said, 'the fact that they prayed individually over him, with none of them leading, is a matter that is agreed upon, there is no difference concerning this. However there is a difference as to why this was so...'

Ash-Shāfi'ī, *al-Umm* [1/244] said, 'they prayed over him individually, one after another, due to the great respect accorded him and due to their ardent desire that none act as Imām over him in the prayer.'

[27] Al-Ḥāfiẓ Ibn Ḥajr, *al-Iṣābah* [1/135] quoted in the biography of Aws (*raḍiyAllāhu 'anhu*) that Ibn Isḥāq mentioned him amongst those who placed him into his grave and that aṭ-ṭabarāni reported this via the same route and that it contains a ḍa'īf narrator.

[28] The *lahd* is a cleft in the side of the grave. From amongst the proofs that he (ﷺ) was buried in a *lahd* is the saying of Sa'd Ibn Abū Waqqāṣ reported by Muslim, 'make a *lahd* for me and construct sun-dried bricks upon me just as was done with the Messenger of Allāh (ﷺ).'

with water being sprinkled over it.[30] He [al-Ḥākim] also said, 'it is said that al-Mughīrah descended into his grave' but this is not authentic.[31]

Al-Ḥākim, Abū Aḥmad said, 'it is said that 'Abdullāh, the father of the Messenger of Allāh (ﷺ) died when the Prophet (ﷺ) was twenty-eight months old. It is also postulated that he was nine months, or seven months or two months or he was not yet born.[32] He passed

---

[29] The correct position is that his grave was made into a convex shape, curving outward, as is proven by the ḥadīth reported by Bukhārī [no. 1390] from Sufyān at-Tammār that he saw the Prophet's (ﷺ) grave in a convex shape.

Ibn Ḥibbān [14/602] reports from Jābir (*raḍiyAllāhu 'anhu*) that, 'the Prophet (ﷺ) was buried in the lahd with sun-dried bricks constructed on top of him. His grave was raised above the level of the earth by a hand-span.'

Shu'ayb al-Arna'ūṭ said that its isnād was Ṣaḥīḥ, meeting the criteria of Muslim.

Benefit: It is necessary that the grave not be raised more than a hand-span above the earth. It is forbidden to excessively raise it, to build on top of it or to place candles on it. This is due to the saying of the Prophet (ﷺ) reported by Muslim [no. 666], 'do not leave an idol except that you destroy it, or a raised grave except that you level it.' From amongst the last words that the Prophet (ﷺ) spoke were, 'Allāh cursed the Jews and Christians, they took the graves of their prophets as Masjids.'—Agreed upon.

[30] Ibn Ḥajr mentioned this in *Talkhīṣ al-Ḥabīr* [2/133] and said that its isnād contained al-Wāqidī. The author of *al-Mishkāt* attributed it to al-Bayhaqī, *Dalā'il an-Nubuwwah* [7/264] and its isnād also contains al-Wāqidī who is *matrūk* in reporting ḥadīth.

With regards to sprinkling water over a grave there is a ḥadīth reported by Ibn Mājah [no. 1551], 'the Messenger of Allāh (ﷺ) eased Sa'd [into his grave] and sprinkled water over it.' However this is ḍa'īf as stated by al-Albānī.

Ibn Qudāmah, *al-Mughnī* [3/436], said, 'it is recommended to sprinkle water over the grave in order to cause its earth to stick together.'

[31] Refer to: *al-Bidāyah wa-n-Nihāyah* [5/290].

[32] The majority of the scholars hold the opinion that the father of our Prophet, Muḥammad (ﷺ), 'Abdullāh Ibn 'Abdu-l-Muṭṭalib died while the Messenger of Allāh (ﷺ) was still in his mothers womb. From amongst the scholars who determined this position to the strongest were: Ibn al-Qayyim, Ibn Kathīr, al-Dhahabī, Ibn Ḥajr and Ibn al-Jawzī. This is the literal sense of His saying, "Did He not find you an orphan and give [you] refuge?" [*al-Ḍuḥā* (93): 6]

The person who is the orphan in the complete sense of the word is the one whose father dies while he is yet unborn.

=

away in Madīnah. Al-Wāqidī and his scribe, Muḥammad Ibn Sa'd, both said: it is not established that he passed away while he (ﷺ) was not yet born.'[33]

His grandfather, 'Abdu-l-Muṭṭalib passed away when he was eight years old, it is also postulated that he was six years, leaving him in the care of Abu Ṭālib.[34]

The mother of the Messenger of Allāh (ﷺ) passed away when he was six years old, it is also postulated that he was four years old, at al-Abwā'—a place falling between Makkah and Madīnah.[35]

He (ﷺ) was commissioned as a Messenger to the whole of mankind when he was forty years old, and it is also postulated that he was forty years and one day.[36]

After receiving Prophethood, he remained in Makkah for thir-

=

Al-Ḥākim [2/605] reports from Qays Ibn Mukhrimah; from his father; from his grandfather that, 'the father of the Messenger of Allāh (ﷺ) died while his mother was still pregnant with him.' Al-Ḥākim said that it was ṣaḥīḥ, meeting the criteria of Muslim and al-Dhahabī agreed.

Refer to: *al-Bidāyah wa-n-Nihāyah* [2/3220323]; al-Dhahabī, *as-Sīrah* [p. 50]; *Fatḥ* [7/163]; *al-Wafā bi Aḥwāl al-Muṣṭaphā* [1/153].

[33] That which was determined to be the strongest position by al-Wāqidī and Muḥammad Ibn Sa'd, as far as I have come across, was that his father died while the Messenger of Allāh (ﷺ) was not yet born. This contradicts what the author mentions [from them].

Refer to: *at-Ṭabaqāt al-Kubrā* [1/99]; *al-Bidāyah wa-n-Nihāyah* [2/323].

[34] The famous opinion being that he (ﷺ) was eight years old.

[35] On her way back from Madīnah, going to Makkah, after having visited the relatives of the father of the Messenger of Allah (ﷺ) from amongst the Banū 'Adī Ibn an-Najjār.

[36] Al-Ḥāfiẓ Ibn Ḥajr, *Fatḥ* [6/164] declared with certainty that his (ﷺ) age was forty and six months when revelation came to him. This is by taking into consideration the narration established in the ṣaḥīḥ that he was commissioned at the turn of the fortieth year, that revelation first came to him in the month of Ramaḍān and the famous position that he was born in Rabī' al-Awwal.

teen years. It is also said that he remained there for ten or fifteen years.[37] Then he migrated to Madīnah and remained there for ten years—there is no difference concerning this. He arrived in Madīnah on Monday, after twelve nights of Rabīʿ al-Awwal had passed.[38]

Al-Ḥākim said, 'the Messenger of Allāh's (ﷺ) pain commenced while he was in the house of Maymūnah[39] on Wednesday, with two nights remaining from the month of Ṣafar.'[40]

His (ﷺ) Fostering

He (ﷺ) was first fostered by Thuwaybah,[41] the freed slave-girl of Abū Lahab, for some days,[42] then he was fostered by Ḥalīmah bint Abū Dhu'ayb 'Abdullāh Ibn al-Ḥārith as-Saʿdiyyah. It is reported from her that she said, 'he would age in one day what another child

---

[37] The correct opinion is that the Prophet (ﷺ) stayed in Makkah for thirteen years after having received Prophethood. This is due to what Bukhārī [no. 3851] reports from Ibn 'Abbās that, 'the Messenger of Allāh (ﷺ) received revelation when he was forty, he then remained in Makkah for thirteen years, then he was commanded to undertake the Hijrah whereupon he migrated to Madīnah. He remained in Madīnah for ten years and then passed away.'

This narration is more established than the one reported by Muslim that the Prophet (ﷺ) remained in Makkah for fifteen years as stated by al-Ḥāfiẓ Ibn ḥajr, *Fatḥ* [7/164]. I say: it is also more established than the narration of Muslim [no. 2350] from 'Urwah that the Prophet (ﷺ) stayed in Makkah for ten years.

[38] It is established in Bukhārī [no. 3906] that the Prophet (ﷺ) arrived in Madīnah on Monday in the month of Rabīʿ al-Awwal. However they have differed as to the precise date and it is said the 1st, 2nd, 7th, 13th, 15th and the 22nd. The majority hold the opinion that it was the 12th.

Refer to: *Fatḥu-l-Bārī* [7/244].

[39] Al-Ḥāfiẓ Ibn Ḥajr, *Fatḥ* [8/148] said, "Abdu-r-Razzāq reports with a ṣaḥīḥ isnād from Asmā' Ibn 'Umays who said, 'the first time he felt pain was in the house of Maymūnā...'"

[40] Al-Ḥāfiẓ Ibn Ḥajr, *Fatḥ* [8/129] said, 'there is a difference concerning how long his illness lasted with the majority taking to the opinion that it lasted thirteen days. It is also mentioned that it was fourteen or twelve days.'

[41] She died in 7H and there is a difference as to whether or not she accepted Islām.

[42] Reported by Bukhārī [no.'s 5101, 5106-5107, 5123, 5372] and Muslim [no. 1449].

would in a month.'[43]

His (ﷺ) Upbringing

He (ﷺ) grew up as an orphan in the care of his grandfather, 'Abdu-l-Muṭṭalib, then [after his death] in the care of his uncle, Abū Ṭālib.

Allāh, the Mighty and Magnificent, purified him from the filth of Jāhiliyyah and therefore he never exalted or worshipped any of their idols in his entire life. Neither did he ever attend any of their events of disbelief even though they would request him to attend, however Allāh, the Exalted, prevented and preserved him from this. It is mentioned in a ḥadīth reported by 'Alī (*raḍiyAllāhu 'anhu*) that the Prophet (ﷺ) said,

مـــا عَـــبَدْتُ صَنَماً قَطُّ ، وَما شَرِبْتُ خَمْراً قَطُّ ، وَما زِلْتُ أَعْرِفُ أَنَّ الَّذي هُمْ عَلَيْهِ كُفْرٌ.

> I have never worshipped an idol and neither have I ever drunk alcohol. I always knew that what they were upon was disbelief.[44]

This is from the great kindness that Allāh, the Exalted, bestowed upon him (ﷺ). He freed him of the filth of Jāhiliyyah, from every lowly trait, and gifted him with every beautiful moral and manner to the point that he was known amongst his people as *al-Amīn*, the

---

[43] Al-Dhahabī, in the section concerning *Sīrah* in *Tārīkh al-Islām* [p. 46] mentions a long narration dealing with the story of Ḥalīmah in which this statement occurs.

He declared its isnād to be good and Ibn Ḥajr, *al-Iṣābah* [12/200], referenced this ḥadīth to Abū Ya'lā and Ibn ḥibbān. However al-Albāni, *Difā' 'an al-ḥadīth an-Nabawī* [p. 38] ruled it to be Ḍa'īf. This is because it has two defects, 1) it is munqaṭi' and 2) it contains Jahm Ibn Abū Jahm who is unknown as per *Mīzān al-I'tidāl* [1/426].

Ibn Kathīr, *al-Bidāyah wa-n-Nihāyah* [2/333-340], stated that his being fostered by Ḥalīmah has been reported via a Ṣaḥīḥ isnād and that he remained with her, with the Banū Sa'd for four years.

[44] As-Suyūṭī, *Khaṣā'iṣ al-Kubrā* [1/150] referenced it to Abū Nu'aym and Ibn 'Asākir.

Trustworthy. This due to what they had witnessed of his trustworthiness, his truthful nature and his cleanliness [from all impurity].

When he was twenty-two years old, he went with his uncle, Abū Ṭālib to Syria. When he reached Buṣrah,[45] he came to the attention of Baḥīrah, the monk, who recognised him [for who he truly was] through his characteristics and descriptions. He came and took hold of him by his hand and said,

هَــذا سَيِّدُ العَالَمِينَ، هَذا رَسُولُ رَبِّ العَالَمِينَ، هَذا يَبْعَثُهُ اللهُ حُجَّةً لِلعَالَمِينَ.

> 'This is the master of all the worlds, this is the Messenger of the Lord of the worlds, this one has been sent by Allāh as a manifest proof for all the worlds.'

They asked, 'how did you come to know this?' He replied, 'when you came from the mountain path, not a single tree or rock remained except that it fell prostrate and they do not prostrate except to a Prophet, indeed we have found him [to be mentioned] in our books.' He then asked Abū Ṭālib to take him back for fear of the Jews.[46]

Then, later, he (ﷺ) left a second time for Syria again stopping at the marketplace of Buṣrah, this time with Maysirah, the servant of

[45] A city in east Syria.

[46] This is one of the narrations dealing with the story of Baḥīrah. It is reported by at-Tirmidhī [no. 3620] and al-Ḥākim [2/615-617] who said that it was ṣaḥīḥ, meeting the criteria of Muslim, but al-Dhahabī said, 'I think it is mawḍū', some of it is bāṭil.' In *Tārīkh al-Islām* [p. 57] he said, 'this ḥadīth is extremely bāṭil.' Ibn Kathīr, *al-Bidāyah wa-n-Nihāyah* [2/348] declared it to be strange due to its mentioning Abū Bakr and Bilāl in some of its versions, and in *as-Sīrah* [p. 36] he said that its narrators were all trustworthy and precise.

Ibn Ḥajr, *al-Iṣabah*, said, 'its narrators are trustworthy are precise but the mention of Abū Bakr and Bilāl is munkar and an error on the part of the narrator.' Al-Albānī, ṣaḥīḥ at-Tirmidhī and Mishkāt, stated that the ḥadīth was ṣaḥīḥ but the mention of Bilāl was munkar.

Khadījah (*raḍiyAllāhu 'anha*) in order to trade on her behalf.[47] This was before he married her.

He (ﷺ) married her at the age of twenty-five.[48]

When he (ﷺ) left Madīnah, undertaking the Hijrah, he was accompanied by Abū Bakr as-Ṣiddīq (*raḍiyAllāhu 'anhu*) and his freed-slave, 'Āmir Ibn Fuhairah. Their guide was 'Abdullāh Ibn al-Urayqiṭ al-Laythī who was a disbeliever and it is not known that he accepted Islām.[49]

His (ﷺ) Description[50]

He (ﷺ) was neither very tall nor short [rather of medium height]. He was not extremely white and neither was he brown. His hair was neither curly nor completely straight,[51] when he passed away the number of white hairs on his head did not reach twenty.

---

[47] Al-Dhahabī, *Tārīkh al-Islām* [p. 64], said, 'al-Mahāmilī reported this narration via 'Abdullāh Ibn Shabīb and he is weak.'

[48] Refer to *Fathu-l-Bārī* [7/133].

As for Khadījah, she is Umm al-Qāsim bint Khuwaylid Ibn Asad Ibn 'Abdu-l-'Uzzah Ibn Quṣayy, and it is at this point that her lineage meets the lineage of the Messenger of Allāh (ﷺ). She is the mother of his children and the first to believe in him, (*raḍiyAllāhu 'anha*). She had many virtues, was intelligent, noble and religious, from amongst the inhabitants of Paradise. The Prophet (ﷺ) used to praise her extensively and miss her to the point that 'Ā'ishah would feel jealous of her, even though she had passed away. She was forty years old when the Prophet (ﷺ) married her and they remained married for fifteen years, with his marrying no other. She died three years before the Hijrah.

Refer to: *Fath* [7/134] and *as-Sīrah* [2/109].

[49] With regards to the Hijrah and the story of Abū Bakr, Allāh, the Exalted says, "If you do not aid him [the Prophet (ﷺ), Allāh has already aided him when those who disbelieved had driven him out [of Makkah] as one of two, when they were in the cave and he [Muḥammad (ﷺ)] said to his companion, 'do not grieve; indeed Allāh is with us.' ... " [*at-Tawbah* (9): 40]

[50] Refer to at-Tirmidhī, *Shamā'il al-Muḥammadiyyah*, summarised by al-Albānī.

[51] And this is the best state for hair to be in.

He was of a goodly stature, finely balanced, having broad shoulders. His hair would reach his shoulders, sometimes to his earlobes and other times it would reach half way down his ears. He had a thick and full beard and his hands were fine, meaning that his fingers were thick.[52] He had a large head and joints. His face was slightly round and he had jet black eyes with speckles of red in their edges with long eyelashes. He had fine hair extending from his chest to navel.

When he walked, he walked briskly as if descending a slope. His face would shine with a resplendence like that of the moon when it was full, as if it was the moon itself. He had a nice voice, he was sociable and good natured. He had a wide mouth[53] and his chest and stomach were level.

He had hair on his shoulders, forearms and upper chest. His wrists were thick with wide palms, his eyes were wide-set and he had thick heels. Between his shoulder blades was the Seal of Prophethood that resembled the tassel of a curtained canopy or a pigeon egg.

When he walked it was as if the earth had gathered together for him and those with him had to hurry to keep up with him while he walked on, unmindful of them.

He used to let his hair hang freely, then later he would part it. He would comb it and the hair of his beard. He would smear his eyes with *ithmad* (antimony) every night when going to sleep, three times.

The most beloved garment to the Messenger of Allāh (ﷺ) was the *qamīṣ* (shirt), white garments and the *ḥabrah*, which is a type of thick outer garment with red in it. The sleeve of the Messenger of Allāh's

[52] This description is praiseworthy in men because it means they have a strong grasp, it is blameworthy in women because their fingers should be slender and delicate.
Refer to: Ibn al-Athīr, *an-Nihāyah* [2/444].

[53] Again this is a characteristic of perfection in men.

(ﷺ) shirt extended to his wrist.[54]

One time he wore two red garments and sometimes he would wear an *izār* (lower garment) and *radā'* (upper garment). Another time he wore two green *thawbs*, another time an outer garment having tight sleeves, and yet another, a *qibā'* (a garment whose ends come together).

One time he wore a black turban, letting its two ends hang between his shoulders and another time he wore a *mirṭ* made of hair, this being a type of garment.

He would also wear a ring,[55] leather socks and sandals.

His (ﷺ) Children

He (ﷺ) had three sons,

1. Al-Qāsim, after whom he was nicknamed. He was born to him before his Prophethood and he died when he was two years old.
2. 'Abdullāh. He was also called Ṭayyib and at-Ṭahir because he was born to him after his Prophethood. It is postulated that Ṭayyib and at-Ṭahir are other than 'Abdullāh but the correct position is the first.
3. Ibrāhīm, and died there in the tenth of year of Hijrah at the age of seventeen or eighteen months.

[54] Reported by Abū Dāwūd [no. 4027] and at-Tirmidhī [no. 1765]. Its isnād contains Shahr Ibn ḥawshab and he is Ḍa'īf. Refer to al-Albānī, *Mukhtaṣar Shama'il al-Muḥammadiyyah* [p. 46].

[55] His ring was made of silver and he would place it on his right little finger and sometimes on the left.

Refer to Bukhārī [no. 5877] and Muslim [no. 2094].

He (ﷺ) had four daughters,

1. Zaynab. He married her to Abū al-'Āṣ Ibn ar-Rabī' Ibn 'Abdu-l-'Uzzah Ibn 'Abd-Shams who was the son of her maternal aunt. His mother was Hālah bint Khuwaylid.
2. Fāṭimah. He married her to 'Alī Ibn Abū Ṭālib (*raḍiyAllāhu 'anhu*).
3. Ruqayyah.
4. Umm Kulthūm. He married both of these to 'Uthmān (*raḍiyAllāhu 'anhu*), first Ruqayyah and then Umm Kulthūm and they both passed away while married to him. It for this reason that he was called the Possessor of Two Lights (*Dhu-n-Nūrayn*). Ruqayyah died on the Day of Badr, in Ramaḍān of the second year of Hijrah. Umm Kulthūm died in Sha'bān of the ninth year of Hijrah.

So his daughters numbered four and there is no difference concerning this, and his sons numbered three according to the correct position.

The first to be born to him was al-Qāsim, then Zaynab, Ruqayyah, Umm Kulthūm, Fāṭimah—it is mentioned that Fāṭimah (*raḍiyAllāhu 'anhā*) was older than Umm Kulthūm as stated by al-Ḥāfiẓ 'Alī Ibn Aḥmad Ibn Sa'īd Ibn Ḥazm, Abū Muḥammad. Then in the epoch of Islām, 'Abdullāh was born to him in Makkah and Ibrāhīm in Madīnah.

All of his children, except Ibrāhīm, were from Khadījah. Ibrāhīm was born to him by Māria, the Copt. All of his children passed away before him except for Fāṭimah who passed away six months after him according to the most correct and famous position.

His (ﷺ) Uncles and Aunts

He (ﷺ) had eleven uncles.

1. Al-Ḥārith who was the oldest son of ʿAbdu-l-Muṭṭalib and it was after him that he was nicknamed.
2. Qutham.
3. Zubair.
4. Ḥamzah.
5. Al-ʿAbbās.
6. Abū Ṭālib.
7. Abū Lahab.
8. ʿAbdu-l-Kaʿbah.
9. Ḥajl.
10. Ḍarār
11. Ghaydāq.[56]

From amongst these, those who accepted Islām were Ḥamzah and al-ʿAbbās. Ḥamzah was the youngest of them because he was foster-brother to the Messenger of Allāh (ﷺ), and al-ʿAbbās was of a close age to him. He was the one who was in charge of distributing Zamzam water [to the pilgrims], inheriting this duty from his father, ʿAbdu-l-Muṭṭalib. He was three years older than the Messenger of Allah (ﷺ).

He (ﷺ) had six aunts,

1. Ṣafiyyah (*raḍiyAllāhu ʿanhā*). She accepted Islām and undertook the Hijrah. She was the mother of az-Zubair Ibn al-ʿAwām and died in Madīnah during the rule of ʿUmar Ibn al-Khaṭṭab. She was the sister of Ḥamzah.
2. ʿĀtikah. It is said that she accepted Islām and she is the one who

[56] ʿAbdu-l-Ghanī al-Maqdisi, *Mukhtaṣar as-Sirah* [p. 51] said, ʻhe was called al-Ghaydāq (the Liberal) because of his generosity and frequent feeding [of the poor].'

had the dream about the Battle of Badr. Her story is famous.[57]

3. Barrah
4. Arwā
5. Umaymah
6. Umm Ḥakīm who was [known as] al-Bayḍā' (the White Woman).

His (ﷺ) Wives

The first was Khadījah, then Sawdah, 'Ā'ishah, Ḥafṣah, Umm Ḥabībah, Umm Salamah, Zaynab bint Jaḥsh, Maymūnah, Juwayriyyah and Ṣafiyyah. We shall mention them in their respective biographies, inshā'Allāh.[58]

He [married] these nine after Khadījah and passed away before them. He did not marry anyone else during the lifetime of Khadījah and neither did he marry a virgin other than 'Ā'ishah.

---

[57] In summary: 'Ātikah sent for al-'Abbās Ibn 'Abdu-l-Muṭṭalib to inform him of a nightmare she had. She had seen a rider coming upon a camel, he halted in the valley and cried out to the people, 'come forth, do not leave your men to the disaster that is to come in three days!' The people followed him to the Masjid, then his camel, with him on it, mounted to the top of the Ka'bah and he cried out again using the same words. Then his camel mounted on top of Mount 'Abd Qubays and he cried out again. Then he grabbed a rock and loosened it and it broke, not a single house remained in Makkah except that a piece of that rock entered it.

This dream was the reason why the enemy of Allāh, Abū Lahab refrained from going to fight at Badr.

Refer to: *Sīrah Ibn Hishām* [1/607]; *Marwiyyāt Ghazwah al-Badr* [p. 128].

[58] i.e later on in the book, *Tahdhīb al-Asmā' wa-l-Lughāt.*

The author, may Allāh have mercy upon him, neglected to mention Zaynab bint Khuzaymah (*raḍiyAllāhu 'anhā*) who was called 'the Mother of the Orphans' due to her good treatment of them. The Prophet (ﷺ) married her after Ḥafṣah (*raḍiyAllāhu 'anhā*). She remained with him for two or three months and then died, none of his wives, other than her and Khadijah, died while he was still alive.

From those matters that were specific to him was that he could have more than four wives as the author shall later mention.

Refer to: *al-Ist?'āb* [1/88]; *al-Iṣābah* [12/280]; *as-Siyar* [2/218].

As for those whom he divorced during his (ﷺ) lifetime, then we have not mentioned them due to the great difference concerning them.

He had two slave girls (*surriyyah*), Māria[59] and Rayḥānah bint Zayd, it also postulated that she was bint Sham'ūn, and he later set her free.[60]

It has been reported to us; from Qatādah who said,

تَـزَوَّجَ النَّـبِيُّ ﷺ خَمْسَ عَشْرَةَ امْرَأَةً، فَدَخَلَ بِثلاث عَشْرَةَ، وَجَمَعَ بَينَ إِحْدَى عَشْرَةَ، وَتُوَفِّيَ عَنْ تِسْعٍ.

> 'The Messenger of Allāh (ﷺ) married a [total of] fifteen women. He entered upon thirteen, combined a total of eleven [at one time], and passed away leaving nine living behind him.'[61]

Those Slaves whom He (ﷺ) Freed[62]

From amongst them were,

1. Zayd Ibn ḥārithah Ibn Sharāḥīl al-Kalbī, Abū Usāmah.

[59] The Copt. She was mother to Ibrāhīm, the son of the Messenger of Allāh (ﷺ) and was gifted to him by the leader of Alexandria, Muqawqis.
Refer to: *al-Iṣābah* [13/125].

[60] She was from Banū an-Nadīr, a Jewish tribe, and she accepted Islām.
Refer to: *al-Iṣābah* [12/268].

[61] Refer to Abū 'Ubaydah, *Tasmiyyah Azwāj an-Nabī* (ﷺ) *wa Awlādihi*' [pp. 70-80] and Ibn 'Abdi-l-Barr, *al-Istī'āb* [1/90] wherein he said, 'with regards those concerning whom there is a difference of opinion, who he had marital relations with and then divorced, or contracted the marriage but did not have marital relations, or proposed to but did not complete the contract, there is such a great deal of difference concerning them and the reasons for divorcing them that it necessitates refraining from being certain of the authenticity of any one of them.'

[62] Refer to as-Sakhāwī, *al-Fakhr al-Mutawālī fīman Intusiba li-n-Nabī* (ﷺ) *min al-Khadam wa-l-Mawālī.*

2. Thawbān Ibn Bujdud.
3. Abū Kabashah. His name was Sulaym and he was present at Badr.
4. Bādhām.[63]
5. Ruwayfi'
6. Qaṣir.[64]
7. Maymūn.[65]
8. Abū Bakrah.[66]
9. Hurmuz.[67]
10. Abū Ṣafiyyah, 'Ubayd.
11. Abū Salmā[68]
12. Anasah.
13. Ṣaliḥ i.e. ash-Shukrān.
14. Rabāḥ Aswad.
15. Yasār ar-Rā'ī, the Nabatean.
16. Abū Rāfi', his name was Aslam, other opinions have also been mentioned
17. Abū Muwayhibah.
18. Faḍālah al-Yamānī.
19. Ar-Rāfi'.[69]
20. Mid'am Aswad who was killed at Khaybar.
21. Kirkirah, who used to carry the belongings of the Prophet (ﷺ) [while travelling].
22. Zayd, the grandfather of Hilāl Ibn Yasār Ibn Zayd.
23. 'Ubaydah.[70]

---

[63] It is said that he is also Dhakwān who will be mentioned later.

[64] I have not found, in any of the references that I have, anyone who mentioned him amongst his (ﷺ) freed slaves.

[65] It is said that he is also Dhakwān who will be mentioned later.

[66] He is the famous Companion, Nufay' Ibn al-Ḥārith and some of the scholars did not include him amongst the freed slaves.

[67] It is said that this was the name of Abū Rāfi', the Copt, or that he was Dhakwān who will be mentioned later.

[68] It is said that he is Yasār ar-Rā'ī whose mention follows.

[69] It is said that he is Abū Rāfi' whose mention has preceded.

[70] It is said that he is 'Ubaid or 'Ubaydah whose mention follows.

24. Ṭahman, or Kaysān, or Mahrān, or Dhakwān, or Marwān.[71]
25. Ma'būr, the Copt.
26. Wāqid.
27. Abū Wāqid.[72]
28. Hishām.
29. Abū Ḍumayrah.
30. Ḥunayn.
31. Abū 'Asīb whose name was Aḥmar.
32. Abū 'Ubaydah.
33. Safīnah.
34. Salmān al-Fārisī.
35. Ayman Ibn Umm Ayman.[73]
36. Aflaḥ.
37. Sābiq.
38. Sālim.[74]
39. Zayd Ibn Bawlā.
40. Sa'īd.
41. Ḍumayrah.
42. 'Ubaydullāh Ibn Aslam.
43. Nāfi'.
44. Nabīh.[75]
45. Wardān.
46. Abū Uthaylah.
47. Abū al-Ḥumrā'[76]

From the females were,

---

[71] These are all names that Dhakwān was known by.

[72] The correct position is that he is either Wāqid or Abū Wāqid as mentioned by Shaykh Mashhūr Salmān, *al-Fakhr al-Mutawālī* [p. 61].

[73] Some of the scholars included him amongst the servants and not the freed slaves.

[74] As-Sakhāwī, *al-Fakhr al-Mutawālī* [p. 44] rejected that he was one of the freed slaves.

[75] In another text [of the book] the name given is Nabīl, and both of these have been mentioned amongst his freed slaves.

[76] Some scholars included him amongst the servants, other amongst the freed slaves and yet others placed him in both categories.

1. Salmā.
2. Umm Rāfi'.
3. Umm Ayman, Barakah. She is the mother of Usāmah Ibn Zayd.
4. Maymūnah bint Sa'd.[77]
5. Khaḍirah.
6. Raḍwah.
7. Umaymah.
8. Rayḥānah.
9. Umm Ḍumayrah.
10. Māria.
11. Shīrīn, sister to Māria.[78]
12. Umm 'Abbās.[79]

Many of the aforementioned names are mentioned in these books[80] and an explanation of their lives follows in their biographies, inshā'Allāh, the Exalted.

Know that all of these freed slaves were not present at the same time, rather some of them were present at different times.

Those who served Him (ﷺ)

From amongst these were,

1. Anas Ibn Mālik.
2. Hind.
3. Asmā' both of whom were the daughters of Ḥārithāh al-

[77] Others said that her name was Maymūnah bint Sa'īd.

[78] Others said that her name was Sīrīn, auntie to Ibrahīm, the son of the Prophet (ﷺ).

[79] Others said that her name was Umm 'Ayyāsh.

[80] i.e books written by the scholars, in particular he is referring to *al-Muzanī*, *al-Muhadhdhab*, *al-Wasīṭ*, *al-Wajīz*, and *ar-Rawḍāh*, these being books written by the Shāfi'īs. The biographies of the above people can be found scattered throughout *Tahdhīb al-Asmā' wa-l-Lughāt* as the author has clarified in the introduction [p.3].

Aslamī.

4. Rabī'ah Ibn Ka'b al-Aslamī.
5. 'Abdullāh Ibn Mas'ūd who used to look after his shoes, when he stood he would put them on for him. When he sat, he would remove them and place them under his arms until he stood once again.
6. 'Uqbah Ibn 'Āmir al-Juhanī who was in charge of his mule.
7. Bilāl, the one who called the adhān.
8. Sa'd the freed slave of Abū Bakr as-Ṣiddīq.
9. Dhū Mikhmar, it is also said Mikhbar, the son of the brother of an-Najāshī, it is also postulated that he was the son of his sister.
10. Bukayr Ibn Shaddākh al-Laythī, it is also postulated that his name was Bakr.
11. Abū Dharr al-Ghifārī.
12. Al-Asla' Ibn Sharīk Ibn 'Awf al-A'rajī.
13. Muhājir, the freed slave of Umm Salamah.
14. Abū as-Samḥ, (*raḍiyAllāhu 'anhum*)

His (ﷺ) Scribes

Al-Ḥāfiẓ Abū al-Qāsim mentioned in *Tārīkh Dimashq* that they numbered twenty-three and he listed all of them with his chains of narration.

They are:

1. Abū Bakr as-Ṣiddīq
2. 'Umar Ibn al-Khaṭṭab.
3. 'Uthmān.
4. 'Alī.
5. Ṭalḥah.
6. Az-Zubair.

7. Ubayy Ibn Kaʿb.
8. Zayd Ibn Thābit.
9. Muʿāwiyah Ibn Abū Sufyān.
10. Muḥammad Ibn Maslamah.
11. Al-Arqam Ibn Abū al-Arqam.
12. Abān Ibn Saʿīd Ibn al-ʿĀṣ.
13. Khālid Ibn Saʿīd Ibn al-ʿĀṣ, his brother.
14. Thābit Ibn Qays.
15. Ḥandhalah Ibn ar-Rabīʿ.
16. Khālid Ibn al-Walīd.
17. ʿAbdullāh Ibn al-Arqam.
18. ʿAbdullāh Ibn Zayd Ibn ʿAbd-Rabbih.
19. Al-ʿAlā' Ibn ʿUqbah.
20. Al-Mughīrah Ibn Shuʿbah.
21. As-Sijil.
22. Others added, Shurḥabīl Ibn Ḥasanah.[81]

They mentioned that the most prolific scribes were Zayd Ibn Thābit and Muʿāwiyah (*raḍiyAllāhu ʿanhum*).

His (ﷺ) Envoys

He (ﷺ) sent:

1. ʿAmr Ibn Umayyah ad-Ḍamrī to an-Najāshī. He took the letter of the Messenger of Allāh (ﷺ), placed it between his eyes, descended from his throne and sat on the floor. He then

[81] There are also others that the author, may Allāh have mercy upon him, did not mention. However there is a difference concerning as-Sijil as to whether he was a scribe or not. This is because the only ḥadīth that is used to prove this is reported by Abū Dāwūd [no. 2935] and an-Nasāʾī, *al-Kabīr*, and it is not authentic. There is no one who was called *as-Sijil* amongst the Companions, those who mentioned him amongst the Companions depended upon this ḥadith.

Refer to: Ibn Kathīr, *Tafsīr* [3/200]; *al-Miṣbaḥ al-Maḍī'* [p. 80]; *Kuttāb an-Nabī* [p. 100]

accepted Islām when later in the presence of Ja'far Ibn Abū Ṭālib and his Islām was good.[82]

2. Diḥyah Ibn Khalīfah al-Kalbī to Heraclius, the leader of Rome.
3. 'Abdullāh Ibn Ḥudhāfah as-Sahmī to Chosroes, the King of Persia.
4. Ḥāṭib Ibn Abū Balta'ah al-Lakhmī to al-Muqawqis, the King of Egypt and Alexandria. He said some good words and almost accepted Islām and gifted the Messenger of Allāh (ﷺ) with Māria, the Copt and her sister Shīrīn. The Messenger of Allāh (ﷺ) in turn gifted Ḥassān Ibn Thābit with Shīrīn.[83]
5. 'Amr Ibn al-'Āṣ to the two kings of 'Umān and they accepted Islām, he remained with them until the Messenger of Allāh (ﷺ) passed away.
6. Salīṭ Ibn 'Amr al-'Āmirī to Hawdhah Ibn 'Alī al-Ḥanafī in al-Yamāmah.
7. Shujā' Ibn Wahb al-Asadī to al-ḥārithah Ibn Abū Shamir al-Ghassānī, the King of al-Balqā', Syria.
8. Al-Muhājir Ibn Abū Umayyah al-Makhzūmī to al-Ḥārith al-Ḥumairī.
9. Al-'Alā' Ibn al-Ḥadramī to al-Mundhir Ibn Sāwā al-'Abadī, the King of Baḥrain (today's al-Ḥaṣa, Saudi Arabia) who believed and accepted Islām.
10. Abū Mūsā al-Ash'arī and Mu'ādh Ibn Jabal to Yemen, calling its people to Islām. The generality of its inhabitants accepted Islām, leader and subject.[84]

[82] Ibn al-Qayyim, *Zād al-Ma'ād* [1/120] said, 'Aṣḥamah an-Najāsh?, for whom the Prophet (ﷺ) prayed [the funeral prayer], was not the one to whom he sent the letter to. This second one is not known to have accepted Islām whereas the first died as a Muslim. This was pointed out by Abū Muḥammad Ibn Ḥazm, *as-Sīrah* [p. 30] and the ḥadīth in ṣaḥīḥ Muslim [no. 1774] reported as a statement of Anas also proves this.'

[83] It is also said that her name was Sīrīn.

[84] Other envoys were also sent that the author, may Allāh have mercy upon him, has not mentioned desiring thereby to summarise his words.

All of these kings accepted Islām except for Heraclius, Muqawqis, Hawdhah, Chosroes, al-Ḥārith Ibn Abū Shamir and an-Najāshī. This Najāshī was not the one to whom the Muslims migrated as has preceded.

Those who called the *Adhān* for Him (ﷺ)

He (ﷺ) had four *Mu'adhdhins*:

1. Bilāl
2. Ibn Umm Maktūm, both in Madīnah.
3. Maḥdhūrah in Makkah.
4. Sa'd al-Qaradh in Qubā'.

An explanation of their lives follows in their respective biographies, inshā'Allāh, the Exalted.

His (ﷺ) *'Umrah*, Ḥajj, Military Expenditions, and Raiding Parties

It is established in the Two Ṣaḥīḥs that the Prophet (ﷺ) performed 'Umrah four times after the Hijrah[85] and he performed the Ḥajj only once in his lifetime, the Farewell Ḥajj in which he bid the people farewell in the tenth year of Hijrah.[86]

He (ﷺ), himself participated in twenty-five military expeditions according to the famous opinions. This is the opinion of Mūsā Ibn 'Uqbah, Muḥammad Ibn Isḥāq, Abū Ma'shar and other scholars of biography and military expeditions. It is also said that he undertook twenty-seven such expeditions.

Abū 'Abdullāh Muḥammad Ibn Sa'd, *at-Ṭabaqat*, quoted an agree-

[85] Bukhārī [no.'s 1778-1780, 3066, 4148] and Muslim [no. 1253].

[86] Bukhārī [no. 1778] and Muslim [no. 1254].

There is a ḥadīth in Bukhārī [no. 1664] and Muslim [no. 1220] that proves that he performed Ḥajj once before the Hijrah as well and this was what Ibn Ḥajr declared to be the strongest position in *Fatḥ* [3/517].

ment that he (ﷺ) undertook twenty-seven military expeditions[87] and fifty-six raiding parties. He then mentioned them one by one in order of occurrence.

They mentioned that he physically fought in nine: Badr, Uḥud, al-Khandaq, Banū Quraydha, Banū Muṭṭaliq, Khaybar, Fatḥ Makkah, Hunain and at-Ṭā'if, this according to the opinion of those who say that Makkah was conquered by force.[88]

It is also said that he fought at Bawādī al-Qurā, al-Ghābah[89] and Banū an-Naḍīr. Allāh knows best.

His (ﷺ) Manners

He (ﷺ) was the most generous of people, and he was never so generous as he was in the month of Ramaḍān. He had the best morals and manners and the best physical constitution. His hands were the softest of hands, he was the most pleasant smelling of them and the

[87] Muslim [no. 1813] reports from Ibn Zubair that he heard Jābir Ibn 'Abdullāh saying, 'I went on nineteen military expeditions with the Messenger of Allāh (ﷺ). I was not present at Badr or Uḥud because my father forbade me. When 'Abdullāh [my father] was killed at Uḥud, I never missed a single military expedition with the Messenger of Allāh (ﷺ).' It is understood from this narration that the number of expeditions undertaken by the Prophet (ﷺ) were twenty-one. This is also what is clearly reported from Jābir by Abū Ya'lā with a Ṣaḥīḥ isnād as stated by Ibn Ḥajr, *Fatḥ*[7/380].

The discrepancy in numbers is explained by some people calling two battles by the same name, or giving one battle more than one name due to its length or the different places in which it was fought and the likes, as pointed out by al-Ḥāfiẓ Ibn Ḥajr. It can also be explained by some people considering only those battles in which fighting actually occurred and others not.

[88] Ibn Taymiyyah, may Allāh have mercy upon him, said, 'it is not known that he physically fought in any battle except for Uḥud, in which he killed Ubayy Ibn Khalaf. It is not to be understood from the statement, 'he fought at such-and-such a battle' that he fought in it himself as understood by some students who have not investigated his (ﷺ) life in detail.' Quoted by the *muḥaqqiq* to al-Qasṭalanī, *Mawāhib al-Laduniyyah* [1/335].

[89] These two places fall between Madīnah and Syria, closer to Syria.—*Mu'jam al-Buldān.*

most intelligent and perspicuous of them. He was the best of them with regards companionship and good-nature, the most courageous of them and the one who had the most knowledge of Allāh. He had the most fear of Allāh, he never became angry for personal motives and neither did he take revenge for personal motives. He only became angry when the sacred laws of Allāh, the Mighty and Magnificent, were violated and nothing would appease his anger until the truth was aided. When he became angry he would turn aside or avert his face.

His manners were the Qur'ān and he was the most humble of people. He would fulfil the needs and requirements of his family and lower his wing in mercy to the weak. He was never asked for anything to which his reply would be in the negative. He was the most forbearing of people, and had a greater sense of modesty and shame than a virgin secluded in her private room. He viewed the near and the far, the strong and the weak all the same.

He never criticised food, if he desired it, he ate it and if not he left it. He would not eat while reclining and neither upon an eating table. He would eat what was easy and readily available. He used to love sweets and honey, gourd used to please him. He (ﷺ) said,

نِعْمَ الإِدامُ الخَلُّ.

What an excellent condiment is vinegar.[90]

وَفَضْلُ عائشَةَ عَلى النِّساءِ كَفَضْلِ الثَّريد عَلى سائِرِ الطَّعامِ.

The superiority of 'Ā'ishah over all women is like the superiority of *ath-Tharīd* (a mixture of bread, meat and broth) over all other food.[91]

---

[90] Muslim [no. 2051].

[91] Bukhārī [no.'s 3770, 549, 5428] and Muslim [no. 2426].

His favourite part of the sheep was the shoulder. Abū Hurayrah (*raḍiyAllāhu ʿanhu*) said,

خَرَجَ رَسُولُ اللهِ مِنَ الدُنيا وَلَمْ يَشْبَعْ مِنْ خُبْزِ الشَّعِيرِ.

> The Messenger of Allāh (ﷺ) left the world without ever eating his fill of barley bread.[92]

A month or two would go by without a fire being lit in any of his houses.

He used to partake of gifts but would not touch that which was given in charity. He would reward a gift with a gift. He would fix his own sandals and sow his own clothes. He would visit the sick and accept the invitation of the rich, poor, noble and lowly alike, he would never look down contemptuously upon anyone.

Sometimes he would sit with his knees drawn up to his chest, holding his shins with his hands, sometimes cross-legged and sometimes reclining. Most of the times he would sit in the first posture. He would eat with three of his fingers and would lick them [clean]. He would drink water in three sips, taking a breath between each outside of the vessel that contained the water.

He would speak in comprehensive and concise words, he would repeat his words three times so that they be understood clearly. His words were clear and understandable to all who heard him and he would not speak unless there was a need to do so.

He would not stand or sit except that he made *dhikr* of Allāh, the Exalted. He rode a horse, camel, donkey and mule, sometimes having Muʿādh sit behind him on a camel and on a donkey, he would not allow anyone to walk behind him.

[92] Bukhārī [no.'s 3770, 5419, 5428] and Muslim [no. 2426].

He would tie a rock firmly on his stomach out of hunger, and he and his family would lie down to sleep while still hungry. His bed was made of leather skin, being filled with palm-fibres. He would seldom partake of the delight and pastime of this world, even when he did, taking only a little. Allāh, the Exalted, had given him the keys to the treasures of the whole world, but he refused to accept them, preferring the Hereafter instead.

He would frequently and consistently perform the *dhikr* of Allāh, constantly would he be in a state of contemplation. Most of the times his laugh would consist of a smile and sometimes he would laugh such that his molar teeth showed. He loved scents and hated distasteful smells. He joked, but would not say ought but the truth. He would accept the excuses presented to him by people and he was as Allāh, the Exalted, described him,

لَقَدْ جَآءَكُمْ رَسُولٌ مِّنْ أَنفُسِكُمْ عَزِيزٌ
عَلَيْهِ مَا عَنِتُّمْ حَرِيصٌ عَلَيْكُم بِٱلْمُؤْمِنِينَ
رَءُوفٌ رَّحِيمٌ ﴿١٢٨﴾

> "Indeed there has come to you a Messenger from amongst yourselves, grievous to him is what you suffer. He is deeply concerned about you and kind and merciful to the believers."
>
> [*At-Tawbah* (9): 128]

وَصَلِّ عَلَيْهِمْ إِنَّ صَلَوٰتَكَ سَكَنٌ لَّهُمْ

> "Pray for them, indeed your prayers bring about relief for them."
>
> [*At-Tawbah* (9): 103]

His censuring would consist of his alluding and hinting at something or someone, [for example],

ما بالُ أُناسٍ يَشْتَرِطُونَ شُرُوطاً لَيسَتْ في كِتابِ اللهِ تَعالى.

What is the matter with people that they set conditions that are not in the Book of Allāh, the Exalted?[93]

and the likes.

He would command with gentleness and he would encourage gentleness while prohibiting rudeness and harshness. He would encourage forgiveness, clemency and all virtuous morals and manners.

He loved starting with his right side when cleaning, putting his shoes on, combing his hair and indeed in all of his affairs. His left hand was reserved for cleaning himself after having relieved himself and for whatsoever was deemed offensive. When he slept or lay down, he would lie down on his right side, facing the Qiblah.

His gatherings would be conducted with forbearance and modesty, conducted with integrity and honesty, and were places of patience and tranquillity. No voice was raised therein, women were not needlessly discussed, rather matters inducing taqwā were discussed and those present would be humble, giving due respect to the elders, showing mercy to the young, giving precedence to the needs of the needy and protecting the stranger. Hence they would leave having been guided to and guiding to the good.

---

[93] Bukhārī [no.'s 2155, 2563] and Muslim [no. 1504].

It is reported by Abū Dāwūd [no. 4788] from 'Ā'ishah (*raḍiyAllāhu 'anhā*) that when something was conveyed to the Prophet (ﷺ) about a person he would not say, 'what is wrong with that person who says such-and-such' rather he would say, 'what is wrong with a people who say such-and-such.'

He would bring his Companions together in unity, he would honour the head of every nation and enjoin him to govern their affairs. He would ask after his Companions. He was not one who spoke indecently or promoted indecent speech and action. He would not recompense an evil with an evil, rather he would forgive and overlook. He never struck a servant or woman, indeed he never struck anything except when he was fighting in the Way of Allāh, the Exalted.

He was never given a choice between two matters except that he would choose the easier matter as long as it did not involve any sin.

The evidences for all that I have mentioned are famous and can be found in the Ṣaḥīḥ. Allāh, the Glorious and Exalted, combined in him perfect manners and beautiful habits and temperament. He granted him the knowledge of the previous and later people[94] and that which contains victory and success. This despite the fact that he was illiterate, not being able to read or write, having no human teacher. Allāh granted him what He had not granted any of the creation and chose him above all the first and later people. Abundant peace and blessings be upon him perpetually until the Day of Judgement.

It is established in the Ṣaḥīḥ from Anas Ibn Mālik (*raḍiyAllāhu*

[94] There is some generality in this sentence [that requires explanation]. The meaning of the author, 'He granted him the knowledge of the previous and later people' i.e. knowledge of the unseen that Allāh conferred upon him. Allāh, the Exalted says, "[He is] the Knower of the unseen and He does not disclose His [knowledge of the] unseen to anyone, except whom He has approved of messengers... " [*Al-Jinn* (72): 26-27]

As for that which Allāh did not confer upon him, then in this portion he is like the remainder of mankind, "Say: I do not tell you that I have the depositories [containing the provision] of Allāh, nor that I know the unseen, nor do I tell you that I am an Angel. I only follow what is revealed to me... " [*Al-An'ām* (6): 50]

The correct statement to say is, "He has taught you that which you did not know. " [*An-Nisā'* (4): 113].

'anhu) who said,

ما مَسَسْتُ ديباجاً وَلا حَريراً أَلْيَنُ مِنْ كَفٍّ رَسُولِ الله ص، وَلا شَمَمْتُ رَائِحَةً قَطُّ أَطْيَبُ مِنْ رَائِحَة رَسُولِ الله، وَلَقَدْ خَدَمْتُ رَسُولَ الله ص عَشْرَ سِنِينَ فَما قالَ لي قَطُّ: أُفٍّ، وَلا قَالَ لِشَيءٍ فَعَلْتُهُ: لِمَ فَعَلْتَهُ، وَلا لِشَيءٍ لَمْ أَفْعَلْهُ: أَلا فَعَلْتَ كَذا.

> I have not touched silk brocade or silk that was finer to touch than the hands of the Messenger of Allāh (ﷺ). I have not smelt anything that was more pleasant than the smell of the Messenger of Allāh. I served the Messenger of Allāh (ﷺ) for ten years and he never once said to me, 'uff,' neither did he ever say to something that I did, 'why did you do it?' or to something that I did not do, 'have you not done such-and-such?'[95]

His (ﷺ) Miracles[96]

The Messenger of Allāh (ﷺ) possesses many manifest miracles and signs demonstrating [his veracity], reaching thousands and they are well known.

From amongst them was the Qur'ān, the manifest and clear miracle and brilliant proof, falsehood cannot approach it from before it or behind it. It is a revelation from One Who is All-Wise and Praiseworthy. It incapacitated the most eloquent of people in the most eloquent of times to produce a single chapter that would be

[95] Bukhārī [no. 3561] and Muslim [no. 2309].

[96] A number of works have been authored concerning this topic or discussing this topic amongst them are: Ibn Taymiyyah, *al-Jawāb as-Ṣaḥīḥ liman Baddala Dīn al-Masīḥ*; what was mentioned by Ibn Kathīr, *Tārīkh* and al-Dhahabī, *Tārīkh al-Islām*; Ibn Ḥajr, *Fatḥu-l-Bārī* [6/582].

Refer also to Khayru-d-Dīn Wānilī, *Mu'jazāt al-Muṣṭapha* [3rd ed., Maktabah as-Sawādī, Jeddah]. Consult this for the evidences for what is mentioned in this chapter.

comparable to it, even if the whole of creation were to gather for that purpose. Allāh, the Exalted says,

قُل لَّئِنِ ٱجۡتَمَعَتِ ٱلۡإِنسُ وَٱلۡجِنُّ عَلَىٰٓ أَن يَأۡتُواْ بِمِثۡلِ هَٰذَا ٱلۡقُرۡءَانِ
لَا يَأۡتُونَ بِمِثۡلِهِۦ وَلَوۡ كَانَ بَعۡضُهُمۡ لِبَعۡضٖ ظَهِيرٗا ﴿٨٨﴾

> "Say: if the whole of mankind and the jinn gathered in order to produce the like of this Qur'ān, they could not produce the like of it, even if they assisted each other."
>
> [*Al-Isrā'* (17): 88]

It challenged them to this despite their large numbers, their eloquence and their severe enmity, and it challenges them to this day.

As for the other miracles, it is not possible to enumerate them all due to their huge number and renewing and increasing nature. However, I will mention some examples:

The splitting of the moon, water flowing from between his fingers, increasing the quantity of food and water, the glorification of the food, the palm tree yearning for him, stones greeting him, the talking of the poisoned leg [of roasted sheep], trees walking towards him, two trees that were far apart coming together and then parting again, the barren [and therefore dry] sheep giving milk, his returning the eye of Qatādah Ibn an-Nuʿmān to its place with his hand after it had slipped out, his spitting lightly into the eye of ʿAlī when it had become inflamed and its being cured almost immediately, his wiping the leg of ʿAbdullāh Ibn ʿAtīq whereupon he was immediately cured.

His informing of the places of death of the polytheists on the Day of Badr saying, 'this is the place of such-and-such a person.'

His informing of his killing Ubayy Ibn Khalaf, that a group of his nation would traverse an ocean and Umm Ḥarām would be amongst them and this occurred. That all that was drawn together for him of the ends of the earth and displayed to him would be opened for his nation, that the treasures of the Chosroes would be spent by his nation in the Way of Allāh, the Mighty and Magnificent. That he feared for his nation that they would be tempted by the wealth and allurement of this world and that the treasures of the Persians and Romans would be ours and that Surāqah Ibn Mālik would wear the trousers of Chosroes.

He informed us that Ḥasan Ibn ʿAlī would reconcile between two large warring parties of the Muslims, that Saʿd Ibn Abū Waqqāṣ would live such that nations would benefit by him and others would be harmed. That an-Najāshī had died on this particular day while he was in Ethiopia and that al-Aswad al-ʿAnsī had been killed on this particular day while he was in Yemen.

That the Muslims would fight the Turks who were described as having small eyes, wide faces and small, chiselled noses and that Yemen, Syria and Irāq would be conquered by the Muslims.

He informed us that the Muslims would comprise three armies, an army in Syria, and army in Yemen and an army in Irāq. That they would conquer Egypt, a land whose [unit of land measurement] was the Qīrāṭ, that they should deal with their people well for they have protection [being Copts] and ties of kinship [through Hajar]. That Awais al-Qarnī would come to you from the auxiliaries of Yemen, he would be afflicted with leprosy and it would be healed except for the space of a dirham, and he indeed arrived during the rule of ʿUmar.

He informed us that a group of his nation would always be upon the truth and that mankind would become many in number and that the Anṣar would diminish in number and that the Anṣar would be not be given their due [with regards distribution of wealth and leadership]. That mankind would keep on asking questions until they would say,

خَلَقَ اللهُ الخَلْقَ...

Allāh created the creation....[97]

He informed us that Ruwayfi' Ibn Thābit would live a long life, that 'Ammār Ibn Yāsir would be killed by the transgressing group, that this nations shall divide into sects and that they would fight each other.

He informed us that a fire would emanate from the land of ḥijāz and the likes of this. All of this occurred exactly as he (ﷺ) said it would.

He said to Thābit Ibn Qays,

تَعِيشُ حَمِيداً...وتُقْتَلُ شَهِيداً.

You will live being praised... and you will die as a martyr.

and he live being praised and was martyred at al-Yamāmah. He said to 'Uthmān,

تُصِيبُهُ بَلوَى شَدِيدَةٌ

He would be afflicted by a severe trial.[98]

[97] Referring to the ḥadīth, "the people will continue asking until they say, 'this is Allāh Who created everything...but who created Allāh?'"

Reported by Bukhārī [no. 7296] and Muslim [no. 136].

[98] The meaning of severe trial is his being imprisoned in his house and his being killed by the transgressors.

He said about a person amongst the Muslims who had just fought a severe fight that

وَإِنَّهُ مِنْ أَهْلِ النَّارِ

He would be from amongst the denizens of the Fire.

and later he committed suicide. Wābiṣah Ibn Maʿbad came to him in order to ask him about righteousness and sin upon which he asked,

جِئْتَ تَسأَل عَنِ الْبِرِّ وَالإِثْمِ؟

Have you come to ask about righteousness and sin?

He (ﷺ) said to ʿAlī, az-Zubair and al-Miqdād,

اذْهَبُوا إِلى رَوْضَةِ خاخ، فَإِنَّ بِها ظَعِينَةً مَعَها كِتابٌ.

Go to the garden of Khākh for indeed there is Dhaʿīnah[99] who has a book with her.

They found her there but she initially denied having the book and then took it out from her within her braids.

He (ﷺ) said to Abū Hurayrah, when Satan had stolen some dates,

إِنَّهُ سَيَعُودُ.

Indeed he shall return.

and he did. He (ﷺ)said to his wives,

[99] This is the woman with whom Ḥāṭib al-Baltaʿah (*raḍiyAllāhu ʿanhu*) sent a letter to the people of Makkah in order to inform them of the plans of the Messenger of Allāh (ﷺ) to fight them. It was concerning this that the first verses of *Sūrah Mumtaḥinah* were revealed.
The garden of Khākh is a place falling between Makkah and Madīnah.
Refer to Bukhārī [no. 3983] and Muslim [no. 2494] and *Tafsīr Ibn Kathīr* [4/344].

أَطْوَلُكُنَّ يَداً أَسْرَعُكُنَّ لِحاقاً بِي.

> The most prolific of you in giving charity will be the quickest of you to join me.[100]

and it was so. He (ﷺ) said to 'Abdullāh Ibn Sallām,

أَنْتَ عَلَى الإِسلامِ حَتَّى تَمُوتَ.

> You will remain upon Islām until you die.

He (ﷺ) supplicated for Anas that his wealth and sons increase and that he should live a long life and it was so. He lived for more than one hundred years and not one of the Anṣar was richer than he and one hundred and twenty of his children had already been buried before the arrival of al-Ḥajjāj [to Baṣrah]. This is detailed further in Ṣaḥīḥ Bukhārī and others.[101]

He (ﷺ) supplicated that Islām be strengthened through 'Umar Ibn al-Khaṭṭab or Abū Jahl, and Allāh strengthened it through 'Umar (*raḍiyAllāhu 'anhu*). He (ﷺ) supplicated against Surāqah Ibn Mālik and the feet of his horse sank into the earth and he was thrown off, he called out asking for safe conduct and was granted it, then he asked the Prophet (ﷺ) to make a supplication for him.

He (ﷺ) supplicated that Allāh remove feeling the bitter cold and heat from 'Alī and so never did he feel cold or hot. He (ﷺ) supplicated for Hudhayfah, the night that he sent him to spy on the Confederates, that he not feel the cold and he did not until he had returned. He (ﷺ) supplicated for Ibn 'Abbās that Allāh grant him understanding of the religion and it was so. He (ﷺ) supplicated against 'Utbah

---

[100] Zaynab bint Jahsh (*raḍiyAllāhu 'anhā*) was the most prolific of them in giving charity and was the first to die. Refer to Muslim [no. 2452].
[101] Bukhārī [no. 1982].

Ibn Abū Lahab[102] that Allāh cause a dog from amongst his dogs to overcome him and he was killed by a lion at az-Zarqā'.

He (ﷺ) supplicated for the descent of rain when they asked him to at the time of drought, there was not a single cloud in the sky, then when he had supplicated, the clouds gathered like mountains and it rained until the next Friday. It rained so much that they had to come back and ask him to supplicate and stop the rain, so he supplicated and the rain stopped and they walked out into the glaring sun.

He (ﷺ) supplicated for Abū Ṭalḥah and his wife, Umm Sulaym, that he bless them in the night they had spent together and she became pregnant and gave birth to 'Abdullāh. He had nine children and all of them were scholars.

He (ﷺ) supplicated for the mother of Abū Hurayrah (*raḍiyAllāhu 'anhu*) that she be guided and Abū Hurayrah left to find her performing the ritual bath because she had accepted Islām. He (ﷺ) supplicated for Umm Qays bint Muḥṣin, the sister of 'Ukkasha, that she live a long life and we do not know of another woman who lived as long as she did. This was reported by an-Nasā'ī in the chapter concerning washing the deceased.

On the Day of Ḥunain he (ﷺ) threw a handful of dirt at the disbelievers and said,

شاهت الوُجُوه.

May the faces be disfigured.

and Allāh, the Exalted, vanquished them, filling their eyes with dirt. He (ﷺ) once went out to one hundred of the Quraysh who were

[102] This is how it is in all of the printed editions, perhaps the author means 'Utaybah Ibn Abū Lahab for this description fits him. As for 'Utbah, he accepted Islām in the year of the Conquest of Makkah.

waiting to do something horrible to him and he put dirt on their head and went on his way without their seeing him.

His (ﷺ) Horses, riding Beasts and Weapons

He (ﷺ) had a number of horses:

1. As-Sakab, which he (ﷺ) owned. It was unique, having a white streak and white hooves and it was the first horse that he undertook a military expedition on.
2. Sabḥah. This is the one he (ﷺ) raced on and won.
3. Al-Murtajiz. This is the one he (ﷺ) bought from the bedouin Arab, Khuzaymah Ibn Thābit testified on his behalf [on timely payment].

Sahl Ibn Sa'd said,

كَانَ لِرَسُولِ اللهِ ﷺ ثَلاثَةُ أَفْرَاسٍ: لِزَازٌ وَالظَّرِبُ وَاللُّحَيفُ.

> The Messenger of Allāh (ﷺ) had three horses: Lizāz, al-Dharib and al-Luḥayf.

As for Lizāz, it was given to him by al-Muqawqis, al-Luḥayf was given to him by Rabī'ah Ibn Abū al-Barā'a, and al-Dharib was given to him by Farwah Ibn 'Amr al-Judhāmī.

He (ﷺ) also had a horse called al-Ward which was given him by Tamīm ad-Dārī which he then gave as a gift to 'Umar, then 'Umar gave it as a gift to another man, and later found it being sold.

He (ﷺ) had a mule called Duldul upon which he used to ride on his journeys. It lived on after his death until it grew old and lost its teeth. He used it to grind barley and it died at Yanbu'.[103] It has been

[103] A famous city today in Saudi Arabia, on the Red Sea coast.

reported to us in *Tārikh Dimask* via a number of routes that it remained alive until ʿAlī (*raḍiyAllāhu ʿanhu*) fought the Khawārij, while riding it during his rule.

He (ﷺ) had a camel called al-ʿAḍbā', also called al-Jadʿā' and al-Qaṣwā'. This is how it has been reported to us from Muḥammad Ibn Ibrāhīm at-Taimī that these three names belonged to one and the same camel. This has also been stated by others and it is also postulated that they are names to three different camels.[104]

He (ﷺ) had a donkey called ʿUfayr which died during the Farewell Pilgrimage. Al-Qāḍī ʿAyāḍ said that it was called Ghufayr but they have agreed that this is an error.

One time he (ﷺ) had twenty she-camels about to give birth and one hundred sheep, three spears, three bows and six swords. From amongst these swords was the one called Dhu-l-Faqār which he appropriated from the war booty on the Day of Badr and it was the sword that he saw in his dream on the Day of Uḥud.[105] He (ﷺ) had two suits of armour, a shield, a ring and a wooden pitcher, a black square standard, a white flag—and it is said that it was black.

Know that the circumstances and events of the Messenger of Allāh (ﷺ), his life, that which Allāh, the Exalted, honoured him with, what He inundated the worlds with of his influence and mark, is beyond enumeration, it is not possible to examine all of it. This is especially true of a book like this whose intent is just to show a glimpse of the

[104] It never lost a race. Once it did lose to a bedouin riding his own young camel, this outcome was difficult for the Companions to bear and they felt despondent. The Messenger of Allāh (ﷺ) said, "it is a duty upon Allāh that He not elevate anything of this world except that He would later lower it."

Refer to Bukhārī [no. 6501].

[105] Wherein he saw himself brandishing it and it breaking, which he interpreted to mean that his Companions would be killed on the Day of Uḥud.

Refer to Bukhārī [no. 4081] and Muslim [no. 2272].

lives of individual personalities and what is related to them. What I have mentioned here should serve as a pointer to what I have left out. This is also true because my purpose was to honour this book by mentioning some of the events during the life of the Messenger of Allāh (ﷺ) and his circumstances at its onset.

This has occurred, and all praise and thanks are due to Allāh, indeed how can a book not be ennobled that commences by mentioning the events of the life of the Chosen Messenger (ﷺ), the Beloved and Elect, the chosen one of the world, the Seal of the Prophets, the Imām of the pious and God-fearing, the Master of the Messengers, the Guide of the nation, the Prophet of Mercy (ﷺ), may Allāh increase him in nobility and excellence with Him.

All praise and thanks are due to the
Lord of the worlds.

APPENDIX TWO

The Legal Rulings that were Specific to the Messenger of Allah (ﷺ)[106]

This is a valuable section, the habit of our companions [the Shāfi'īs] is to mention it at the beginning of the Book of Marriage [in their books of *fiqh*]. This is because the rulings specific to him alone are more with regards to marriage than any other topic. I have gathered them in ar-Rawḍah in some detail and all praise and thanks are due to Allāh.

This book is not the place to detail them so I will just mention

[106] After investigation and research one finds that many of the aspects that are mentioned as being specific to the Prophet (ﷺ) in this chapter are not actually so, indeed some of them contradict his (ﷺ) Sunnah.

The basic principle here is that he (ﷺ) is the same as any other man except for that which is established through evidence. The proof for this is His saying, "Say: I am a man like yourselves to whom it has been revealed... " [*Al-Kahf* (18): 110]

and his (ﷺ) saying, "I am only a man...".

How excellent is what the author, may Allāh have mercy upon him, quoted at the end of this chapter that the specific qualities cannot be established through analogy and that they can only be proven through textual evidences. As for that which has no text, then to have a difference of opinion concerning it is to guess at the unseen, so pay attention to this!

them in brief inshā'Allāh, the Exalted.

Our companions have stated that those things specific to him (ﷺ) are of four types:

1. That which is specific to the Messenger of Allāh (ﷺ) with regards the obligations. They said that the wisdom behind this was to increase his closeness to Allāh and to raise his lofty ranking. None of those desiring to come close to Allāh can do so as they do through performing that which Allāh, the Exalted, has obligated upon them as has been clarified in the authentic ḥadīth. [107]

Imām al-Ḥaramain quoted from some of our companions that the reward of an obligation is seventy times greater than the reward of an optional act, conforting themselves with a ḥadīth. Included in this category are: the prayer of *al-Ḍuḥā*, sacrifice, the *witr* prayer, the night prayer (*tahajjud*), employing the miswāk and taking consultation.

The correct opinion according to our companions is that the above are obligatory upon him, it is also postulated that they are recommended. The most correct opinion according to our companions is that the *witr* prayer is not the same as the *tahajjud* prayer. The correct opinion with regards *tahajjud* is that its obligation was abrogated with regards to him (ﷺ) just as it was abrogated with regards his nation. This is what is textually reported from al-Shāfi'ī, may Allāh have mercy upon him. Allāh, the Exalted says,

وَمِنَ ٱلَّيْلِ فَتَهَجَّدْ بِهِۦ نَافِلَةً لَّكَ

[107] Reported by Bukhārī [no. 6502] wherein the Messenger of Allāh (ﷺ) said, "Allāh says, 'whosoever has mutual animosity with a friend (*waliy*) of Mine, then I declare war on him. My servant does not draw close to Me with anything as he does by carrying out what I have made obligatory upon him....'

> "And [stay awake] some of the night for pray, an optional worship for yourself. "
>
> [*Al-Isrā'* (17): 79]

The ḥadīth in Ṣaḥīḥ Muslim, reported from 'Ā'ishah also proves this.[108]

Included in this category is bearing [the harm afflicted upon him] by his enemy with patience, even if they be many, even if they be more than double in number.

Included in this category is the obligation to pay the debt of those who have passed away in the case that there is no one to pay it off. It is postulated that he paid debts off as a generous and noble action on his part and not as an obligation, however the most correct opinion according to our companions is that it was obligatory.

It is also said that it was obligatory upon him (ﷺ), when he saw something that pleased him to say,

لَبَّيكَ إِنَّ العيشَ عيشُ الآخرَة.

> Labbayk, indeed the true livelihood is the livelihood of the Hereafter[109]

Included amongst this category are issues related to marriage, that it was made obligatory upon him to make his wives choose between leaving him or choosing him. Some of our companions said that

---

[108] Reported by Muslim [no. 746] from 'Ā'ishah (*raḍiyAllāhu 'anhā*) who said, 'Allāh, the Mighty and Magnificent, obligated the night prayer in the beginning of this chapter—i.e. *al-Muzzammil*—and the Prophet and his Companions observed this with eagerness. Allāh refrained from revealing its conclusion for twelve months, then He revealed an easing [of the ruling] at the end of this chapter. Hence the night prayer became optional after having been obligatory...'.

[109] Bukhārī [no. 2834] and Muslim [no. 1805].

this was only recommended, however the correct opinion was that it was obligatory. So when he gave them the choice, they chose him and the abode of the Hereafter, thereupon Allāh made it unlawful for him to marry any other or to exchange them as a fitting reward for their excellent choice. Allāh, the Exalted says,

لَّا يَحِلُّ لَكَ ٱلنِّسَآءُ مِنۢ بَعْدُ وَلَآ أَن تَبَدَّلَ بِهِنَّ مِنْ أَزْوَٰجٍ

> "Not permissible for you are any [additional] women after [this], nor may you exchange them for [other] wives..."
> [*Al-Aḥzāb* (33): 52]

Then this ruling was abrogated, so that this could be a favour and grace bestowed upon the Messenger of Allāh (ﷺ), so that he could marry additional women. Allāh, the Exalted says,

إِنَّآ أَحْلَلْنَا لَكَ أَزْوَٰجَكَ ٱلَّٰتِىٓ ءَاتَيْتَ أُجُورَهُنَّ
وَمَا مَلَكَتْ يَمِينُكَ

> "Indeed We have made lawful for you your wives to whom you have given dowries and any slave-girls you own... "
> [*Al-Aḥzāb* (33): 50]

Our companions have differed as whether or not it became unlawful for him (ﷺ) to divorce them after having given them the choice. The most correct opinion is that it was not unlawful, the only thing that was unlawful was to exchange them which is something different to mere divorce.

2. That which was specific to the Messenger of Allāh (ﷺ) with regards to prohibitions, so that his reward could increase through his avoiding them. This is of two types:

THE FIRST: Those issues outside of marriage. Included in this is poetry, writing[110] and [the acceptance of] *zakāh*. With regards to [the acceptance of] optional charity, two opinions have been voiced by al-Shāfiʿī, the most correct of which is that it is unlawful for him. As for eating in a reclining posture, eating onion, garlic and leek then this was disliked for him but not unlawful according to the most correct opinion. Some of our companions said that it was unlawful for him.

When he had made his preparations for war, it was unlawful for him to put his war-items aside until he had engaged the enemy in battle. It is also postulated that it was disliked, however the correct opinion according to our companions is that it was unlawful. Some of our companions said, by way of extrapolating upon this, that when he commenced an optional action of worship, it was necessary for him to complete it but this a is weak opinion.

It was unlawful for him to look desirously at that which Allāh had provided people from the allurements of this world.

It was unlawful for him to commit 'treachery with the eye', which is to motion with the hand or head, indicating permission for a person to be killed or beaten or the likes in a way that contradicts the outward appearance or perception of things.

Initially he would not pray upon those who has died while having a debt, having none to pay it off on his behalf, instead allowing his Companions to pray over him. Our companions have differed as whether or not it was unlawful for him to pray over them. [If it was unlawful] was it then abrogated? Then, later, he would pray over them and pay off their debts himself.

---

[110] Allāh, the Exalted says, "And you did not recite any scripture before it, nor did you inscribe one with your right hand..." [*al-ʿAnkabūt* (29): 48] and "And We did not give knowledge of poetry and neither is it befitting for him. " [*Yāsīn* (36): 69].

THE SECOND: Concerning issues of marriage. Included in this is keeping anyone who disliked to marry him, the correct opinion according to our companions being that it was unlawful for him [to keep her], some of them said that he should leave her by way of a noble gesture on his part.

Included amongst this is marrying a woman from amongst the People of the Book, the most correct opinion according to our companions being that it was unlawful for him. This was the opinion of Ibn Suraij, Abū Saʿīd al-Iṭṭakhri and Qāḍī Abū Ḥāmid al-Marwadhī. Abū Isḥāq al-Marwazī said that it was not unlawful. There are two opinions voiced [by the Shāfiʿīs] concerning sexual relations with a slave-girl from amongst the People of the Book and marrying a Muslim slave-girl. The most correct opinion concerning the slave-girl from the People of the Book is that it was lawful and with regards the Muslim slave-girl that it was unlawful. With regards the slave-girl of the People of the Book, the majority declared decisively that it was unlawful for him to marry her. Al-Ḥannāṭī dismissed both these opinions while our companions extrapolated many issues from this, but it is not fitting to mention them in this book.

3. Concessions and allowance that were granted specifically to him (ﷺ). These are of two types:

THE FIRST: That which does not relate to marriage. Included amongst this is continual fasting, choosing that which he preferred from the war booty before its distribution such as a slave-girl or the likes. This chosen portion was called as-Ṣafī and as-Ṣafiyyah, the plural of which is Ṣafāyah.

Included amongst this is the one-fifth war booty [apportioned for Allāh and His Messenger (ﷺ)] from the spoils of war acquired through victory (*ghanīmah*) and one-fifth of one-fifth of the spoils of war acquired through the enemy surrendering (*fai'*) along with an additional four-fifths.

Included amongst this is entering Makkah without *iḥrām* and the permissibility of fighting therein at the time he entered it during the Conquest of Makkah. He was allowed to pass judgement based upon what he already knew [of a case without the need of the plaintiff or the accused testifying], with regards to other than him there is a difference of opinion. He was allowed to pass verdicts with regards himself and his children and bear testimony on his own behalf and on behalf of his children. He was allowed to accept the witness of one who testified on his behalf. He was allowed to cultivate land on his own behalf. His ablution would not be broken were he to sleep in a lying down position. Some of our companions have mentioned two opinions with regards his ablution breaking upon touching a woman, the most correct opinion being that it does break.[111]

With regards the permissibility of his staying in the Masjid while in a state of major impurity, our companions have voiced two opinions. Abū al-ʿAbbās Ibn al-Qāṣṣ, *at-Talkhīṣ*, said that it was permissible whereas al-Qaffāl and others said that it was not permissible. Imām al-Ḥaramain and others declared the author of *at-Talkhīṣ* to be in error with regards his considering it permissible.

To prove its permissibility it could be possible to depend upon the ḥadīth of ʿAṭiyyah; from Abū Saʿīd that the Prophet (ﷺ) said,

يا عَلِيُّ لا يَحِلُّ لِأَحَدٍ يَجْنُبُ فِي هذا المَسْجِدِ غَيرِي وَغَيرُكَ.

[111] The correct opinion is that touching a woman does not nullify the ablution, this fact holds true for the Prophet (ﷺ) and those other than him, even if one were to touch her with desire. This is due to what is established from ʿĀ'ishah (*raḍiyAllāhu ʿanhā*) that the Messenger of Allāh (ﷺ) used to kiss his wives, then go for prayer without performing ablution.
Reported by Abū Dāwūd [no. 178], Tirmidhī [no. 86], Ibn Mājah [no. 502] and declared Ṣaḥīḥ by al-Albānī.

> O ‘Alī, it is not allowed for anyone who is in a state of major impurity to be in this *masjid* except for you and I.

At-Tirmidhī ruled the ḥadīth to be ḥasan.

It is possible to object to this ḥadith by stating that ‘Aṭiyyah is considered to be weak by the majority. It could be replied to this by saying that at-Tirmidhī ruled the ḥadīth to be ḥasan and perhaps he found supports for it that led to this ruling.[112]

It was permissible for him to take food and drink for its owner who was in need of it, if he (ﷺ) himself was in need of it and it was obligatory upon the owner to give him them, giving precedence to his (ﷺ) needs over his own. This due to the saying of Allāh, the Exalted,

وَأَزْوَٰجُهُۥٓ أُمَّهَٰتُهُمْ

> "The Prophet is more worthy of the believers than themselves... "
>
> [*Al-Aḥzāb* (33): 6]

Know that the Prophet (ﷺ) did not actually carry out the majority of these permissible matters, even though they were permissible for him and Allāh knows best.

THE SECOND: Those issue related to marriage. Included amongst this is the permissibility of having nine wives, the correct opinion

---

[112] The ḥadīth is Ḍa‘īf, its isnād contains ‘Aṭiyyah al-‘Awfī, who is Ṣadūq, makes mistakes, a shia and a *mudallis* as mentioned in *at-Taqrīb*. At-Tirmidhī alluded to its weakness for he said after quoting it, ‘this ḥadīth is *gharīb*, we only know it via this route. Muḥammad Ibn Ismā‘īl [al-Bukhārī] heard this ḥadīth from me and declared it strange.’

From amongst those who declared it ḍa‘īf was al-Albānī.

being that he was allowed even more, his marriage being considered valid by using the word 'gift', and limiting his divorce [to taking effect with] three proclamations, it is also postulated that this is not limited. In the case that the marriage has been contracted with the wording 'gift', it was not obligatory upon him to give the mahr upon the completion of the contract or after having marital relations, this is not the case with those other than him.

Included amongst this is the validity of marriage without a legal guardian [for the woman] or any witnesses and in the state of iḥrām[113] according to the most correct opinion in all of these. In the case that he desired to marry an unmarried woman, it is necessary for her to respond according to the correct opinion and it is unlawful for any other to offer his hand in marriage to her. With regards to distribution of time between his wives and female-slaves there are two opinions. Al-Iṭṭakhrī said that it was not obligatory and therefore this would fall under the matters specific to him whereas other said that it was obligatory and therefore this would not fall under the matters that were specific to him.

The companions [of the Shāfi'ī *madh'hab*] have built the majority of these issues and their likes upon the premise that is his (ﷺ) marrying like our marrying or is it like sexual relations (*tasarri*)?[114]

He freed Ṣafiyyah and then married her and appointed her freedom as her mahr. It is also said that he freed her upon the condition that he marry her and therefore it was obligatory upon him to fulfil it,

[113] It seems clear that the author, may Allāh have mercy upon him, depended upon the opinion of those who say that he married Maymūnah while in a state of iḥrām. The correct opinion, however, is that he married her while not in a state of iḥrām, as stated by Maymūnah herself and by Abū Rāfi', their mediator.

Refer to: *Zād al-Ma'ād* [1/113].

[114] The basic principle here is that he (ﷺ) is as Allāh said, "Say: I am a man like yourselves to whom it has been revealed... " [*Al-Kahf* (18): 110]

Therefore whoever claims specificity then let him bring an evidence.

this is not the case with those other than him. It is also said that he made the very action of freeing be the *mahr* and that this was valid for him, but not valid for any other. It is also said that he freed her without any sort of return and married her without giving her a *mahr* at all, this is the most correct opinion.

The companions have mentioned many issues in this category but I have omitted them.

4. His noble virtues and respect due to him that was specific to him (ﷺ).

Included amongst these was the fact that it was unlawful to marry his wives who lived after him. As for the ones that he divorced during his lifetime, there are a number of opinions, the most correct of which is that it is unlawful to marry them. This has been textually stated by ash-Shāfi'ī, may Allāh have mercy upon him, in *Aḥkām al-Qur'ān* and this was also the opinion of Abū 'Alī Ibn Abū Hurayrah due to the saying of Allāh, the Exalted,

وَأَزْوَٰجُهُۥٓ أُمَّهَٰتُهُمْ

"...and his wives are their mothers."

[*Al-Aḥzāb* (33): 6]

The second opinion mentioned concerning this is that it is lawful to marry them and the third that it is unlawful to marry those whom he had marital relations with. If we say that it is unlawful then their ensue two opinions with regards to marrying his slave-girls that lived on after his death, or he left, after having sexual relations with them.

Included amongst these is that his wives are the mothers of the believers regardless of whether they died before him or after him. This relationship applies with regards to marrying them, respecting them, obeying them and the prohibition of disobeying them and being rude to them. It does not apply to the rules of looking at them, being alone with them, and their children being unlawful to marry. Therefore it is not said that their daughters are the sisters of the believers and neither is it said that their mothers and fathers are the grandmothers and grandfathers of the believers and so on. Some of our companions said that the term denoting brotherhood can be applied to their daughters and uncle and aunt can be applied to their brothers and sisters. This is the clear sense of what al-Shāfiʿī textually stated in *Mukhtaṣar al-Muzani*.

Are they the mothers of the male and female believers? There are two opinions voiced by our companions, the most authentic of which being no, rather they are the mothers of the male believers to the exception of the female believers and this is what is reported from ʿĀ'ishah (*raḍiyAllāhu ʿanhā*), building upon the premise of the preferred opinion that the feminine gender is not included in the male pronoun.[115]

Al-Baghawī, from amongst our companions, said that it can be said that the Prophet (ﷺ) was the father of the male and female believers while al-Wāḥidī quoted some of our companions saying that this should not be said due to the saying of Allāh, the Exalted,

مَّا كَانَ مُحَمَّدٌ أَبَآ أَحَدٍ مِّن رِّجَالِكُمْ

"Muḥammad is not the father of any of your men."

[*Al-Aḥzāb* (33): 40]

He said, ash-Shāfiʿī, may Allāh have mercy upon him, textually stated that it was permissible with the meaning their father with regards the respect accorded him and his sanctity. He said that the

[115] The opinion of the majority, and the correct opinion, is that females are indeed included in the male pronoun as long as their exists no evidence indicating that it specifically refers to men. There is no evidence in this case.

Refer to: Ibn Qudāmah, *Rawḍah an-Nādhir* [2/148-150].

meaning of the verse was that not one of you are his children from his loins. It is reported in the Ṣaḥīḥ ḥadīth in Abū Dāwūd and elsewhere that the Prophet (ﷺ) said,

إِنَّما أنا لَكُمْ مِثْلُ الوَالِدِ.

Indeed I am like a father to you.[116]

It is said [in commentary to this] i.e. in mercy and compassion; and it is said i.e. they should not be embarrassed to ask him about personal questions whose answers they are in need of knowing; and it said i.e. both the aforementioned matters. I have clarified this further in the *Kitāb al-Istiṣābah of Shar'ḥ al-Muhadhdhab.*

Included amongst this is the superiority of his (ﷺ) wives over all other women. Their reward and punishment was doubled and it was prohibited to ask them except from behind a veil, whereas it is permissible to ask other women directly. The best of his wives were Khadījah and 'Ā'ishah and Abū Sa'd al-Mutawallī said, 'our companions have differed as which of these two was the better.'

With regards to issues outside of marriage then he (ﷺ) was the Seal of the Prophets and the best of creation. His nation is the best of nations and his Companions consisted the best of generations. His nation is preserved from uniting upon error and his Sharī'ah is valid for all time, abrogating all other laws. His Book is a miracle, preserved from distortion and alteration and it is the proof against mankind after his passing away whereas the miracles of all the other Prophets have vanished. He was aided by having fear of him planted [into the hearts of his enemies] to the distance of one months journey. The earth was made as a *masjid* for him and its dust was purifying, war booty was made lawful for him and he was granted the rank of intercession and the Praiseworthy Station. He was sent to the whole of mankind.

[116] Abū Dāwūd [no. 8] and it was declared ḥasan by al-Albānī.

He is the Master of the Children of Ādam and the first one who the earth will give up, the first to intercede and the first to have his intercession accepted and he is the first to knock on the gates of Paradise. He will have the largest following from amongst the Prophets and he was granted concise and comprehensive speech. The rows of his followers in prayer reflect the rows of the Angels. His heart never slept and he would see those behind him in the same way that he saw those in front of him.[117] It is not permissible for anyone to raise his voice over his voice, neither is it permissible for anyone to shout for him from beyond his private quarters, neither is it permissible for anyone to call him by his name by saying, 'O Muḥammad' rather he should say, 'O Prophet of Allāh, O Messenger of Allāh.'[118] The one who is praying should address him by saying,

السَّلامُ عَلَيكَ أَيُّها النَّبِيُّ وَرَحْمَةُ اللهِ وَبَرَكاتُهُ.

> Peace be upon you, O Prophet and the mercy of Allāh and His blessings.

If the person praying were to address any other human in his prayer, his prayer is rendered invalid. If somebody is praying and he (ﷺ) was to call him, it is necessary to respond to him and his prayer would not be rendered invalid.

Blessings can be sought with his urine and blood,[119] his hair was

[117] i.e in prayer due to the ḥadīth reported by Anas Ibn Mālik (*raḍiyAllāhu 'anhu*) that, 'the Messenger of Allāh (ﷺ) said: complete the rows for indeed I see you behind me.'

Reported by Bukhārī [1/176] and Muslim [no. 433].

[118] i.e. during his (ﷺ) life.

[119] The basic principle here is that he (ﷺ) is like the rest of the nation as Allāh aid, "Say: I am a man like yourselves to whom it has been revealed... " [*Al-Kahf* (18): 110]

The aḥādīth that are used to prove this particular issue cannot be used as proof because they are either weak, or do not clearly prove the point. Therefore the clear sense of the verse is not to be left by a mere possibility that is subject to weakness. This is true love of the Prophet (ﷺ)—that we hold firm to the evidence, that we follow and that we do not innovate. May Allāh delight our eyes by being allowed to see him (ﷺ) and by being resurrected amongst his group of followers.

pure even if we rule that the hair of the nation is impure.[120]

Our companions have differed concerning the purity of his blood, urine and all other remnants related to him.

Presents donated to him were permissible for him to accept, but this is not the case with the other leaders for it is not lawful for them to accept presents from their subjects subject to the well-known specifications. It is not possible for Prophets to lose their senses but is permissible for them to faint for this is a state different to the first. They have differed concerning the possibility of their having wet-dreams and the most famous opinion is that this is not possible.

He (ﷺ) once missed the two rakʿahs after *Zuhr* and he made them up after the *ʿAṣr* prayer and he continued to pray them after *ʿAṣr*. With regards to his persistence in praying them at this time there is a difference as to whether this was specific to him or not, with the most correct opinion being that it was.[121]

He (ﷺ) said,

تَسَمَّوا باِسْمِي وَلا تَكَنَّوا بِكُنْيَتِي.

> Name yourselves with my name, but do not use my agnomen (*kunyā*).[122]

[120] The correct opinion is that hair is pure with respect the whole of the nation, it is not specific to him (ﷺ) as there is not clear evidence proving the impurity of hair.

[121] The proof of specificity lies in what is established from Umm Salamah (*raḍiyAllāhu ʿanhā*) who said, 'I asked, "O Messenger of Allāh, should we make them up if we miss them?" He replied, "no." '

'Abdu-l-'Azīz Ibn Bāz said, 'this is a ḥasan ḥadīth, it is reported by Aḥmad with a good isnād and constitutes proof that making up the sunnahs of *Zuhr*, after *ʿAṣr*, was specifically allowed for him.'

[122] Bukhārī [no.'s 3539, 6188] and Muslim [no. 2134].

With regards the permissibility of taking the agnomen Abū al-Qāsim there is a difference that I have clarified in *ar-Rawḍah* and *al-Adhkār.*

He (ﷺ) said,

كُلُّ سَبَبٍ وَنَسَبٍ يَنْقَطِعُ يَومَ القِيامَةِ إلاَّ سَبَبِي وَنَسَبِي

> Every relationship and lineage will be severed on the Day of Judgement except for my relationship and my lineage.[123]

It is said [in commentary to this] that his nation attribute themselves to him and it also said that on that day the only attribution that would be of benefit is the attribution to him and none other.

Our companions said that whoever mocks him or commits fornication while he is alive becomes a disbeliever. This is what they said, however their claim with regards to fornication is problematic.

Ibn al-Qāṣṣ and al-Qaffal al-Marwazī said, 'from those matters specific to him is that he was removed from the world when he was receiving revelation, but despite this the obligation of prayer and other such matters were not lifted from him.'

Included amongst this is that whosoever sees him in a dream has truly seen him for Satan cannot impersonate him. However if the dreamer hears anything in his dream with regards rules and regulation then he should not act upon them if they contradict what the Sharīʿah has already established. This is due to the absence of precision and accurate conveyance on the part of the dreamer, not that there is any doubt in the dream. Narrative is only acceptable from a narrator who is trustworthy, precise and legally responsible, however

[123] Reported by Aḥmad [4/323, 332] and it was declared Ṣaḥīḥ by al-Albānī, *al-Ṣaḥīḥah* [no. 2036], by taking into consideration its many routes of narration.

the one who is dreaming is not in this condition.

Included amongst this is that the earth cannot consume the flesh of the Prophets as is established in the famous ḥadīth.[124]

Included amongst this is his (ﷺ) saying,

إنَّ كَذِباً عَلَيَّ لَيسَ كَكَذِبٍ عَلى أحَدٍ.

> Indeed a lie against me is not like a lie perpetrated against another.[125]

Our companions and others have stated that deliberately lying against him is from the major sins and anyone who believes that this is permissible becomes a disbeliever, otherwise this sin is like all other major sins, the perpetrator does not become a disbeliever through committing it. Shaykh Abū Muḥammad al-Juwaynī, the father of Imām al-Ḥaramain, said that a person does become a disbeliever [through committing this sin] but the correct opinion is the first and this was the opinion of the majority. Allāh knows best.

Know that this category of matters specific to him cannot be enumerated, however what we have mentioned should serve as a pointer to what we have left.

We will conclude this section by making two points:

1. Imām al-Ḥaramain said that the researching scholars stated that mentioning the differences of opinion concerning those matters specific to him (ﷺ) is useless containing no benefit.

---

[124] Reported by Aḥmad [4/8], Abū Dāwūd [no. 1047], Nasā'ī [3/91] and Ibn Mājah [no. 1085] that the Prophet (ﷺ) said, 'Allāh has prohibited the earth from consuming the bodies of the Prophets.'

[125] Bukhārī [no. 1291] and Muslim [no. 4—the introduction].

This is because there is no implementable ruling connected to it that one is in need of. The difference of opinion occurs in those issues whose rulings we are in need of knowing. The rules specific to him can only be discerned through following the texts and there is no room for analogies. When there is no text concerning an issue then having a difference of opinion concerning it only comprises guessing at the unseen, having no benefit.

2. Al-Ṣaymari said that Abū ʿAlī Ibn Khayrān prevented any discussion concerning those matters specific to him because they relate to a matter that is over and done with. He said, 'however the totality of the companions [of the Shāfiʿī madhʿhab] said that there is no harm in discussing them and this is the correct opinion.'

This is the discussion concerning this issue as presented by our companions, the correct stance is to be certain of its permissibility, rather its recommendation. If someone were to say it is obligatory, it would not be far-fetched, provided that there were to exist no consensus opposing this. This is because an ignoramus could see some matters specific to him mentioned in the Ṣaḥīḥ and act by them taking to the basic principle of following him, therefore it becomes obligatory to clarify them so that they become known because no one can share in them. So what benefit is there greater than this?

This is the end of what I have selected regarding various glimpses into the life of the Messenger of Allāh (ﷺ), the beloved (*ḥabīb*)[126] of the Lord of the worlds and the best of the first and last people.

---

[126] The level of beloved friend (*khalīl*) is higher than the level of *ḥabīb*. Allāh has taken Muḥammad (ﷺ) as a *khalīl* as is shown by the ḥadīth, 'and Allāh has taken your comrade as a *khalīl*.' Reported by Muslim [no. 2383].

Refer to: *al-Mawāhib al-Laduniyyah* [3/314-317].

Abundant peace and blessing be upon him and upon all of the Prophets, the families of all of them and upon all the righteous.

Allāh suffices for me and what an excellent disposer of affairs is He.